Epistemologies of t

Epistemologies of the South

Justice against Epistemicide

BOAVENTURA DE SOUSA SANTOS

Routledge
Taylor & Francis Group

LONDON AND NEW YORK

First published 2014 by Paradigm Publishers

Published 2016 by Routledge
2 Park Square, Milton Park, Abingdon, Oxon OX14 4RN
711 Third Avenue, New York, NY 10017, USA

Routledge is an imprint of the Taylor & Francis Group, an informa business

Library of Congress Cataloging-in-Publication Data

Santos, Boaventura de Sousa.
  Epistemologies of the South : justice against epistemicide / Boaventura De Sousa Santos.
     pages cm
  Includes bibliographical references and index.
  ISBN 978-1-61205-545-9 (pbk.   )
  ISBN 978-1-61205-565-7 (consumer e-book)
  1. Knowledge, Sociology of. 2. Social epistemology. 3. Social justice—Developing countries.
I. Title.
  HM651.S2483 2013
  303.3'72—dc23

                                                                    2013030574

ISBN 13: 978-1-61205-545-9 (pbk)
ISBN 13: 978-1-61205-544-2 (hbk)

Contents

Part Two
Toward Epistemologies of the South:
Against the Waste of Experience

Preface

THREE BASIC IDEAS underlie this book. First, the understanding of the world by far exceeds the Western understanding of the world. Second, there is no global social justice without global cognitive justice. Third, the emancipatory transformations in the world may follow grammars and scripts other than those developed by Western-centric critical theory, and such diversity should be valorized.

A critical theory is premised upon the idea that there is no way of knowing the world better than by anticipating a better world. Such anticipation provides both the intellectual instruments to unmask the institutionalized, harmful lies that sustain and legitimate social injustice and the political impulse to struggle against them. Critical theory is therefore meaningless without a search for truth and healing, even if in the end there is no final truth or definitive cure. History shows that the most entrenched social lies have been limited in scope and duration, even if, while in force and dominant, they appear to be the very source of truth and healing.

Viewed from the perspective of the excluded and discriminated against, the historical record of global capitalism, colonialism, and patriarchy is full of institutionalized, harmful lies. It is a record of social regulation in the name of social emancipation, appropriation in the name of liberation, violence in the name of peace, the destruction of life in the name of the sanctity of life, violation of human rights in the name of human rights, societal fascism in the name of political democracy, illegal plundering in the name of the rule of law, assimilation in the name of diversity, individual vulnerability in the name of individual autonomy, constitution of subhumanities in the name of humanity, putting price tags on convictions in the name of priceless values, commodification in the name of redemption, standardization in the name of choice, massification in the name of freedom, racism in the name of tolerance, constitutional wrongs in the name of constitutional rights, ontologies of inferiority in the name of Immanuel Kant's *Was ist die Aufklärung?*, inequalities after the law in the name of equality before the law, compulsive consumption in the name of happiness, and hypocrisy in proclaiming principles (St. Thomas's *habitus principiorum*) in order to cover up for the most hideous negations of *recta vita*.

Given the peculiar pervasiveness and intensity of the institutionalized, harmful lies running our contemporary world, the adequate recognition of injustice and the possible overcoming of oppression can only be achieved by means of an epistemological break. The focus on such an epistemological break is what best distinguishes the theory expounded in this book from the Western-centric critical tradition. The latter, of which the most brilliant exemplar is the Frankfurt School, has failed to account for the emancipatory struggles of our time, in part at least because it shares with the bourgeois thinking it criticizes the same epistemological foundations that suppress the cognitive dimension of social injustice, and thus renders universal the Western understanding and transformation of the world. Moreover, it sees itself as a vanguard theory that excels in knowing about, explaining, and guiding rather than knowing with, understanding, facilitating, sharing, and walking alongside.

This book aims to depart from this Eurocentric critical tradition. It proposes a *teoria povera*, a rearguard theory based on the experiences of large, marginalized minorities and majorities that struggle against unjustly imposed marginality and inferiority, with the purpose of strengthening their resistance. The critical theorizing laid out in this book seeks to be non-Eurocentric because it prepares the ground for both valorizing non-Eurocentric conceptions of emancipation or liberation and for proposing counterhegemonic understandings and uses of Eurocentric concepts, such as human rights, the rule of law, democracy, and socialism. This book stands on its own but it will benefit from a reading in conjunction with my forthcoming *Epistemologies of the South: Reinventing Social Emancipation.* The wager of this latter book is that vast political landscapes of emancipation and liberation will emerge once the epistemological work proposed in the current book is accomplished.

This volume starts with a preamble presented in a counterpoint mode, a counterpoint between an imagined manifesto for good living/*buen vivir* and a minifesto thus designated in order to challenge the grandiose purposes underlying modernist manifestos. The manifesto presents the imagined voices of social movements with which I have been working over the years. The minifesto presents my own response, highlighting the limitations of writing at a time of impossible radicalism, as this book intends to show. In order best to visualize the counterpoint structure, the manifesto is printed on the even pages, the minifesto on the odd pages.

In the introduction I defend the need for creating a distance in relation to Western-centric political imagination and critical theory. I show the reasons why the Western-centric critical tradition (Marxism included) fails to account for the forms of struggle, social actors, and grammars of liberation that have developed in the last twenty years. In the past decade the World Social Forum has provided a dramatic illustration of this failure.

The book is divided into two parts. In the first part, I show that in order to be solid and convincing the critique of Western modernity must take into account the complexity and internal diversity of this social, political, and cultural paradigm. What is usually called Western modernity is a very complex set of phenomena in which dominant and subaltern perspectives coexist and constitute rival modernities. Critiques of predominant Western modernity tend to ignore this fact. To that extent they run the risk of becoming reductionist and of being like the very conceptions of modernity they criticize, that is, mere caricatures. In Chapter 1, drawing on a famous essay by the nineteenth-century Cuban intellectual-activist José Martí, I identify some Calibanesque views on America and Western modernity. In Chapter 2, I resort to Walter Benjamin's *Angelus Novus* in order to analyze the turbulence that is currently shaking one of the grounding metaphors that underlies modern identities (or, rather, modern processes of identification): the double metaphor of roots and options. In Chapter 3, I ask whether a non-Occidentalist West is possible. Resorting to two early modern philosophers, Nicholas of Cusa and Blaise Pascal, I show how alternative understandings of Western modernity were set aside because they failed to fit the capitalist-colonial enterprise.

In the second part, by means of various approximations, I expound my criticisms of the dominant epistemologies (Northern epistemologies) and present my own epistemological proposal, which I have been calling epistemologies of the South, a set of inquiries into the construction and validation of knowledge born in struggle, of ways of knowing developed by social groups as part of their resistance against the systematic injustices and oppressions caused by capitalism, colonialism, and patriarchy. In Chapter 4, the central chapter of my postcolonial or decolonial approach, I analyze the abyssal lines drawn by the dominant abyssal thinking of our time through which both human and nonhuman realities existing on the other side of the line are made invisible or even actively produced as nonexistent. This results in the most radical forms of social exclusion. In Chapter 5, I approach invisibility from another angle, which I call the *epistemology of blindness.* Taking the epistemological foundations of modern economics as an extreme example, I show the different mechanisms through which the immense lot of the unseen is generated. In Chapter 6, and still from another perspective, which I term the sociology of absences and the sociology of emergences, I show how the laziness of dominant modern forms of reason leads to an enormous waste of social experience that otherwise might be useful to identify emancipatory possibilities. In Chapter 7, I focus on ecologies of knowledges; I present the outline of the epistemologies of the South by showing how the sociology of absences and the sociology of emergences open up the possibility both for ecologies of knowledges and for intercultural translation. Finally, in Chapter 8, I deal with intercultural translation that I conceive of as the alternative both to the abstract universalism grounding Western-centric general theories and to the idea of incommensurability between cultures.

This is a book soaked in tragic optimism, neither radical pessimism nor radical hope. Nothing is so oppressive as to eliminate the sense of a nonoppressive alternative. But, on the other hand, no such alternative is strong or convincing enough to avoid running the risk of somehow conflating itself with oppression.

If the human condition were slavery, there would be no need for the institution of slavery. Conversely, if the human condition were freedom, there would be no need for constitutions and human rights. The human condition is the condition of humans carrying a heavy load of history on their shoulders and half-blindly choosing ways of making the load easier to carry.

I have worked on this book for many years. I am indebted to much precious support from many colleagues and collaborators over the course of that time. I am afraid I will not be able to mention them all. This book owes a lot to Maria Irene Ramalho, to our many stimulating dialogues and challenging interdisciplinary exchanges, and to her inspiration regarding my incursions into literary theory. She has also helped on occasion to render some of my ideas into English. My committed research assistant of many years, Margarida Gomes, has once again brought competence and professionalism to support my research and to prepare the manuscript for publication. Over the years my books in English have benefited from the invaluable support of Mark Streeter as an outstanding copy editor. The invisible hand of my devoted secretary, Lassalete Simões, makes itself present, directly or indirectly, in everything I have written for the past twenty years. My colleagues João Arriscado Nunes and Maria Paula Meneses were precious collaborators in crucial moments of my research. Over the years, my doctoral and postdoctoral students at the Universities of Coimbra, Wisconsin–Madison, Warwick, and London were a constant source of inspiration for me to embark on novel topics and perspectives. At different moments of my research, I could always count on the unfailing support of collaborators, colleagues, and friends: Agustin Grijalva, Alison Phipps, Allan Hunter, Ana Cristina Santos, António Casimiro Ferreira, António Sousa Ribeiro, Armando Muylema, Bill Whitford, Carlos Lema, Cesar Baldi, César Rodríguez-Garavito, Claire Cutler, Conceição Gomes, Cristiano Gianolla, David Larraz, David Schneiderman, Diane Soles, Efua Prah, Élida Lauris, Emilios Christodoulidis, Erik O. Wright, Gavin Anderson, Heinz Klug, Immanuel Wallerstein, Ivan Nunes, James Tully, Javier Couso, Jeremy Webber, João Pedroso, Joaquin Herrera Flores, John Harrington, José Luis Exeni, José Manuel Mendes, Joseph Thome, Juan Carlos Monedero, Juan José Tamayo, Len Kaplan, Liliana Obregón, Luís Carlos Arenas, Marc Galanter, Margarida Calafate Ribeiro, Maria José Canelo, Mario Melo, Mary Layoun, Michael Burawoy, Michael Wall, Neil Komesar, Raul Llasag, Raza Saeed, Rebecca Johnson, Sara Araújo, Sílvia Ferreira, Tiago Ribeiro, and Upendra Baxi. My heartfelt thanks to all of them, and I just hope the end result will not disappoint them. Last but not least, a very special word of gratitude to Dean Birkenkamp of Paradigm Publishers for the extraordinary incentive he gave me for the swift completion of this book and its timely publication.[1]

1. This book was completed in the framework of the research project "ALICE—Strange Mirrors, Unsuspected Lessons" (alice.ces.uc.pt), coordinated by me at the Centre for Social Studies (CES) of the University of Coimbra, Portugal. The project has received funding from the European Research Council under the European Union's Seventh Framework Programme (FP/2007-2013)/ERC Grant Agreement n. 269807.

Epistemologies of the South

Manifesto for Good Living/
Buen Vivir[1]

It is time to change the conversation. The past had better be large and demand little. The future had better come closer. Let's enlarge the present and the space of the world. Let's move on. Let's travel with crude maps. Between theory and action there may be correspondence, but there is no sequence. We will not necessarily reach the same place, and many of us will not even reach any recognizable place, but we share the same starting point, and that's enough. We are not all headed to the same address, but we believe we can walk together for a very long time. A few of us speak colonial languages; the large majority of us speak other languages. Since only a small number of us have voice, we resort to ventriloquists, whom we call rearguard intellectuals, because they go on doing what they have always done well: looking back. But they have now received a new mission from us: to care for those of us who lag behind and bring them back into the fight and to identify whoever keeps betraying us at the back and help us find out why.

We know Marx, even though Marx may not know us. The grand theory is a recipe book for famished people. We are neither universal nor eternal. We discard all the philosophies that do not value what we are. We know Gandhi, and Gandhi knows us. We know Fanon, and Fanon knows us. We know Toussaint L'Ouverture and Toussaint L'Ouverture knows us. We know Patrice Lumumba, and Patrice Lumumba knows us. We know Bartolina Sisa, and Bartolina Sisa knows us. We know Catarina Eufémia, and Catarina Eufémia knows us. We know Rosa Parks, and Rosa Parks knows us. But the large majority of those who know us are not well known. We are revolutionaries with no papers.

We have heard that there are many accredited intellectuals who specialize in certifying ideas that supposedly concern us. They dwell on what for them is this side of the line, that is to say, in inaccessible neighborhoods and fortified institutions they call universities. They are erudite libertines and cherish impunity.

Who are we? We are the global South, that large set of creations and creatures that has been sacrificed to the infinite voracity of capitalism, colonialism, patriarchy,

---

1. The concept of good living/*buen vivir* derives from the Quechua word *sumak kawsay* and is central to the conception of social emancipation whose epistemological foundations are laid out in this book. The political implications of this concept are analyzed in detail in my forthcoming *Epistemologies of the South: Reinventing Social Emancipation*.

Minifesto for Intellectual-Activists

This book begins by acknowledging its limited capacity to contribute to the success of all those rallying for good living/*buen vivir*—if for no other reason than because it is written on this side of the line. To be sure, its thinking is on the other side of the line, but its life, as a book, cannot but be on this side of the line. It will be read by those who least need it. Those who, in my judgment, might benefit from it will not be able to read it. If they could, they would probably have no interest in doing so, and if they did, they would most probably not understand it. This book is thus, at best, a reluctant ally, even if the solidarity it expresses is not reluctant at all. In any case, an ally is, at most, a relative.

The second reason for its scanty contribution is that, unlike in other eras—for instance, the extraordinary seventeenth and eighteenth centuries in Europe—in the global North of our time radical ideas are not translated into radical practices, and vice versa; radical practices do not recognize themselves in available radical ideas. This double opacity is due to several reasons that will be analyzed in the book. One of the most important is no doubt the fact that the established powers today have efficient means with which to prevent the encounter between ideas and practices beyond what befits the genetic code of the status quo. Radicalism has become antinature, *aberratio entis*. It has been a long time since 1677, when the European powers mobilized (for example, by hiring spies) to find out if, in his last living moments, Spinoza had renounced his "pantheistic atheism" and converted to Christianity; the impact of Spinoza's capitulation to the "evidence" that human beings are natural believers was eagerly expected.

In our time, genuine radicalism seems no longer possible in the global North. Those who proclaim themselves as radical thinkers are either fooling themselves or fooling someone else, since their practices are bound to contradict their theories. Most of them work in institutions such as universities that require protective hats and gloves to deal with reality. One of the tricks that Western modernity plays on intellectuals is to allow them only to produce revolutionary ideas in reactionary institutions. On the other hand, those who act radically seem to be silent. Either they have nothing intelligible to say, or if they were to speak, nobody would understand them outside their circle of action, or they might even be thrown in jail or killed.

Given the above circumstances, how is one to write about social emancipation? To avoid misleading anyone and being misled in turn, it would be better and all their satellite-oppressions. We are present at every cardinal point because our geography is the geography of injustice and oppression. We are not everyone; we are those who do not resign themselves to sacrifice and therefore resist. We have dignity. We are all indigenous peoples because we are where we have always been, before we had owners, masters, or bosses, or because we are where we were taken against our will and where owners, masters, or bosses were imposed on us. They want to impose on us the fear of having a boss and the fear of not having a boss, so that we may not imagine ourselves without fear. We resist. We are widely diverse human beings united by the idea that the understanding of the world is much larger than the Western understanding of the world. We believe that the transformation of the world may also occur in ways not foreseen by the global North. We are animals and plants, biodiversity and water, earth and Pachamama, ancestors and future generations—whose suffering appears less in the news than the suffering of humans but is closely linked to theirs, even though they may be unaware of it.

The most fortunate of us are alive today but afraid of being killed tomorrow; they have food today but are afraid of having none tomorrow; they till the land they inherited from their ancestors today but fear lest they be expropriated tomorrow; they talk with their friends in the streets today but are afraid that tomorrow there will be only wreckage; they care for their families today but are afraid of being raped tomorrow; they have jobs today but are afraid of being laid off tomorrow; they are human beings today but are afraid of being treated like animals tomorrow; they drink pure water and enjoy virgin forests today but fear lest tomorrow there will be neither water nor forests. The least fortunate of us are those whose fears have long since become reality.

Some of us were able to participate in the meetings of the World Social Forum in the first decade of the third millennium. We are solidary with the participants, even though they have not said everything about us, let alone the most important things. In any case, they have shown that we are many more than our enemies think, that we think better than they do about their world and ours, and that we are bold enough to act under the conviction that, in certain circumstances, it is possible to fight aircraft-carrier-ideas with kite-ideas, even though an aircraft carrier is an aircraft carrier and a kite is a kite. This is exactly what some of us have been demonstrating while venting our outrage at the beginning of the second decade of the millennium, in the streets of Cairo and Tunis, Madrid and Athens, New York and Johannesburg—in a word, in the streets of the world where it has recently been discovered that the wealthy countries are merely the countries of the wealthy people (whereas the 99 percent, the poor and their families, live outside the neofeudal enclaves that belong to the 1 percent, the superrich families). Many of those outraged at indignity are not, like us, on the other side of the line, but we hope to be able to build alliances with them.

Where are we going? Some of us are headed toward social emancipation, others to socialism of the twenty-first century, *buen vivir* socialism, others to communism, others to *sumak kawsay* or *sumak qamaña*, others to Pachamama or *umma*, others to acknowledge the impossibility of being radical and to write from such an acknowledgment. The radical acknowledgment of said impossibility is all that is left over from the radicalism of Western modernity. What is left over is not negligible and therefore must not be viewed with nostalgia. It is, on the contrary, the sole way of imagining the new. Before us there are more ruins than well-defined plans. But ruins may be creative too. Starting anew means rendering creativity and interruption possible under hostile conditions that promote reproduction and repetition. The point is not so much to imagine new theories, new practices, and new relations among them. The point is mainly to imagine new ways of theorizing and of generating transformative collective action. By acknowledging how powerful the constituted impossibility of radicalism is, we will be better equipped to imagine new constituent possibilities.

To write from the perspective of the impossibility of radicalism means to start by acknowledging two impossibilities and to go on writing between them: the *impossibility of communicating the unsayable* and *the impossibility of collective authorship.*

The impossibility of communicating the unsayable. For the last two hundred years, the relation between knowing and acting has lost its general character and been reduced to the relation between knowledge validated by modern science and rational social engineering (Santos 2007b). As a result, all that was arbitrarily conceived of as being outside this highly intellectualized and rationalized field was ignored or stigmatized. Outside was the dark world of passions, intuitions, feelings, emotions, affections, beliefs, faiths, values, myths, and the world of the unsayable, which cannot be communicated save indirectly, as Kierkegaard would say. Various kinds of positivism managed to demonstrate that what was left out either did not exist (was an illusion) or was unimportant or dangerous. Such reductionisms allowed for geometrical correspondences between theory and practice. However, as both theory and practice became disembodied from their unsayable "halves," it became impossible to account for the complexity and contingency of the relationships between them. Being imagined as reflected in the same mirror, both theory and practice became reciprocally blind. Now, blind people guided by blind people are not doubly blind, but they do not see better either.

Theoreticians and intellectuals in general are not prepared for either joys or sorrows, for either mourning or the celebration that the ralliers for good living/ *buen vivir* talk about. The former know how to name these affections, as Spinoza called them, but do not live them; moreover, they are incapable of making the absence of such affections into a problem for thought or reason. They are not prepared to integrate that which thought has separated, meaning life itself. If life could make distinctions, it would make many, but certainly not this one between affections and reason, lest it deny itself as life. This is particularly true of the life of transformative action in which the reality consists of giving life to what does not yet exist and can only come about by reasonable affections and affectionate to *ubuntu*, still others to human rights, others to real and true democracy, others to dignity and respect, others to plurinationality, others to interculturality, others to social justice, others to *swadeshi*, others to *demokaraasi*, others to *minzhu*, others to food sovereignty, others to solidary economy, others to ecosocialism and the fight against large dams and megaprojects. We have been warned that every concept tends to become a conceptual monster. We are not afraid.

What we all have in common is that we all have to fight against many obstacles in order to live with dignity—that is to say, to live well. There are many obstacles, but they all have a family resemblance: capitalism among humans and between humans and nature, colonialism, patriarchy, fetishism of commodities, monocultures of knowledge, the linear time of progress, naturalized inequalities, the dominant scale, and the productivism of economic growth and capitalist development. The obstacles to a life with dignity are very different, but they all have something in common: to wit, the infinite accumulation of unequal differences on the unjust behalf of very few. We are the dispossessed of the earth because we are considered ignorant, inferior, local, particular, backward, unproductive, or lazy. The immensurable suffering we get from this and the waste of world experience it brings about are unjust, but they are not historical fatalities. We fight against them under the conviction that they can be eliminated. But our struggle depends less on our objectives than on the quality of our actions and emotions in striving to attain them.

What do we want? The world is full of opportunities to live well, both regarding ourselves and mother earth. We want to have the opportunity to take advantage of them. We know better what we do not want than what we want. Those living in what they themselves call "this side of the line" think a lot about us. For the most fortunate of us, they organize fairs in our villages with many bazaars and stalls for counseling. They display transgenic foodstuffs, bibles, intellectual copyrights, certified consultants, empowerment recipes, structural adjustments, human rights, private property, nicely wrapped democracy, bottled water, and environmental concerns. We read once that Socrates, walking through the square and seeing many deluxe products, remarked, "So many things in the world that I do not want!" Socrates would be today a rallier for good living/*buen vivir*. We do not want to be spoken about. We want to speak for ourselves. We do not want to be seen on the other side of the line. We want to eliminate the line.

Where do we live? We live in Chiapas, in the Andes, in Amazonia, in the squatter settlements of big cities, in the lands coveted by new and old colonizers in Africa and Asia, in the ghettos of global cities, on the banks of rivers where they want to build dams and on the hills where they want to mine for ore and minerals and destroy life, in the new plantations using slave labor in the United States, Brazil, and Bangladesh, in the world's maquiladoras, where we produce, with sweat and sorrow, the consumerist pleasure of the masters. We actually live where tourists never go or, if they do, where they would never deign to live. The world is divided by two kinds of borders: those we accept with reservations and those we refuse without reservation. The former are the national borders wherein reasons. The concern of intellectuals is the life of thought, and that has little to do with the life of life. *Lived life*—as much as Spinoza's *natura naturata*—is supposed to be less than thought, but *living life* and *natura naturans* are surely more than thought.

By calling myself an intellectual-activist I wish to suggest a possible way of living the impossibility of communicating the unsayable in a productive way, thereby creating new possibilities. This book resorts frequently to indirect communication; it was itself thought through on the basis of much indirect communication.

The impossibility of collective authorship. As far as authorship goes, this book has diffuse limits. In recent years I have been an activist in the World Social Forum process and have been deeply involved in the struggles of the indigenous peoples of Latin America. I am unable to determine to what extent my thoughts are part of a collective without a name and without clear outlines. Of my own is only what is expressed individually and with full awareness of a double absence: the absence of that which could be formulated only collectively, were it susceptible to rational formulation, and the absence of that which cannot be rationally formulated, either individually or collectively. Half this book will forever remain unwritten. I write what I am able to write with this in mind. I am part of a collective by being aware of how I separate myself from it in order to write.

To write from the perspective of the impossibility of radicalism is today more promising than before owing to three factors: *the end of the game of dogmas*; *the mission of the rearguard theory* with which the ralliers have entrusted the intellectuals; and *the inexhaustible diversity of the world* and what it shows, or what it lets be seen, regardless of the possibility of its being spoken.

The end of the game of dogmas. For the past two hundred years the social struggles against the old dogmas have almost always been fought on behalf of new dogmas. As a consequence, social emancipation became a new social regulation, and the old orthodoxy was replaced by the new one. What was a means became an end; what was rebellion became conformity. Now the social movements rallying for good living/*buen vivir* show that it is possible to fight against old dogmas without doing it in the name of new dogmas.

According to such movements, social emancipation presupposes social regulation; an emancipated society that is not regulated is not conceivable. But there is a difference between regulating emancipation and emancipating regulation. Regulating emancipation consists of applying to the new conditions the same logic of regulation (if not necessarily the same kind of regulation) that presided over the old conditions, now overcome; emancipating regulation, on the other hand, consists of establishing as a new kind of regulation the condition for that which it aims to regulate. If the purpose of social emancipation is to build a democracy-without-end, emancipating regulation involves deepening and diversifying democratic solutions as transformative practices create the need for them. Only this will prevent means from becoming ends; new idols from replacing old ones and demanding of citizens the same kind of submission as before;

we were born or raised. We accept them to save our energies and because we think they are a lesser obstacle compared to the other borders. The others are the walls, trenches, ditches, barbwire fences, cordons of police cars, and checkpoints; above all, they are the maps that have traced the abyssal lines in people's minds, laws, and politics and banished us to the other side of the line. The worst borders are the borders that cannot be seen, read, heard, or felt on this side of the line, that is to say, in Kakania, whose capital is Excrementia. We live on the other side of the line that someone traced while thinking of us but aiming at not thinking of us anymore. We are invisible, inaudible, and illegible because the success of previous revolutions decided not to include us. If our here is invisible, our now is even more so. According to those revolutions, we have, at most, a past, but no future. We were never allowed to write the history books.

How do we live? Always at risk of dying for causes other than illness, of being wounded or killed but not in friendly games; on the verge of losing home, land, water, sacred territories, children, grandparents; always at risk of being displaced long distances to flee war or of being confined in our barrios or in concentration camps; at risk of finding that our popular, solidary, cooperative savings may be worth nothing because they do not count toward the GDP; at risk of seeing our rivers contaminated and our forests deforested in the name of what they call development; at risk of being humiliated, without the power to respond because we are of an inferior gender, race, class, or caste; at risk of being the target of wealthy kids' tricks, which may prove fatal to us; at risk of impoverishment, of being helped as poor without giving a bad conscience to those helping us; at risk of being considered terrorists for wanting to defend our mother earth; at risk, indeed, for facing so many risks, of ending up conforming.

What kind of passion urges us? The most subjective and diverse passion because grounded in the most intensely and diversely lived truth: that we deserve a life with dignity, a free life because free from the fear of violence and dispossession, a life to which we are entitled, and that fighting for it is possible and that we might succeed. We are the children of a passionate truth and a truthful passion. We passionately know that reality is not reduced to what exists and that most of what does not exist could and deserves to exist. Time does not allay our passion. Our brother Evo Morales had to wait five centuries to become president after Pope Paul III stated in his 1537 bull that Indians had souls. It was a cunning bull from which we started to arrive at where we are now.

Against whom do we fight? On this side of the line everything is seductive; on the other side of the line everything is scary. We are the only ones who know, from experience, that there are two sides to the line, the only ones who know how to imagine what they do not live. Our context is the urgency of a life with dignity as a condition for everything else to be possible. We do know that only a civilizational change can guarantee it, but we also know that our urgency can bring about such change. We must live today in order to live a long time, and vice versa; we have to live a long time in order to live today. Our *durées* and times new rules from being naturalized as necessities of life, as was the case with the old rules; the struggles against the elimination of alternatives from leading to a society without alternatives; political actions adopted to restore politics vis-à-vis technical solutions from becoming a solution of political technique; limits to freedom of action and creativity from becoming exactly the same as the old ones; nonconformity, which made change possible, from turning into change-hindering conformity; the emotions, fantasies, and aspirations invested in social change from being condemned for what they are; the new functions that broke with the old ones from becoming structures blocking new functions; the historicization of that which was considered ahistorical from turning into a new ahistorical truth; the necessarily relative unconsciousness of all those engaged in change involving risks from becoming the maximum possible consciousness of those benefiting from the change. The aim is, in sum, to prevent the weapons of the once oppressed from becoming the weapons of the new oppressors. I believe that, according to the good-living ralliers, this is the only way to turn the journey toward the end in view into a journey without end.

This new stance poses a huge challenge to intellectual-activists. Particularly in the global North, the protagonism of intellectuals has been largely due to games of dogmas and orthodoxies. Dogmas are as intense concerning formulation (precise words) as direction (precise and binding instructions for action and behavior). They are so intensely directive that they confuse the reality of direction with the direction of reality. They create autonomous forms of life. Intellectuals living inside and off such games have no need of any other life. They were trained for that sort of life, and their mission is to reproduce it. Under these conditions, the challenge posed to the intellectuals by the ralliers is almost dilemmatic: either they must untrain and reinvent themselves, or they will continue to be what they already are—irrelevant. Before they choose untraining, intellectuals do wonder about the dilemma: how is it possible to fight against dogmas without resorting to other and more potent dogmas? Would leaving everything open not be the same as letting the enemy loose? Can the attempt to integrate life and thought not bring about the disintegration of both? Is anti-dogma not another kind of dogma after all?

What is promising at the beginning of the new millennium is that the ralliers for good living/*buen vivir* have created possibilities not previously foreseen or deemed admissible theoretically. These new possibilities show that irrationality is not the only alternative to what is currently considered rational, that chaos is not the only alternative to order, and that concern about what is less than true (the messy reasons and affections underlying the struggles for uncertain results) must be balanced by concern about what is more than true (the *habitus* of disproved grand theories of claiming truthfulness in their explanations of previous failures). The new possibilities emerge from new actions acted out by new players with new discourses and conceptions. They are actually not new; some of them are very old indeed; they are ancestral. They became more visible because only stress what is useful for our struggles. Our times are not flat or concentric; they are passages between the No Longer and the Not Yet.

To a certain extent, the age of our side of the line coincides with the age of their side of the line, but the two ages are not to be confused. We and they are contemporaneous in distinct ways. Our age is potentially more revolutionary than all the previous ones. Never was so much unjust suffering caused to human and nonhuman beings; never were the sources of power and oppression so diverse and so powerful. Never as today was it possible for human beings on this planet to have any idea, however vague and distorted, of what is happening.

This is a time of reckoning at a planetary level, involving humans and mother earth. It is a time of reckoning as yet without any rules. On the one side, capitalism, colonialism, patriarchy, and all their satellite-oppressions. This is what we call the global North, a political, not geographical, location, increasingly more specialized in the transnationalization of suffering: workers losing their jobs in displaced plants; peasants in India, Africa, and Latin America expropriated by the megaprojects, agribusiness, and the mining industry; indigenous peoples of the Americas and Australia who survived genocide; women murdered in Ciudad Juárez; gays and lesbians of Uganda and Malawi; people of Darfur, who are so poor and yet so rich; Afro-descendents murdered and displaced to the confines of the Colombian Pacific; mother earth struck in her vital cycles; those accused of being terrorists, tortured in secret prisons all over the world; undocumented immigrants facing deportation; Palestinians, Iraqis, Afghans, and Pakistanis who live, work, and celebrate under constant bombardments; the impoverished North Americans, shocked by the fact that capitalism and colonialism treat them with exactly the same contempt and arbitrariness with which they have treated all the other peoples of the world; the retired, unemployed, and unemployable who are prey to the law of pillaging of the financial pirates.

On the other side, our time is the time of the return of the humiliated and degraded. This is what we call the global South. We are not victims; we are victimized and offer resistance. We are many, and we use our new learning in very different ways. We do not always agree, and we even suspect that there are traitors among us. We are experts at exposing them.

Despite everything else, we have problems in common with our enemies, and our destinies have some affinities. The suffering they inflict on us and have recently increased will end up turning against them. The sanest of them have already realized as much. As the sage Voltaire used to say, the cause of all wars is theft. Now those who learned how to steal outside the house are stealing from the people inside it. If suffering, murder, humiliation, and destruction continue to escalate, the survival of the planet may be at stake. Could our enemies be already thinking of colonizing another planet where they won't need closed condominiums?

We know that the first of our struggles is against ourselves. The sage Marx said that after the philosophers were done with interpreting the world, the world would have to be changed. But there is no change without self-change, for the

the repertoire of social emancipation that had been intellectually certified has collapsed, because the fashion show of the new, which actually is the old-in-new-forms, has failed totally.

The absence of dogmas is not easy to describe, but it is felt in the pulse and easy to see. It can be seen in the urge not to squander actions, energies, aspirations, or knowledges. It can be seen in the changes in conversation and in the agreed upon silence to facilitate joint action.

To acknowledge the ralliers' novelty does not mean much. It is just a solidary manner of protecting them from being silenced. To be sure, the ralliers know by their own experience the extent to which Western modernity has specialized in techniques for silencing insurgent actions. According to dominant common sense, they deserve being silenced because they are being carried out by ignorant, inferior, backward, retrograde, local, unproductive people—in sum, by people who are supposed to be obstacles to progress and development. How to counter this powerful silencing machine without giving rise to an alternative but also silencing machine—such is the greater challenge facing intellectual-activists. Herein lie their untraining and self-reinvention.

The rearguard theory. The second reason why I consider that writing from the perspective of the impossibility of radicalism is promising has to do with the mission ascribed to intellectual-activists by ralliers for good living/*buen vivir*: to contribute to the elaboration of theories of the rearguard (more on this throughout the book). This mission is almost impossible, but to the extent that it can be accomplished, it constitutes the greatest novelty at the beginning of the millennium and is the best piece of news for those who genuinely believe that capitalism, colonialism, patriarchy, and all other satellite-oppressions can be overcome.

These political experiences witnessed by ralliers for good living/*buen vivir* cause surprise because they were not conceived of, let alone foreseen, by the political theories of Western modernity, including Marxism and liberalism. Particularly significant, among many other examples, is the case of the indigenous peoples' movements in Latin America and their contribution to recent political changes in some countries. The surprise is due to the fact that both Marxism and liberalism have ignored the indigenous peoples, both as social and political actors. The great Peruvian Marxist José Mariátegui was stigmatized as "romantic" and "populist" by the Communist International for having ascribed a role to the Indians in the construction of Latin American societies. Such a surprise poses a new question to theoreticians and intellectuals in general—namely, whether they are prepared to experience surprise and wonder. This question has no easy answer. Critical theoreticians are particularly trapped in this difficulty since they have been trained in vanguard theorizing. Vanguard theory, by its nature, does not let itself be taken by surprise or feel wonderment. Whatever does not fit the vanguardists' previsions or propositions either does not exist or is not relevant.

To answer positively to the challenge of allowing oneself to be surprised presupposes that the process of untraining and reinvention is in progress and obstacles to life with dignity, or to living well, reside in ourselves, to the extent that we conform to indignity and deny that the difference between what is imposed on us and what we desire is much smaller than we think.

What certainties do we have? As all human and nonhuman animals, we specialize in possibilities, passages between the No Longer and the Not Yet. The only certainties we have concern possibility and the wager. All other certainties are paralyzing. We have partial knowledge of the conditions that allow us to proceed and believe that such conditions are partial themselves. We follow the sage Fanon, according to whom each generation must find its own mission from within relative opacity and then go on to fulfill or betray it. Our possibilities are far from being infinite, and they only become definite according to how we move. We reflect as we run. Our way is semi-invisible and semiblind. The very certainty concerning the shackles from which we wish to free ourselves is treacherous because, with time, the shackles may feel comfortable and turn into ornaments. And they may also induce us to put shackles on those close to us.

What kinds of knowledge are available to us? Our knowledge is intuitive; it goes straight to what is urgent and necessary. It is made of words and silences-with-actions, reasons-with-emotions. Our life does not allow us to distinguish life from thought. All our everydayness is thought of every day in detail. We think of our tomorrow as if it were today. We have no important questions, only productive questions.

Our knowledge flies at low altitude because it is stuck to the body. We feel-think and feelact. To think without passion is to make coffins for ideas; to act without passion is to fill the coffins. We are voracious in getting the diversity of the knowledges we are interested in. There are many knowledges looking for people eager to know them. We squander no knowledges that might help us in our struggle to live well. We mix knowledges and combine them according to logics that are not limited to them. We do not want authors' copyrights; we want to be authors of rights.

Our kind of knowledge is existential and experiential; it is therefore both resilient and flexible, disturbed by all that happens to us. Unlike what goes on in Kakania, here among us, ideas are people; they have weight and pay fines for excess weight; they wear clothes and may be incarcerated for indecent exposure; they make appeals and get killed for that.

How do we get educated? We are the educators with the fewest credentials in the world. Our bodies and our lives are the squandered knowledge of the world, the knowledge that is objective vis-à-vis ourselves and subjective vis-à-vis our enemies. All we know of them is theirs and ours; all they know of us is theirs. Universities have a full inventory of departments, books, careers, computers, reams of papers, uniforms, privileges, erudite discourses, chancellors, and officials; yet they do not educate at all. Their mission is to turn us into ignorants so that we may be treated as ignorants in conscience. At most, they teach us how to choose proceeds successfully. Intellectuals willing to let themselves be taken by surprise are those who are no longer surprised by the imagined novelties, however extravagant and seductive, of vanguard theories, having reached the conclusion that the time of vanguard theories (the time of linearity, simplicity, unity, totality, and determination) is over. Once intellectuals enter the untraining process, the academicist, overintellectualized, and stagnated character of vanguard theories becomes gradually more obvious.

I wrote this book having in mind the creation of an affective-intellectual horizon in which rearguard theories may emerge through their contributions to the success of the struggles of ralliers for good living/*buen vivir*. Rearguard theories can only validate themselves by their practical results, by the evaluation of the changes made by all their protagonists, among whom the intellectual-activist is always a minor figure. That is to say, rearguard theories are, borrowing from Schopenhauer, *parerga* and *paralipomena*, minor parts of nontheoretical forms of life. They are actions of theoretical intervention woven inside forms of life. They do not wash their hands like Pontius Pilate; nor are they a Greek chorus. They specialize in skeletons, drawings, registrations, envelopes, and postal addresses—important things but far from important enough.

The inexhaustible experience of the world and indirect communication. The third reason why I consider the present moment promising for writing from the perspective of the impossibility of radicalism is today's increased awareness that the cultural, cognitive, social, ethnic-racial, productive, political, and religious diversity of the world is immense; besides its capacity to be described and represented, such diversity can be seen, shown, felt, and poetically expressed. Many factors account for this, and some of them will be analyzed in the book, but the most important one is the recent visibility of ralliers for good living/*buen vivir* and the internal diversity they reveal and celebrate. This is a kind of diversity that totally subverts the monocultural diversity of *National Geographic* or eco-ethno-cultural tourism. It is diversity with its own criteria for diversity, which, unlike monocultural diversity, turns inert simultaneity into complex contemporaneity. Unlike the touristic or entertaining gaze, which creates acts of simultaneity among noncontemporaneous people, the diversity of the ralliers for good living/*buen vivir* creates encounters among different contemporaneities—that is to say, among different forms of being contemporaneous. It reveals the polychromy and polyphony of the world without turning them into discontinuous and incommensurable, radical heterogeneity.

Unity lies in no essence. It lies in the task of building good living/*buen vivir*. Herein reside the novelty and the political imperative: to enlarge contemporaneity means to amplify the field of reciprocity between the principle of equality and the principle of the recognition of difference. Thus, the struggle for social justice expands in unsuspected ways. To the injustice regarding wealth distribution, based on the conventional concept of social justice, many other dimensions of injustice are added, having varied temporal durations and hence carrying distinct between two evils. We educate ourselves by learning how not to choose between either. When some day we enter the university—that is to say, when we occupy and decolonize it—we will not merely open the doors and redecorate the walls. We will destroy both so that we may all fit in.

What are our weapons? All weapons of life, none of death. In truth, only those weapons with proper names in our own languages belong to us. All the others are taken from our enemies as war trophies or unintended heirlooms: democracy, human rights, science, philosophy, theology, law, the university, the state, civil society, constitutionalism, and so on. We learn that, when we wield them autonomously, they frighten the enemy. However, borrowed weapons are efficacious only when used together with our own weapons. We are competent rebels. We follow sage Subcomandante Insurgente Marcos, according to whom top politicians do not understand anything; above all, they do not understand the essential: that their time is over.

Joy and celebration are what the victims feel when they stop being victims, when their suffering is turned into resistance and fight. We are artists embodied in life, and ascendant is our art. The only ugly and sad truths are those imposed on us. The truths with which we offer resistance are beautiful and joyous.

On which kinds of allies can we count? Even if we are a large majority, there are very few of us. We must get together before others try to come together with us. We ask for help but use it only to become independent of it. As we free ourselves from help, we free help itself. We ask democracy for help in order to free democracy. Democracy was invented out of fear of us, and we have always been afraid of it. Today we are not afraid, but neither do we have any illusions. We know that when we take possession of democracy, our enemies will go back to their old inventions: dictatorship, violence, theft, the arbitrary manipulation of legality and illegality. We will fight for the democratization of democracy until it frees itself from the fraud into which they have turned it. We will ask the help of human rights in order to render them unnecessary. They turned us into a global multitude of objects of human rights discourses. When we all become subjects of human rights, who will remember the concept of human rights? Could the human contain the nonhuman? We ask for the help of liberation theology to free us from theology.

Our allies are all those who are solidary with us and have a voice because they are not on our side of the line. We know that "solidarity" is a trap word. To decide unilaterally with whom one is solidary and how one is solidary is to be solidary with oneself alone. Unlike what has been the case up until now, we put conditions on solidarity. Alliance with us is demanding because our allies have to fight against three kinds of enemies: our enemies, their enemies, and the commonsensical view that there is no connection at all between the two previous kinds of enemies. Specific enemies include comfort and discomfort once certified by the same indifference-producing factory; laziness and its older sister, the laziness of whoever commands action; temporary apathy and equally modes of contemporaneity: the historical injustice of colonialism and slavery; the sexual injustice of patriarchy, gynophobia, and homophobia; the intergenerational injustice of hatred against the young and against sustainable models of development; the ethnic-racial injustice of racism and xenophobia; and the cognitive injustice committed against the wisdom of the world on behalf of the monopoly of science and the technologies sanctioned by science.

Structural (not functional) diversity is as seductive as it is threatening. It is seductive for those who see in it the reason for the end of dogmas and the opportunity to imagine and create other life possibilities. If the diversity of the world is inexhaustible, then utopia is possible. All possibilities are finite, but their number is infinite. The constituted experience is nothing more than a provisional and localized concretization of the constituent experience. The fact that the existing reality is so far away from ideals does not prove the impossibility of the latter; rather, it only proves that current reality is without ideals. However, such diversity is also threatening, particularly in the global North, because it reveals the isolation of the West. The affirmation of the diversity of the world marks a turning point in Western exceptionalism. Once seemingly originary (*archetypus*) and ascendant, showing the way forward to the "rest," it has become derivative (*ectypus*) and descendent, a conception of the world and a mode of experiencing society and nature that are being proven unsustainable.

Acknowledging this autonomous and enabling diversity is perhaps the crucial feature of the process of untraining, as partly reported in this book. It is from this perspective that I propose epistemologies of the South. Such an acknowledgment works as a safety net against the abysses into which one falls when one loses the certainty that scientific knowledge is the only valid kind of knowledge and that beyond it there is only ignorance. It is the most efficacious antidote against Wittgensteinian silencing, which is totally prey to monolanguage and monoculture. What cannot be said, or said clearly, in one language or culture may be said, and said clearly, in another language or culture. Acknowledging other kinds of knowledge and other partners in conversation for other kinds of conversation opens the field for infinite discursive and nondiscursive exchanges with unfathomable codifications and horizontalities.

The three reasons mentioned above as favoring writing from the perspective of the impossibility of radicalism may indirectly facilitate the emergence of intellectual-activist or rearguard intellectuals, as ralliers for good living/*buen vivir* call them. On the other hand, some ralliers may eventually read this book and even become interested in their reading. As far as I am concerned, however, what remains written in this book is a thought-action experiment, a gym of ideas in which I prepare myself to become a rearguard intellectual, hence a competent rebel. What the ralliers may learn from me is but a faithful mirror of what I go on learning from them.

temporary enthusiasm; the paradox of running risks just in order not to run risks; lack of arguments and excess of arguments to justify both action and inaction; abstract thought without body or passion; catalogues of principles to read rather than to live; understanding and representations geared to statistical homogeneity; criticism without irony, satire, or comedy; the belief that it is normal to be thought of as a whole and only act individually; the desire to please those who despise us while despising everybody else; a preference for still life and dread of living nature; the twin obsessions of being a client or having clients; the twin fears of losing wealth or loosing poverty; the twin uncertainties of whether the worst is over or about to come; the obsession of obsession, the uncertainty of uncertainty, the fear of fear. Only later come our enemies, those against whom we must rebel together.

In part, the enemies against whom our allies have to fight are themselves, how they came to be what they are and have to stop being themselves if they want to be our honest allies. As our comrade Amílcar Cabral once said, they will have to commit suicide as a class, which cannot be easy.

How do we build our alliances? The world is oversized for human beings and nature. The oppressive world is oversized for the oppressed. No matter how many the oppressed are, they will always be few, and fewer they will be if they are not united. Unity makes strength, but the best strength is the strength that builds unity. We have neither leaders nor followers. We organize ourselves, mobilize ourselves, reflect, and act. We are no multitude, but we do aspire to be a multitude of organizations and movements. We follow the sage Spinoza, but only to the extent that he does not contradict the sages Gandhi and Rosa Luxemburg: spontaneity disorganizes the status quo only to the extent that it organizes itself in order not to turn itself into a new status quo.

We start from purpose and action. Our problems are practical, our questions productive. We share two premises: our suffering is not reduced to the word "suffering," and we do not accept unjust suffering and instead fight for the something better to which we are entitled. Ambiguity does not paralyze us. We do not have to coincide; we have to converge. We do not have to unify; we must generalize. We translate into one another reciprocally and are very careful lest some engage more in translation than others. It is not important to agree on what it means to change the world. It is enough to be in agreement about the actions that contribute to changing it. To such an agreement many emotions and sensations contribute, which assert and criticize without words. Translation helps us define the limits and possibilities of collective action. We communicate directly and indirectly by means of smiles and affects, by the warmth of hands and arms, and by dancing, until we reach the threshold of joint action. The decision is always autonomous; different reasons may lead to convergent decisions. Nothing is irreversible, except the risks we run.

I hope this book will be read by others besides the ralliers. The latter may not be able to buy it or, in any case, have enough interest in it. Although this book was written on this side of the line, it was generated on the other side of the line. It will be intelligible and promising only for those who can imagine the end of the abyssal line I will be writing about in the following pages.

The attempt to contribute to the emergence of rearguard theories calls for repeated exercises of self-reflexivity about the ongoing untraining and reinvention. The context is similar to St. Augustine's eloquent statement as he was writing his *Confessions*: *Quaestio mihi factus sum* ("I have become a question for myself"). The difference is that the question is no longer the confession of past errors but rather participation in the construction of a personal and collective future, without ever being sure that past errors will not be repeated again.

Readers are no doubt aware that my writing from the perspective of the impossibility of radicalism is still an attempt, albeit hopeless or hopelessly honest, to retrieve radicalism by ways that catch the established powers distracted or off guard. Let me add right away: I have no way of knowing if I have succeeded. I do not know, therefore, if I am a competent rebel. I do not feel the pressing urge to write what I write, which is not troublesome. What is troublesome is not to feel the need to silence what should be silenced. The last sentence of Spinoza's *Ethics* is terrifying: *Sed omnia praeclara tam difficilia quam rara* ("All things excellent are as difficult as they are rare").

This is why this book, to a large extent, will remain incomplete.

Introduction

*Creating a Distance in Relation
to Western-centric Political Imagination
and Critical Theory*

T HE GLOBAL NORTH is getting smaller and smaller in economic as well as political and cultural terms, and yet it cannot make sense of the world at large other than through general theories and universal ideas. Observed from the outside, such a *habitus* is less and less convincing and can be viewed as the expression of a somewhat anachronistic manifestation of Western exceptionalism, even if it remains very destructive when translated into imperial politics. In sum, from this perspective, the global North seems to have little to teach the world. Is this all that important?[1] Would not the historical opportunity for the global North to learn from the experiences of the global South lie precisely here? The truth of the matter is that, after five centuries of "teaching" the world, the global North seems to have lost the capacity to learn from the experiences of the world. In other words, it looks as if colonialism has disabled the global North from learning in noncolonial terms, that is, in terms that allow for the existence of histories other than the universal history of the West.

This condition is reflected in all the intellectual work produced in the global North and, most specifically, in Western, Eurocentric critical theory.[2] A sense of exhaustion haunts the Western, Eurocentric critical tradition. It manifests itself in a peculiar and diffuse uneasiness expressed in multiple ways: irrelevance, inadequacy, impotence, stagnation, paralysis. Such uneasiness is all the more disquieting because we are living in a world in which there is so much to be criticized, in a world, moreover, in which an ever-growing number of people live in critical

---

1. Presently, I coordinate a research project, "ALICE—Strange Mirrors, Unsuspected Lessons: Leading Europe to a New Way of Sharing World Experiences," funded by the European Research Council (http://alice.ces.uc.pt/en). This project aims to develop a new theoretical paradigm for contemporary Europe based on two key ideas: the understanding of the world by far exceeds the European understanding of the world; and the much-needed social, political, and institutional reform in Europe may benefit from innovations taking place in regions and countries that European colonialism viewed as mere recipients of the civilizing mission.
2. On the difficulties of constructing a new critical theory, see Santos (1995, 1998).

conditions that imply both crisis and critique. If there is so much to criticize, why has it become so difficult to build convincing, widely shared, powerful, critical theories, theories that give rise to effective and profound transformative practices?

For the past thirty years, growing difficulties—often presented as perplexities before unintelligible political repertoires, unpredicted mobilizations and solutions, impasses attributed to a supposed lack of alternatives, and a variety of more or less sophisticated protocols of surrendering—have beset Western critical thinking both in its Marxist and libertarian streams. Three such difficulties are somewhat dilemmatic insofar as they occur at the level of the very political imagination that sustains both critical theory and, in the last instance, emancipatory politics. Three others refer to the impact of perplexities and political impasses on theory making. Taken together these difficulties call for some distance vis-à-vis the Western critical tradition.

In this introduction I analyze these difficulties and show the root causes of the uneasiness they generate. The first set of difficulties concerns the shrinking of the emancipatory political imagination. In short, they may be designated as strong questions and weak answers, the end of capitalism without end, and the end of colonialism without end.

Strong Questions and Weak Answers

One reason for the need to create a distance from the Eurocentric critical tradition is that the latter is providing only weak answers for the strong questions confronting us in our time. Strong questions address not only our specific options for individual and collective life but also the societal and epistemological paradigm that has shaped the current horizon of possibilities within which we fashion our options, the horizon within which certain options are possible while others are excluded or even unimaginable. Such questions are paradigmatic in nature since they confront the very criteria for inclusion and exclusion of specific options. They arouse, therefore, a particular kind of perplexity.

Weak answers, on the contrary, are those answers that do not challenge the horizon of possibilities. They assume that the current paradigm provides answers for all the relevant questions. They therefore fail to abate the perplexity caused by the strong questions and may, in fact, increase it. Indeed, they discard and stigmatize this perplexity as the symptom of an irrational refusal to travel according to historically tested maps. But since perplexity derives in the first place from questioning such maps, the weak answers are an invitation to immobility.

The first strong question can be formulated in this way: If humanity is one alone, why are there so many different principles concerning human dignity and social justice, all of them presumably unique, yet often contradictory? At the root of the perplexity underlying this question is a recognition that much has been left out of the modern and Western understanding of the world. The

Western-centric critical answer to this question is that such diversity is only to be recognized to the extent that it does not contradict universal human rights.[3] This is a weak answer because, by postulating the abstract universality of the conception of human dignity underlying the concept of human rights, it dismisses the perplexity underlying the question, which precisely questions the possibility of such an abstract universality.[4] The fact that such a conception is Western-based is considered irrelevant, as the historicity of human rights discourse does not interfere with its ontological status.[5]

However fully embraced by conventional political thinking and also by critical theory, particularly in the global North, this is a weak answer because it reduces the understanding of the world to the Western understanding of the world, thus ignoring or trivializing other non-Western understandings of the world, for example, decisive cultural and political experiences and initiatives in the countries of the global South. This is the case of movements or grammars of resistance that have been emerging against oppression, marginalization, and exclusion, whose ideological bases often have very little to do with the dominant Western cultural and political references prevalent throughout the twentieth century. When they resort at all to the grammar of human rights to formulate their struggles, these movements do so in terms that fully contradict the dominant understanding of human rights. The most salient examples of such movements and grammars are those of the indigenous and Afro-descendent peoples who have become very politically active in the last thirty years, particularly in Latin America. But we could also mention movements and grammars focusing on the revival of non-Western ethical, cultural, and political imaginations in Africa, Asia, and the Islamic world. They start out from cultural and political references that are non-Western, even if constituted by a resistance to Western domination. Conventional human rights thinking lacks the theoretical and analytical tools to position itself in relation to such movements; even worse, it does not understand the importance of doing

---

3. We know that human rights are not universal in their application. Four international regimes of human rights are consensually distinguished in the world in our time: the European, the Inter-American, the African, and the Asian regimes. For an extended analysis of the four regimes, see Santos (1995: 330–337, 2002b: 280–311) and the bibliographies cited there.

4. The conventional understanding of human rights includes some or all of the following characteristics: they are universally valid irrespective of the social, political, and cultural contexts in which they operate and the different human rights regimes existing in different regions of the world; they are premised on a conception of human nature as individual, self-sustaining, and qualitatively different from nonhuman nature; what counts as a violation of human rights is defined by universal declarations, multilateral institutions (courts and commissions), and established, global (mostly North-based) nongovernmental organizations; the recurrent phenomenon of double standards in evaluating compliance with human rights in no way compromises the universal validity of human rights; the respect for human rights is much more problematic in the global South than in the global North.

5. See more on this in Santos (2007b: 3–40).

so. It applies the same abstract recipe across the board, hoping that thereby the nature of alternative ideologies or symbolic universes will be reduced to local specificities with no impact on the universal canon of human rights.

The second strong question confronting our time is the following: What degree of coherence is to be required between the principles, whatever they may be, and the practices that take place in their name? This question gains a particular urgency in contact zones between the global North and the global South, or between the global West and the global East, because it is there that the discrepancy between principles and practices tends to be highest. More and more frequently we witness the massive violation of human rights in the name of human rights, the destruction of democracy in the name of democracy, the killing of innocent civilians in the name of supposedly protecting them, the devastation of liveli-hoods in the name of development, and the massive deployment of surveillance techniques and restrictions of basic freedoms in the name of preserving freedom and security. The ideological investments used to conceal such a discrepancy are as massive as the brutality of such practices.

In this case, too, the answer given by Eurocentric critical theory is a weak one. Though it denounces the discrepancy between principles and practices, it tends to subscribe uncritically to the idea that the principles of human rights, democracy, development, humanitarian intervention, and so on do not lose credibility despite their increasingly more systematic and glaring violation in practice, both by state and nonstate actors alike. Eurocentric critical thinking continues to visit with curiosity the fairs of the human rights industry, which feature ever-more new products (the Global Compact, the Millennium Goals, the War on Poverty, the War on Terror, and so forth), even though on its way there it must travel through an increasingly ungraspable graveyard of betrayed promises.

A *third strong question* emerges out of the rising presence of spirituality and religion in political struggles and the ways in which they confront the Western critical tradition. Is the process of secularization, considered to be one of the most distinctive achievements of Western modernity, irreversible? What, if any, might be the contribution of religion to social emancipation? Again, the Eurocentric critical tradition answers on the basis of Enlightenment premises and the conventional human rights they give rise to. Thus understood, human rights take secularization for granted, including the secular nature of their own foundation. Religion belongs to the private sphere, the sphere of voluntary com-mitments; therefore, from a human rights perspective, its relevance is that of a human right among others: the right to religious freedom.[6] This is a weak answer because it assumes as a given precisely what is being questioned, that is, the idea that freedom of religion is only possible in a world free of religion. What, then, if that is not the case?

---

6. For an extensive analysis, see Santos (2009).

The fourth strong question asks, Is the conception of nature as separate from society, so entrenched in Western thinking, tenable in the long run? It is becoming widely accepted that one of the novelties of the new millennium is that it will see capitalism reach its ultimate, ecological limits, that the insatiable exploitation of nature must have an end, lest human life on the planet become unsustainable. This is perhaps the strong question that raises the most perplexity, since all Western thinking, whether critical or not, is grounded on the Cartesian idea that nature is a *res extensa* and, as such, an unlimited resource unconditionally available to human beings.

The answer that Western thought gives to this question is weak because it only recognizes the problems that can be discussed within the Cartesian epistemological and ontological model. Evidence of this is found in the ideas of sustainable, integral, or human development, as well as in the environmental policies derived therefrom. No matter how many qualifiers are added to the concept of development, development keeps intact the idea of infinite growth and the unstoppable development of productive forces. Actually, global capitalism has never been so avid for natural resources as today, to the extent that it is legitimate to speak of a new extractivist imperialism. Land, water, and minerals have never been so coveted, and the struggle for them has never had such disastrous social and environmental consequences.

Thus, the Cartesian paradigm does not at all address the fundamental problem underlying this strong question. Moreover, and most importantly, it fails to understand the strength and logic of the social movements that for the past few decades have been organizing their struggles on the basis of a non-Eurocentric conception of the relation between nature and society, according to which nature appears as mother earth, a living organism to which we belong and that is entitled to its own rights. From a Cartesian point of view, the fact that the Ecuadorian constitution includes a whole section devoted to the rights of nature is juridically and ontologically absurd, a true *aberratio entis* (more on this below).

The fifth strong question may be formulated like this: Is there any room for utopia in our world? After the historical failure of so many attempts to build noncapitalist societies, and with such tragic consequences, is there really an alternative to capitalism? For how long will we continue to "solve" the problems caused by capitalism with more capitalism? Why is the economy of reciprocity and cooperation not a credible alternative to the economy of greed and competition? The perplexity caused by these questions is grounded on an even stronger question: Is it not below human dignity—if not even below human intelligence—to accept that there is no alternative to a world in which the five hundred richest individuals take in as much income as the poorest forty countries, meaning 416 million people? Is it not below Mexican human dignity that the wealth of a single Mexican citizen, Carlos Slim, constitutes 4 to 6 percent of the country's GDP and equals the combined wealth of several million Mexicans?

The concept of an alternative society and the struggle for it were the backbones of both critical theory and left politics throughout the twentieth century. The historical strength of Marxism has resided in its unique capacity to articulate the idea of an alternative future with an oppositional way of living in the present. But in recent decades, much of critical thinking and left politics, particularly in the global North, seems to have lost the capacity to formulate the idea of a credible postcapitalist future (see section below). The problem is that without a conception of an alternative society, the current state of affairs, however violent and morally repugnant, will not generate any impulse for strong or radical opposition and rebellion. This fact has certainly not escaped the political Right, which has grounded its exercise of power since the 1980s not in political consensus (based on preferences among alternatives) but rather in political resignation (based on the absence of alternatives).

The End of Capitalism without End

The second difficulty haunting the Western political imagination is a specification of the fifth strong question mentioned in the preceding section. It may be formulated in the following way: it is as difficult to imagine the end of capitalism as it is difficult to imagine that capitalism has no end. If it is true that the fall of the Berlin Wall had a devastating effect on the idea of postcapitalist futures, it is no less true that it is hard to believe that capitalism may escape the fatality of all historical phenomena, that is, the fatality of having a beginning and an end. Hence, the double difficulty. This difficulty has split Eurocentric critical thinking, both in the global North and in the global South, into two strands that have been sustaining two different political options for the Left.

The first strand gets blocked by the first difficulty (imagining the end of capitalism). As a consequence, it has stopped worrying about the end of capitalism, focusing its creativity, rather, on developing a modus vivendi with capitalism capable of minimizing the social costs of capitalist accumulation and its grounding principles of possessive individualism, competition, and the infinite expansion of exchange values. Social democracy, Keynesianism, the welfare state, and the developmentalist state of the 1960s in what was then called the Third World are the main political forms of such a modus vivendi. The bankruptcy of this strand is today dramatically evident in the financial and economic crises of Europe and the United States. It has found a second life in the Latin American subcontinent, particularly in Brazil, first under President Lula da Silva and now under President Dilma Roussef. It points to a new kind of strong state involvement in economic development, based on public/private partnerships, and wealth redistribution, based not on universal rights, as in the case of European social democracy, but rather on significant, means-tested money transfers targeted to vulnerable social groups. It leads to a new state form, the neodevelopmentalist state. This state form combines a mitigated economic nationalism—based on a strong economic public sector and an active economic diplomacy on behalf of Brazilian multinational corporations—with either passive compliance or active complicity with the institutions of global capitalism. Contrary to its European precedent, this model does not aim at confronting the fault line between rich and poor and indeed may deepen it. It believes in neoliberal economic growth as much as it disbelieves in trickle-down economics.

The other, minority strand of the Eurocentric critical tradition does not allow itself to be blocked by the first difficulty. On the contrary, it is strongly convinced that capitalism will end one day and better sooner than later. But it experiences very intensely the second difficulty (imagining how the end of capitalism will come about and what will follow it). The Latin American subcontinent offers the most vivid political manifestations of this difficulty. It is experienced in two very contrasting ways. On the one hand, it consists of imagining postcapitalist alternatives after the collapse of "real socialism" (the debate over the "socialism of the twenty-first century");[7] on the other, it consists of imagining postcapitalist alternatives by reinventing precapitalist alternatives prior to the conquest and colonialism.

Imagining postcapitalism after capitalism haunts the Eurocentric Left in its multiple forms, as illustrated in the last ten years by the governments of Venezuela, Bolivia, and Ecuador. Imagining postcapitalism before capitalism haunts the indigenous movements throughout Latin America. The debates and political struggles over the plurinational state, the *sumak kawsay*, the *sumak qamaña*, and the rights of nature in Ecuador and Bolivia are telling examples.[8] Attempts at combining the two imaginations are visible in such hybrid conceptions as the "socialism of *sumak kawsay*" in Ecuador or "communitarian socialism" in Bolivia. They seem to be failing because imaginings of postcapitalism on the basis of the current capitalist state of affairs (privileged by the governments) and postcapitalism on the basis of real or invented precapitalist ways of life (privileged by the indigenous movements) are reciprocally unintelligible without an effort at intercultural translation, which so far has not been attempted (more on this below). However, common to both is the idea that capitalism and colonialism belong together as forms of domination.

The two responses to the difficulties facing emancipatory political imagination, as exemplified by the case of Brazil, on one side, and the cases of Venezuela, Bolivia, and Ecuador, on the other, while quite distinct, share the fact that they came about through political processes based on very strong popular mobilizations. By dramatically raising the expectations of the popular classes, they make

---

7. On the topic of socialism of the twenty-first century, see Boaventura de Sousa Santos, "Socialism, 21st Century," CES, www.ces.uc.pt/opiniao/bss/182en.php.

8. This topic will be developed in *Epistemologies of the South: Reinventing Social Emancipation* (forthcoming).

new demands on the democratic mandate that, if not met, may lead to intense social frustration and possibly to violent repression. The two responses take advantage of a certain leeway that global capitalism has created (mainly through the rise of the exchange value of commodities, land, and minerals typical of extractivist imperialism) without challenging it in any significant way, even when the official rhetoric is anticapitalist and anti-imperialist, as in the cases of Venezuela, Bolivia, and Ecuador. In different ways, they reflect the current limits of counterhegemonic globalization as illustrated by the process of the World Social Forum (WSF) during the past decade.

The End of Colonialism without End

The third difficulty confronting Eurocentric emancipatory political imagination has to do with colonialism. It can be formulated in this way: it is as difficult to imagine the end of colonialism as it is to imagine that colonialism has no end. Postcolonial or decolonial studies and struggles in the past three decades have shown how entrenched colonialism is in both private and public life, even many decades after the end of historical colonialism. On the other hand, as in the case of the end of capitalism without end, it is hard to believe that colonialism will escape the fate of other social phenomena and have no end. In this case as well, Eurocentric emancipatory imagination and politics have been split into two main responses. A first strand is blocked by the first difficulty; incapable of imagining the end of colonialism, it denies the existence of colonialism itself. According to this strand, the political independence of the colonies meant the end of colonialism; since then, anticapitalism has been the only legitimate political objective of emancipatory politics. This line of Eurocentric critical thinking focuses on class struggle and hence does not acknowledge the validity of ethno-cultural-racial struggles. On the contrary, it valorizes hybridity (*mestizaje*)—which, for instance, it identifies as a key feature of Iberian colonialism—as extra proof that colonialism has been overcome. Accordingly, the idea of racial democracy,[9] rather than being defended as a legitimate aspiration, is celebrated as being already fully accomplished.

On the other hand, a second strand of the critical tradition reads the historical processes leading to independence as showing that internal colonialism has continued to exist after independence until today. It is very difficult to imagine an alternative to colonialism because internal colonialism is not only, or mainly, a state policy; it is rather a very wide social grammar that permeates social relations, public and private spaces, culture, mentalities, and subjectivities. In sum, it is a way of life, a form of unequal conviviality that is often shared by both those who benefit from it and those who suffer its consequences. According to this

---

9. In Brazil's case, racial democracy was first systematized by the anthropologist Gilberto Freyre (1946).

strand of the critical tradition, the anticapitalist struggle must be fought side by side with the anticolonial struggle. Class domination and ethno-cultural-racial domination feed on each other, which means that the struggle for equality cannot be separated from the struggle for the recognition of difference. According to this strand, the postcolonial challenge has been inscribed in all the regions of the world that were once subjected to European colonialism, and the inscription has lasted from the conquest, invasion, or occupation into our time. It has been formulated most eloquently by Frantz Fanon (1967a) and before him by José Mariátegui, when, while referring to Peruvian society (though his statement is applicable to other Latin American societies as well), he mentioned the original sin inscribed in it by the conquest: "the sin of emerging and becoming without the Indian and against the Indian" (1974a [1925]: 208).

In a paradoxical way, the militant postcolonial, decolonizing struggles and movements of the last thirty years, which have been so influential in discrediting the first strand, have also contributed to discrediting the second strand due to their inability (glaring in the case of indigenous and Afro-descendent movements) to articulate ethno-cultural struggles with class-based struggles and thus to build broader political alliances that might prevent their social and political isolation.

These difficulties confronting the progressive political imagination are reflected in four other difficulties that have an even more direct impact upon the theories that have been developed to account for emancipatory social transformation. In short, they can be designated thus: urgency versus civilizational change; the very old and the very new; the loss of critical nouns; and the ghostly relation between theory and practice.

The Paradox of Urgency and Civilizational Change

We live in a time torn apart by two extreme and contradictory temporalities disputing the time frame of collective action. On the one hand, there is a sense of urgency. A long series of phenomena seems to demand that absolute priority be given to immediate or short-term action because the long term may not even exist if the trends expressed in those phenomena are allowed to evolve without control. Here are some of the phenomena that come to mind: global warming and the imminent ecological catastrophe; the destructive impact of unregulated financial capital upon the lives and expectations of people; the vanishing sustainability of the livelihoods of vast populations (as in the case of water, for example); the uncontrolled drive for eternal war and the violence and unjust destruction of human life it causes; the increasing scale of the depletion of natural resources; and, finally, the exponential growth of social inequality that gives rise to new forms of social fascism, that is, social regimes regulated only by extreme power differences or status hierarchies of a new kind, the seemingly neofeudal hierarchies. To be sure, the specific phenomena and the mixes among them that create the pressure of urgency vary in the global North and the global South, but most of them seem to be present everywhere, albeit in different forms and with different intensities.

On the other hand, there is a sense that our time calls for deep and long-term civilizational changes. The phenomena mentioned above are symptoms of deep-seated structures and agencies, which cannot be confronted by short-run interventionism insofar as the latter is as much a part of the civilizational paradigm as the state of affairs it fights. The twentieth century proved with immense cruelty that to take power is not enough and that, rather than taking power, it is necessary to transform power.[10] This double and paradoxical uncertainty poses new epistemological, theoretical, and political challenges. It invites open-ended formulations of an alternative society whose strength relies more on the intensity with which it rejects the current state of affairs than on the precision of alternatives advanced. Such open-ended formulations consist of affirming the possibility of a better future and another possible world without knowing for sure if the latter is possible and what it will be like. It is therefore a very different utopia from the modern utopias that are at the foundation of the Eurocentric critical tradition.

The coexistence of these polar temporalities is producing great turbulence in old distinctions and cleavages that were at the core of Eurocentric critical theory and politics, such as those between tactics and strategy, the short term and the long term, and reform and revolution. While the sense of urgency calls for tactics and reform in the short term, the sense of civilizational paradigmatic change calls for long-term strategy and revolution. But the fact that both senses coexist and are pressing disfigures the terms of the distinctions and cleavages and makes them more or less meaningless and irrelevant. At best, they become loose signifiers prone to contradictory appropriations. There are reformist processes that seem revolutionary (Hugo Chávez in Venezuela) and revolutionary processes that seem reformist (Neozapatismo in Mexico) and reformist processes whose reformism is highly questionable (Brazil, India, and South Africa, for instance).

The fall of the Berlin Wall, while dealing a mortal blow to the idea of revolution, struck a silenced but no less deadly blow to the idea of reform. Since then we live in a time that turns reformism into counterreformism with an astonishing lack of democratic accountability and with a no less astonishing passivity on the part of citizens. It is a time that is either too late to be postrevolutionary or too premature to be prerevolutionary. As a result, political polarizations become relatively unregulated and exhibit meanings that have very little to do with the names attached to them. Under these circumstances, theoretical reconstruction in the Eurocentric tradition and style becomes difficult, messy, and unconvincing; moreover, no one seems to be very much concerned about it.

---

10. The idea of refusing to take power was popularized on the basis of a wrong interpretation of the ideas of Subcommandante Marcos, leader of the Neozapatistas. See Holloway (2002). More on this below.

In my view, the World Social Forum has shown the bankruptcy of this theoretical tradition and style by responding pragmatically to these unresolved tensions between contradictory temporalities and theoretical claims. With all its limitations, which became more evident as the decade progressed (Santos 2006b, 2008), the WSF fostered the expression of campaigns, coalitions of discourses, and practices focused either on immediate action or, to the contrary, on long-term transformation. Calls for immediate debt cancellation got articulated with long-lasting campaigns of popular education concerning HIV/AIDS; denunciations of the criminalization of social protest by indigenous peoples before the courts went hand in hand with the struggle for the recognition of the cultural identity and ancestral territories of the same peoples; the struggle for immediate access to sufficient potable water by the people of Soweto (South Africa) in the wake of the privatization of water supplies became part and parcel of a long-term strategy to guarantee sustainable access to water throughout the African continent, as illustrated in the Constitution of the Africa Water Network[11] in Nairobi during the WSF-2007.

These different time frames of struggle came to coexist peacefully in the WSF for three main reasons. First, they translated themselves into struggles that shared the same mix of institutional and postinstitutional/direct collective action. This was a significant departure from the Eurocentric leftist theorizing that dominated throughout the twentieth century. For the latter, the struggle for short-range objectives was always framed as legal gradualism, as nonradical, institutional activism. Second, mutual knowledge of such diverse temporalities among movements and organizations led to the idea that the differences among them were much wider in theory than in practice. A radical call for immediate action could be the best way of giving credibility to the need for a civilizational change, if for no other reason than because of the unsurpassable obstacles it would be bound to run up against. The WSF also drew attention to untheorized possibilities such as those brought about by some major movements that combined in their overall activism both immediate-time and civilizational-time frameworks. This was (and is) the case with the MST (movement of landless rural workers in Brazil), which combined illegal land occupations to feed hungry peasants with massive actions of popular political education aimed at a much broader transformation of the Brazilian state and society.[12] It is also the case with indigenous movements in Latin America and India, which are calling for the validity of non-Eurocentric cosmovisions and conceptions of the state while also fighting to stop the megaprojects that are already under way and that have ruined their livelihoods.

The final reason for the pragmatic coexistence of contradictory temporalities was that the WSF did not set priorities between them; it simply opened a space

---

11. Available online at the Transnational Institute website (www.tni.org).
12. See also Santos and Carlet (2010).

for discussion and coalition building among the movements and organizations, the outcomes of which could be most diverse. An overriding sense of a common purpose, however vaguely defined, to build another possible world tended to deemphasize theoretical polarizations among the movements and invite the latter to concentrate on building more intense coalitions wherever and whenever the affinities were more inviting. Selectivity in coalition building became a way of avoiding unnecessary polarization.

Very Old or Very New? The Example of the Yasuní Project

The second difficulty confronting Eurocentric critical theory has also to do with conflicting temporalities, this time not short term versus long term but rather the nature of the temporal trajectory of the political innovation emerging in the present: innovation as the very new or as the reinvention of the very old. In order to illustrate this difficulty in valorizing adequately new/old fields of alternatives (up until now "wasted" or ignored by the Western critical tradition), I will refer briefly to one of the transformations that has recently been proposed in Latin America: the Yasuní ITT project in Ecuador, a highly disputed project. The Yasuní ITT project, presented for the first time in 2007 by the then minister of energy and mines, Alberto Acosta,[13] is an alternative to the developmentalist-extractivist capitalist model of development that is today prevalent in Latin America and Africa and, actually, in most of the global South. It calls for an international coresponsibility of a new type, a new relation among more- and less-developed countries, and it aims at a new, postoil model of development. Ecuador is a poor country in spite of—or because of—its being rich in oil. Its economy depends heavily on oil exports: oil income constitutes 22 percent of the GNP and 63 percent of exports. The human and environmental destruction in Amazonia caused by this economic model is truly impressive. As a direct consequence of oil exploitation by Texaco and later Chevron, between 1960 and 1990 two entire Amazonian peoples disappeared: the Tetetes and the Sansahauris.

The Ecuadorian initiative tries to break loose from this past and proposes the following: The Ecuadorian state vouches to leave unexploited in the subsoil oil reserves estimated at 850 million barrels in three blocs of the National Amazonian Park of Yasuní, one of the richest biodiversity regions of the planet, on the condition that the more developed countries reimburse Ecuador by half the income Ecuador would surrender as a consequence of this decision. According to government estimates, the exploitation would generate, in the course of thirteen years, an income of €4 billion to €5 billion, while emitting 410 tons of CO_2 into the atmosphere. This could be avoided if Ecuador were to be compensated with

---

13. Acosta later became the president of the Constitutional Assembly that promulgated the Constitution of 2008.

€2 billion. This money would go to environmentally correct investments such as renewable energies, reforestation, and so on; the money would be received as warrantee certificates, or credits that the "donor" countries would retrieve, with interest, should Ecuador decide to engage in oil exploitation.

Unlike the Kyoto Protocol, this proposal does not aim to create a carbon market; rather, it aims to prevent carbon emissions. It does not limit itself to appealing to the diversification of energy sources; it suggests the need to reduce energy demands. It combines Western-centric environmental concerns with indigenous conceptions of the Pachamama (mother earth). It vindicates the right of nature to be protected as a living entity whenever the stability and regeneration of its vital cycles are threatened. It proclaims the idea of *sumak kawsay*, good living, as an alternative to the Western conceptions of development, all of them considered unsustainable because they rely on infinite growth. It must be assessed as an indigenous contribution to the entire world. It has actually earned more and more followers among citizens and movements as it has become clearer and clearer that environmental degradation and the unfair pillaging of irreplaceable natural resources are leading to the collective suicide of humankind.

The internal political turmoil provoked by this proposal is a clear sign of the magnitude of what it entails.[14] At stake is the first great, concrete break with the developmentalist-extractivist economic model. The possibility of its becoming a precedent for other, similar initiatives in other countries is very threatening to global capitalism, particularly to the powerful oil interests. On the other hand, the proposal demands an equally new pattern of international cooperation, a cooperation sustainable over the course of many years and capable of addressing two equally legitimate interests: Ecuador's interest in preserving its national sovereignty, given the risks it incurs in internationalizing its development plans, and the interests of the international taxpayers, concerned that their contributions not be used for ends not previously agreed upon. This will be a very different type of cooperation from the one that has prevailed in center-periphery relations in the modern world-system, dominated by imperialism, double standards, structural adjustments, unequal exchange, forced alignment, and so on.

This proposal raises several theoretical and political challenges. The first probably is how to deal with the temporal identity of this initiative. Is it new because it aims at a postcapitalist future and constitutes an unprecedented novelty

---

14. In August 2010, with the purpose of going ahead with the project, Ecuador signed an agreement with the United Nations Development Project that will be administrated by the Multi-Donor Trust Fund. Until now it has received contributions from Chile, Spain, Belgium, Italy, and France. Germany failed to assume its contribution and is still debating about whether to participate. As expected, the most polluting countries of the world are absent from this initiative. Under these circumstances, the government of Ecuador faces a dilemma: keep waiting for the support of the international community or, if that fails (and it seems the needed percentage will not be reached), explore the oil in ITT. However, many social sectors in the country demand a coherent position with regard to the rights of nature and call for the interdiction of ITT oil exploration or even a general extractive ban.

within the logic of modern development, or rather, is it new because it calls for an unprecedented return to or reinvention of an ancient precapitalist past grounded on indigenous, non-Western conceptions of nature? In the first case, the novelty approaches a utopia; in the second case, it approaches an anachronism. In the following I present some of the analytical dilemmas.

It is not easy to analyze new or innovative social, political, and cultural processes. There is the real risk of submitting them to old conceptual and analytical frameworks that are incapable of capturing their novelty and are therefore prone to devalue, ignore, or demonize them. This difficulty carries a dilemma not immediately obvious: it is only possible to create new analytical and conceptual frameworks on the basis of the processes that generate the very need to create them. How is this need to be identified? How is it to be felt? This need is metatheoretical and meta-analytical; that is to say, it implies the political choice to consider such processes as new rather than as extensions of old processes. How to theorize this choice if exactly the same processes, save the rare case of total structural ruptures, may call for either political option for equally credible reasons? Behind the choice there is a wager, an act of will and imagination, rather than an act of speculative reason.[15] Choosing novelty implies willing novelty. Grounding this will is a sense of uneasiness and nonconformism vis-à-vis our present based on the conviction that we deserve better. Of course, for the wager to be credible, it is necessary to invoke reasonable arguments. But such arguments are made against a background of uncertainty and ignorance, the very ingredients of the wager. The matter becomes even more complex once the novelty aims at the future by pointing to the past, even to an ancient past. For a mode of thinking molded by the modern conception of linear time, this is absurd: whatever aims at going back to the past is old, not new. To be minimally consistent, it must involve an invention of the past, in which case the why and how of the invention become the issue. That brings us back to the question of novelty.

The difficulty may perhaps be even greater: a successful wager on novelty does not imply the sustainability of successful novelty. In other words, an unequivocally new or novel process may fail precisely on account of its being new. The new has to confront not only the old theories and concepts but also the social and political forces that mobilize themselves with particular efficacy when faced with something new. The ultimate meaning of conservatism resides in its resistance to the new, which, at its best, is conceived of as a threat to what can be reached by means of the old. This conservatism can emerge from the right as well as from the left. Here again the possible dual nature of novelty returns. Conservatism will confront it in two contrasting ways, either because the new has no precedent in the past or because the new resorts to a past too ancient to belong to the conservative conception of the past. In the particular case of Latin America, to claim a precolonial past is a revolutionary proposition for conservatives since they are

---

15. On the wager, see Chapter 3.

the children of the colonizers. For the same reason, for Eurocentric progressives, to claim a precolonial past is an embarrassment at best and an exposure of false consciousness at worst.

There is yet another difficulty. The new or novel can only be analyzed on its own terms as it is occurring. Once the occurrence is over—the moment and the nature of closure are usually highly disputable—it is no longer new. The old takes hold. To resist against closure, the wager on the new has to be followed by the wager on nonclosure, on the Not Yet. The second wager requires that the analysis always be as open and incomplete as what is being analyzed. It goes along with the ongoing processes in analytical real time, so to speak. What is being analyzed today may no longer exist tomorrow. Even the political meaning of the analysis may change rapidly, as rapidly as different political forces destroy, co-opt, or subvert the agendas of their adversaries. Any theoretical-analytical construction thus necessarily has a programmatic dimension. Such a dimension is nevertheless not to be conceived of as the vanguard of an ongoing social and political process always on the verge of being betrayed by a mediocre reality. On the contrary, it is rather a rearguard construction that examines how the most exhilarating social and political processes accumulate forgotten themes, lost alliances, unacknowledged mistakes, unfulfilled promises, and disguised betrayals.

The Loss of Critical Nouns

The third difficulty in generating powerful and convincing critical-theoretical work in the Eurocentric political imagination is what I call the *loss of critical nouns*. There was a time when Eurocentric critical theory "owned" a vast set of nouns that marked its difference from conventional or bourgeois theories. These nouns included socialism, communism, revolution, class struggle, dependency, alienation, fetishism of commodities, and so on. In the past thirty years the Eurocentric critical tradition seems to have lost "its" nouns and now distinguishes itself from conventional or bourgeois theories by the adjectives it uses to subvert the meaning of the proper nouns it borrows from such theories. Thus, for instance, if conventional theory speaks of development, critical theory refers to alternative, integral, inclusionary, democratic, or sustainable development; if conventional theory speaks of democracy, critical theory proposes radical, participatory, or deliberative democracy. The same happens with cosmopolitanism, which ends up being called subaltern, oppositional, insurgent, or rooted cosmopolitanism; human rights turns into radical, collective, or intercultural human rights.

These changes must be carefully analyzed. Hegemonic concepts (nouns) are not, at the pragmatic level, an inalienable property of conventional or bourgeois thinking. As I have suggested elsewhere (Santos 2002b) and will elaborate upon in a later chapter, one of the distinctive features of current grassroots collective action in different parts of the world is precisely the capacity shown by social movements to use hegemonic tools or concepts, such as the rule of law, democracy, and human rights, in counterhegemonic ways and for counterhegemonic purposes. Adjectives may subvert the meaning of nouns. As Voltaire said, "Adjectives are the enemies of nouns." On the other hand, we must bear in mind that nouns establish the intellectual and political horizon of that which is sayable, credible, legitimate, or realistic and, by implication, of that which is unsayable, incredible, illegitimate, or unrealistic. In other words, by taking refuge in adjectives, critical theory believes in the creative use of what I would call *conceptual franchising*, while at the same time accepting the need to frame its debates and proposals within a horizon of possibilities that initially is not its own. Critical theory thus assumes a derivative character that allows it to engage in debate but does not allow it to discuss the terms of the debate, let alone why one might opt for one kind of debate and not for another. In fact, the efficacy of the counterhegemonic use of hegemonic concepts or tools depends on the consciousness of such limits.

As I will discuss in the next section, such limits are now becoming more highly visible as social struggles in different regions of the world are introducing new concepts that have no precedent in Eurocentric critical theory and, indeed, no adequate expression in any of the colonial languages in which critical theory has been formulated.

The Ghostly Relation between Theory and Practice

The final difficulty confronting Eurocentric critical theory and political imagination consists in the huge discrepancy between what is stated or foreseen in theory, on the one hand, and the most innovative, transformative practices taking place in the world, on the other. For the past thirty years, the most advanced struggles have had as their protagonists social groups whose political existence Eurocentric critical theory (and the political Left it founded) has not acknowledged: women, indigenous peoples, peasants, Afro-descendents, *piqueteros*, the unemployed, gays and lesbians, the *indignados*, and the Occupy movement. These social groups organize themselves very often in ways totally different (social movements, grassroots communities, rallies, self-government initiatives, land and building occupations, popular economic organizations, petitions, popular assemblies, referenda, collective presences in public spaces, and so forth) from those privileged by Eurocentric critical theory (the workers' party and the union, institutional action, armed struggle, and the strike). Most of them dwell not in industrial urban centers but rather in remote sites, whether in the forests and river basins in India or up in the Andes and in the large plains of Amazonia.

This discrepancy between theory and practice had a moment of great visibility at the World Social Forum at the beginning of the first decade of the millennium. The WSF, whose first meeting took place in Porto Alegre, Brazil, in 2001, has shown that the gap between the practices and classical theories of the Left is deeper than ever. The truth is that the WSF is not alone, as evidenced by the political experiences of the last decade in Latin America, the region where the WSF emerged. Consider the grassroots organizations developed by liberation theology, the Zapatista Army of National Liberation (EZLN) in Chiapas, and the transformative constitutionalism that began with the 1988 Constitution of Brazil and was followed by many other constitutions in the 1990s and 2000s; the collapse of the traditional oligarchic parties and the emergence of parties of a new type; the Argentinian *piqueteros* and the MST in Brazil; the indigenous movements of Bolivia, Ecuador, Colombia, Peru, and the Frente Amplio of Uruguay; the emergence of self-designated revolutionary processes out of liberal democratic elections; the successive victories of Hugo Chávez in Venezuela and the coexistence of popular power organizations with liberal democratic institutions; the election of Evo Morales in Bolivia, Rafael Correa in Ecuador, Fernando Lugo in Paraguay, and José Mujica in Uruguay; the struggle of the whole subcontinent against the Free Trade Area of the Americas (ALCA); and the alternative project of regional integration (the Bolivarian Alternative for the Americas, or ALBA). These are all political practices and initiatives that cannot but be recognized as progressive, although most of them do not really fit the major theoretical traditions of the Eurocentric Left and may even contradict them. As an international event and a meeting point for so many practices of resistance and alternative-society projects, the World Social Forum has added a new dimension to this mutual blindness—the blindness of practice vis-à-vis theory and of theory vis-à-vis practice—and has created the conditions for a broader and deeper reflection on this problem.

The blindness of theory renders practice invisible or undertheorized, whereas the blindness of practice renders theory irrelevant. The blindness of theory can be seen in how the parties of the conventional Left, together with the intellectuals at their service, have initially refused to pay attention to the WSF and minimized its significance, as well as in the often racist views of the Eurocentric Left with regard to the indigenous movement. The same blindness can equally be traced in the current evaluations of the movements of the *indignados*[16] throughout Europe

---

16. Excerpt from the Real Democracy Now! manifesto: "We are ordinary people. We are like you: people, who get up every morning to study, work or find a job, people who have family and friends. People, who work hard every day to provide a better future for those around us. Some of us consider ourselves progressive, others conservative. Some of us believe in socialism, others in laissez faire. Some of us have clearly defined ideologies, others are apolitical however all of us are concerned, troubled and angry about the political, economic, and social outlook in our society: politicians, businessmen, bankers, with a monopoly on power leaving us helpless, without a voice. Our powerless situation has become normal, a daily suffering, without hope. Yet if we join forces, we can change our communities, our society, our country, our world. It's time. We must build a better world together and start here at home, we must protest, camp, demonstrate and occupy for the future, peacefully always." Available at "Our Manifesto," Real Democracy Now! www.realdemocracynow.webeden.co.uk/#/our-manifesto/4551801662.

or of the Occupy movement in North America, according to which the affective proximity cannot be theoretically expressed without grossly distorting what the *indignados* or Occupy do and think about what they are doing.

The blindness of practice, in turn, is clearly present in the scorn shown by the large majority of WSF activists, by the indigenous leaders, and most recently by the *indignados* for the rich theoretical tradition of the Eurocentric Left and their utter indifference to its self-proclaimed need for renewal. This mutual misencounter generates, on the practice side, an extreme oscillation between revolutionary spontaneity and innocuous, self-imposed restriction and, on the theory side, an equally extreme oscillation between the postfactum reconstructive zeal and arrogant indifference to what is not amenable to reconstruction.

In such conditions, the relation between theory and practice assumes strange characteristics. On the one hand, theory is no longer at the service of the future collective actions it potentially contains and rather serves to legitimate (or not) the current collective actions that have emerged despite it. Thus, vanguard thought stops being orientation and rather serves as either ratification of the successes obtained by default or confirmation of preannounced failures. On the other hand, practice justifies itself by resorting to a theoretical bricolage that responds to the needs of the moment, made up of heterogeneous concepts and languages that, from the point of view of theory, are no more than opportunistic rationalizations or rhetorical exercises. From the point of view of theory, theoretical bricolage never qualifies as theory. From the point of view of practice, a posteriori vanguard theorization is mere parasitism if not altogether a *contradictio in adjecto*. This ghostly relation between theory and practice yields three political facts, all of which were made evident by the WSF process decisive for our understanding of the situation of the Left today.

Who Is the Enemy?

The first political fact is the discrepancy between short-term certainties and long-term uncertainties, which has never been so wide. To an unprecedented extent, for the last three decades neoliberal capitalism has been subjecting more and more social relations to the laws of the market. The exponential growth of social inequality, the brutal intensification of exploitation and exclusion in both peripheral and core countries, confers to the resistance struggles a strong sense of short-term urgency and allows for ample convergences regarding short-term goals (struggles against savage privatizations, social and economic injustice, bailouts of the banking system, unregulated financial markets, budget cuts in social policies, scandalous fiscal bonanzas for mining companies, the International Monetary Fund's one-size-fits-all recipes, landgrabbing, neoextractivism, and so forth). What remains unclear is if the struggles are aimed at confronting capitalism on behalf of socialism or some other postcapitalist future or, on the contrary, against this type of capitalism (neoliberalism) on behalf of a type of capitalism with a more human face.

This lack of clarity is not a new problem, but it gains now a new intensity. The impetus of neoliberal capitalism is so overwhelming that what actually ends up conniving with it can credibly be seen as struggling against it. By the same token, the uncertainty regarding the long term now has a new dimension: whether there is indeed a long term at all. That is to say, the long term in itself has become so uncertain that conflicts about it cease to be important or mobilizing. As a consequence, the short term expands, and concrete political polarizations occur in the light of short-term certainties. Discrediting the long term favors tactics and prevents polarizations about the long term from interfering with short-term mobilization. The other side of the total opening to the long-term future is the latter's total irrelevance.

The increasing uncertainty and open-endedness of the long term in left politics are expressed in the transition from the certainty in Marx of the socialist future as the scientific result of the development of the productive forces, to the binary socialism or barbarism formulated by Rosa Luxemburg, to the idea that "another world is possible" that presides over the WSF. The long term has always been the strong horizon of critical theory and left politics. In the past, the greater the distance of that horizon from the realities of present-day capitalism, the more radical the political strategy, hence the cleavage between revolution and reform. Nowadays, this cleavage seems to suffer from an erosion that goes along with that of the long term. As I said above, the long term is still there, but it is no longer very consistent or pregnant with consequences.

How to Measure Success or Failure?

The second consequence of the ghostly relationship between theory and practice is the impossibility of a consensual account regarding the performance of transformative politics. Again, this is not a new problem, but it is now more dilemmatic. For some, the crisis of the Left since the 1970s is manifested in a certain retrogression of the class struggle and in its partial replacement by the so-called identity and cultural turns and the struggles they privilege. The WSF has been both a symptom and a confirmation of this transformation. For others, this was a period teeming with innovation and creativity, in which the Left renovated itself through new struggles, new forms of collective action, and new political goals. According to the latter position, there was certainly a retrogression, but it concerned rather the classical forms of political organization and action; also, thanks to this retrogression new forms of political organization and action emerged. For those who sustain the idea of the general retrogression, the balance is negative, and the supposed novelties result in a dangerous and surrendering deviation from primary objectives (class struggle in the domain of production) to secondary objectives (identity, culture, or, in a word, objectives in the domain of social reproduction). According to this view, this was no more than a yielding to the enemy, no matter how radical the discourses of rupture. On the contrary, for those who defend the idea of innovation and creativity, the balance is positive, because the blocking dogmatisms have been shattered, the forms of collective action and the social bases supporting them have been enlarged, and, above all, the struggles, by their forms and range, have managed to reveal new vulnerabilities in the enemy. Among the protagonists of the struggles in the last decade, the latter position prevails, even though the former, arguing the idea of the general retrogression, is quite visible in the participation of some organizations (mainly trade unions) in the WSF or in the *indignados* mobilizations.

In the assessment of the last thirty years, resorting to the fallacy of hypothetical pasts is very common, be it to show that if the bet on the class struggle had prevailed, the results would have been better or, on the contrary, that without the new struggles the results would have been much worse.

Inconsequent Extremisms?

The third consequence deriving from the ghostly relationship between theory and practice is theoretical extremism of a new kind, relatively uncoupled from the long-term horizon debate mentioned above. It concerns polarizations that are simultaneously much larger and much more inconsequential than the ones that characterized the debates until the 1970s. The uncertainty and open-endedness of the long term, while preventing polarizations-with-consequences, invite extreme polarizations-without-consequences. Compared with these more recent positions, the extreme positions of the past seem less distant among themselves. And yet choosing between them yielded at the time far more concrete consequences in the life of the organizations, militants, and societies than what happens today. The current polarizations, on the contrary, are not directly linked to concrete political organizations; nor do they carry significant consequences. The main dimensions of present-day theoretical extremism are three.

As regards the subjects of social transformation, the polarization is between those for whom the struggles for social emancipation are to be fought by a well-defined historical subject, the working class and its allies, on the one hand, and those for whom such struggles are open to a plurality of ill-defined collective subjects, be they all the oppressed, "common people therefore rebels" (Subcomandante Marcos), the movement of movements (WSF), or the *multitude* (Toni Negri and Michael Hardt). This is a huge difference compared to that of the past. Until the 1970s, the polar positions focused "only" on the delimitation of the working class (the industrial vanguard versus retrograde sectors), on the identification of allies, be they the peasants or the petty bourgeoisie, on the move from "class in itself" to "class for itself," and so on and so forth. But the options they led to had a decisive (sometimes fatal) impact on the lives of the militants. To stick to the example given above of José Mariátegui, suffice it to remember the threats he received from the Comintern[17] on account of his "romantic deviance" in favor of the indigenous peoples.[18] His premature death saved him from such threats.

Concerning the goals of the social struggle, the polarization is between the seizure of power and the total rejection of the concept of power, that is to say, between the statism that has prevailed on the Left, in one way or another, and the most radical antistatism, as in John Holloway's (2002) problematic interpretation of the Zapatista movement, namely, that it is possible to change the world without seizing power. Until the 1970s, the polarization occurred around the means of seizing power (armed struggle or direct action versus institutional struggle) and the nature and goals of the exercise of power once seized (popular democracy/ dictatorship of the proletariat versus participatory/representative democracy).

Concerning organization, the polarization is between those for whom some kind of centralized organizations, such as parties and trade unions, are necessary to carry out successful struggles and those who reject any kind of centralism or even any kind of organization beyond that which emerges spontaneously in the course of the collective action, by the initiative of the actors themselves as a whole. Until the 1970s, the distance among polar positions was much narrower, but the option for one or the other carried concrete and often tragic consequences. The polarization occurred between communist and socialist parties, between one single party and a multiparty system; it addressed the relation between party and the masses or the forms of organization of the workers' party (democratic centralism versus decentralization and internal pluralism).

We are facing, therefore, polarizations of a different kind, between new and more demarcated positions. This does not mean that the previous ones have disappeared; they have just lost their exclusivity and centrality. The new polarizations do have consequences for political action; yet these are certainly more diffuse than those of previous polarizations. The reason is twofold. On the one hand, the aforementioned ghostly relationship between theory and practice contributes to rendering political activism relatively immune to theoretical polarizations or encourages it to use them selectively and instrumentally. On the other, actors in extreme positions do not dispute the same social bases and do not militate in

---

17. Abbreviation for the Communist International, also known as the Third International. The International intended to fight "by all available means, including armed force, for the overthrow of the international bourgeoisie and for the creation of an international Soviet republic as a transition stage to the complete abolition of the State."

18. Victorio Codovilla, the leader of the Comintern's South American Secretariat, instructed Mariátegui to prepare a document for a 1929 Latin American Communist Conference analyzing the possibility of forming an Indian republic in South America. This republic was to be modeled on similar Comintern proposals to construct black republics in the southern United States and South Africa. Mariátegui rejected this proposal, asserting that existing nation-state formation was too advanced in the South American Andes to build a separate Indian republic. From Mariátegui's point of view, it would be better for the subaltern Indians to fight for equality within existing state structures instead of further marginalizing themselves from the benefits of modernity in an autonomous state (Becker 2006). See also Löwy (2005b).

the same organizations or even in the same nonorganizations. The contours of political options, therefore, look rather like the parallel lives of the Left.

To a great extent, such disjunctions are due to the fact that transformative political mobilizations in our time are not confined to the cultural universe of the Eurocentric Left as we have known it. On the contrary, they go far beyond it. They belong to very distinct cultural, symbolic, and linguistic universes, and the disjunctions they give rise to will not be mutually intelligible without intercultural translation.[19]

In my view, herein lies the most important factor behind the ghostly relationship between theory and practice. While Eurocentric critical theory and left politics were historically developed in the global North, indeed in only five or six countries of the global North (Germany, England, France, Russia, Italy, and, to a smaller extent, the United States), the most innovative and effective transformative left practices of recent decades, as I mentioned above, have been occurring in the global South. The Western critical tradition developed in light of the perceived needs and aspirations of European oppressed classes, not in light of those of the oppressed classes of the world at large. Both from a cultural and a political economy point of view, the "European universalism" that this tradition embodied and that the Frankfurt School celebrated was indeed a particular reading of a particular reality that, for instance, did not include colonialism as a system of oppression, even though the majority of the world population was subjected to it.[20]

Today, a wide variety of transformative progressive practices occur in the former colonial world outside Europe or North America, in unfamiliar places, carried out by strange people who often speak very strange noncolonial languages (Aymara,[21] Quechua,[22] Guaraní,[23] Hindi,[24] Urdu,[25] IsiZulu,[26] Kikongo,[27] or Kiswahili[28]) or less hegemonic colonial languages such as Spanish and Portuguese, and their cultural and political references are non-Western. Moreover, when we translate their discourses into a colonial language, there is often no trace of the familiar

---

19. On intercultural translation, see Chapter 8.

20. To be sure, the anticolonial struggles and the movement of the nonaligned countries, founded in Bandung in 1955, also contributed important new concepts and ideas to the hegemonic northern, left script.

21. Aymara is an Aymaran language with about 2.2 million speakers in Bolivia, Peru (where it is an official language), Chile, and Argentina.

22. Quechua is an indigenous language of the Andean region, spoken today by approximately 13 million people in Bolivia, Peru, Ecuador, northern Chile, Argentina, and southern Colombia. It was the official language of Tawantinsuyu, the Inca Empire.

23. Guaraní is a Tupí-Guaraní language spoken by about 4.6 million people in Paraguay, where it is one of the official languages. There are also small communities of Guaraní speakers in Bolivia, Brazil, and Argentina.

24. More than 180 million people in India regard Hindi as their mother tongue. Another 300 million use it as a second language. Outside India, Hindi speakers number 100,000 in the United States; 685,170 in Mauritius; 890,292 in South Africa; 232,760 in Yemen; 147,000 in Uganda; 5,000 in Singapore; 8 million in Nepal; 20,000 in New Zealand; and 30,000 in Germany.

concepts with which Western left politics were historically built, such as revolution, socialism, the working class, capital, democracy, and human rights. Instead, we encounter concepts such as land, water, territory, self-determination, dignity, respect, good living, and mother earth.

It is therefore not surprising that Eurocentric critical theory and left politics do not recognize or understand the counterhegemonic grammars and practices emerging in the global South. Indeed, the Eurocentric tradition becomes provincialized by the emergence of critical understandings and transformative practices in the world that do not fit their frameworks. Moreover, such movements in the global South often refuse to refer their experiences to what they see as the unproductive Northern binary of left or right. If a distance vis-à-vis Eurocentric critical theory is not successfully maintained, one runs the risk of not adequately identifying or valorizing the political novelties occurring worldwide and their eventual contribution to emancipatory politics at large.

Theorizing after the WSF

The WSF originated in the global South based on cultural and political premises that defied all the hegemonic traditions of the Eurocentric Left. Its novelty, which was strengthened as the WSF moved from Porto Alegre to Mumbai and later to Nairobi and more recently to Dakar, lay in inviting these left traditions to be present but not as the sole legitimate traditions. They were invited along with many other traditions of critical knowledge, transformative practices, and conceptions of a better society. Movements and organizations could interact over the course of several days and plan for collaborative actions even though they came from disparate critical traditions and were united only by a very broadly defined purpose to fight against neoliberal globalization and for "another possible world." This had a profound impact on the relationship between theory and practice.

The experience of the WSF, no matter how it evolves in the future (if the current version of the WSF has a future at all), has made an important contribution to unraveling the ghostly relationship between theory and practice. It has made

---

25. Urdu is an Indo-Aryan language with about 104 million speakers, including those who speak it as a second language. It is the national language of Pakistan.

26. One of the official languages of South Africa, it is spoken by about 9 million people, mainly in Zululand and northern Natal in South Africa and also in Botswana, Lesotho, Malawi, Mozambique, and Swaziland.

27. There are more than 7 million native speakers of Kikongo, many of whom live in western Congo (Kinshasa), where Kongo is a national language. The remaining native speakers live in Congo (Brazzaville) and northern Angola. An additional 7 million Africans claim Kongo as a second language.

28. This is a Bantu language spoken by about 35 million people in Burundi, Congo (Kinshasa), Kenya, Mayotte, Mozambique, Oman, Rwanda, Somalia, South Africa, Tanzania, Uganda, United Arab Emirates, and the United States. Kiswahili is an official language of Kenya, Tanzania, and Uganda and is used as a lingua franca throughout East Africa.

clear that the discrepancy between the Left in books and the Left in practice is one more Western problem. In other parts of the world and even among non-Western populations of indigenous peoples and immigrants in the West, there are other understandings of collective action for which such a discrepancy does not make sense. The world at large is full of transformative experiences and actors who are not educated in the Western left. Moreover, scientific knowledge, which has always been granted absolute priority in the Western critical tradition, is considered by the new popular movements as only one kind of knowledge among many others. It is more important for certain movements and causes than for others, and in many instances it is deployed in articulation with other knowledges—lay, popular, urban, peasant, indigenous, women's, and religious, to name a few.

In this way, the WSF generated a new epistemological issue: if social practices and collective actors resort to different kinds of knowledge, an adequate evaluation of their value for social emancipation must be premised upon a new epistemology, which, contrary to hegemonic epistemologies in the West, does not grant a priori supremacy to scientific knowledge (heavily produced in the North). It must allow for a more just relationship among different kinds of knowledge. In other words, there is no global social justice without global cognitive justice. Therefore, in order to capture the immense variety of critical discourses and practices and to valorize and maximize their transformative potential, an epistemological reconstruction is needed. This means that we do not need alternatives so much as we need an alternative thinking of alternatives.

Such an epistemological reconstruction must start from the idea that hegemonic left thinking and the hegemonic critical tradition, in addition to being (or precisely because they are) North-centric, are colonialist, imperialist, racist, and sexist as well. To overcome this epistemological condition and thereby decolonize left thinking and practice, it is imperative to go South and learn from the South, though not from the imperial South (which reproduces in the South the logic of the North taken as universal) but rather from the anti-imperial South (Santos 1995: 479–520). Such an epistemology in no way suggests that North-centric critical thinking and left politics must be discarded and thrown into the dustbin of history. Its past is in many respects an honorable one and has significantly contributed to the liberation of the global South. Rather, it is imperative to start an intercultural dialogue and translation among different critical knowledges and practices: South-centric and North-centric, popular and scientific, religious and secular, female and male, urban and rural, and so forth. This intercultural translation is at the roots of what I call the *ecology of knowledges* (more on this in later chapters).

The other WSF contribution to the theory/practice conundrum lies in the way it has refused to reduce its openness for the sake of efficacy or political coherence. While there is an intense debate inside the WSF about this issue, I am convinced that the idea that there is no general theory of social transformation capable of capturing and classifying the immense diversity of oppositional ideas and practices present in the WSF has been one of its most innovative and productive principles. This potentially unconditional inclusiveness has contributed to the creation of a new political culture that privileges commonalities to the detriment of differences and fosters common action even in the presence of deep ideological differences, once the objectives are limited, well defined, and adopted by consensus. In this respect, we can identify a strong continuity between the WSF and the more recent movements of *indignados* in North Africa, southern Europe, and the Occupy movement in the United States and other countries.

The coalitions and articulations made possible among individual participants and among social movements are generated from the bottom up and tend to be pragmatic and to last as long as they are seen as furthering each movement's objectives. While in the tradition of the conventional Left, particularly in the global North, politicizing an issue tends to polarize it, often leading to factionalism, in the political mobilizations of the last fifteen years, particularly in the global South, another political culture seems to be emerging in which politicization goes hand in hand with depolarization, with the search for common grounds, and with agreed-on limits to ideological purity or ideological messiness.

This new political culture represents an attempt at overcoming the ghostly relationship between theory and practice. As a result of a virulent, theoretical extremism that dominated the conventional Left throughout much of the twentieth century, left politics gradually lost contact with the practical aspirations and options of the activists engaged in concrete political action. Between concrete political action and theoretical extremism, a vacuum formed.

In his overview of the peoples' history of the Latin American subcontinent, and in particular of the various subversive and emancipatory "conceptions of the world" prevailing in Bolivia for the last two centuries, Álvaro García Linera, vice president of Bolivia, has insightfully shown how the "modernist and teleological narrative of history" ended up becoming a theoretical blindness and an epistemological blockage vis-à-vis the new social movements. Here is García Linera in his own words:

> This modernist and teleological narrative of history, largely adopted from economics and philosophy course books, will create a cognitive blockage and an epistemological impossibility concerning two realities that will be the starting point of a different emancipatory project, one superseding Marxist ideology itself: the peasant and ethnic thematics of our country. (2009: 482)

Conclusion

The antinomies, difficulties, and hard cases analyzed in this introduction demand that at the beginning of the new millennium we distance ourselves from

Eurocentric critical thinking. To create such a distance is the precondition for the fulfillment of the most crucial theoretical task of our time: that the unthinkable be thought, that the unexpected be assumed as an integral part of the theoretical work. Since vanguard theories, by definition, do not let themselves be taken by surprise, I submit that, in the current context of social and political transformation, rather than vanguard theories we need rearguard theories. I have in mind theoretical work that follows and shares the practices of the social movements very closely, raising questions, establishing synchronic and diachronic comparisons, symbolically enlarging such practices by means of articulations, translations, and possible alliances with other movements, providing contexts, clarifying or dismantling normative injunctions, facilitating interaction with those who walk more slowly, and bringing in complexity when actions seem rushed and unreflective and simplicity when action seems self-paralyzed by reflection. The grounding ideas of a rearguard theory are craftsmanship rather than architecture, committed testimony rather than clairvoyant leadership, and intercultural approximation to what is new for some and very old for others.

The aim of creating distance in relation to the Eurocentric tradition is to open analytical spaces for realities that are "surprising" because they are new or have been ignored or made invisible, that is, deemed nonexistent by the Eurocentric critical tradition. They can only be retrieved by what I call the *sociology of absences* (more on this in later chapters).

As I will explain in the following chapters, keeping a distance does not mean discarding the rich Eurocentric critical tradition and throwing it into the dustbin of history, thereby ignoring the historical possibilities of social emancipation in Western modernity. It means, rather, including it in a much broader landscape of epistemological and political possibilities. It means exercising a hermeneutics of suspicion regarding its "foundational truths" by uncovering what lies below their "face value." It means giving special attention to the suppressed or marginalized smaller traditions within the big Western tradition.

It means, above all, assuming our time to be an unprecedented, transitional time in which we face modern problems for which there are no modern solutions. The modern problems are those highlighted by the bourgeois revolutions of the eighteenth century: the problem of freedom, the problem of equality, the problem of fraternity. The bourgeois "solutions" to such problems are irreversibly discredited. We live in a "post-" or "neo-" Westphalian world in which the state shares the field of international relations with frequently more powerful nonstate actors. Sovereignty is being eroded while powerful states and nonstate actors coalesce to take control of natural resources and people's lives in less powerful states. Social contractualism is being replaced by individual contractualism among ever more unequal parties, while rights are being "legally" violated in the name of the twin imperatives of economic austerity and national security and while a global attack against social and economic rights is orchestrated. Capitalism is today experiencing one of the most destructive moments in its recent history as witnessed in new forms of primitive accumulation by dispossession, from land-grabbing to the theft of wages and bank bailouts; in the subjection to capitalist law of the value of common goods and resources, resulting in the displacement of millions of poor peasants and indigenous peoples and in environmental devastation and ecological disasters; and in the eternal renewal of colonialism, revealing, in old and new guises, the same genocidal impulse, racist sociability, thirst for appropriation, and violence exerted on resources deemed infinite and on people deemed inferior.

On the ruins of the idea of the civic nation, the suppression of ethnic-cultural nations and cultural diversity has become more visible and, with it, the untold human suffering and social destruction thereby produced. Individual autonomy turns into a cruel slogan as the conditions for effectively exercising autonomy are being destroyed. Ideological differences underlying democracy have been replaced by amorphous centrism and institutionalized corruption. As politicians turn into money launderers, hijack democracy, and allow it to be occupied by corporate greed, people are forced to occupy democracy outside democratic institutions. The criminalization of social protest, paramilitarism, and extrajudicial executions complement the scene. Social conflicts both within and among states become less and less institutionalized, human rights are violated in the name of human rights, and civilian lives are destroyed under the pretence of defending civilian lives.

Of course, Western modernity also produced a critical tradition that from the beginning questioned both the problems and the solutions proposed by bourgeois and liberal politics, Marxism being the most prominent exemplar of such a tradition. The problem is that Marxism shared too much with bourgeois Western modernity. Furthermore, Marxism shared not only the philosophical and epistemological foundations of bourgeois Western modernity but also some of its proposed solutions, such as the belief in linear progress or the unlimited use of natural resources as part of the infinite development of the forces of production, or even the idea that colonialism might be part of the progressive Western narrative, albeit with some qualifications. This explains why the bankruptcy of liberalism, although bearing witness to the analytical accuracy of Marxism, does not make the latter more persuasive, as one might expect. On the contrary, as it becomes more apparent that liberal "solutions" were originally fraudulent and are patently exhausted, another transitional dimension of our time gets unveiled: we face Marxist problems for which there are no Marxist solutions.

In light of this, the need for creating a distance vis-à-vis the Eurocentric tradition seems increasingly urgent. This need, however, is not determined by a sudden intellectual or political awareness. Its formulation is in itself a historical process deriving from the ways in which Western modernity, in both its bourgeois and Marxist versions, came to be embodied in political processes across the globe in the last two hundred years. As global capitalism and its satellite forms of oppression and domination expanded, more and more diversified landscapes of peoples, cultures, repertoires of memory and aspiration, symbolic universes, modes of livelihood and styles of life, conceptions of time and space, and so on, were dialectically included in the conversation of humankind through untold suffering and exclusion. Their resistance, often through subaltern, clandestine, insurgent cosmopolitan networks, managed to confront public suppression carried out by capitalist and colonialist forms of physical, symbolic, epistemological, or even ontological violence. The end result of this exclusionary inclusion was a tremendous expansion of hermeneutic communities, some public, some clandestine, some worldwide, some local, some Western based, some non-Western based.

In my view, this is the core characteristic of our time, one condition that is still to be fully acknowledged, theorized, and accounted for. This being the case, it follows that the repertoire of the modes, models, means, and ends of social transformation are potentially much vaster than those formulated and recognized by Western modernity, including its Marxist versions. Ultimately, keeping a distance vis-à-vis the Eurocentric tradition amounts to being aware of the fact that the diversity of world experience is inexhaustible and therefore cannot be accounted for by any single general theory. Keeping a distance allows for what I call the *double transgressive sociology of absences and emergences*. Such transgressive sociology is, in fact, an epistemological move that consists of counterposing the epistemologies of the South with the dominant epistemologies of the global North.

PART ONE

Centrifugal Modernities and Subaltern Wests: Degrees of Separation

CHAPTER 1

Nuestra America

Postcolonial Identities and Mestizajes

I N THIS CHAPTER I argue that there were at least two twentieth centuries, the European American twentieth century and the *Nuestra America* twentieth century. I am aware that there were others in Africa and Asia and even in Europe, but I will focus here on the first two and mainly on the second. My argument is that the European American twentieth century, which carried so many promises of democracy and welfare and experienced devastating wars in Europe and elsewhere, ended with the disturbing rise of what I call *societal fascism*, very often disguised under the name of hegemonic globalization. On the margins of this century, another evolved, the *Nuestra America* century. I argue that the alternative to the spread of societal fascism is the construction of a new pattern of local, national, and transnational relations. Such a pattern entails a new transnational political culture embedded in new forms of sociability and subjectivity. Ultimately, it implies a new insurgent cosmopolitan politics, law, and culture. I see in the *Nuestra America* century the seeds of new emancipatory energies, which I have been calling counterhegemonic globalization (Santos 1995: 252–268).

The European American Century and the Rise of Societal Fascism

According to G. W. F. Hegel, we recall, universal history goes from the East to the West. Asia is the beginning, while Europe is the ultimate end of universal history, the place where the civilizational trajectory of humankind is fulfilled. The biblical and medieval idea of the succession of empires (*translatio imperii*) becomes for Hegel the triumphal way of the Universal Idea. In each era a people takes on the responsibility of conducting the Universal Idea, thereby becoming the historical universal people, a privilege that has in turn passed from the Asian to the Greek, to the Roman, and, finally, to the German peoples. America, or rather, North America, carries, for Hegel, an ambiguous future in that it does not collide with the utmost fulfilling of the universal history in Europe. The future of (North) America is still a European future, made up of Europe's left-over population.

This Hegelian idea was behind the dominant conception of the twentieth century as the American century: the European American century. Herein implied was the notion that the Americanization of the world, starting with the Americanization of Europe itself, was but an effect of the European, universal cunning of reason, which, having reached the Far West and being unreconciled with the exile to which Hegel had condemned it, was forced to turn back, walk back upon its own track, and once again trace the path of its hegemony over the East. Americanization, as a hegemonic form of globalization, was thus the third act of the millennial drama of Western supremacy. The first act, to a large extent a failed act, was the Crusades, which initiated the second millennium of the Christian era; the second act, beginning halfway through the millennium, comprised the "discoveries" and subsequent European expansion. In this millennial conception, the European American century carried little novelty; it was nothing more than one more European century, the last of the millennium. Europe, after all, had always contained many Europes, some of them dominant, others dominated. The United States of America was the last dominant Europe; like the previous ones, it exerted its uncontested power over the dominated Europes. The feudal lords of eleventh-century Europe had and desired as little autonomy vis-à-vis Pope Urban II, who recruited them for the Crusades,[1] as the European Union countries of our time have vis-à-vis the United States, as illustrated by the multiple NATO missions in the Balkans, Afghanistan, and Libya.

In these conditions it is hard to think of any alternative to the current regime of international relations, which has become a core element of what I call *hegemonic globalization* (Santos 1995). However, such an alternative is not only necessary but urgent, since the current regime, as it loses coherence, becomes more violent and unpredictable, thus enhancing the vulnerability of subordinate classes, social groups, regions, and nations. The real danger, as regards both intra- and international relations, is the emergence of what I call societal fascism. Fleeing from Germany a few months before his death, in 1940 Walter Benjamin (1968) wrote his "Theses on the Philosophy of History" prompted by the idea that European society lived at that time in a moment of danger. I think today we live in a moment of danger as well. In Benjamin's time the danger was the rise of fascism as a political regime. In our time, the danger is the rise of fascism as a societal regime. Unlike political fascism, societal fascism is pluralistic and coexists easily with the democratic state; its privileged time-space is, rather than national, both local and global.

---

1. On the relations between the pope and the feudal lords concerning the Crusades, see Gibbon (1928: 6:31).

Societal fascism is a set of social processes by which large bodies of populations are irreversibly kept outside or thrown out of any kind of social contract. They are rejected, excluded, and thrown into a kind of Hobbesian state of nature, either because they have never been part of any social contract and probably never will (I mean the precontractual underclasses everywhere in the world, the best example of which are probably the youth of urban ghettos, the *indignados*, and participants in the Occupy movement) or because they have been excluded from or thrown out of whatever social contract they had been part of before (I mean the postcontractual underclasses, millions of post-Fordist workers, and peasants after the collapse of land-reform or other development projects).

As a societal regime, fascism manifests itself as the collapse of the most trivial expectations of the people living under it. What we call society is a bundle of stabilized expectations from the subway schedule to the salary at the end of the month to employment at the end of a college education. Expectations are stabilized by a set of shared scales and equivalences: for a given amount of work, a given amount of pay; for a given crime, a given punishment; for a given risk, a given insurance. The people who live under societal fascism are deprived of shared scales and equivalences and therefore of stabilized expectations. They live in a constant chaos of expectations in which the most trivial acts may meet with the most dramatic consequences. They run many risks, and none of them are insured. The case of Gualdino Jesus, a Pataxó Indian from northeastern Brazil, symbolizes the nature of such risks. It happened some years ago and is mentioned here as a parable of societal fascism. He had come to Brasília to take part in the march of the landless. The night was warm, and he decided to sleep on a bench at a bus stop. In the early morning hours, he was killed by three middle-class youths, one the son of a judge and another the son of an army officer. As the youngsters confessed later to the police, they killed the Indian for the fun of it. They "didn't even know he was an Indian, they thought he was a homeless vagrant." Elsewhere I distinguish five main forms of societal fascism:[2] the fascism of social apartheid, contractual fascism, territorial fascism, the fascism of insecurity, and financial fascism (more on this in Chapter 4).

One possible future is therefore the spread of societal fascism. There are many signs that this is a real possibility. If the logic of the market is allowed to spill over from the economy to all fields of social life and to become the sole criterion for successful social and political interaction, society will become ungovernable and ethically repugnant, and whatever order is achieved will be fascistic, as indeed Joseph Schumpeter (1962 [1942]) and Karl Polanyi (1957 [1944]) predicted decades ago.

---

2. I analyze in detail the emergence of societal fascism as a consequence of the breakdown of the logic of the social contract in Santos (2002b: 447–458).

The *Nuestra America* Century

At the margins of the European American century, as I argue, another century, a truly new and American century, emerged. I call it the *Nuestra America* century. While the former carried hegemonic globalization, the latter contained in itself the potential for counterhegemonic globalizations. In the following section I analyze the baroque ethos, conceived of as the cultural archetype of *Nuestra America* subjectivity and sociability. My analysis highlights some of the emancipatory potential of a new insurgent cosmopolitan politics, culture, and law based not on the ideas of European universalism but rather on the social and political culture of social groups whose everyday lives are energized by the need to transform survival strategies into sources of innovation, creativity, transgression, and subversion. In the last sections of the chapter I try to show how this emancipatory counterhegemonic potential of *Nuestra America* has so far not been realized and how it may be realized in the twenty-first century. Finally, I identify five areas, all of them deeply embedded in the secular experience of *Nuestra America*, that in my view will be the main contested terrains of the struggle between hegemonic and counterhegemonic globalizations, thus the playing field for a new transnational political culture and the insurgent cosmopolitan law that legitimates it. In each of these contested terrains the emancipatory potential of the struggles is premised on the idea that a politics of redistribution of social and economic wealth cannot be successfully conducted without a politics of recognition of difference, and vice versa.

To my mind, the *Nuestra America* century has best formulated the idea of social emancipation based on the metaright to have rights and on the dynamic equilibrium between recognition and redistribution presupposed by it. It has also most dramatically shown the difficulty of constructing successful emancipatory practices on that basis.

The Founding Ideas of *Nuestra America*

"Nuestra America" is the title of a short essay by José Martí, published in the Mexican paper *El Partido Liberal* on January 30, 1891. In this article, which is an excellent summary of his thinking as found in several Latin American papers at the time, Martí expresses the set of ideas that I believe were to preside over the *Nuestra America* century, ideas later pursued by many others, among them José Mariátegui and Oswald de Andrade, Fernando Ortiz, and Darcy Ribeiro, and influential in many grassroots movements and revolutionary changes that occurred throughout the twentieth century.

The main ideas in this agenda are as follows. First, *Nuestra America* is at the antipodes of European America. It is the *mestiza* America founded at the often violent crossings of European, Indian, and African blood. It is the America that is capable of delving deeply into its own roots and thereby of edifying the kinds of knowledge and government that are not imported but rather are adequate to its reality. Its deepest roots are the struggle of the Amerindian peoples against their invaders, where we find the true precursors of the Latin American *independentistas* (Retamar 1989: 20). Asks Martí, "Is it not evident that America itself was paralyzed by the same blow that paralyzed the Indian?" And he answers, "Until the Indian is caused to walk, America itself will not begin to walk well" (1963–1966: 8:336–337). Although in "Nuestra America" Martí deals mainly with anti-Indian racism, elsewhere he refers also to blacks: "A human being is more than white, more than mulatto, more than black. Cuban is more than white, more than mulatto, more than black.... Two kinds of racist would be equally guilty: the white racist and the black racist" (1963–1966: 2:299).

The second idea about *Nuestra America* is that in its mixed roots resides its infinite complexity, its new form of universalism from below that made the world richer. Says Martí, "There is no race hatred because there are no races" (1963–1966: 6:22). In this sentence reverberates the same radical liberalism that had encouraged Simon Bolívar to proclaim that Latin America was "a small humankind," a "miniature humankind." This kind of situated and contextualized universalism was to become one of the most enduring leitmotivs of *Nuestra America*.

In 1928, the Brazilian poet Oswald de Andrade published his *Anthropophagous Manifesto*. By "anthropophagy" Andrade meant the American's capacity to devour all that was alien to him and to incorporate all so as to create a complex identity, a new, constantly changing identity:

> Only what is not mine interests me. The law of men. The law of the anthropophagous.... Against all importers of canned consciousness. The palpable existence of life. Pre-logical mentality for Mr. Levy-Bruhl to study.... I asked a man what is law. He said it is the guarantee of the exercise of possibility. This man's name was Galli Mathias. I swallowed him. Anthropophagy. Absorption of the sacred enemy. To turn him into totem. The human adventure. Earthly finality. However, only the pure elites managed to accomplish carnal anthropophagy, the one that carries with itself the highest meaning of life and avoids the evils identified by Freud, the catechetical evils. (1990 [1928]: 47–51)

This concept of anthropophagy, ironic in relation to the European representation of the "Carib instinct," is quite close to the concept of transculturation developed by Fernando Ortiz (1973) in Cuba somewhat later (1940). For a more recent example, I quote the Brazilian anthropologist Darcy Ribeiro in a burst of brilliant humor:

> It is quite easy to make an Australian: take a few French, English, Irish, and Italian people, throw them on a deserted island, they kill the Indians and make

a second-rate England, damn it, or third-rate, that shit. Brazil has to realize that that is shit, Canada is shit, because it just repeats Europe. Just to show that ours is the adventure of making the new humankind, mestizaje in flesh and spirit. Mestizo is what is good. (1996: 104)

The third founding idea of *Nuestra America* is that for *Nuestra America* to be built upon its most genuine foundations, it has to endow itself with genuine knowledge. Martí again: "The trenches of ideas are worth more than the trenches of stone" (1963–1966: 6:16). But, to accomplish this, ideas must be rooted in the aspirations of oppressed peoples. Just as "the authentic mestizo has conquered the exotic Creole ... the imported book has been conquered in America by the natural man" (1963–1966: 6:17). Hence Martí's appeal:

> The European university must yield to the American university. The history of America, from the Incas to the present, must be taught letter perfect, even if that of the Argonauts of Greece is not taught. Our own Greece is preferable to that Greece that is not ours. We have greater need of it. National politicians must replace foreign and exotic politicians. Graft the world into our republics, but the trunk must be that of our republics. And let the conquered pedant be silent: there is no homeland of which the individual can be more proud than our unhappy American republics. (1963–1966: 6:18)

This situated knowledge, which demands a continuous attention to identity, behavior, and involvement in public life, is truly what distinguishes a country, not the imperial attribution of levels of civilization. Martí distinguishes the intellectual from the man whose life experience has made wise: "There is no fight between civilization and barbarism, rather between false erudition and nature" (1963–1966: 6:17).

Nuestra America thus carries a strong epistemological component. Rather than importing foreign ideas, one must find out about the specific realities of the continent from a Latin American perspective. Ignoring or disdaining them has helped tyrants accede to power, as well as grounded the arrogance of the United States vis-à-vis the rest of the continent. "The contempt of the formidable neighbor who does not know her is the major threat to Nuestra America; and he must know her urgently to stop disdaining her. Being ignorant, he might perhaps covet her. Once he knew her, he would, out of respect, take his hand off her" (Martí 1963–1966: 6:22).

A situated knowledge is therefore the condition for a situated government. As Martí says elsewhere, one cannot

> rule new peoples with a singular and violent composition, with laws inherited from four centuries of free practice in the United States, and nineteen centuries of monarchy in France. One does not stop the blow in the chest of

the plainsman's horse with one of Hamilton's decrees. One does not clear the congealed blood of the Indian race with a sentence of Sieyes. (1963–1966: 6:16–17)

And, Martí adds, "In the republic of Indians, governors learn Indian" (1963–1966: 6:21).

A fourth founding idea of *Nuestra America* is that it is Caliban's America, not Prospero's.[3] Prospero's America lies to the North, but it abides also in the South with those intellectual and political elites who reject the Indian and black roots and look upon Europe and the United States as models to be imitated and upon their own countries with the ethnocentric blinders that distinguish civilization and barbaric wilderness. Martí has particularly in mind one of the earliest Southern formulations of Prospero's America, the work of Argentinian Domingo Sarmiento, titled *Civilization and Barbarism* and published in 1845. It is against this world of Prospero that Andrade pushes with his "Carib instinct":

However, not the Crusaders came, rather the runaways from a civilization we are now eating up, for we are strong and vengeful like the Jabuti.[4]... We did not have speculation. But we did have divination. We had politics, which is the science of distribution. It is a social-planetary system.... Before the Portuguese discovered Brazil, Brazil had discovered happiness. (1990 [1928]: 47–51)

The fifth basic idea of *Nuestra America* is that its political thinking, far from being nationalistic, is rather internationalistic and strengthened by an anticolonialist and anti-imperialist stance, aimed at Europe in the past and now at the United States. Those who think that neoliberal globalization from NAFTA[5] to the Free Trade Initiative for the Americas and the World Trade Organization is something new should read Martí's reports on the Pan-American Congress of 1889–1890 and the American International Monetary Commission of 1891. Here are Martí's remarks on the Pan-American Congress:

Never in America, since independence, was there subject matter demanding more wisdom, requiring more vigilance or calling for clearer and closer attention than the invitation that the powerful United States, filled with unsalable products and determined to expand domination over America, addresses to

---

3. In this chapter, I use the names of Prospero and Caliban, from Shakespeare's *The Tempest* (1611), to signify that the colonial contact zone emerged as a contact zone between the "civilized" and the "savage."

4. A medium-sized tortoise described in Brazilian Indian folk tales as being very strong, patient, and resilient.

5. The North American Free Trade Agreement between the United States, Canada, and Mexico entered into force in 1994, the same date as the uprising of the Zapatista Army of National Liberation of Chiapas.

the American nations with less power, linked by free, Europe-friendly trade, to form an alliance against Europe and cut off their contacts with the rest of the world. America managed to get rid of Spain's tyranny; now, having looked with judicious eyes upon the antecedent causes and factors of such an invitation, it is imperative to state, because it is true, that the time has come for Spanish America to declare her second independence. (1963–1966: 6:46)

According to Martí, the dominant conceptions in the United States concerning Latin America must incite the latter to distrust all proposals coming from the North. Outraged, Martí accuses,

They believe in necessity, the barbaric right, as the only right, that "this will be ours because we need it." They believe in the incomparable superiority of the "Anglo-Saxon race as opposed to the Latin race." They believe in the baseness of the Negro race that they enslaved in the past and now-a-days humiliate, and of the Indian race, which they exterminate. They believe that the peoples of Spanish America are mainly constituted of Indians and Negros. (1963–1966: 6:160)

The fact that *Nuestra America* and European America are geographically so close, as well as the former's awareness of the dangers issuing from the power imbalance between both, soon forced *Nuestra America* to claim her autonomy in the form of a thought and a practice from the South: "The North must be left behind" (Martí 1963–1966: 2:368). Martí's insight derives from his many years of exile in New York, during which he became well acquainted with "the monster's entrails":

In the North there is neither support nor root. In the North the problems increase and there is no charity and patriotism to solve them. Here, men don't learn how to love one another, nor do they love the soil where they are born by chance.... Here are piled up the rich on one side and the desperate on the other. The North clams up and is full of hatred. The North must be left behind. (1963–1966: 2:367–368)

It would be difficult to find a more clairvoyant preview of the European American century and the need to create an alternative to it.

According to Martí, such an alternative resides in a united *Nuestra America* and the assertion of her autonomy vis-à-vis the United States. In a text dated 1894, Martí writes, "Little is known about our sociology and about such precise laws as the following one: the farther away they keep from the United States, the freer and more prosperous will the peoples of America be" (1963–1966: 6:26–27). More ambitious and utopic is Oswald de Andrade's alternative: "We want the Caribbean Revolution greater than the French Revolution. One unification of all efficacious revolts on behalf of man. Without us, Europe would not even have its poor declaration of the rights of man" (1990 [1928]: 48).

In sum, for Martí the claim of equality grounds the struggle against unequal difference as much as the claim of difference grounds the struggle against inequality. The only legitimate cannibalization of difference (Andrade's anthropophagy) is the subaltern's because only through it can Caliban recognize his own difference with regard to the unequal differences imposed upon him. In other words, Andrade's anthropophagus digests according to his own guts.

The Baroque Ethos: Prolegomena for an Insurgent Cosmopolitan Politics and Culture

Nuestra America is no mere intellectual construct for discussion in the salons that gave so much life to Latin American culture in the first decades of the twentieth century. It is a political project, or rather, a set of political projects and a commitment to the objectives therein contained. That was the commitment that dragged Martí into exile and later to death fighting for Cuba's independence. As Oswald de Andrade was to say epigrammatically, "Against the vegetal elites. In contact with the soil" (1990 [1928]: 49). But before it becomes a political project, *Nuestra America* is a form of subjectivity and sociability. It is a way of being and living permanently in transit and transitoriness, crossing borders, creating borderland spaces, open to risk—with which it has lived for many years, long before the invention of the "risk society" (Beck 1992)—accustomed to enduring a very low level of stabilization of expectations in the name of a visceral optimism before collective potentiality. Such optimism led Martí to assert in a period of fin-de-siècle Viennese cultural pessimism, "A governor in a new nation means a creator" (1963–1966: 6:17). The same kind of optimism made Andrade exclaim, "Joy is counterproof" (1990 [1928]: 51).

The subjectivity and sociability of *Nuestra America* are uncomfortable with institutionalized, legalistic thought and comfortable with utopian thinking. By utopia I mean the imagination's exploration of new modes of human possibility and styles of will and the confrontation by imagination of the necessity of whatever exists—just because it exists—on behalf of something radically better that is worth fighting for and to which humanity is fully entitled (Santos 1995: 479). This style of subjectivity and sociability is what I call, following Bolívar Echeverría (1994, 2011), the *baroque ethos*.[6]

Whether as an artistic style or as a historical epoch, the baroque is most specifically a Latin and Mediterranean phenomenon, an eccentric form of modernity,

---

6. The baroque ethos I propound here is very different from Scott Lash's "baroque melancholy" (1999: 330). Our differences are due in part to the different loci of the baroque we base our analysis in, Europe in the case of Lash, Latin America in my case.

the South of the North, so to speak. Its eccentricity derives, to a large extent, from the fact that it occurred in countries and historical moments in which the center of power was weak and tried to hide its weakness by dramatizing conformist sociability. The relative lack of central power endows the baroque with an open-ended and unfinished character that allows for the autonomy and creativity of the margins and peripheries. Because of its eccentricity and exaggeration, the center reproduces itself as if it were a margin. I mean a centrifugal imagination that becomes stronger as we go from the internal peripheries of the European power to its external peripheries in Latin America. The whole of Latin America was colonized by weak centers, Portugal and Spain. Portugal was a hegemonic center during a brief period, between the fifteenth and sixteenth centuries, and Spain started to decline but a century later. From the seventeenth century onward, the colonies were more or less left alone, a marginalization that made possible a specific cultural and social creativity, now highly codified, now chaotic, now erudite, now vernacular, now official, now illegal. Such *mestizaje* is so deeply rooted in the social practices of these countries that it came to be considered as grounding a cultural ethos that is typically Latin American and has prevailed since the seventeenth century until today.[7] This form of baroque, inasmuch as it is the manifestation of an extreme instance of the center's weakness, constitutes a privileged field for the development of a centrifugal, subversive, and blasphemous imagination.

As an epoch in European history, the baroque is a time of crisis and transition. I mean the economic, social, and political crisis that is particularly obvious in the case of the powers that fostered the first phase of European expansion. In Portugal's case, the crisis implies even the loss of independence. Due to issues of monarchic succession, Portugal was annexed to Spain in 1580 and only regained its independence in 1640. The Spanish monarchy, particularly under Filipe IV (1621–1665), underwent a serious financial crisis that was actually also a political and cultural crisis. As José Antonio Maravall has pointed out, it begins as a certain awareness of uneasiness and restlessness, which "gets worse as the social fabric is seriously affected" (1990: 57). For instance, values and behaviors are questioned, the structure of classes undergoes some changes, banditism and deviant behavior in general increase, and revolt and sedition are constant threats. It is indeed a time of crisis, but also of transition toward new modes of sociability made possible by emergent capitalism and the new scientific paradigm, as well as toward new modes of political domination based not only on coercion but also on cultural and ideological integration. To a large extent, baroque culture is one such instrument for the consolidation and legitimation of power. What nonetheless seems to me inspiring in baroque culture is its grain of subversion and eccentricity, the weakness of the centers of power that look for legitimation in it,

---

7. See below the postcolonial critique of *mestizaje*.

the space of creativity and imagination it opens up, and the turbulent sociability that it fosters. The configuration of baroque subjectivity that I wish to advance here is a collage of diverse historical and cultural materials, some of which in fact cannot be considered technically as belonging to the baroque period.

Baroque subjectivity lives comfortably with the temporary suspension of order and canons. As a subjectivity of transition, it depends both on the exhaustion and the aspiration of canons; its privileged temporality is perennial transitoriness. It lacks the obvious certainties of universal laws—in the same way that baroque style lacked the classical universalism of the Renaissance. Because it is unable to plan its own repetition ad infinitum, baroque subjectivity invests in the local, the particular, the momentary, the ephemeral, and the transitory. But the local is not lived in a localist fashion, that is, it is not experienced as an orthotopia; the local aspires, rather, to invent another place, a heterotopia, if not even a utopia. Since it derives from a deep feeling of emptiness and disorientation caused by the exhaustion of the dominant canons, the comfort provided by the local is not the comfort of rest but a sense of direction. Again, we can observe here a contrast with the Renaissance, as Heinrich Wölfflin has taught us: "In contrast to the Renaissance, which sought permanence and repose in everything, the baroque had from the first moment a definite *sense of direction*" (1979: 67, emphasis added).

Baroque subjectivity is contemporaneous with all the elements that it integrates and hence contemptuous of modernist evolutionism. Thus, we might say, baroque temporality is the temporality of interruption. Interruption is important on two accounts; it allows for reflexivity and surprise. Its reflexivity is the self-reflexivity required by the lack of maps (without maps to guide our steps, we must tread with double care). Without self-reflexivity, in a desert of canons, the desert itself becomes canonical. Surprise, in turn, is really suspense; it derives from the suspension accomplished by interruption. By momentarily suspending itself, baroque subjectivity intensifies the will and arouses passion. The "baroque technique," argues Maravall, consists of "suspending resolution so as to encourage it, after that provisional and transitory moment of arrest, to push further more efficiently with the help of those retained and concentrated forces" (1990: 445).

Interruption provokes wonder and novelty and impedes closure and completion—hence the unfinished and open-ended character of baroque sociability. The capacity for wonder, surprise, and novelty is the energy that facilitates the struggle for an aspiration that is all the more convincing because it can never be completely fulfilled. The aim of baroque style, says Wölfflin, "is not to represent a perfect state, but to suggest an incomplete process and a moment towards its completion" (1979: 67).

Baroque subjectivity has a very special relationship with forms. The geometry of baroque subjectivity is not Euclidean; it is fractal. The suspension of forms results from the extreme uses to which they are put: Maravall's "extremosidad" (1990: 421). As regards baroque subjectivity, forms are the exercise of freedom par excellence. The great importance of the exercise of freedom justifies that forms be treated with extreme seriousness, though the extremism may result in the destruction of the forms themselves. The reason Michelangelo is rightly considered one of the baroque's forefathers is, according to Wölfflin, "because he treated forms with a violence, a terrible seriousness which could only find expression in formlessness" (1979: 82). This is what Michelangelo's contemporaries called *terribilità*. Extremism in the use of forms is grounded on a will to grandiosity that is also the will to astound so well formulated by Bernini: "Let no one speak to me of what is small" (Tapié 1988: 188). Extremism may be exercised in many different ways, to highlight simplicity or even asceticism as well as exuberance and extravagance, as Maravall has pointed out. Baroque extremism allows for ruptures emerging out of apparent continuities and keeps the forms in a permanently unstable state of bifurcation, in Ilya Prigogine's (1997) terms. One of the most eloquent examples is Bernini's *The Mystical Ecstasy of Santa Teresa*. In this sculpture, St. Teresa's expression is dramatized in such a way that the most intensely religious representation of the saint is one with the profane representation of a woman enjoying a deep orgasm. The representation of the sacred glides surreptitiously into the representation of the sacrilegious. The extremism of forms alone allows baroque subjectivity to entertain the turbulence and excitement necessary to continue the struggle for emancipatory causes, in a world in which emancipation has been collapsed into or absorbed by hegemonic regulation. To speak of extremism is to speak of an archaeological excavation of the regulatory magma in order to retrieve emancipatory fires, no matter how dim.

The same extremism that produces forms also devours them. This voracity takes on two forms: sfumato and *mestizaje*. In baroque painting, sfumato is the blurring of outlines and colors among objects, as clouds and mountains or the sea and the sky. Sfumato allows baroque subjectivity to create the near and the familiar among different intelligibilities, thus making cross-cultural dialogues possible and desirable. For instance, only by resorting to sfumato is it possible to give form to configurations that combine Western human rights with other conceptions of human dignity existing in other cultures (Santos 2007a: 3–40). As the coherence of monolithic constructions disintegrates, their free-floating fragments remain open to new coherences and the invention of new multicultural forms. Sfumato is like a magnet that attracts the fragmentary forms into new constellations and directions, appealing to their most vulnerable, unfinished, open-ended contours. Sfumato is, in sum, an antifortress militancy.

Mestizaje, in its turn, is a way of pushing sfumato to its utmost or extreme. While sfumato operates through the disintegration of forms and the retrieval of fragments, *mestizaje* operates through the creation of new constellations of meaning, which are truly unrecognizable or blasphemous in light of their constitutive fragments. *Mestizaje* resides in the destruction of the logic that presides over the formation of each of its fragments and in the construction of a new logic. This productive-destructive process tends to reflect the power relations among the original cultural forms (that is, among their supporting social groups), and this is why baroque subjectivity favors the *mestizajes* in which power relations are replaced by shared authority (*mestiza* authority). Latin America has provided a particularly fertile soil for *mestizaje*, and so the region is one of the most important excavation sites for the construction of baroque subjectivity.[8] The postcolonial critique of *mestizaje* allows for new and empowering forms of *mestizaje* (more on this below).

Sfumato and *mestizaje* are the two constitutive elements of what I call, following Fernando Ortiz, *transculturation*. In his justly famous book, *Contrapunteo cubano*, originally published in 1940, Ortiz proposes the concept of transculturation to define the synthesis of the utterly intricate cultural processes of deculturation and neoculturation that have always characterized Cuban society. In his thinking, the reciprocal cultural shocks and discoveries, which in Europe occurred slowly throughout more than four millennia, occurred in Cuba by sudden jumps in less than four centuries (Ortiz 1973: 131). The pre-Colombian transculturations between paleolithic and neolithic Indians were followed by many others after the European "hurricane" among various European cultures and between those and various African and Asian cultures. According to Ortiz (1973: 132), what distinguishes Cuba since the sixteenth century is the fact that all its cultures and peoples were equally invaders, exogenous, all of them torn apart from their original cradles, haunted by separation and transplantation to a new culture being created. This permanent maladjustment and transitoriness allowed for new cultural constellations that cannot be reduced to the sum of the different fragments that contributed to them. The positive character of this constant process of transition between cultures is what Ortiz designates as *transculturation*.[9] To reinforce this positive, new character, I prefer to speak of sfumato instead of deculturation and *mestizaje* instead of neoculturation. Transculturation designates, therefore, the voraciousness and extremism with which cultural forms are processed by baroque sociability. This selfsame voraciousness and selfsame extremism are also quite present in Oswald de Andrade's concept of anthropophagy.

The extremism with which forms are lived by baroque subjectivity stresses the rhetorical artifactuality of practices, discourses, and modes of intelligibility. Artifice (*artificium*) is the foundation of a subjectivity suspended among fragments. Artifice allows baroque subjectivity to reinvent itself whenever the sociabilities

---

8. Among others, see Pastor et al. (1993) and Alberro (1992). With reference to the Brazilian baroque, Coutinho (1990: 16) speaks of "a complex baroque *mestiçagem*." See also the concept of the "Black Atlantic" (Gilroy 1993) to express the *mestizaje* that characterizes black cultural experience, an experience that is not specifically African, American, Caribbean, or British but all of them at one and the same time. In the Portuguese-speaking world, the *Anthropophagous Manifesto* of Oswald de Andrade remains the most striking exemplar of *mestiçagem*.

9. From a postcolonial perspective, the concept of transculturation is highly questionable since it does not duly valorize the claim of difference. Cuban emergent black movements, for example, raise many questions in this regard.

to which it leads transform themselves into micro-orthodoxies. Through artifice, baroque subjectivity is ludic and subversive at one time, as the baroque feast so well illustrates. The importance of the feast in baroque culture, both in Europe and in Latin America, is well documented.[10] The feast turned baroque culture into the first instance of a mass culture of modernity. Political and ecclesiastical powers used its ostentatious and celebratory character to dramatize their greatness and reinforce their control over the masses. However, through its three basic components—disproportion, laughter, and subversion—the baroque feast is invested with an emancipatory potential.

The baroque feast is out of proportion; it requires an extremely large investment that is nevertheless consumed in an extremely fleeting moment and an extremely limited space. As Maravall says, "Abundant and expensive means are used, a considerable effort is exerted, ample preparations are made, a complicated apparatus is set up, all only to obtain some extremely short-lived effects, whether in the form of pleasure or surprise" (1990: 488). Nevertheless, disproportion generates a special intensification that in turn gives rise to a will for motion, a tolerance for chaos, and a taste for turbulence, without which the struggle for the paradigmatic transition cannot take place.

Disproportion makes wonder, surprise, artifice, and novelty possible. But, above all, it makes playful distance and laughter possible. Because laughter is not easily codifiable, capitalist modernity declared war on mirth, and so laughter was considered frivolous, improper, and eccentric, if not blasphemous. Laughter was to be admitted only in highly codified contexts of the entertainment industry. This phenomenon can also be observed among modern anticapitalist social movements (labor parties, unions, and even the new social movements), which banned laughter and play lest they subvert the seriousness of resistance. Particularly interesting is the case of unions, whose activities in the beginning had a strong ludic and festive element (workers' feasts) that, however, was gradually suffocated, until at last union activity became deadly serious and deeply antierotic. The banishment of laughter and play is part of what Max Weber calls the disenchantment (*Entzäuberung*) of the modern world.

The reinvention of social emancipation, which I suggest can be achieved by delving into baroque sociability, aims at the reenchantment of common sense, which in itself presupposes the carnivalization of emancipatory social practices and the eroticism of laughter and play. The carnivalization of emancipatory social practice has an important self-reflective dimension; it makes the decanonization and subversion of such practices possible. A decanonizing practice that does not

---

10.   On the baroque feast in Mexico (Vera Cruz), see León (1993); in Brazil (Minas Gerais), see Ávila (1994). The relationship between the feast, particularly the baroque feast, and utopian thinking remains to be explored. On the relationship between *fouriérisme* and *la société festive*, see Desroche (1975).

know how to decanonize itself falls easily into orthodoxy. Likewise, a subversive activity that does not know how to subvert itself falls easily into regulatory routine.

And now, finally, the third emancipatory feature of the baroque feast: subversion. By carnivalizing social practices, the baroque feast displays a subversive potential that increases as the feast distances itself from the centers of power and that is always there, even when the centers of power themselves are the promoters of the feast. Little wonder, then, that this subversive feature was much more noticeable in the colonies. Writing about carnival in the 1920s, the great Peruvian intellectual Mariátegui asserted that, even though it had been appropriated by the bourgeoisie, carnival was indeed revolutionary because, by turning the bourgeois into a wardrobe, it was a merciless parody of power and the past (1974b [1925–1927]: 127). Antonio García de León also describes the subversive dimension of baroque feasts and religious processions in the Mexican port of Vera Cruz in the seventeenth century. Up front marched the highest dignitaries of the viceroyalty in their full regalia—politicians, clergymen, and military men; at the end of the procession followed the populace, mimicking their "betters" in gesture and attire and thus provoking laughter and merriment among the spectators (León 1993). This symmetrical inversion of the beginning and end of the procession is a cultural metaphor for the upside-down world—*el mundo al revés*—that was typical of Vera Cruz sociability at the time: *mulattas* dressed as queens, slaves in silk garments, whores pretending to be honest women and honest women pretending to be whores, Africanized Portuguese and Indianized Spaniards.[11] The same *mundo al revés* is celebrated by Oswald de Andrade in his *Anthropophagous Manifesto*: "But we have never admitted to the birth of logic among us. . . . Only where there is mystery is there no determinism. But what have we to do with this? We have never been catechized. We live in a sleepwalking law. We made Christ be born in Bahia. Or in Belém-Pará" (1990 [1928]: 48).

In the feast, subversion is codified, in that it transgresses order while knowing the place of order and not questioning it; yet, the code itself is subverted by the sfumatos between feast and daily sociability. In the peripheries, transgression is almost a necessity. It is transgressive because it does not know how to be order, even as it knows that order exists. That is why baroque subjectivity privileges margins and peripheries as fields for the reconstruction of emancipatory energies.

All these characteristics turn the sociability generated by baroque subjectivity into a subcodified sociability; somewhat chaotic, inspired by a centrifugal imagination, positioned between despair and vertigo, this is a kind of sociability that celebrates revolt and revolutionizes celebration. Such sociability cannot but be emotional and passionate, the feature that most distinguishes baroque

---

11. Ávila concurs, stressing the mixture of religious and heathen motifs: "Amongst hordes of negroes playing bagpipes, drums, fifes, and trumpets, there would be, for example, an excellent German impersonator 'tearing apart the silence of the air with the loud sound of a clarinet,' while the believers devoutly carried religious banners or images" (1994: 56).

subjectivity from high modernity, or first modernity in Scott Lash's (1999) terms. High modern rationality, particularly after René Descartes, condemns the emotions and the passions as obstacles to the progress of knowledge and truth. Cartesian rationality, says Stephen Toulmin, claims to be "intellectually perfectionist, morally rigorous and humanly unrelenting" (1990: 198). Not much of human life and social practice fits into such a conception of rationality, but it is nonetheless quite attractive to those who cherish the stability and hierarchy of universal rules. Albert Hirschman, in his turn, has clearly shown the elective affinities between this form of rationality and emergent capitalism. Inasmuch as the interests of people and groups began centering on economic advantage, the interests that before had been considered passions became the opposite, and even the tamers, of passion. From then on, says Hirschman, "in the pursuit of their interests men were expected or assumed to be steadfast, single-minded and methodical, in total contrast to the stereotyped behavior of men who are buffeted and blinded by their passions" (1977: 54). The objective was, of course, to create a "one-dimensional" human personality. And Hirschman concludes, "In sum, capitalism was supposed to accomplish exactly what was soon to be denounced as its worst feature" (1977: 132).

Cartesian and capitalist recipes are of little use for the reconstruction of a human personality with the capacity and desire for social emancipation. The meaning of the emancipatory struggles at the beginning of the twenty-first century can be deduced neither from demonstrative knowledge nor from an estimate of interests. Thus, the excavation undertaken by baroque subjectivity in this domain, more than in any other, must concentrate on suppressed or eccentric traditions of modernity, representations that occurred in the physical or symbolic peripheries where the control of hegemonic representations was weaker—the Vera Cruzes of modernity—or earlier, more chaotic representations of modernity that occurred before the Cartesian closure. For example, baroque subjectivity looks for inspiration in Montaigne and the concrete and erotic intelligibility of his life. In his essay "On Experience," after saying that he hates remedies that are more troublesome than the disease, Montaigne writes,

> To be a victim of the colic and to subject oneself to abstinence from the pleasure of eating oysters, are two evils instead of one. The disease stabs us on one side, the diet on the other. Since there is the risk of mistake let us take it, for preference, in the pursuit of pleasure. The world does the opposite, and considers nothing to be useful that is not painful; facility rouses suspicions. (1958: 370)

As Ernst Cassirer (1960, 1963) and Toulmin (1990) have shown for the Renaissance and the Enlightenment, respectively, each era creates a subjectivity that is congruent with the new intellectual, social, political, and cultural challenges. The baroque ethos is the building block of a form of subjectivity and sociability interested in and capable of confronting the hegemonic forms of globalization, thereby opening the space for counterhegemonic possibilities. Such possibilities are not fully developed and cannot by themselves promise a new era. But they are consistent enough to provide the grounding for the idea that we are entering a period of paradigmatic transition, an in-between era and therefore an era that is eager to follow the impulse of *mestizaje*, sfumato, hybridization, and all the other features that I have attributed to the baroque ethos, hence to *Nuestra America*. The progressive credibility conquered by the forms of subjectivity and sociability nurtured by such an ethos will gradually translate into new interstitial normativities. Both Martí and Andrade have in mind a new kind of law and a new kind of rights. For them the right to be equal involves the right to be different, as the right to be different involves the right to be equal. Andrade's metaphor of anthropophagy is a call for such a complex interlegality. It is formulated from the perspective of subaltern difference, the only "other" recognized by Eurocentric high modernity. The interstitial normative fragments we collect in *Nuestra America* will provide the seeds for a new insurgent cosmopolitan politics and law, a politics and law from below, to be found in the streets where survival and creative transgression fuse in an everyday-life pattern.

The Limits of *Nuestra America*

The *Nuestra America* century was one of counterhegemonic possibilities, many of them following the tradition of others in the nineteenth century after the independence of Haiti in 1804. Among such possibilities, we might count the Mexican Revolution of 1910; the indigenous movement headed by Quintin Lame in Colombia in 1914; the Sandinista movement in Nicaragua in the 1920s and 1930s and its triumph in the 1980s; the radical democratization of Guatemala in 1944; the rise of Peronism in 1946; the indigenous, peasant, and miners revolution of 1952 in Bolivia, followed in recent years by the election of the first indigenous president, Evo Morales; the triumph of the Cuban Revolution in 1959; Salvador Allende's rise to power in 1970; the Landless Workers' Movement in Brazil since the 1980s; the rise of the indigenous movement in Ecuador in 1990 and the long road to the 2008 Montecristi constitution; the Zapatista movement since 1994; the World Social Forum born in Porto Alegre, Brazil, in 2001; and the progressive governments of the first decade of the new century in Brazil, Venezuela, Argentina, Bolivia, and Ecuador, among others.

However, the list of the defeats of the popular movements caused by internal oligarchies and imperial powers is much greater and includes civil and military dictatorships, foreign interventions, the war on communism, massive violations of human rights, extrajudicial executions by paramilitary militias, and so on. As a result, throughout the twentieth century *Nuestra America* became a fertile field of cosmopolitan, emancipatory, counterhegemonic experiences, as exhilarating as painful, as radiant in their promises as frustrating in their fulfillments.

What failed and why in the *Nuestra America* century? It would be silly to propose an inventory before such an open future as ours. Nonetheless, I will risk a few thoughts. In the first place, to live in the "monster's entrails" is no easy matter. It does allow for a deep knowledge of the beast, as Martí so well demonstrates; on the other hand, it makes it very difficult to come out alive, even when one heeds Martí's admonishment: "The North must be left behind" (1963–1966: 368). To my way of thinking, *Nuestra America* has been living doubly in the monster's entrails because it shares with European America the continent that the latter has always conceived of as its vital space and zone of privileged influence and because, as Martí says in "Nuestra America," "nuestra America is the working America" (1963–1966: 6:23), and thus, in its relations with European America, it shares the same tensions and sorrows that plague the relations between workers and capitalists. In this latter sense, *Nuestra America* has failed no more and no less than the workers of the whole world in their struggle against capital.

Second, *Nuestra America* did not have to fight only against the imperial visits of its northern neighbor. The latter took over and became at home in the South, not just socializing with the natives but itself becoming native in the form of local elites and their transnational alliances with US interests. The Southern Prospero was present in Domingo Sarmiento's political-cultural project, in the interests of the agrarian and industrial bourgeoisie, especially after World War II, in the military dictatorships of the 1960s and 1970s, in the fight against the communist threat, and in the drastic neoliberal structural adjustment. In this sense, *Nuestra America* has had to live trapped in and dependent on European America, just like Caliban vis-à-vis Prospero. That is why Latin American violence has taken the form as much of civil war as of the Bay of Pigs.

The third thought concerns a certain triumphalist postmodernism *avant la lettre* about the novel social value of *mestizaje*, which left unexamined the social processes through which *mestizaje* came about. Untold violence and destruction of life were thereby swept under the facade of a benevolent *mestizaje*. The latter became the self-serving narrative of whites and white mestizos. Not surprisingly, this concept of *mestizaje* became a target of the indigenous peoples and Afro-descendent movements and struggles. The colonial *mestizaje* was to be strictly distinguished from a postcolonial or decolonial *mestizaje*, the white mestizo *mestizaje* from the dark mestizo *mestizaje*. The above movements and struggles were instrumental in forcing into the open such distinctions, and Frantz Fanon provided them with the most eloquent and forceful arguments. Such distinctions were crucial to identify differences on the basis of which alliances could be sought. In fact, one of the weaknesses of *Nuestra America*, actually quite obvious in Martí's work, was its overestimation of the communality of interests and the possibilities of uniting around them. Because of the unexamined differences and the conflicts they could generate, rather than uniting, *Nuestra America* underwent a process of political fragmentation.

My final thought concerns the cultural project of *Nuestra America* itself. To my mind, contrary to Martí's wishes, the European and North American university never gave way entirely to the American university, as witness the

> pathetic bovaryism of writers and scholars … which leads some Latin Americans … to imagine themselves as exiled metropolitans. For them, a work produced in their immediate orbit … merits their interest only when it has received the metropolis' approval, an approval that gives them the eyes with which to see it. (Retamar 1989: 82)

Contrary to Ortiz's claim, transculturation was never total, and in fact it was undermined by power differences among the different components that contributed to it. For a very long time (and perhaps even more so today, at a time of vertiginous deterritorialized transculturation in the guise of hybridization) the questions about the inequality of power remained unanswered: Who hybridizes whom and what? With what results? And to whose benefit? What, in the process of transculturation, did not go beyond deculturation or sfumato and why? In sum, the crucial differences between a colonial *mestizaje* and a decolonial *mestizaje* were never examined. If indeed it is true that most cultures were invaders, it is no less true that some invaded as masters, some as slaves. It is perhaps not risky today, eighty years later, to think that Oswald de Andrade's anthropophagous optimism was exaggerated: "But no Crusaders came. Only runaways from a civilization that we are eating up, because we are strong and vengeful like the Jabuti" (1990 [1928]: 50).

Counterhegemonic Possibilities for the Twenty-First Century

In the light of the preceding, we must ask whether in fact *Nuestra America* harbors the conditions necessary to continue to symbolize a utopian will to emancipation and counterhegemonic globalization based on the mutual implication of equality and difference. My answer is positive but depends on the following condition: *Nuestra America* must be deterritorialized and turned into a metaphor for the struggle of the victims of hegemonic globalization wherever they may be, North or South, East or West. If we revisit the founding ideas of *Nuestra America*, we observe that the transformations of the last decades have created conditions for them to occur and flourish today in other parts of the world. Let us examine some of them.

First, the exponential increase of transborder interactions—of emigrants, students, and refugees, as well as executives and tourists—is giving rise to new forms of *mestizaje*, anthropophagy, and transculturation all over the world. The world becomes increasingly a world of invaders who are cut off from an origin they never had, or if they did have such an origin, who suffered there the original experience of being invaded. More attention must be paid than in the first century of *Nuestra America* to the power of the different participants in the processes of *mestizaje*. Such inequalities accounted for the perversion both of the politics of difference (recognition became a form of miscognition) and the politics of equality (redistribution ended up as the new form of poverty relief advocated by the World Bank and International Monetary Fund). Second, the recent ugly revival of racism in the global North and even in the global South points to an aggressive defense against the unstoppable construction of the multiple little humankinds Bolívar talked about, in which races cross and interpenetrate in the margins of repression and discrimination. As the Cuban, in Martí's voice, could proclaim to be more than black, mulatto, or white, so the South African, the Mozambican, the New Yorker, the Parisian, and the Londoner can proclaim today to be more than black, white, mulatto, Indian, Kurd, Arab, and so on.[12] Third, the demand to produce or sustain situated and contextualized knowledge is today a global claim against the ignorance and silencing effect produced by modern science as it is used by hegemonic globalization. This epistemological issue gained enormous relevance in recent times with the newest developments in biotechnology and genetic engineering and the consequent struggle to defend biodiversity from biopiracy. In this domain, Latin America, one of the great holders of biodiversity, continues to be the home of *Nuestra America*, but many other countries are in this position in Africa and in Asia (Santos, Meneses, and Arriscado 2007).

Fourth, as hegemonic globalization has deepened, the "entrails of the monster" have gotten closer to many other peoples on other continents. The closeness effect is today produced by information and communication capitalism and by consumer society. Hereby are multiplied both the grounds for cynical reason and the postcolonial impulse. In a word, as a metaphor, the new *Nuestra America* today has the conditions necessary to globalize itself and thereby propose new emancipatory alliances to the old *Nuestra America*.

The counterhegemonic nature of *Nuestra America* lies in its potential to develop a progressive transnational political culture.[13] Such a political culture will concentrate on (1) identifying the multiple local/global linkages among struggles, movements, and initiatives; (2) promoting the clashes between hegemonic globalization trends and pressures, on one side, and the transnational coalitions to resist against them, on the other, thus opening up possibilities for counterhegemonic globalizations; and (3) promoting internal and external self-reflexivity

---

12. According to both Martí and Bolívar, and in tune with Enlightenment postulates, the crucial step toward emancipation was to eliminate difference, rather than to take it as a constellation of equal differences. Later, the pan-Africanists assumed negritude as a condition to acquire equality, that is to say, the difference that does not erase history, the colonial wound.

13. It was surely no coincidence that the most consistent manifestation of counterhegemonic globalization in the first decade of the twenty-first century—the World Social Forum—occurred in Latin America (Santos 2006b).

so that the forms of redistribution, recognition, and accountability inside the movements mirror the forms of redistribution, recognition, and accountability that the insurgent cosmopolitanism and its emancipatory politics wish to see implemented in the world.

Conclusion: Which Side Are You On, Ariel?

Starting from an analysis of *Nuestra America* as the subaltern view of the American continent throughout the twentieth century, I identified *Nuestra America*'s counterhegemonic potential and indicated some of the reasons why it failed to fulfill itself. Revisiting the historical trajectory of *Nuestra America* and its cultural conscience, the baroque ethos, I then reconstructed the forms of sociability and subjectivity that might be interested in and capable of confronting the challenges posed by counterhegemonic globalizations. The symbolic expansion made possible by a metaphorical interpretation of *Nuestra America* allows one to view the latter as the blueprint of the new transnational political culture called for in the new century and millennium. The normative claims of this political culture are embedded in the lived experiences of the people for whom *Nuestra America* speaks. Such claims point to a new kind of situated, insurgent, decolonial, intercultural, bottom-up, cosmopolitan culture and politics.

However, in order not to repeat the frustrations of the last century, this symbolic expansion must go one step further and include the most neglected trope in the *Nuestra America* mythos: Ariel, the spirit of air in Shakespeare's *The Tempest*. Like Caliban, Ariel too is Prospero's slave. However, besides not being deformed like Caliban, he gets much better treatment from Prospero, who promises him freedom if he serves Prospero faithfully. As we have seen, *Nuestra America* has looked upon itself predominantly as Caliban in constant and unequal struggle against Prospero. This is how Andrade, Aimé Césaire, Edward Brathwaite, George Lamming, Roberto Retamar, and many others see it (Retamar 1989: 13). While this is the dominant vision, it is not the only one. For instance, in 1898 the Franco-Argentinian writer Paul Groussac spoke of the need to defend the old European and Latin American civilization against the "Calibanesque Yankee" (Retamar 1989: 10). On the other hand, the ambiguous figure of Ariel inspired several interpretations. In 1900, the writer José Enrique Rodó published his essay titled "Ariel," in which he identifies Latin America with Ariel, while North America gets identified implicitly with Caliban. In 1935, the Argentine Aníbal Ponce saw in Ariel the intellectual, tied to Prospero in a less brutal way than Caliban but nonetheless at his service, much according to the model that Renaissance humanism conceived for intellectuals: a mixture of slave and mercenary, indifferent to action and conformist vis-à-vis the established order (Retamar 1989: 12). This is the intellectual Ariel reinvented by Aimé Césaire in his play of the late 1960s: *Une tempête: Adaptation de "La tempête" de Shakespeare pour un theatre nègre.* Now turned into a mulatto, Ariel is the intellectual permanently in crisis.

This said, I suggest it is high time we gave a new symbolic identification to Ariel and ascertain his usefulness for the promotion of the emancipatory ideal of *Nuestra America.* I shall conclude, therefore, by presenting Ariel as a baroque angel undergoing three transfigurations.

His first transfiguration is as Césaire's mulatto Ariel. Against racism and xenophobia, Ariel represents transculturation and multiculturalism, a *mestizaje* of flesh and spirit, as Darcy Ribeiro would say. In this *mestizaje* the possibility of interracial and intercultural dialogue is inscribed. The mulatto Ariel is the metaphor of a possible synthesis between recognition and equality. But this *mestizaje* is different from the one that dominated the first century of *Nuestra America.* The old *mestizaje* was the white mestizo's *mestizaje*, not the dark mestizo's *mestizaje.* It was a *mestizaje* with little concern for the relations of production of *mestizaje* and, to that extent, served as a cover-up for much violence and discrimination. The new *mestizaje* is a decolonial *mestizaje*, and the mestizo Ariel cannot but be a Fanonian Ariel.

Ariel's second transfiguration is as Antonio Gramsci's intellectual, who exercises self-reflectivity in order to know on whose side he is and of what use he can be. More than that, he must become the rearguard theorist. This Ariel is unequivocally on the side of Caliban, on the side of all the oppressed peoples and groups of the world, and keeps a constant epistemological and political vigilance over himself, lest his help become useless or even counterproductive. This Ariel is an intellectual trained in Martí's university.

Following from this, the third transfiguration is an epistemological one. Once Ariel joins Caliban in the quest for liberation, the knowledge born in struggle becomes the most reliable source of insight and orientation. As the African proverb goes, it is time for the story of the hunting to be told from the standpoint of the lion rather than from that of the hunter, as has always been the case under colonialism. This demands a profound change in the ways knowledge is produced and validated. It amounts to a break with what I call, in the following chapters, *Northern epistemologies.*

In these symbolic transfigurations reside the foundations for transnational emancipatory politics and thus for counterhegemonic globalizations. Following the symbolic expansion of the *Nuestra America* metaphor proposed here, the second century of *Nuestra America* only makes sense as a broad constellation of *Nuestras Americas* in Africa, Asia, and Europe, all of them depending on deep, enduring, and truly decolonizing alliances between Ariel and Caliban.

CHAPTER 2

Another *Angelus Novus*

*Beyond the Modern Game
of Roots and Options*

Introduction

In 1841, Charles Fourier launched an attack against social scientists—whom he called "the philosophers of the uncertain sciences"—for systematically neglecting the fundamental problems of the sciences they deal with.

> When dealing with industrial economy, they forget to study the associations of people that are the basis of the economy itself.... Dealing with administration, they fail to consider the means of accomplishing the administrative unity of the globe, without which empires will never have permanent order or guaranty of future.... Dealing with morals, they forget to recognize and demand the rights of women, whose oppression undermines the basis of justice.... Dealing with human rights, they forget to recognize the right to work, which is actually not possible in the present society but without which all the other rights are useless. (1967: 86, 129)

Fourier's conclusion is that social scientists have the *étourderie méthodique*, the "odd property," of neglecting precisely the fundamental problems, the primordial questions. Now, 170 years later, the reasons and examples invoked by Fourier are still so convincing that it seems appropriate to ask if the situation has changed significantly at all. Are the social sciences today better equipped to deal with the fundamental problems, or, on the contrary, are they still forgetting them systematically? And if such forgetting still goes on, what should be done in the next few decades to put an end to it?

I shall start by identifying the most fundamental problem confronting us, in my view, in the first decades of the twenty-first century. This problem is the failure to acknowledge the permanence of an abyssal line dividing metropolitan

70

from colonial societies decades after the end of historical colonialism. Such a line divides social reality in such a profound way that whatever lies on the other side of the line remains invisible or utterly irrelevant. All the generalizations of the Western social sciences, Fourier's theories included, are flawed to the extent that they take into account only the social reality of metropolitan societies, that is, the social reality on this side of the line. The European universalism so celebrated by the Frankfurt School is based on this truncated view that leaves out the social reality of the other side of the line, which in the 1920s happened to cover the majority of the world's population. In later chapters I address this issue in greater detail. Here I focus on the problems that such an abyssal line today creates for the social conditions prevailing on this side of the line. The most important problem is the collapse of social emancipation into social regulation.

The paradigm of Western modernity postulates a dialectical tension between social regulation and social emancipation, according to which each crisis of social regulation would presumably lead to new forms of social emancipation, which would in turn give rise to more progressive forms of social regulation, and so on and so forth (Santos 1995).[1] Emancipation is thus conceived of as the other of regulation, the emancipatory will and energy being the driving force of historical development. The cognitive-instrumental rationality of science and technology has been gradually entrusted with providing the tools for the social engineering called for by this theory of history. Sociology and the social sciences have developed as part and parcel of this historical project.

At the beginning of the second decade of the twenty-first century, it is not difficult to conclude that, in historical practice, the relationship between regulation and emancipation has never been a dialectical tension at all. More often than not, emancipatory projects and energies have led to forms of social regulation that, no matter how new, could hardly be conceived of as more progressive than the previously existing ones. Nowadays, if it is at all legitimate to speak of the exhaustion of the paradigm of Western modernity, it is in the sense that despite the generalized crisis of current forms of social regulation, with strident calls for "deregulation," no new emancipatory projects are emerging, let alone the energy to fight for them. Rather than being the other of social regulation, social emancipation has become its double. As the collapse of emancipation into regulation becomes common sense, social regulation does not have to be effective in order to flourish; it flourishes simply because individuals and groups find it increasingly difficult to desire beyond regulation.

In my view, our fundamental problem is how to reinvent emancipation as the other of regulation in such a way that the degenerative conflation of both is unlikely to occur. In light of the social experience of the last two hundred

---

1. The positivistic creed of order and progress is a decadent version of this dialectics. In later chapters I show that, on the other side of the line, the dialectical tension is not between social regulation and social emancipation but rather between appropriation and violence.

years, this means that we are facing a modern problem that, nevertheless, cannot be solved in modern terms. In this sense, we may see ourselves entering a period of paradigmatic transition. Because science and hence the social sciences as we know them are part and parcel of the project of Western modernity, they are much more part of the problem that we are facing than part of the solution we are seeking. At the most, they may help us to elucidate and bring analytical precision to the different dimensions of our problem. However, short of an epistemological transformation, they will be of little help in solving it. The paradigmatic transition must therefore be understood in both epistemological and societal terms.[2] The call is not just for a new epistemology and a new politics but for a new relationship between epistemology and politics. Moreover, as Ernst Cassirer has clearly shown for both the Renaissance and the Enlightenment, a new epistemology always goes together with or entails a new subjectivity, thus a new psychology (1960, 1963). The call is therefore also for a new relationship between epistemology and subjectivity.

The challenge confronting us is thus a double one: on the one hand, the need to reinvent an emancipatory map that will not, like an Escher drawing, turn gradually and insidiously into the same map of regulation; on the other, the need to reinvent an individual and collective subjectivity able and willing to use such a map. This challenge questions sociology and the social sciences in general in fundamental ways. In order to help us face this challenge, the social sciences must undergo radical change. In this chapter I address one dimension of such change: the theory of history that underlies social scientific knowledge and the hegemonic forms of sociability the latter has contributed to consolidating.

The idea of progress lies at the core of the theory of the history of modernity. The meaning of social experience, which before depended on its linkage to the past, had to be sought in a new linkage between present experience and expectations about the future. Such linkage was provided by the idea of progress. As Reinhart Koselleck argues, "Progress is the first genuinely historical concept which reduces the temporal difference between experience and expectation to a single concept" (1985: 282). The idea of progress applies to both scientific and societal development and grounds a universalistic conception of both truth and ethics. Modern emancipation is unthinkable without the ideas of progress and universalism. As I show in Part II, the discrediting of both these ideas is at the core of our current difficulty in conceptualizing emancipation, let alone investing emancipatory projects with social and political credibility. Indeed, in the last two decades, contingency and relativism have often been advanced as evidence of the impossibility of emancipation. Contingency and relativism stem from the most powerful critique of the modern theory of history, Friedrich Nietzsche's notion of the eternal recurrence of the same. However, as I try to show in the following, after two centuries of the hegemony of the idea of progress, historical repetition or circularity

---

2. In Part II, I deal at great length with the epistemological issues.

cannot but involve a certain kind of regression, liable therefore to melancholy and denial, hence to social and political withdrawal—in other words, to a will to power on the verge of "degenerating" into a will to powerlessness.

In this chapter I present the prolegomena of a social scientific contribution to the construction of an emancipatory project free from the idea of both progress and universalism.

The Past in a Cage

We live in a time without fulgurations, a time of repetition. The grain of truth in the theory of "the end of history" is that the latter is the possible maximum consciousness of an international bourgeoisie that has finally seen time transformed into the automatic and infinite repetition of its own domination. The long term thus collapses into the short term, and the latter, which has always been the time frame of capitalism, finally allows the bourgeoisie to produce a theory of history that is truly bourgeois—namely, the theory of the end of history. That this theory is not at all credible in no way interferes with its success as the spontaneous ideology of the victors. The other side of the end of history is the slogan of the celebration of the present, so much favored by the dominant versions of postmodern thought.[3]

The notion of repetition is what allows the present to spread back into the past and forward into the future, thereby cannibalizing them both. Are we facing a new situation? Up until now, the bourgeoisie had not yet been capable of elaborating a theory exclusively according to its own interests. The bourgeoisie had always seen itself as struggling against strong adversaries, first the dominant classes of the ancien régime and later the working classes. The outcome of this struggle was in the future, and for that reason the future could not be seen as a mere repetition of the past. This future-oriented movement was given several names, such as revolution, progress, and evolution. Since the outcome of the struggle was not predetermined, the revolution could be both bourgeois and working-class; progress could be seen as both the apotheosis of capitalism and its supersession; evolutionism could be claimed both by Herbert Spencer and Karl Marx. Common to the various theories of history were the devaluation of the past and the hypertrophy of the future. The past was seen as past, hence, as incapable of erupting in the present. By the same token, the power of revelation and fulguration was wholly transposed into the future.

Such was the background against which social transformation, the rationalization of individual and collective life, and social emancipation were then thought. To the extent that the victory of the bourgeoisie was being constructed, the space

---

3. The idea of "the end of history" and the impossibility of the capitalist system's renewing itself are not new, but they gained wide notoriety after Francis Fukuyama's 1992 book of the same title. Fukuyama's thesis is that the West is incapable of reinventing itself.

of the present as repetition kept expanding, but such expansion never reached the idea of the future as progress. The crisis of the idea of revolution in the 1920s resulted in the strengthening of reform as a model of social transformation and emancipation, a model based on the coexistence of repetition and amelioration,[4] whose most accomplished political form was to be the welfare state.

The difficulty we acknowledge today in thinking social transformation and emancipation resides in the fact that the theory of history that has brought us this far has gone bankrupt as a consequence of the erosion of all the assumptions that once gave it credibility. The global bourgeoisie feels that its historical victory has been accomplished, and the accomplished victor is only interested in the repetition of the present. Indeed, the future as progress may well turn out to be a dangerous threat. Paradoxically, in these circumstances, the most conservative consciousness is the one most interested in retrieving the idea of progress, but only because it refuses to accept the fact that the victory is final. It therefore construes external enemies that are as powerful as they are incomprehensible and seem like a kind of external ancien régime. Such is the case of Samuel Huntington (1993, 1997) and the threat he sees in non-Western civilizations, Islam in particular.

On the other hand, the utterly defeated in this historical process—the workers and the large majorities in the global South—put even fewer stakes in the idea of the future as progress, for that is precisely where their defeat was generated. Even the softer version of the future, the repetition/amelioration model typical of reformism, seems today untenable, albeit still desirable, given the apparently irreversible erosion of the welfare state. If the repetition of the present is intolerable, the idea of its closure is even more intolerable. Repetition and controlled regression suddenly seem the lesser evil. But if, on the one hand, the future appears meaningless, on the other, the past remains as unavailable as ever. The capacity for fulguration, for irruption, for explosion, for revelation, or, as Walter Benjamin (1968: 255) would call it, the messianic capacity, was entirely conferred on the future by Western modernity. Disenabling the future in no way enables the past. We no longer know how to envision the past in an enabling way. I believe we cannot go back to thinking social transformation and emancipation without reinventing the past. I engage in such a reinvention in the following sections and in Chapter 6.

The Parable of the *Angelus Novus*

I begin with Walter Benjamin's allegory of history. It reads like this:

> A Klee painting named *Angelus Novus* shows an angel looking as though he is about to move away from something he is fixedly contemplating. His eyes

---

4. On the concepts of amelioration and repetition as articulated moves of the modern state, see Santos (1995: 96–107).

are staring, his mouth is open, his wings are spread. This is how one pictures the angel of history. His face is turned toward the past. Where we perceive a chain of events, he sees one single catastrophe which keeps piling wreckage upon wreckage and hurls it in front of his feet. The angel would like to stay, awaken the dead, and make whole what has been smashed. But a storm is blowing from Paradise; it has got caught in his wings with such violence that the angel can no longer close them. This storm irresistibly propels him into the future to which his back is turned, while the pile of debris before him grows skyward. This storm is what we call progress. (1968: 257)

Impotent, the angel of history contemplates the pile of wreckage and suffering at his feet. He would like to remain with the catastrophe and grow roots so as to awaken the dead and summon the defeated; however, his will has been expropriated by the power that forces him to opt for the future against which his back is turned. A surplus of lucidity is matched by a deficit of efficacy. What the angel knows best and could transform has become strange, and he yields instead to what he does not know. Roots do not hold; options are blind. Thus, the past is a report, never a resource—never a power capable of irrupting at a moment of danger in favor of the defeated. Benjamin says this much in another of his theses on the philosophy of history: "To articulate the past historically does not mean to recognize it 'the way it really was.' ['The way it really was' is Ranke's motto for a scientific history.] It means to seize hold of a memory as it flashes up at a moment of danger" (1968: 255). The past's capacity for redemption lies in this possibility of emerging unexpectedly at a moment of danger as a source of nonconformity.

According to Benjamin, the nonconformity of the living would not exist without the nonconformity of the dead, for "even the dead will not be safe from the enemy if he wins"; Benjamin adds, "This enemy has not ceased to be victorious" (1968: 255). Tragic it is, then, that the angel of history has deprived the past of its capacity for explosion and redemption. By rendering impossible the nonconformity of the dead, he also renders impossible the nonconformity of the living.[5]

What are the consequences of this tragedy? Like Benjamin, we too face a moment of danger. We must therefore change the position of the angel of history. And we must reinvent the past so as to return to it the capacity for explosion and redemption. To the extent that we have no other viewpoint from which to look upon the past than the stance given us by the angel, this seems like an impossible task. However, I dare to think that the beginning of the new millennium grants us an opportunity to address this dilemma creatively. The storm blowing from Paradise is still felt, but much less intensely. The angel is still poised the same way, but the power sustaining him is weakening. It may even be that his stance

---

5. For recent analyses of Walter Benjamin's theory of history, see Echeverría (1996, 2011); Steinberg (1996); Ribeiro (1995); Callinicos (1995: 150); Löwy (2005a); Gandler (2010).

is merely the result of inertia and that Klee's angel has stopped being a tragic angel and become a puppet in repose. I shall begin by proposing a narrative of Western modernity and then go on to present the preface to a new narrative.

Roots and Options

The social construction of identity and change in Western modernity is based on an equation of roots and options. Such an equation confers a dual character on modern thought: on the one hand, it is a thought of roots; on the other, a thought of options. The thought of roots concerns all that is profound, permanent, singular, and unique, all that provides reassurance and consistency; the thought of options concerns all that is variable, ephemeral, replaceable, and indeterminate from the viewpoint of roots. The major difference between roots and options is scale (Santos 2002b: 426–434).[6] Roots are large-scale entities. As in cartography, they cover vast symbolic territories and long historical durations but fail to map the characteristics of the field in detail and without ambiguity. As any other map, theirs is a map that misguides as much as it guides. On the contrary, options are small-scale entities. They cover confined territories and short durations but do so in enough detail to allow for the assessment of the risk involved in the choice of alternative options. Because of this difference of scale, roots are unique while options are multiple, and yet the equation remains possible without being trivialized.

The root/option duality is a founding and constituting duality; that is to say, it is not subjected to the play it itself institutes between roots and options. In other words, one does not have the option not to think in terms of roots and options. The efficacy of the equation lies in a double cunning. First, there is the cunning of equilibrium between the past and the future. The thought of roots presents itself as a thought of the past as opposed to the thought of the future, which the thought of options alone is supposed to be. I speak of cunning because, in fact, both the thought of roots and the thought of options are thoughts of the future.

---

6. Roots and options are also distinguished according to time. Societies, like social interactions, are built upon a multiplicity of social times and differ according to the specific combinations and hierarchies of social times that they privilege. Drawing freely on Georges Gurvitch's (1969: 340) typology of social times, I suggest that roots are characterized by a combination of (1) long duration time and time *au ralenti* (*temps de long durée et au ralenti*); (2) cyclical time (*temps cyclique*), the time that *danse sur place*; and (3) belated time (*temps en retard sur lui même*), time whose unfolding keeps in wait. Options, on the other hand, are characterized by a combination of (1) accelerated time (*temps en avance sur lui même*), the time of contingency and discontinuity; and (2) explosive time (*temps explosive*), the time without past or present and only with future. In a continuum between glacial time and instantaneous time, modern roots tend to cluster around glacial time, while modern options tend to cluster around instantaneous time. If in roots the tempo tends to be slow, in options it tends to be fast.

In this equation, the past remains largely underrepresented. Underrepresentation does not mean oblivion. On the contrary, it may manifest itself, to use Charles Maier's expression, as "excessive memory" (1993: 137).[7] There is underrepresentation whenever memory becomes an exercise in melancholy, which, rather than recovering the past, neutralizes its redemptive potential by substituting evocation for the struggle against failing expectations.

The second kind of cunning concerns the equilibrium between roots and options. The equation presents itself as a symmetry: equilibrium of roots and options and equilibrium in the distribution of options. Indeed, it is not so. On the one hand, options are overwhelmingly predominant. Of course, certain historical moments or certain social groups consider roots predominant while others consider options so. But, as a matter of fact, it is always a question of options. While certain kinds of options imply the discursive primacy of roots, others imply their marginalization. Equilibrium is impossible. Depending on the historical moment or social group, roots precede options, or, on the contrary, options precede roots. The play is always from roots to options and from options to roots; the only variable is the power of each term as a narrative of identity and change. On the other hand, there is no equilibrium or equity in the social distribution of options. Quite the opposite, roots are but constellations of determinations that, as they define the field of options, also define the social groups that have access to it and those that do not.

A few examples will help to detail this historical process. To begin with, it is in the light of this equation of roots and options that modern Western society sees and distinguishes itself from medieval society. Medieval society is seen as one in which the primacy of roots is total, be the root religion, theology, or tradition. Medieval society is not necessarily static, but it evolves according to the logic of roots. On the contrary, modern society sees itself as dynamic, evolving according to the logic of options. The first major sign of this change in the equation is perhaps the Lutheran Reformation. With the Reformation it became possible, starting from the same root—the Bible of Western Christianity—to create an option vis-à-vis the Church of Rome. By becoming optional, religion as root loses intensity, if not even status.

Seventeenth-century rationalist theories of natural law restore the root/option equation in an entirely modern way. The root is now the law of nature by exercise of reason and observation. The intensity of this root is that it supersedes God. In *De jure belli ac pacis*, Grotius, the best spokesman for the new equation, states, "What we have been saying would have a degree of validity even if we should concede that which cannot be conceded without the utmost wickedness, that there is no God, or that the affairs of men are of no concern to Him" (1964:

---

7. Maier uses this expression in analyzing the proliferation of Holocaust museums in the United States and elsewhere. According to him (1993: 150), the surfeit of memory is a sign not of historical confidence but of a retreat from transformative politics.

11–13).[8] Upon this formidable root, the most disparate options are possible. For this reason, and not for the reasons he invokes, Richard Tuck is right when he says that Grotius's treatise "is Janus-faced and its two mouths speak the language of both absolutism and liberty" (1979: 79). This is exactly what Grotius had in mind. Firmly supported by the root of the law of nature, law may well opt for promoting either hierarchy (what Grotius calls *jus rectorium*) or equality (what he calls *jus equatorium*).

In the selfsame historical process through which religion goes from roots to options, science goes the opposite way, from options to roots. Giambattista Vico's "new science" is a decisive landmark in the transition that started with Descartes and would find its accomplishment in the nineteenth century. Unlike religion, science is a root that originates in the future; it is an option that, by radicalizing itself, turns into a root, thereby creating a wide field of possibilities. This shifting of stances between roots and options reaches its peak with the Enlightenment. In a large cultural field, which includes science and politics, religion and art, roots clearly presume to be the radicalized other of options, of both those options they render possible and those they render impossible. This is why Enlightenment reason, thus turned into the ultimate root of individual and collective life, has no other foundation but the creation of options, and this is what distinguishes it, as a root, from the roots of the ancien régime (religion and tradition). It is an option that, by radicalizing itself, makes possible a wide range of options.

In any case, options are not infinite. This is particularly obvious concerning the other great root of the Enlightenment: the social contract and the general will sustaining it (Santos 1995: 63–71). The social contract is the founding metaphor of a radical option—the option to leave the state of nature and inaugurate civil society—which turns into a root that makes everything possible, except to go back to the state of nature.[9] The contractuality of roots is irreversible, such being the limit of the reversibility of options. That is why, in Jean-Jacques Rousseau, the general will cannot be challenged by the free men it creates. Says Rousseau in *The Social Contract*, "Whoever refuses to obey the general will shall be compelled to do so by the whole body. This means nothing less than that he will be forced to be free" (1973 [1762]: 174).

The contractualization of roots is a long and eventful historical process. Romanticism, for example, is basically a reaction against the contractualization of roots as well as the assertion of their uniqueness and unavailability.[10] But romantic

---

8. Elsewhere, I deal at greater length with Grotius's theories and rationalist theories of natural law in general (Santos 1995: 60–63).

9. Like many other matrices of Western modernity (see Chapter 4), the social contract excludes colonized peoples. Actually, the material conditions for the construction of civil society reside largely in the state of nature being imposed on colonized peoples.

10. Hence the Janus face of romanticism, now reactionary, now revolutionary. See Gouldner (1970); Brunkhorst (1987); Löwy (2005a).

roots are as future oriented as the roots underlying the social contract. At stake in both cases is the opening up of a field of possibilities so as to allow for the distinction between possible and impossible, legitimate and illegitimate options.

It can therefore be said that from the Enlightenment onward, the root/option equation becomes the hegemonic way of thinking both social transformation and the place of individuals and social groups in such transformation. One of the most eloquent manifestations of this paradigm is the travel motif as a core metaphor for the modern way of being in the world. From the real voyages of European expansion to the real or imaginary voyages of Descartes, Montaigne, Montesquieu, Voltaire, and Rousseau, travel always appears as doubly symbolic: on the one hand, it is the symbol of progress and material or cultural ameliora- tion; on the other, it is the symbol of danger, insecurity, and loss. Such duplicity implies that travel contains its own opposite; that is to say, it implies the idea of a fixed point, the home (*oikos* or *domus*); travel has both a point of departure and a point of arrival. As Georges van der Abeele says, the *oikos* functions "as a transcendental point of reference that organizes and domesticates a given area by defining all other points in relation to itself" (1992: xviii). Similarly, Gaston Bachelard speaks of the "original fullness of the house's being," the fact that "a great many of our memories are housed" (1969: 8), which leads him to suggest that psychoanalysis should be complemented by topoanalysis.

The *oikos*, in a word, is that part of travel that does not travel so that travel may occur and make sense. The *oikos* is the root that both sustains and limits the possibilities for life or knowledge that travel makes possible. Travel in turn strengthens the original root because the exoticism of the places it visits deepens the familiarity of the home-point of departure. The cultural relativism aimed at by the comparative stance of the Enlightenment's imaginary travelers has its boundary in the assertion of the identity and, in general, of the superiority of European culture. Even if Montaigne never really traveled to America, or Mon- tesquieu to Persia, or Rousseau to Oceania, the truth is that they all traveled to Italy in search of the roots of European culture and that such roots were all the more revered for their sharp contrast with Italy's degradation at the time of the journey.

The travel motif excels in revealing the discriminations and inequalities that the modern root/option equation both hides and attempts to justify at the same time. On the one hand, voyaging to exotic places was not for many a voluntary gesture; nor did it aim at deepening any cultural identity whatsoever. On the contrary, it was a forced journey aimed at destroying identity. Just think of the slave trade. On the other hand, the travel motif is phallocentric. Traveling implies, as I have suggested, the fixity of the point of departure and arrival, the home (*oikos* or *domus*). Now, the home is the woman's place. That the woman does not travel makes travel possible. As a matter of fact, this sexual division of labor as regards the travel motif is one of the most resilient topoi of Western culture, if not of other cultures as well. In Western culture, its archetype is the

Odyssey. Domestic Penelope takes care of the home while Ulysses goes about his interminable voyaging. Penelope's long wait spent weaving is the right metaphor for the soundness of the point of departure and arrival that guarantees the possibility of Ulysses's aleatory journeys and adventures.

The travel motif is important in this context in that it helps to identify the sexist, racist, and classist definitions of the modern equation of roots and options. The range of possibilities created by the equation is not equally available to all. Some, perhaps the majority, are excluded. For these, roots are, rather than the possibility of new options, the very instrument of their denial. Those same roots that grant options to men, whites, and capitalists deny them to women, blacks, and workers. From the nineteenth century onward, the mirror play of roots and options has been consolidated and becomes the *ideologie savante* of the social sciences. The two outstanding examples are unquestionably Karl Marx and Sigmund Freud.

In Marx, the base is the root, and the superstructure the options. This is no vulgar metaphor, as some nonvulgar Marxists wanted us to believe. It is rather a logical principle of social intelligibility running through Marx's work, and indeed even through the work of many social scientists who disagreed with Marx. It will suffice to mention the case of Émile Durkheim, who believed that collective consciousness is the ever-threatened root in a society based on the division of social labor and on the options that such a division goes on duplicating endlessly. This is also Freud's and Carl Jung's frame of thought. The centrality of the unconscious in depth psychology resides precisely in the fact that the unconscious is the deep root that grounds both the options of the ego and their neurotic limitation. In Peter Homans's cultural reading of Freud and Jung, "Interpretation discerns the unconscious infrastructure of culture thereby freeing the interpreter from its oppressive and coercive powers" (1993: xx).

The communist and introspective revolutions[11] have in common that both are creative responses to the profound social and individual disorganization of a society that experiences the loss of ideals, symbols, and ways of life that constitute their common heritage. Furthermore, the future-oriented stance as regards the equation of roots and options is as strong in Marx as in Freud. If for Marx the base is the key to social transformation, for Freud or Jung it does not make any sense to study the unconscious except in the context of therapy. Likewise, both historical materialism and depth psychology wish to go back to the roots of modern society—of capitalism and Western culture, respectively—in search of new and ampler options. In either case, the success of the underlying theory is measured by its becoming the foundation and instrument of change. In a world that had long lost its "deep past"—the root of religion—science becomes in either

---

11. On the introspective revolution as a radical value change taking place at the beginning of the twentieth century and involving, aside from Freud, writers such as Proust, Joyce, and Kafka and philosophers such as Bergson, see Weinstein and Platt (1969: 137).

case the only root capable of sustaining a new beginning in modern Western society. On that basis, good options are the options legitimated by science. This is what grounds, in Marx, the distinction between reality and ideology and, in Freud, the distinction between reality and fantasy. In this distinction also resides the possibility of modern critical theory. As Nietzsche says, if realities disappear, appearances vanish too. And the opposite is also true.[12]

In our century, sociology and social sciences in general have developed as disciplines on the basis of the new roots/options equation, converted into the master narrative of social intelligibility: structure and agency in sociology and anthropology, the *longue durée* and *l'événement* in history, and *langue* and *parole* or deep structure and surface structure in linguistics are different versions of the same equation. Even when some theoretical currents in the different disciplines positioned themselves against these schemata (phenomenological and poststructuralist currents) or looked for mediations between or sublations of the terms of the equation (Anthony Giddens's theory of structuration, Pierre Bourdieu's concept of *habitus*), their analytical claims remained prey to the equation due to the specific ways they distanced themselves from it.

Concerning the modern political field, the liberal political equivalent of this new equation of roots and options is the nation-state and positive law, now turned into the roots that create the wide range of options in the market and in civil society. In order to function as a root, law must be autonomous, meaningful, and scientific. There was some resistance to this transformation. In Germany, for example, the historical school claimed for law the old root/option equation: law as an emanation of the *Volksgeist*. But what prevailed was the new equation: the juridical root constituted by codification and positivism and prone to turn law into a tool of social engineering (Santos 1995: 73). The liberal state, in its turn, constituted itself as a root by imagining homogeneous nationality and national culture (Anderson 1983). The state becomes, then, the guardian of a root that does not exist beyond the state.

The End of the Equation

We are living at a moment of danger in Benjamin's sense. To my mind, it consists largely in the fact that the modern equation of roots and options, from which we have learned how to think social transformation, is undergoing a process of profound destabilization that seems to be irreversible. Such destabilization presents itself under three main forms: the turbulence of scales, the explosion of roots and options, and the interchangeability of roots and options. I shall briefly characterize each of these forms.

---

12. Given its anti-Kantian obsession, this idea recurs in Nietzsche. See, for example, Nietzsche (1973).

The Turbulence of Scales

As regards the turbulence of scales, we must recall what I said above about the difference in scale between roots (large scale) and options (small scale). The root/option equation rests on this difference and on its stability. Today we are living in turbulent times whose turbulence manifests itself through a chaotic confusion of scale among phenomena. Urban violence is here paradigmatic. When a street kid is looking for shelter for the night and is for that reason murdered by a policeman, or when a person is approached in the street by a beggar, refuses to give money, and is for that reason murdered by the beggar, what happens is an unpredictable explosion of the scale of the conflict: a seemingly trivial phenomenon seemingly without consequences is equated with another one—now dramatic and with fatal consequences. This abrupt and unpredictable change in the scale of phenomena occurs today in all the various domains of social praxis, and that is why I dare to consider it as one of the basic features of our time.

Following Ilya Prigogine (1980, 1997; Prigogine and Stengers 1979), I believe that our societies today are characterized by bifurcation. Bifurcation occurs in unstable systems whenever a minimal change can bring about qualitative changes in an unpredictable and chaotic way. This sudden explosion of scale creates tremendous turbulence and leaves the system in a state of irreversible vulnerability. I believe that the turbulence of our time is of this kind and that in it resides the vulnerability affecting all forms of subjectivity and sociability, from labor to intimacy, from citizenship to ecosystems. This state of bifurcation reverberates on the root/option equation, rendering chaotic and reversible the scale difference between roots and options. The political instability of our time has largely to do with sudden changes in scale, both as regards roots and options: from the collapse of the Soviet Union to ethnic cleansing in the Balkans; from the ever more brutal and immoral occupation of Palestine to the Arab Spring; from the partition of Sudan to the imperialist intervention in Iraq, Afghanistan, and Libya by the United States and its allies and the French imperialist intervention in Côte d'Ivoire; from the horrendous attack against the Twin Towers and Pentagon in the United States to the global war on terror that developed therefrom; from the extrajudicial execution of rival leaders (Osama bin Laden, Mu'ammar Gadhafi) as a new doctrine of international law to the neocolonial disciplining of the martyred people of Haiti under the supposedly benevolent stewardship of the United Nations. When the Soviet Union fell apart, the roughly 25 million Russians living outside Russia in the USSR's various republics suddenly saw their identity shrinking to the status of a local identity like that of an ethnic minority. On their part, the Serbs of the former Yugoslavia, initially with the assistance of the Western countries, sought to expand the scale of their national roots by cannibalizing the national roots of their neighbors. An attack on one city becomes a global phenomenon of the highest order. While the mostly Christian South Sudanese people achieve the status and the scale of a nation-state, the same is denied to Palestinians. National conflicts in Libya, Egypt, Syria, Tunisia, and Yemen become regional or global or remain national without clear reasons. These changes in scale are nothing new. They had already occurred after World War II, during the decolonization process and with the creation of the new, so-called national, postcolonial states. What is new about these changes is precisely the fact that they took place upon the ruins of the states that had claimed to be the sole entitlement of identity roots.

The same seemingly erratic explosion in scale also occurs in the realm of options. In the field of economics, the manner in which such options (such as those concerning structural adjustment) are imposed as a fatality and the drastic results they produce cause the small scale to expand into the large scale and the short term to turn instantly into the long term. The adoption of the neoliberal structural adjustment programs by the countries subjected to the International Monetary Fund, far from being an option, is a transnational root that invades and stifles national roots, reducing them to local excrescences. On the other side, the social contract, which is the metaphor for the contractualization of the political roots of modernity, is subjected today to great turbulence, if not totally dismantled. The social contract is a root contract based on the commonly shared option of abandoning the state of nature. Two hundred years later, we faced structural unemployment, precarious work, work without rights, and slave-like labor, alongside scandalous salaries in the financial sector; bailouts granted to banks, yet denied to people unable to pay their mortgages or debts incurred in obtaining an education; the return of reactionary ideologies that substitute the principle of individual culpability for the principle of social responsibility and fill the political agenda with calls for the sick, poor, or elderly to die fast in order to lower public spending on health; and the abysmal increase in social and economic inequalities within and among the countries of the world-system. Considering the famine, poverty, and disease that beleaguer the global South and the internal Third World of the global North, it seems obvious that we are opting for excluding from the social contract a significant percentage of the population of the world, both on the periphery and in the core of the world-system, forcing it to go back to the state of nature.

The Explosion of Roots and Options

The second manifestation of the destabilization of the equation of roots and options is the explosion of roots and options alike. In point of fact, what is commonly called globalization, in relation to the consumer and media society, has given rise to a seemingly infinite multiplicity of options. The range of possibilities has expanded tremendously, legitimated by the very forces that make possible such expansion, be they technology, the market economy, the global culture of advertising and consumerism, the information technology revolution, or democracy. Each increase of options becomes automatically a demand for (and a right to) the further increase of options. However, in blatant contradiction to all this, we live in a time of localisms and territorializations of identities and singularities, genealogies and memories. These have become all the more visible with the struggles of indigenous people and of Afro-descendents in defense of their territories, of peasants in defense of their land and against landgrabbing, of tribal peoples against megaprojects, and of movements for the right to memory after the atrocities of apartheid and dictatorship or movements for cultural identity and the right to speak one's own language. In sum, the time we live in is also a time of limitless multiplication of roots.

But the explosion of roots and options does not occur merely by means of the endless multiplication of both. It also occurs in the process of searching for particularly deep and strong roots capable of sustaining particularly dramatic and radical options. In this case, the range of possibilities may be drastically reduced, but the remaining options are dramatic and full of consequences. The two most telling examples of this explosion of roots and options by means of the intensification of both are fundamentalism and DNA research. Religious or political fundamentalism is usually understood as any extreme version of the politics of identity considered, explicitly or implicitly, non-Western. In fact, its most common form derives from extreme versions of Eurocentric universalism. The hegemonic character of this latter form of fundamentalism is signaled by its capacity to designate the extreme versions of the politics of identity as the sole forms of fundamentalism: there is no fundamentalism in the global North except that of non-Western social groups living there. Against this self-serving ideology, I suggest that, of all fundamentalisms, neoliberal fundamentalism is undoubtedly the most intense. Now that Marxism has only just begun to recover from a deep crisis, capitalism has become truly Marxist. In the course of the last few decades, the ideology of the free markets and privatization has become a kind of new social contract, that is to say, the universal economic base or root that forces the majority of countries, individuals, and communities into dramatic and radical options, which very often boil down to the option between the chaos of exclusion and the chaos of inclusion.

On the other hand, DNA research, conducted within the scope of the human genome project, signifies, in cultural terms, the transformation of the body into the ultimate root whence sprout the dramatic options of genetic engineering. The boom of neuroscience—the research on the brain over the past few years, the so-called brain decade, and on personalized biotech medication—can also be interpreted as another way of converting the body into the ultimate root. We began the twentieth century with the socialist and the introspective revolutions, of Marx and Freud, respectively, and we are now starting the new century with the body revolution. The centrality then assumed by class and the psyche is now being assumed by the body (corporeality), itself now converted, like enlightened reason before, into the root of all options.

The Interchangeability of Roots and Options

This extensive and intensive explosion of roots and options only destabilizes the root/option equation to the extent that it interconnects with the interchangeability of roots and options. Today we see that many of the roots in which we have been mirroring ourselves were but disguised options. In this field, major contributions have been provided by feminist theory and epistemology, critical race theory, postcolonial studies, and the new historicism. By considering the West/East option of primatology as studied by Donna Haraway (1989), the sexist and racist option of the welfare state as analyzed by Linda Gordon (1991, 2007), the option, denounced by Cheik Anta Dioup (1967) and Martin Bernal (1987), to eliminate the African roots of Greek antiquity so as to intensify its purity as the root of European culture, and the option to whiten the crossings of the Atlantic Ocean so as to hide the syncretisms of modernity, as Paul Gilroy (1993) has shown, we realize that the roots of our sociability and intelligibility are in fact optional and address the hegemonic idea of the future that gave them meaning, rather than the past that, after all, only existed to function as the anticipated mirror of the future.

However, paradoxically, as they become more and more elaborate, this unmasking and this denunciation also become trivialized. As Captain Ahab discovered at his own cost, behind the mask there is but another mask. Knowing that the hegemonic roots of Western modernity are disguised options gives the hegemonic culture the opportunity to impose its options as roots, this time without any need for disguise and with increased arrogance. The most eloquent case may well be Harold Bloom's *The Western Canon* (1994). Here, roots are a mere effect of the right to options. In sociology, the explosion of roots and options in recent times has taken the form, among others, of the proliferation of revisionism concerning the founders of the discipline, their identification, and their contributions (Alexander 1982a, 1982b, 1987, 1995; Alexander and Thompson 2008; Collins 1994, 2008; Cuin and Gresle 1992; Hedström 2005; Giddens 1993, 1995; Karsenti 2005; Joas and Knöbl 2009; Rawls 2004; Ritzer 1990, 1992, 2010; C. Turner 2010; J. Turner 2010a, 2010b; P. Wagner 2012; S. Wagner 1992).

The interchangeability of roots and options is not exclusive of the cultural and scientific fields. It is rather taking place at all levels of sociability and everyday life. It has even become constitutive of our life trajectories and histories. The debates on adoption and on the negotiation of motherhood are probably one of the best examples.[13] The wall of secrecy that for many years separated the birth mother (root) from the adoptive mother (option) has been questioned by the "open adoption" policy "in which the birth parents meet adoptive parents, participate in the separation and placement process [and] retain the right to continuing contact and to knowledge of the child's whereabouts and welfare" (Yngvesson 1996:

---

13. A fine analysis of negotiated motherhood, interweaving scientific analysis and personal life trajectory, can be read in Yngvesson (1996). See also Mandell (2007) and Sales (2012).

14). The interdependence of birth and adoptive mothers gives the adopted child the possibility to opt between biological and socially constructed genetic roots or even to opt to keep both of them as a kind of bounded root life contingency.

In the new constellation of meaning, roots and options are no longer qualitatively distinct entities. Being a root or an option is just an effect of scale and intensity. Roots are the continuation of options on a different scale and intensity; the same goes for options. The outcome of this circularity is that the rights to roots and to options are reciprocally translatable. All in all, it has become very often a question of style. The mirror play of roots and options reaches its climax in cyberspace. On the Internet (most dramatically on Facebook), identities are doubly imagined, as flights of imagination and as sheer images. People are free to create roots at their pleasure and then reproduce their options ad infinitum. Thus, the same image can be seen as a root without options or as an option without roots. Hence, it no longer makes sense to think in terms of the root/option equation. Actually, we come to realize that the equation only makes sense in a conceptual, logocentric culture that speculates on social and territorial matrixes (space and time), subjecting them to criteria of authenticity. As we move on to an imagocentric culture, space and time are replaced by instances of velocity, matrixes are replaced by mediatrixes, and at this level the authenticity discourse becomes an incomprehensible gibberish. There is no depth but the succession of screens. All that is below or behind is also above and in front. At this stage, perhaps, Gilles Deleuze's (1968) analysis of the rhizome gains a new up-to-datedness. In point of fact, Mark Taylor and Esa Saarinen, two media philosophers, have stated that "the imaginary register transforms roots into rhizomes. A rhizomic culture is neither rooted nor unrooted. One can never be sure where rhizomes will break new ground" (1994: "Gaping," 9).

The condition of our condition is that we are in a period of transition. Matrixes coexist with mediatrixes, space and time with the instances of velocity, the intelligibility of the discourse of authenticity with its unintelligibility. The root/option equation now makes sense, now makes no sense at all. Ours is a more complex situation than Nietzsche's, for, in our case, realities and appearances pile up one moment, and in the next moment they disappear. Perhaps these drastic oscillations of meaning are the ultimate cause of the trivialization of the equation of roots and options. Herein lies our difficulty today in thinking social transformation on this side of the abyssal line. The truth is that the pathos of the distinction between roots and options is constitutive of the modern Western way of thinking social change. The more intense the pathos, the more easily the present evaporates into an ephemeral moment between the past and the future.[14] On the contrary, in the absence of the pathos, the present tends to be eternalized, devouring both past and future. Such is our present condition on this side of the line. We live in a time of repetition. The acceleration of repetition provokes a feeling of

---

14. This pathos was largely responsible for the irrelevance of the social realities on the other side of the line, the colonial societies, as I show in Chapter 4.

vertigo and a feeling of stagnation at the same time. Because of its acceleration and media treatment, repetition ends up subjecting even those groups that assert themselves by the pathos of roots.[15] It is as easy and irrelevant to yield to the retrospective illusion of projecting the future into the past as it is to yield to the prospective illusion of projecting the past into the future. The eternal present renders the two illusions equivalent and neutralizes both. Thus, our condition takes on a Kafkan dimension: what exists can be explained by neither the past nor the future. It exists only in a chaotic web of indefinition and contingency. While modernity deprived the past of its capacity for irruption and revelation, handing it on to the future, the Kafkan present deprives the future of this capacity. What irrupts in the Kafkan present seems erratic, arbitrary, fortuitous, and indeed absurd. In fact, the eternalization of the present goes together with the operation of highly selective criteria that define what counts as relevant present at any given historical moment. In other words, it is the result of the workings of the abyssal line dividing social reality into two reciprocally unintelligible fields, as I show in Chapter 4.

But there are some who read the eternalization of the present as the new storm blowing from Paradise and holding the *Angelus Novus*. According to Taylor and Saarinen, in the global "compu-telecommunications network" of digitalized realities, "space seems to collapse into a presence that knows no absence and time seems to be condensed in a present undisturbed by past or future. If ever achieved, such enjoyment of presence in the present would be the fulfillment of the deepest and most ancient dreams of the western religio-philosophical imagination" (1994: "Speed," 4). To my mind, the digital storm quivering on the wings of the angel is virtual and can be connected and disconnected at our pleasure. Our condition is therefore far less heroic than the storm requires. However idealistically formulated, presence, whose fruition is imagined by religion and philosophy, is the unique and unrepeatable fulguration of a substantive relation; it is the product of a permanent interrogation, be it the mystical experience, dialectical supersession, the fulfillment of the *Geist*, *Selbstsein*, existential being, or communism. On the contrary, digital presence is the fulguration of a relationship, endlessly repeatable, a permanent reply to all possible interrogations. It opposes history without realizing that it is historical itself. Hence, it imagines the end of history without having to imagine its own end.

A Future for the Past

It is not easy to get rid of a situation that is as convincing in its contradictions as it is in its ambiguities, a situation that is as comfortable as it is intolerable. The

---

15. The resistance against the trivialization of the pathos of roots inspires indigenous movements worldwide. See Santos, *Epistemologies of the South: Reinventing Social Emancipation* (forthcoming).

eternalization of the present implies the end of the permanent interrogations discussed by Maurice Merleau-Ponty (1968: 50). The time of repetition can be conceived of as progress or its opposite. Without the pathos of the tension between roots and options, it is not possible to think social change, but such an impossibility loses much of its dramatism if social change, besides being unthinkable, is considered unnecessary. This ambiguity brings about intellectual appeasement, which in turn brings about conformity and passivity. Walter Benjamin's admonishment, though written in 1940, is still quite relevant: "The current amazement that the things we are experiencing [i.e., Nazi fascism] are 'still' possible in the twentieth century is *not* philosophical. This amazement is not the beginning of knowledge—unless it is the knowledge that the view of history which gives rise to it is untenable" (1968: 257).

In my view, we must start from here, from the verification that the theory of history of modernity is untenable and that, for that reason, it is necessary to replace it with another, one capable of helping us to live this moment of danger with dignity and to survive it by strengthening our emancipatory energies. What we most urgently need is a new capacity for wonder and indignation capable of grounding a new, nonconformist, destabilizing, and indeed rebellious theory and practice.

Following Merleau-Ponty's suggestion, we must begin with the most open and incomplete meanings or representations of modernity. They are the ones that ignite passion and open new spaces for human creativity and initiative (Merleau-Ponty 1968: 45). Since the theory of history of modernity was entirely oriented toward the future, the past remained underrepresented and undercodified. The dilemma of our time is that not even the fact that the future is discredited makes it possible, within this theory, to revive the past. For the theory of history of modernity, the past has never stopped being the fatalist accumulation of catastrophes that the *Angelus Novus* looks upon, powerlessly and absently.

Our task consists of reinventing the past in such a way as to make it recapture the capacity for the fulguration, irruption, and redemption so clairvoyantly imagined by Benjamin. "Historical materialism," says Benjamin, "wishes to retain that image of the past which unexpectedly appears to man singled out by history at a moment of danger" (1968: 255). This capacity for fulguration can only flourish once the past stops being the fatalist accumulation of catastrophes in order to become the preview of our nonconformity and outrage. In a modernist conception, fatalism is the other side of faith in the future. The past is thereby doubly neutralized because only what had to happen did happen and because whatever happened in a given moment has already been, or will soon be, superseded. In this constellation of retrospective and prospective illusions, nothing is learned from the past except to trust the future.

We need therefore to fight for another conception of the past, one in which the past becomes a fore-reason of our rage and nonconformity. In lieu of a neutralized past, we need a past as irretrievable loss resulting from human initiatives that had a choice of alternatives, that is, a past of empowering memories, one revived for us by the suffering and oppression caused in the presence of other alternatives that could have avoided them.[16] It is in the name of a similar conception of the past that Benjamin criticizes German social democracy: "Social Democracy thought fit to assign to the working class the role of the redeemer of future generations, in this way cutting the sinews of its greatest strength. This training made the working class forget both its hatred and its spirit of sacrifice, for both are nourished by the image of enslaved ancestors rather than that of liberated grandchildren" (1968: 260).

Perhaps even more than in Benjamin's time, we have lost the capacity for rage and amazement vis-à-vis the grotesque realism of what is accepted only because it exists. We have lost the spirit of sacrifice. In order to retrieve them both, we need to reinvent the past as negativity, as a product of human initiative, and on that basis to construct new, powerful interrogations and passionate stands capable of inexhaustible meanings. We must therefore identify the meaning of powerful interrogations at a moment of danger like ours. Such identification occurs at two moments. First, the efficacy required for powerful interrogations. Resorting to a somewhat idealist expression of Merleau-Ponty's (1968: 44), I suggest that, in order to be efficient, powerful interrogations must be like monograms of the spirit engraved upon things. They must irrupt by the intensity and concentration of the internal energy that they carry within themselves. Under the conditions of the present time, such irruption will only occur if powerful interrogations translate themselves into destabilizing images. Only destabilizing images can give back to us our capacity for wonder and outrage. To the extent that the past stops being automatically redeemed by the future, human suffering and the exploitation and oppression that inhabit it become a merciless commentary on the present time; they become unforgivable because they are still taking place, whereas they could have been prevented by human initiative. Images are destabilizing only to the extent that everything depends on us, and everything could be different and better. Human initiative, then, rather than any abstract idea of progress, is what grounds Ernst Bloch's principle of hope. Nonconformity is the will's utopia. As Benjamin says, "Only that historian will have the gift of fanning the spark of hope in the past who is firmly convinced that even the dead will not be safe from the enemy if he wins" (1968: 255).

Destabilizing images will be efficacious only if they are amply shared. And thus I come to the second moment of the meaning of powerful interrogations. How to interrogate so that the interrogation is more shared than the answers to it? At the present moment of danger, within Western culture today, powerful interrogations, in order to be widely shared, must address as much what unites us

---

16. This empowering conception of the past is well illustrated in indigenous peoples' movements and struggles. More on this in Santos, *Epistemologies of the South: Reinventing Social Emancipation* (forthcoming).

as what separates us. Once the causes of separation are identified, it is necessary to focus on uniting by going to the roots of such separation. We are left today with many theories and practices of separation and various degrees of separation. Since the primacy of options has manifested itself, among other things, through the (optional) affirmation and proliferation of roots, the explosion of particularism in the politics of identity in the last three decades has contributed to strengthening the theories of separation in the very process of building new theories of union. For this reason, what we lack most are theories about uniting, a lack that is particularly serious at a moment of danger. But as I said, uniting can only be brought about on the basis of a radical inquiry into the epistemological, political, cultural, and historical conditions that ground and promote separation. Only thus will a necessary balance between theories of separation and theories of union be accomplished.

The hegemonic powers that govern consumer and information society have been promoting theories and images appealing to a totality, whether of the species, the world, or even the universe, that stands above the divisions that constitute it. We know that they are manipulatory theories and images that ignore the various circumstances and aspirations of peoples, classes, sexes, races, regions, and so on, as well as the unequal relations of exploitation and victimization that have brought together the different parts of that pseudototality. However, the grain of credibility of such theories and images consists of their appeal, albeit in a manipulative way, to an imagined community of humanity as a whole, the universality of suffering. Suffering is everywhere. It is the individuals who suffer, not the societies.

The counterhegemonic forces, in their turn, have been expanding the arenas of political understanding, but their coalitions and alliances have hardly succeeded in superseding the theories of separation. They have, however, been more successful in overcoming territorial separation than separation derived from the different forms of discrimination and oppression. Transnational coalitions have been easier to accomplish by feminist, ecological, or indigenous groups than among all these different groups. The explanation lies in the lack of balance between theories of separation and theories of union. The latter need to be reinforced so as to make visible what is common among the various forms of discrimination and oppression: human suffering. Counterhegemonic globalization, which I designate *insurgent cosmopolitanism*, is grounded on the global and multidimensional character of human suffering. The notion of *totus orbis*, formulated by one of the founders of modern international law, Francisco de Vitoria, must today be reconstructed as counterhegemonic globalization, that is to say, as insurgent cosmopolitanism. Respect for difference cannot prevent the communication and complicity that render possible the struggle against indifference. The moment of danger we traverse demands that we deepen communication and complicity. We must do it not in the name of an abstract *communitas* but spurred, rather, by the destabilizing image of multiform suffering, caused by human initiative, which is as overwhelming as it is unnecessary. At this moment of danger, the theories of separation must be reformulated keeping in mind what unites us; conversely, the theories of union must be reformulated keeping in mind what separates us. Borders must be constructed with lots of entrances and exits. At the same time, we must bear in mind that what unites us only does so a posteriori. It is not human nature but human initiative that unites us.

Communication and complicity must occur in an anchored way and at various levels to allow for a dynamic equilibrium between the theories of separation and the theories of union. To each level corresponds a potential for indignation and nonconformity nourished by a destabilizing image. I suggest we distinguish three levels: cultural, political, and juridical.

The first orientation is cultural. The theories about what unites us proposed by the consumer and information society are based on the idea of globalization. Hegemonic globalizations are in fact globalized localisms[17]—the new cultural imperialisms. Hegemonic globalization can be defined as the process by which a given local phenomenon—be it the English language, Hollywood, fast food, and so on—succeeds in extending its reach over the globe and, by doing so, develops the capacity to designate a rival social phenomenon as local. The communication and complicity allowed for by hegemonic globalization are based on an unequal exchange that cannibalizes differences instead of facilitating the dialogue among them. They are trapped in silences, manipulations, and exclusions.

Against globalized localisms I offer, as a methodological orientation, a *diatopical hermeneutics*.[18] I mean a hermeneutical procedure based on the idea that all cultures are incomplete and that the topoi of a given culture, however strong, are as incomplete as the culture to which they belong. Strong topoi are the main premises of argumentation within a given culture, the premises that make possible the creation and exchange of arguments. By this function, topoi create an illusion of totality based on the figure of synecdoche, or *pars pro toto*. That is why the incompleteness of a given culture can only be assessed on the basis of the topoi of another culture. Seen from another culture, the topoi of a given culture stop being premises of argumentation to become mere arguments.[19] The aim of diatopical hermeneutics is to maximize the awareness of the reciprocal incompleteness of cultures by engaging in a dialogue, as it were, with one foot in one culture and the other in another—hence, its diatopical character. Diatopical hermeneutics is an exercise in reciprocity among cultures that consists in transforming the premises

---

17. On my conception of globalizations, see Santos (1995: 252–264, 2002a, 2002b).

18. I return to this topic in Chapter 8 when dealing with intercultural translation.

19. At moments of great turbulence, the "demotion" of topoi from premises of argumentation into mere arguments can be observed within a given culture. In a way, this is what is happening with the root/option equation. In this chapter, I have challenged this equation as a strong topos of Eurocentric culture, by "demoting" it from premise of argumentation to mere argument and refuting it with other arguments.

of argumentation in a given culture into intelligible and credible arguments in another. Elsewhere (Santos 1995: 337–347, 2007a: 17–21), by way of example, I have proposed a diatopical hermeneutics to study the topos of human rights in Western culture and the topos of *dharma* in Hindu culture, as well as the topos of human rights and the topos of *umma* in Islamic culture, in the latter case in dialogue with Abdullahi Ahmed An-Na'im (1992, 1995, 2000).

Raising incompleteness to the maximum possible consciousness opens up unsuspected possibilities for communication and complicity. It is, however, a difficult procedure. It is a postcolonial, postimperial, and, to a certain extent, even postidentity procedure. The very reflexivity of the conditions that make it possible and necessary is one of the most demanding conditions of diatopical hermeneutics. An idealistic conception of cross-cultural dialogue will easily forget that such a dialogue is only made possible by the temporary simultaneity of two or more different contemporaneities. The partners in the dialogue are only superficially contemporaneous; indeed, they feel contemporaneous only with the historical tradition of their respective culture. This is most likely the case when the different cultures involved in the dialogue share a past of interlocked unequal exchanges. What are the possibilities for a cross-cultural dialogue when one of the cultures *in presence* has itself been molded by massive and long-lasting violations of human rights perpetrated in the name of the other culture? When cultures share such a past, the present they share at the moment when they start the dialogue is at best a quid pro quo and at worst a fraud. The cultural dilemma is the following: Since in the past the dominant culture rendered unpronounceable some of the subordinate culture's aspirations to human dignity, is it now possible to pronounce them in the cross-cultural dialogue without thereby further justifying and even reinforcing their unpronounceability?

The energy that propels diatopical hermeneutics comes from a destabilizing image that I designate *epistemicide*, the murder of knowledge. Unequal exchanges among cultures have always implied the death of the knowledge of the subordinated culture, hence the death of the social groups that possessed it. In the most extreme cases, such as that of European expansion, epistemicide was one of the conditions of genocide. The loss of epistemological confidence that currently afflicts modern science has facilitated the identification of the scope and gravity of the epistemicides perpetrated by hegemonic Eurocentric modernity. The more consistent the practice of diatopical hermeneutics, the more destabilizing the image of such epistemicides (more on this in Chapters 4 through 6).

The second orientation for a dynamic equilibrium between the theories of separation and the theories of union is political. I designate it, following Richard Falk (1995), *humane governance*. The hegemonic theories of union, beginning with the market economy and liberal democracy, are creating barbaric forms of exclusion and destitution that amount to veritable practices of neofeudalism and neocolonialism. By the same token, the counterhegemonic theories of separation, such as those underlying many contemporary identity politics, because they lack the counterbalance of theories of union, have often amounted to fundamentalist or neotribal practices. By these two opposite, though convergent, ways, we live in a time of excess of separatism and segregationism. The destabilizing image that must be constructed out of this excess is the image of a *global apartheid*, a world of ghettos without entrances or exits, swirling in a sea of colonialist and fascist currents. This destabilizing image constitutes the energy for the political orientation of humane governance. By humane governance I mean, after Falk, every normative criterion that "facilitates communication across civilizational, nationalist, ethnic, class, generational, cognitive, and gender divides," but does so with "respect and celebration of difference and an attitude of extreme skepticism toward exclusivist alarms that deny space for expression and exploration of others, as well as toward variants of universalism that ignore the uneven circumstances and aspirations of peoples, classes and regions" (1995: 242). In other words, humane governance is a normative project that is "constantly identifying and reestablishing the various interfaces between the specific and the general in each and every context, yet keeping its spatial and mental borders open for entry and exit, being wary of any version of truth claim as the foundation of extremism and political violence" (1995: 242).

Stimulated by a destabilizing image—global apartheid—that is powerful because it is associated with extreme social inequalities, the principle of humane governance has a strong oppositional potential. Perhaps more than the other two orientations, it has a Eurocentric character by virtue of its aspiration to totality. And yet it represents the maximum possible of centrifugal consciousness of Eurocentrism in that it commits itself to join the struggles against imperial Eurocentrism and the suffering it has historically caused.

Finally, I draw the juridical orientation for our moment of danger from international law. I mean the doctrine of the common heritage of humankind,[20] no doubt the most innovative but also the most vilified substantive doctrine of international law in the second half of the last century and today virtually abandoned due to the overwhelming dominance of neoliberalism and the new imperialisms it has given rise to, such as extractivist or mining imperialism. The concept of the common heritage of humankind was formulated for the first time in 1967 by Malta's ambassador to the United Nations, Arvid Pardo, in relation to UN negotiations on the international regulation of the oceans and the deep seabed. Pardo's purpose was

> to provide a solid basis for future worldwide cooperation ... through the acceptance by the international community of a new principle of international

---

20. The concept of the common heritage of humankind signifies that the struggle of oppressed social groups for a decent life under the new conditions of globalization promoted by capitalism will be fully successful only in terms of a new pattern of development and sociability that will necessarily include a new social contract with the earth, nature, and future generations.

law ... that the seabed and ocean floor and their subsoil have a special status as a common heritage of mankind and as such should be reserved exclusively for peaceful purposes and administered by an international authority for the benefit of all peoples. (1968: 225–226)

Since then, the concept of the common heritage of humankind has been applied not only to the ocean floor but also to other "common areas," such as the moon and outer space. The idea behind this concept is that these natural entities belong to humankind in its entirety and that all people are therefore entitled to have a say and a share in the management and allocation of their resources. Five elements are usually associated with the concept of the common heritage of humankind: nonappropriation; management by all peoples; international sharing of the benefits obtained from the exploitation of natural resources; peaceful use, including freedom of scientific research for the benefit of all peoples; and conservation for future generations.[21]

Although formulated by international lawyers, the concept of the common heritage of humankind transcends by far the field of traditional international law. International law deals traditionally with international relations among nation-states, which are supposed to be the main beneficiaries of the regulation agreed upon. Such relations are based chiefly on reciprocity, that is, granting advantages to another state or states in return for equivalent advantages for oneself (Kiss 1985: 426). The concept of the common heritage of humankind is different from traditional international law on two accounts: as far as the common heritage of humankind is concerned, there is no question of reciprocity; further, the interests to be safeguarded are the interests of humankind as a whole rather than the interests of states. To be sure, as Alexandra Kiss points out, since the nineteenth century states have been signing conventions containing no implication of reciprocity (prohibition of the slave trade, freedom of navigation, regulation of labor conditions, and so on) and whose concern is to safeguard "a benefit for all mankind which can be obtained only by international cooperation and the acceptance of obligations by all governments, even if they receive no immediate return" (1985: 426–427). But the concept of the common heritage of humankind reaches much further inasmuch as both its object and subject of regulation transcend the state. Humankind emerges, indeed, as the subject of international law, entitled to its own heritage and the autonomous prerogative to manage the spaces and resources included in the global commons (Pureza 1998).

The acknowledgment of social fields, whether physical or symbolic, that are *res communes* and can only be administered in the interest of all is a *conditio sine qua non* of the communication and complicity between part and whole intended

---

21. Pureza (1998, 2009); Payoyo (1997); Baslar (1998); Zieck (1992: 177–197); *Pacem in Maribus XX* (1992); Blaser (1990); Weiss (1989); Joyner (1986); Kiss (1985); White (1982); Dupuy (1974).

to bring about a greater balance between the theories of separation and union. If the whole—be it the species, the world, or the universe—does not have a juridical space of its own, it will be subjected to the two basic separation criteria of modernity: the property that grounds world capitalism and the sovereignty that grounds the interstate system.

The juridical monopoly held by these two criteria has destroyed or threatened to destroy natural and cultural resources of the utmost importance for the sustainability and quality of life on earth. The deep seabed, Antarctica, the moon and other celestial bodies, outer space, the global sphere, and biodiversity are some of the resources that, if they are not governed by trustees of the international community on behalf of present and future generations, will be damaged to such an extent that life on earth will become intolerable, even inside the deluxe ghettos that make up the global apartheid (Santos 1995: 365–373). To these resources we must also add the cultural heritage that UNESCO has been proposing as the common heritage of humankind. In this case, however, it is the heritage itself and not its degradation that, in my view, must constitute a destabilizing image: the image of the barbaric conditions in which cultural treasures have been produced. Therefore, cultural heritage can only be considered the common heritage of humankind in the sense of Walter Benjamin's assertion that "there is no document of civilization which is not at the same time a document of barbarism" (1968: 256). The destabilizing image that emerges out of the deterioration of the resources that sustain the quality of life on earth is the parable of the tragedy of the commons as formulated by Garrett Hardin (1968), even though the moral to be drawn from it differs from Hardin's.[22] Since the costs of the individual use of common goods are always inferior to the benefits, common resources, because they are exhaustible, are on the verge of a tragedy. The stronger the global ecological consciousness, the more destabilizing this image will be. It alone generates the energy of the common heritage of humankind.

The archetypal dimension of the common heritage of humankind is that, long before it was formulated, this idea already represented the dialectics of communication between the parts and the whole at a moment in which the abyssal thinking underlying Western modernity and its colonialist constitution was still a problem rather than a solution. I refer to the Iberian School of the sixteenth century and its awareness that to divide the world into "this side of the line" and "the other side of the line" would bring about barbaric destruction (more on this in Chapter 4). The distinction drawn by Francisco de Vitoria between *jus inter omnes gentes* and *totus orbis* and Francisco Suarez's distinction between *jus gentium inter gentes* and *bonnum commune humanitatis* are the archetypes of matricial equilibrium between the theories of separation and the theories of union. That this equilibrium has been upset in favor of the doctrines of separation endows the common-heritage-of-humankind doctrine with a utopian nature, indeed, a messianic nature, in

---

22. A fine analysis of this parable appears in Pureza (1998, 2005, 2009).

Benjamin's sense. One needs only to list its main attributes: nonappropriation; management by all peoples; international sharing of the benefits obtained from the exploitation of natural resources; peaceful use, including freedom of scientific research for the benefit of all peoples; and conservation for future generations (Santos 1995: 366). For this utopian character to develop, it is imperative that the common-heritage-of-humankind idea escape juridical discourse and the practices of international law, wherein it will always remain ensnared by the property and sovereignty principles, and become a new emancipatory juridical common sense that will encourage the action of counterhegemonic social movements and non-governmental organizations for transnational advocacy.

Destabilizing Subjectivities

Destabilizing images are not destabilizing by essence. They merely contain a destabilizing potential, which may be made concrete only to the extent that the images are captured by individual or collective subjectivities that understand correctly the signs they emit, feel outraged at the messages they carry, and turn their outrage into emancipatory energy. As I have already mentioned, the close relationship between knowledge and subjectivity has been amply recognized today in the great paradigmatic transitions of the Renaissance and Enlightenment (Cassirer 1960, 1963; Toulmin 1990). The Enlightenment is the transition that most concerns us here. The great influence exerted by John Locke's (1956) concept of action and human understanding was due to the fact that its elective affinity with the new constellation of meaning was so strong that what it said about human action was understood not as speculation but as discovery or revelation. Voltaire acknowledges this much when he writes admiringly of Locke, "After so many random reasoners had been thus forming what might have been called the romance of the soul, a sage appears who has modestly presented us with the history of it. Mr. Locke has developed human reason to man, just as a skillful anatomist explains the springs and structure of the human body" (1950: 177). The reason for Voltaire's enthusiasm is that Locke opened up a new perspective that posited that the investigation of the function of experience should precede any determination of its object and that the exact insight into the specific character of human understanding could not otherwise be attained but by tracing the whole course of its development from its first elements to its highest forms. According to Locke, the origin of the critical problem was genetic, the history of the human mind providing an adequate explanation of it.[23]

Writing at a crucial moment of the constitution of the paradigm of Western modernity, Locke asked questions and provided answers that are of little use for us today, now that we have probably reached the last phase of the paradigm he

---

23. See also Cassirer (1960: 93–133).

helped to consolidate. What can be of use to us, however, is the archaeology of both Locke's questions and his answers. Locke was able to ask radically for a kind of subjectivity able and willing to create a new scientific knowledge, whose infinite possibilities loomed on the horizon, a kind of subjectivity, indeed, willing also to recognize itself in its own creations. He saw the answer to his question in an unstable correspondence between two extremes: a knowledge that positioned itself on the brink of an exhilarating future could only be willed by a subjectivity that represented the culmination of a long-ascending evolution.

Today, we, like Locke, must raise the question of subjectivity in a radical, though radically different, way. Unlike Locke, we ask about a subjectivity that culminates with no evolution, a subjectivity whose self-reflexivity is focused on a past that never was and on the conditions that prevented it from ever being. A sociology of absences is thus as important as a sociology of presences in the social construction of the destabilizing subjectivity. That dual sociology, which still very much remains to be produced,[24] is at the core of the emancipatory will of the emergent subjectivity. Such will can be traced to Etienne Bonnor de Condillac's "uneasiness" (1984: 288), that kind of disquietude that he considered to be the point of departure not only of our desires and wishes but also of our thinking and judging, willing and acting. In a time of explosion of roots and options, as well as of the interchangeability of roots and options, this disquietude translates itself into a capacity both for unmasking and for meaning: on the one hand, the unmasking of the options of power, which for so long have been concealed by the dominant powers that define and limit options; on the other, the meaning of new possibilities opened up by the self-reflexivity thus enhanced. The issue is, then, to defamiliarize the canonic tradition (the sociology of absences) without stopping there, as if such defamiliarization were the only possible familiarity. In other words, the coupling of unmasking and meaning prevents the emergent subjectivity from falling into Nietzsche's extremes when he states, in *On the Genealogy of Morals*, that "only what has no history is definable" (1973: 453). The destabilizing project must engage in a radical critique of the politics of the possible without yielding to an impossible politics.

Central to the social sciences, knowledge engaged in this kind of project is not the distinction between structure and agency but rather the distinction between conformist action and what I propose to call *action-with*-clinamen. Conformist action is the routinized, reproductive, repetitive practice that reduces realism to what exists and just because it exists. For my notion of action-with-*clinamen*, I borrow from Epicurus and Lucretius the concept of *clinamen*, understood as the inexplicable "quiddam" that upsets the relations of cause and effect, that is to say, the swerving capacity attributed by Epicurus to Democritus's atoms. The *clinamen* is what makes the atoms cease to appear inert and rather to be seen as invested with a power of inclination, a power, that is, of spontaneous movement

---

24. On the sociology of absences, see Chapters 4 and 6.

(Epicurus 1926; Lucretius 1950).[25] Unlike what happens in revolutionary action, the creativity of action-with-*clinamen* is not based on a dramatic break but rather on a slight swerve or deviation whose cumulative effects render possible the complex and creative combinations among atoms, hence also among living beings and social groups.[26]

The *clinamen* does not refuse the past; on the contrary, it assumes and redeems the past by the way it swerves from it. Actually, the swerving is a liminal practice occurring in the borderline of a past that did exist and a past that was not allowed to exist. By virtue of such swerving, which in itself may be imperceptible, the past's capacity for interpellation enlarges to such an extent that it becomes the fulguration Benjamin talks about—an intense *Jetztzeit* that renders possible new emancipatory practices. The occurrence of action-with-*clinamen* is in itself inexplicable. The role of the social sciences in this regard will be merely to identify the conditions that maximize the probability of such an occurrence and, at the same time, define the horizon of possibilities within which the swerving will "operate."

A destabilizing subjectivity is a subjectivity endowed with a special capacity, energy, and will to act with *clinamen*. Bearing Bloom's use of the term in mind, we might say that a destabilizing subjectivity is a poetic subjectivity. The social construction of such subjectivity itself must be an exercise in liminality. It must entail experimenting with eccentric or marginal forms of sociability or subjectivity in modernity. Viewed as an open field of reinvention and experimentation, the baroque, as reconstructed in the previous chapter, is one such form. It may contribute to generate social and cultural fields capable of promoting the formation of subjectivities with a capacity for and will to *clinamen*.

---

25. The concept of *clinamen* was made current in literary theory by Harold Bloom. It is one of the revisionary ratios Bloom proposes in *The Anxiety of Influence* to account for poetic creativity as what he calls "poetic misprision" or "poetic misreading": "A poet swerves away from his precursor, by so reading his precursor's poem as to execute a *clinamen* in relation to it" (1973: 14).

26. As Lucretius says, the swerve is *per paucum nec plus quam minimum* (Epicurus 1926).

CHAPTER 3

Is There a Non-Occidentalist West?

I N THIS CHAPTER I argue that, despite the apparently unshakable hegemony of the arguments invoked by Eurocentric world history to demonstrate the uniqueness of the West and its superiority, there is room to think of a non-Occidentalist West. By that I mean a vast array of conceptions, theories, and arguments that, though produced in the West by recognized intellectual figures, were discarded, marginalized, or ignored because they did not fit the political objectives of capitalism and colonialism that act as a foundation for the construction of the uniqueness and superiority of Western modernity.

Three specific topics are dealt with: the concepts of antiquity, modern science, and the teleology of the future. Among many others that might be selected, I resort to three eccentric figures—Lucian of Samosata, Nicholas of Cusa, and Blaise Pascal—to exemplify some of the paths that might guide us in the construction of a noncapitalist, noncolonialist, intercultural dialogue. Such paths are here designated as learned ignorance, the ecology of knowledge, the wager on another possible world, and the artisanship of practices.

In order to show what I mean specifically by Occidentalism and whether a non-Occidentalist West is possible or not, I shall first discuss an author, Jack Goody, whose work has been dedicated to dismantling every one of the historical and sociological arguments invoked by the canonical history of Europe and the world to demonstrate the uniqueness of the West. My focus will be on his book *The Theft of History* (2006). Throughout this book, the author refers to the "west," meaning Europe, "often western Europe," a small region of the world that, for various reasons and mainly from the sixteenth century onward, managed to impose its conceptions of past and future, of time and space, on the rest of the world. It thus has made its values and institutions prevail, turning them into expressions of Western exceptionalism and thereby concealing similarities and continuities with values and institutions existing in other regions of the world. The hegemony of this position reached such proportions that it is surreptitiously present even in the authors who have given more credit to the achievements of other regions of the world. Goody mentions Joseph Needham, Norbert Elias, Fernand Braudel, and Edward Said, who, he argues, end up being Occidentalist in their struggle against Eurocentrism—"a trap," he adds, that "postcolonialism and postmodernism frequently fall into" (2006: 5). According to Goody, a true "global history" is only possible to the extent that both Eurocentrism and Eurocentric anti-Eurocentrism, both Occidental-ism and Orientalism, are superseded. Such a history is more accurate on the epistemological level and more progressive on the social, political, and cultural levels. Only this kind of history will allow the world to recognize itself in its infinite diversity, which includes as well the infinite diversity of similarities and continuities. This kind of history puts an end to all teleologies because these always presuppose selecting a specific past as the condition for the legitimiza-tion of a unique future.

Is such a history possible? Yes, if it is understood as being situated in the plurality of places and times from which it is written, hence as always having a partial nature. To what extent is the global history proposed by Goody partial? Goody thinks that the best way to fight Eurocentrism in a non-Eurocentric way is to show that all the things attributed to the West as being exceptional and unique—be it modern science or capitalism, individualism, or democracy—have parallels and antecedents in other world regions and cultures. The West's pre-ponderance, therefore, can be explained not by means of categorical differences but rather by means of processes of elaboration and intensification.

Goody's conception of history has the great merit of proposing a humble West, a West sharing with other world regions a much broader mosaic of human creativ-ity. Acknowledging that Western creativity is relative implies negating the power of the reasons invoked to impose it worldwide. A more plausible explanation lies in the reasons of power, the "guns and sails," with which the West knew how to arm itself. The partiality of this history consists of the fact that the humbleness of the West vis-à-vis the world is reached by concealing the processes, themselves not humble at all and indeed quite arrogant, by means of which some versions of the achievements of the West managed to impose themselves internally at the same time as they imposed themselves on the rest of the world. To be sure, Goody is aware of this, but by not giving it emphasis enough, he suggests that the West's geographical unity (problematical in itself) is transferred to the unity of its political, cultural, and institutional achievements. Thus, what is questioned is the exceptionalism of the West's achievements, not the historical processes that led to our understanding of them today. Continuity with the world conceals the internal, categorical discontinuities. In a word, a humble West may turn out to be an impoverished West.

Could this be an insidious form of Occidentalism? The very term *Occidental-ism* has generated some controversy in recent years. At least two very distinct conceptions can be identified: first, Occidentalism as a counterimage of Oriental-ism, the image that the "others," the victims of Western Orientalism, construct concerning the West;[1] second, Occidentalism as a double image of Orientalism, the image that the West has of itself when it subjects the "others" to Orientalism.[2] The first conception carries the reciprocity trap: the idea that the "others," as victims of Western stereotypes, have the same power—because they have the same legitimacy—to construct stereotypes regarding the West. The second conception and the critique of the hegemonic West it implies are now a legacy of critical theory and underlie Jack Goody's oeuvre. To pursue it further, two paths are conceivable. The first one, pursued by Goody in *The Theft of History*, consists of identifying the West's external relativity, that is to say, the continuity between the innovations attributed to the West and similar experiences in other world regions and cultures. The second consists of identifying the West's internal relativity, that is to say, the infinite diversity of Western experiences and the continuity or discontinuity among those that succeeded and ended up being identified as specific to the West and those that were abandoned, suppressed, or simply forgotten. Either of these paths is legitimate. However, since either can be pursued ad infinitum, the global history or sociology to which either leads will be always partial. In spite, or perhaps because, of this, it is worth pursuing both with equal perseverance.

In this chapter I focus on the second path, taking off from Goody's own arguments. Again, among the many thefts of history analyzed by Goody, I isolate three: the conceptions of antiquity, modern science, and the teleology of the future. I will try to show that these thefts against alien, non-Western property also took place among Western coproprietors and that from these inside thefts the West emerged greatly impoverished. We live in a time in which criticizing the West in the West comes close to self-flagellation. To my mind, this stance is necessary and healthy, given the damage brought about by the imperialism and neocolonialism upon which the hegemonic West feeds itself. I believe, nonetheless, that devolving some of the objects stolen inside the West itself is crucial to create a new pattern of interculturality, both globally and inside the West. There is little to be expected from the interculturality currently maintained by many in the West if it does not entail retrieving an originary experience of interculturality. In the beginning was interculturality, and from there we went on to culturality. Only an intercultural West will desire and understand the interculturality of the world and contribute to it actively. The same is probably true of other world cultures, past and present.

To my way of thinking, it is imperative to enlarge the historical experience of the West, namely, by giving voice to Western traditions and experiences that were forgotten or maginalized because they did not conform to the imperialist

---

1. See Buruma and Margalit (2004). For a critique, see Bilgrami (2006) and for a critique of Bilgrami, see Robbins (2007). For a very different version of this conception, Chinese Occidentalism, see Chen (1992).

2. See Carrier (1992); Coronil (1996); Venn (2001); and, most recently, Gregory (2006).

and orientalist objectives prevailing after the convergence of modernity and capitalism.[3] I convene these experiences and traditions not out of historical interest. The aim is to intervene in the present as if it had other pasts beyond the past that made it into what it is today. If it could have been different, it can be different. My concern is to show that many of the problems confronting the world today result from the waste of experience that the West imposed not only upon the world by force but also upon itself to sustain its own imposing upon the others.

As regards antiquity, Goody (2006: 26–67) argues that the idea of the uniqueness of classical antiquity—polis, democracy, freedom, economy, the rule of law, art, logos—is a Hellenocentric and teleological construction that, against the truth of the facts, aims to attribute the uniqueness of modern Europe to a beginning as unique as modern Europe itself. Such reasoning loses sight of the continuity between the achievements of classical Greece and the cultures with which it had close relations, from Persia to Egypt and from Africa to Asia, and neglects the latter's contribution to the cultural legacy appropriated by the West. In this chapter I resort to Lucian of Samosata (125–180 CE) to illustrate the existence of another classical antiquity, an antiquity that is centrifugal vis-à-vis Greece's canonical achievements and multicultural in its roots. I am interested in Lucian of Samosata because I believe he can assist us with one of the tasks I consider crucial to reinventing social emancipation: distancing ourselves from the theoretical traditions that led us to the dead end in which we find ourselves.

Regarding modern science, Goody engages in a dialogue with Joseph Needham in his monumental *Science and Civilization in China* (1954–2008). According to Needham, up until 1600, as far as science is concerned, China was as advanced as Europe, if not more so. Only after the Renaissance, a cultural process exclusive to Europe, was Europe able to gain advantage over China by converting science into exact knowledge, based on mathematized hypotheses about nature and systematic experimental verification. Goody (2006: 125–153) refutes this break or categorical differentiation based on the Renaissance and its alleged affinity with the capitalist ethos (the relation between exact knowledge and profit established by the bourgeoisie). According to him, there was no scientific revolution, and modern science is not qualitatively different from previous science; it is rather the intensification of a long-lasting scientific tradition. I am not engaging in this debate. Instead, I contest the fact that, although duly highlighting the antecedents of the Renaissance and the existence of other renaissances in other cultures and times, Goody nonetheless agrees with Needham—and indeed with the conventional history of European modernity—as regards the Renaissance's homogeneous characteristics and their relations with modern science. The truth is that in the Renaissance there were many different conceptions, some of them swerving substantially from the ones that came to ground the notion of exact knowledge underlying modern science. In order to

---

3. On this topic, see, among others, Santos (1995, 2004).

illustrate one such conception, I resort to Nicholas of Cusa (1401–1464), a great Renaissance philosopher, whose theories had no followers because they could never be used to support the arrogance with which the West engendered Orientalism and its double image, Occidentalism.

Finally, *The Theft of History* is a radical critique of the teleology prevailing in the canonical, Eurocentric tradition of European and world history. Teleology consists of projecting into the West's more or less remote past some unique characteristic or asset that explains the West's preponderance in the present world and the linear certainty of its future trajectory. Goody critiques teleology by questioning, one by one, every originary asset or characteristic lying supposedly at the origin of the categorical or qualitative difference of the West in relation to the rest of the world. In this regard as well, my aim is not to question Goody but rather to introduce another tradition of Western modernity, a tradition that has been forgotten or marginalized precisely because it rejects history's teleology and so cannot be put at the service of the West's religious and civilizing certainties. The tradition I mean is Blaise Pascal's wager.

Lucian of Samosata, Nicholas of Cusa, and Blaise Pascal are my points of departure to reflect on the theoretical and epistemological conditions to supersede Occidentalism and put an end to the theft of history.

Philosophy for Sale

Let us suppose that, because they stopped being useful to their followers, the philosophies and theories that have accompanied us for the past decades or, in some cases, centuries were offered for sale: determinism, free will, universalism, relativism, realism, constructivism, Marxism, liberalism, structuralism, functionalism, poststructuralism, deconstruction, pragmatism, postmodernism, postcolonialism, and so on and so forth. Let us likewise suppose that the followers of given theories had come to the conclusion that not only their own theories had become useless but so had all the others. They would therefore not be interested in buying any of them. Potential buyers, if any, would necessarily be outsiders vis-à-vis the world—let us call it the academic world—in which the different theories had developed. Before deciding to buy, they would naturally ask two questions: How useful is this or that theory for me? How much does it cost? To avoid being left unsold, the different theories or their creators would have to reply persuasively, so as to suggest to the calculating mind of the potential buyer a good relation between utility and price. To be sure, since a large number of theories would be offered for sale, the competition among them would be very high. The difficulty the theories would have in answering those questions would depend greatly on the fact that theories are used to imposing their usefulness, not to offering it and defining it in terms of truth, the truth, of course, being priceless. The outcome of the sale would depend not only on the buyers' purse but also on the value they ascribed to the uses of the theories; the latter would have no way of influencing either the purse, the value, or the decisions.

I am sure we all agree that if such a sale would in itself be a great scandal, the hierarchy of value-price it would establish among the theories would be an even greater one. But the scandal of scandals would be if lucky buyers, finding utility in theories that we consider rival (for instance, determinism and free will), were to buy them as one lot for the sake of complementary uses. Lest the scandal turns on me, let me add that, if such a sale were to take place, it would not be unheard of. Precisely such a sale was proposed around 165 CE by a centrifugal figure of classical antiquity, a marginal classic of Western culture, a man who was born a "barbarian," a "Syrian," in Samosata, by the river Euphrates. I mean Lucian of Samosata (1905: 190) and refer to his dialogue "The Sale of Creeds," in which Zeus, with the assistance of Hermes, offers for sale the various schools of Greek philosophy, some of them brought in by their own founders: Pythagoreanism, Diogenes, Heraclitus, and Democritus (one lot), Socrates, Chrysippus, Epicureanism, Stoicism, and Peripatetic Scepticism (a second). Hermes attracts the potential buyers, all of them merchants, by shouting loudly, "For sale. A varied assortment of live creeds. Tenets of every description. Cash on delivery; or credit allowed on suitable security!" (1905: 190). The "merchandise" gets displayed, and the merchants keep coming. The latter have the right to question every philosophy offered for sale, and they invariably begin by asking how useful each may be to the buyer, his family, or his group. The price is set by Zeus, who oftentimes simply accepts the offers made by the buying merchants. The sale is totally successful. Hermes orders the theories to stop offering resistance and follow their buyers and makes a final announcement: "Gentlemen, we hope to see you here tomorrow, when we shall be offering some lots suitable for plain men, artists and shopkeepers" (1905: 206).

In this as in other satirical works, Lucian of Samosata aims to create distance vis-à-vis established knowledge. He turns the theories into objects rather than subjects, creates a field of externality about them, and submits them to tests for which they were not designed. He does not allow them to argue among themselves, urging them rather to contend for the attention of strangers whose preferences they have no way of controlling. He subjects them to the chaos of the society in which they are produced and shows them that the truth to which they aspire—the truth described by Lucian as "this shadowy creature with the indefinite complexion . . . all naked and unadorned, shrinking from observation, and always slipping out of sight" (1905: 213)—lies not in corresponding to a given reality but rather in corresponding to a reality yet to be given, to utility in terms of social criteria and objectives in a broad sense.

This distance vis-à-vis the theoretical canon is inscribed in Lucian of Samosata's own origin and trajectory. Samosata, the city where he was born, now flooded by the Atatürk Dam in Turkey, had been part of the Commagene kingdom, in ancient Armenia, later absorbed by the Roman Empire as part of the Syrian province. This was a region of very intense commercial and cultural crossings, endowed with a lively *Mischkultur* in which Greek philosophy and literature coexisted with Christianism and Judaism, as well as with many other cultures of the Near and Middle East. Lucian, a Hellenized Syrian who called himself "barbarian," left his homeland to pursue his career as a rhetorician in the cultural centers of the Roman world.[4]

In my view, our time, as much as Samosata's, calls for a distance vis-à-vis the received theoretical tradition. In the introduction I have dealt in detail with the conditions that justify such a distance. In particular, the discrepancy between strong questions and weak answers is very apt for a comparison across such disparate times. As in Samosata's time, the problems of our time—the problems that call for strong questions—no longer concern the privileged knowledge of our time, that is, modern science, to the extent that it became institutionalized and professionalized. In its origin, science was fully aware that the most important problems of existence escaped it, such as, at the time, the problem of God's existence, the meaning of life, the model or models for a good society, and the relations between human beings and other creatures, which, not being human, shared with humans the dignity of likewise being creations of God. All these problems converged with another one and with one far more dilemmatic for science: the problem that science cannot account for the foundation of its scientificity, that is to say, of scientific truth as truth. From the nineteenth century onward, however, as a result of the increasing transformation of science into a productive force of capitalism, a double reduction of such a complex relation among ways of knowing occurred. On the one hand, the epistemological hegemony of science turned it into one single, accurate, and valid kind of knowledge. As a result, only the problems for which science could have an answer were deemed worthy of consideration. Existential problems were reduced to what could be said scientifically about them, which entailed a dramatic conceptual and analytical reconversion. Thus emerged what I call, after José Ortega y Gasset (1987: 39), *orthopedic thinking*: the constraint and impoverishment caused by reducing such problems to analytical and conceptual markers that are foreign to them. With the increasing institutionalization and professionalization of science—concomitant with the evolution pointed out by Michel Foucault from the "universal intellectual" to the "specific intellectual"—science began to give answers to problems raised by itself alone. The immensity of the underlying existential problems disappeared, due to another reduction meanwhile occuring. As is usually the case regarding any hegemony, the hegemony of science spread beyond science, subjecting philosophy, theology, and the humanities in general to a process of scientificization with as many multiple forms as the multiple faces of positivism. As orthopedic

---

4. Lucian of Samosata is still today an eccentric figure of classical antiquity. Some classicists consider him a mere "journalist" or "artist." For an opposing view, see, for example, Jones (1986); Zappala (1990). A polemical treatment of Lucian as a satirist can be read in Sloterdijk (1987).

thinking stretched beyond science and the disciplines became institutionalized and professionalized, the problems they dealt with were only the problems they themselves raised. The result was academic answers for academic problems that were increasingly more distant and reductive vis-à-vis the existential problems they were meant to address.

This vast process of epistemological monopolization did not occur without contradictions. These can be seen precisely in the discrepancy between strong questions and weak answers that characterizes our time. To be sure, as I mention in the introduction, the discrepancy between strong questions and weak answers is a general feature of our time; indeed, it constitutes its epochal spirit, but its impacts on the global North and the global South are very different. Weak answers have some credibility in the global North because that is where orthopedic thinking developed most and also because, once translated into politics, weak answers secure the continuation of the global North's neocolonial domination of the global South, allowing the citizens of the global North to benefit from such domination without being aware of it. In the global South, weak answers translate themselves into ideological impositions and all kinds of violence in the daily lives of citizens, excluding the elites, the small world of the imperial South that is the "representation" of the global North in the global South. The feeling that this difference in impacts, even if real and abyssal, conceals the tragedy of a common condition grows deeper and deeper: the saturation of the *junk knowledge* incessantly produced by an orthopedic thinking that has long stopped thinking of ordinary women and men. This condition expresses itself in the ungraspable lack of credible and prudent knowledge capable of securing for us all—women, men, and nature—a decent life.[5] This lack does not allow us to identify, let alone define, the true dimension of the problems afflicting the epoch. The latter appear as a set of contradictory feelings: exhaustion that does not conceal lack, unease that does not conceal injustice, and anger that does not exclude hope. Exhaustion results from an incessant rhetoric of victory where citizens endowed with the simple lights of life see only defeat, solutions where they see problems, expert truths where they see interests, and consensus where they see resignation. Unease derives from the increasingly more apparent absence of reasonableness from the rationality proclaimed by orthopedic thinking, an injustice-producing machine that sells itself as a machine of happiness. Anger emerges at social regulation disguised as social emancipation, individual autonomy used to justify neoslavery servitude, and the reiterated proclamation of the impossibility of a better world to silence the idea, very genuine if diffuse, that humanity and nature both are entitled to something much better than the current status quo. The masters of orthopedic thinking take advantage of exhaustion to turn it into total fulfilment: the end of history (Fukuyama 1992). As to unease and anger, they are "treated"

---

5. The problematics of constructing a prudent knowledge for a decent life are analyzed in Santos (2007b).

with medical prostheses, the anesthesia of consumption, and the vertigo of the entertainment industry. None of these mechanisms, however, seems to function in such a way as to successfully disguise, by functioning efficaciously, the abyssal dysfunction from which its necessity and efficacy stem.

This epochal spirit suggests the same distancing vis-à-vis the theories and disciplines as the one displayed in Lucian of Samosata. The theories and disciplines are too much concerned with themselves to be able to answer the questions our time poses to them. Distancing implies the predominance of a negative epistemology and a concomitant, equally negative ethics and politics. The reasons to reject what exists ethically, politically, and epistemologically are far more convincing than those invoked to define alternatives. Even if the imbalance between rejection and finding alternatives is probably common to all ages, it seems to be disproportionately large in our time. To fully assume our time means to acknowledge this disproportion and act from there. In other words, it means to radicalize rejection and look for alternatives while recognizing their radical uncertainty.

On the epistemological level, the only one I deal with here, rejection implies a certain kind of epistemological direct action.[6] It consists of taking over the theories and disciplines regardless of their owners (schools, trends of thought, institutions) with a threefold objective: first, to show that the theories and disciplines lose their composure and serenity when they are interpellated by questions, no matter how simple, that they did not ask themselves; second, to identify complementarities and complicities where the theories and disciplines see rivalries and contradictions; and third, to show that the efficaciousness of theories and disciplines lies as much in what they show as in what they conceal, as much in the reality they produce as existent as in the reality they produce as nonexistent.

To accomplish the first objective it is useful to conceive of experiments in which the theories and disciplines are put in the same situation as the apes of the Egyptian king in the story told by Lucian of Samosata in another of his dialogues, titled "The Fisher":

> There is a story of an Egyptian king who taught some apes the sword-dance; the imitative creatures very soon picked it up, and used to perform in purple robes and masks; for some time the show was a great success, till at last an ingenious spectator brought some nuts with him and threw them down. The apes forgot their dancing at the sight, dropped their humanity, resumed their apehood and, smashing masks and tearing dresses, had a free fight for the provender. Alas for the corps de ballet and the gravity of the audience. (1905: 222)

My hypothesis is that the theories and disciplines will have nontheoretical and nondisciplinary responses to questions they themselves have not foreseen. When questioned, their orthopedic manipulation of reality will be of no use to

---

6. The following chapters are dedicated to carrying out the epistemological tasks ahead.

them. The answer will not be orthopedic. To accomplish the two remaining objectives, let us resort to Lucian of Samosata and metaphorically offer for sale, just like Zeus and Hermes, the different theories and disciplines. The latter, having consolidated themselves by dictating various forms of utility to society, will not readily accept their utility becoming the object of assessment. Likewise, the theories and disciplines that, on behalf of capitalism, have theorized the universality of competition as opposed to cooperation, the economy of egoism as opposed to the economy of altruism, and buying/selling as opposed to the gift will not accept being themselves offered for sale.

Assuming that the condition of our time requires not only rejecting orthopedic thinking but also looking for alternatives from the point of view of their radical uncertainty, it is crucial to characterize the roots of such radical uncertainty, what I have called the *paradox of finitude and infinitude.* The uncertainty concerns the inexhaustible and ungraspable diversity of social experiences in the world. The liberation movements against colonialism, the new social movements—feminism, ecology, the indigenous and Afro-descendent movements, peasant movements, decolonial movements, liberation theology, urban movements, LGBT movements—and the newest movements or collective presences of the *indignados* and the Occupy movement, besides enlarging the scope of the social struggles, brought along new conceptions of life and human dignity, new symbolic universes, new cosmogonies, gnoseologies, and even ontologies. Paradoxically, this process, pointing as it does to the infinitude of human experience, occurred alongside another seemingly contradictory one that has gradually revealed the finitude of the planet Earth, the unity between the humanity and the nature inhabiting it (the Gaia hypothesis), and the limits of life sustainability on earth. What we call globalization has contributed, in a contradictory way, to deepen a twofold experience of infinitude and finitude.

How is it that in a finite world the diversity of human experience is potentially infinite? This paradox places us, in turn, face-to-face with an epistemological lack: the knowledge we lack to capture the inexhaustible diversity of the world. The uncertainty caused by this lack is even greater if we keep in mind that the diversity of world experience includes the diversity of knowledge existing in the world. Which kinds of knowledge could reveal the diversity of world experience? How to go about identifying, evaluating, and hierarchizing the many and diverse kinds of knowledge constituting the experience of the world? How to articulate and compare the kinds of knowledge we do know with the kinds of knowledge we do not know?

This paradoxical uncertainty poses new epistemological and political challenges. It invites open-ended formulations of an alternative society, the strength of which has more to do with rejecting the current state of affairs than with defining alternatives. They consist of affirming the possibility of a better future and another possible world without knowing if the latter is possible and what it will be like. It is, therefore, a very different utopia from modern utopias.

In order to face these challenges, I resort to two forgotten traditions of Western modernity: Nicholas of Cusa's learned ignorance and Pascal's wager. Both
conceptions were formulated by authors who lived the uncertainties of their time
very intensely. Their doubts were not methodical, as in Descartes, but rather
epistemological or even ontological. Both were ignored precisely because they
did not go well with the certainties that Western modernity aimed to guarantee.
That is to say, they are at the antipodes of the orthopedic thinking that prevailed
in the following centuries. They were ignored, but by the same token, they were
not colonized either. They are therefore more transparent as regards both their
potential and their limits. Since they did not take part in the modern adventure,
they stayed in the West but remained marginal to the West. They would have
been useless, if not dangerous, for an adventure that was as much epistemological as political: I mean the imperial project of global colonialism and capitalism
that created the abyssal divide between what today we designate as global North
and global South.[7] The traditions created by Nicholas of Cusa and Pascal are the
South of the North, as it were, and are thus better prepared than any other to
learn from the global South and collaborate with it toward building epistemologies capable of offering credible alternatives to orthopedic thinking.

Learned Ignorance

Nicholas of Cusa, philosopher and theologian, was born in Germany in 1401
and died in Umbria in 1467; he wrote the work titled *De docta ignorantia* (1985)
between 1438 and 1440. Confronted with the infinitude of God (whom he called
the "Absolute Maximum"), he engages in a reflection on the idea of knowledge
in not knowing. The important thing is not to know, he argues, but to know
that you do not know. "Indeed," says Nicholas of Cusa, "no greater knowledge
can endow any man, even the most studious, than to discover himself supremely
learned in his ignorance, which is proper to him, and he will be the more learned,
the more ignorant he knows himself to be" (1985: 6). What is new about Nicholas of Cusa is that he uses the excuse of God's infinitude to propose a general
epistemological procedure that is valid for the knowledge of finite things—the
knowledge of the world. Since it is finite, our thought cannot think the infinite—
there is no ratio between the finite and the infinite—but it is limited even in its
thinking of finitude, in its thinking of the world. All we know is subject to this
limitation; thus to know is, above all, to know the limitation, hence the notion
of knowledge in not knowing.

The designation "learned ignorance" may sound contradictory, for the learned
person is, by definition, not ignorant. The contradiction is, however, only

_____

7. This abyssal division itself became an epistemological condition. On abyssal thinking,
see Chapter 4.

apparent, since learnedly not-knowing requires a laborious process of knowing the limitations of what we know. In Nicholas of Cusa there are two kinds of ignorance: ignorant ignorance, which is not even aware that it does not know, and learned ignorance, which knows it does not know what it does not know. We may be tempted to think that Nicholas of Cusa simply parrots Socrates, but this is really not the case.[8] Socrates is not aware of the idea of infinitude, which only appears in Western thought through Christian-based Neoplatonism.[9] This idea, undergoing multiple metamorphoses (progress, emancipation), is to play a crucial role in the construction of the paradigm of Western modernity. But its fate inside this paradigm is completely different from that in Nicholas of Cusa's thought. The dominant versions of the paradigm of modernity turned the infinite into an obstacle to overcome: the infinite is the infinite zeal to overcome it, control it, tame it, and reduce it to finite proportions. Thus, infinitude, which from the outset ought to arouse humility, becomes the ultimate foundation of the triumphalism underlying the hegemonic rationality of orthopedic thinking. On the contrary, in Nicholas of Cusa infinitude is accepted as such, as consciousness of a radical ignorance. The aim is not to control or master it but to acknowledge it in a twofold way: through our total ignorance of it and through the limitations it imposes on the accuracy of the knowledge we have of finite things. Before the infinite, no arrogance, only humility, is possible. Humility does not mean negativity or skepticism. Reflective acknowledgment of the limits of knowledge implies an unsuspected positivity. Indeed, to acknowledge the limits is somehow to be already beyond them (André 1997: 94). The fact that it is not possible to reach the truth with accuracy does not release us from searching for it. Quite the opposite, what lies beyond limits (the truth) rules what is possible and demandable within the limits (veracity, as the search for the truth).

It comes as no surprise that, almost six centuries later, the dialectics of finitude/infinitude characterizing the present time are very different from Nicholas of Cusa's. The infinitude we face is not transcendental, resulting, rather, from the inexhaustible diversity of human experience and the limits to knowing it. In our time, learned ignorance will entail a laborious work of reflection and interpretation of those limits, of the possibilities they open and the exigencies they create for us. Moreover, the diversity of human experience includes the diversity of ways of knowing human experience. Our infinitude has thus a contradictory epistemological dimension: an infinite plurality of finite ways of knowing human experience in the world. The finitude of each way of knowing is thus twofold: it is made up of the limits of what it knows about human experience in the world and the limits (albeit much larger) of what it knows about the world's other ways

8. Both concur, however, that what you know is far less important than what you do not know, hence the need to give ignorance epistemological priority. See also C. L. Miller (2003: 16).

9. See André (1997: 94).

of knowing, hence about the knowledge of the world supplied by other ways of knowing. The knowledge that does not know is the knowledge that fails to know the other ways of knowing that share with it the infinite task of accounting for the experiences of the world. Orthopedic thinking is no adequate guide for us in this uncertainty, because it grounds a kind of knowledge (modern science) that does not know well enough the limits of what it allows one to know of the experience of the world and knows even less well the other kinds of knowledge that share with it the epistemological diversity of the world. Actually, besides not knowing the other kinds of knowledge, orthopedic thinking refuses to acknowledge their very existence. Among the available experiences of the world produced as nonexisting, the kinds of knowledge that do not fit orthopedic thinking become particularly important. Thus, one of the main dimensions of the sociology of absences is the sociology of absent ways of knowing, that is to say, the act of identifying the ways of knowing that hegemonic epistemology reduces to nonexistence.[10]

To be a learned ignorant in our time is to know that the epistemological diversity of the world is potentially infinite and that each way of knowing grasps it only in a very limited manner. In this respect too our condition is very different from Nicholas of Cusa's. Whereas the not-knowing knowledge he postulates is singular and hence entails one learned ignorance alone, the learned ignorance appropriate to our time is infinitely plural, as plural as the possibility of different ways of knowing. At any rate, just as in the case of Nicholas of Cusa's learned ignorance, the impossibility of grasping the infinite epistemological diversity of the world does not release us from trying to know it; on the contrary, it demands that we do. This demand, or exigency, I call the *ecology of knowledges*. In other words, if the truth exists only in the search for truth, knowledge exists only as an ecology of knowledges. Once we are aware of the differences that separate us from Nicholas of Cusa, it is easier to learn his lesson. I dedicate Chapters 6 and 7 to developing the concept of the ecology of knowledges.

The Wager

To face the uncertainty of our time I propose still another philosophical suggestion of Western modernity now totally forgotten: Pascal's wager. Sharing the same forgetfulness and marginalization as Nicholas of Cusa's learned ignorance, Pascal's wager can also serve as a bridge to other, non-Western philosophies and to other practices of social interpretation and transformation than those eventually sanctioned by orthopedic thinking. Actually, there is a basic affinity between learned ignorance and Pascal's wager. They both assume the uncertainty and precariousness of knowledge as a condition, which, being a constraint and

---

10. On the sociology of absences, see Chapter 6.

a weakness, is also a strength and an opportunity. They both struggle with the "disproportion" between the finite and the infinite and try to push to the maximum limit the potentialities of what it is possible to think and make within the limits of the finite.

Pascal starts from a radical uncertainty: the existence of God cannot be demonstrated rationally. Pascal says, "If there is a God, he is infinitely beyond our comprehension, since, being indivisible, and without limits, he bears no relation to us. We are therefore incapable of knowing either what he is or whether he is" (1966: 150). This leads him to ask how to formulate the reasons that might persuade a nonbeliever to change his mind and start believing in God. The answer is the wager. Although we cannot determine rationally that God exists, we can at least find a rational way to determine that to wager on his existence is more advantageous than to believe in his nonexistence. The wager involves a certain risk of winning or losing, as well as the possibility of an infinite gain. To wager on God's existence compels us to be honest and virtuous. And, of course, it also compels us to renounce noxious pleasures and worldly glories. If God does not exist, we will have lost the wager but gained in turn a virtuous life, full of good deeds. By the same token, if he does exist, our gain will be infinite: eternal salvation. Indeed, we lose nothing by wagering, and the gain can be infinite: "In the end you will realize that you have wagered on something certain and infinite for which you have paid nothing" (1966: 153).

The wager is rational because, in order to wager on the existence of God, you don't have to have faith. Its rationality is, however, very limited, for it tells us nothing about the real existence of God, let alone about God's nature. Since belief in the existence and nature of God is always an act of faith, Pascal has to find some kind of mediation between faith and rationality. He finds it in custom. Says Pascal, "Custom is our nature. Anyone who grows accustomed to faith believes it" (1966: 153). That is to say, by wagering repeatedly on the existence of God, the wagerer will end up believing in it.

As in the case of Nicholas of Cusa, the concern derived from the uncertainty of our time is very different from that of Pascal's. What is at stake now is not eternal salvation, the world beyond, but rather an earthly world better than the present one. Since there is no necessity or determinism in history, there is no rational way of knowing for sure if another world is possible, let alone how life would be there. Our infinite is the infinite uncertainty regarding the possibility of another and better world. As such, the question confronting us may be formulated in the following way: What reasons could lead us to fight for such a possibility if the risks are certain and the gains so uncertain? The answer is the wager, the only alternative to both the theses of the end of history and the theses of vulgar determinism. The wager is the metaphor for the precarious yet minimally credible construction of the possibility of a better world, that is to say, the possibility of social emancipation, without which the rejection of or nonconformity before injustice in our world makes no sense. The wager is the metaphor for social transformation in a world in which negative reasons and visions (what is rejected) are far more convincing than positive ones (identifying what we want and how to get there).

The truth is that the wager of our time on the possibility of a better world is very different and far more complex than Pascal's wager. The conditions of the wager are different, as is the ratio between the chances of winning and losing. What we have in common with Pascal are the limits of rationality, the precariousness of calculations, and the awareness of risks. Who is the wagerer in our time? While for Pascal the wagerer is the rational individual, in our time the wagerer is the excluded, discriminated against, in a word, oppressed class or social group and its allies. Since the possibility of a better world occurs in this world, only those with reasons to reject the status quo of the present world will wager on this possibility. The oppressors tend to experience the world in which they live as the best possible world. The same is true for all those who, not being directly oppressors, benefit from oppressive practices. As far as they are concerned, it is rational to wager on the impossibility of a better world.

The conditions of the wager in our time also differ largely from those of Pascal's wager. While with Pascal God's existence or nonexistence does not depend on the wagerer, in our time the possibility or impossibility of a better world depends on the wager and the actions resulting therefrom. Paradoxically, however, the risks the wagerer runs are higher. Indeed, the actions resulting from the wager will occur in a world of conflicting classes and groups, of oppressors and oppressed, and so there will be resistance and retaliation. The risks (the possibilities of loss) are thus twofold: risks deriving from the struggle against oppression and risks deriving from the fact that another and better world is, after all, not possible. Hence, the demonstration that Pascal offered his wagerer is not convincing: "Whenever there is infinity and where there are not infinite chances of losing against that of winning there is no room for hesitation, you must give everything" (1966: 151).

In our time there are therefore many reasons to hesitate and not to risk everything. They are the other side of the prevalence of reasons for rejecting the current state of affairs over reasons for specific alternatives to it. This has several consequences for the project of the wager on social emancipation. The first concerns the wager's pedagogy. Unlike Pascal's wager, the reasons for the wager on social emancipation are not transparent. To become convincing, they must be the object of argumentation and persuasion rather than the wager's demonstrative rationality, the wager's argumentative reasonableness. Since reasonableness is not the monopoly of any single type of knowledge, the wager's pedagogy must take place in conformity with the ecology of knowledges through a new type of popular education adequate to the needs of intermovement politics.[11] The second

---

11. Such a project of popular education underlies the proposal for the creation of the popular university of social movements that I have been defending (Santos 2006b: 148–159). See also "Highlights," Popular University of Social Movements, www.universidadepopular.org/site/pages/en/highlights.php?lang=EN.

consequence of the wager's condition of our time concerns the kinds of action that derive from the wager. The radical uncertainty about a better future and the risks involved in fighting for it result in privileging actions focused on the everyday and amount to improvements here and now in the lives of the oppressed and excluded. In other words, the wager privileges *actio in proximis*. Because of its success, this kind of action strengthens the wager's will and satisfies the sense of urgency for changing the world, that is to say, the need to act now lest later be too late. The wager does not fit *actio in distans*, for this would be an infinite risk before an infinite uncertainty. This does not mean that *actio in distans* is not there. It is, but not on its own terms. The changes in the everyday only ratify the wager to the extent that they too signal the possibility of social emancipation. In order to do so, they must be radicalized. Radicalization consists of searching for the subversive and creative aspects of the everyday, which may occur in the most basic struggle for survival. The changes in the everyday have thus a double valence: concrete improvement in the everyday and the signals they give of far larger possibilities. Through these signals, *actio in distans* becomes present in *actio in proximis*. In other words, *actio in distans* only exists as a dimension of *actio in proximis*, that is, as the will and reason of radicalization. Through the wager, it is possible to bring the everyday and utopia together, without their dissolving into one another. Utopia is what is missing in the everyday to exempt us from thinking about utopia. Ortega y Gasset teaches us that the human being is the human being and her circumstance. I think we must go beyond him and say that the human being is also what is missing in her circumstance for her to be fully human.

Conclusion

To have shown the possibility of conceiving a non-Occidentalist West is one of Jack Goody's major contributions for our time. In this chapter, I have tried to enhance such a possibility. Obviously, there is a wide gap between conceiving of a non-Occidentalist West and transforming such a conception into a political reality. Actually, I am convinced that it will not be possible to bridge that gap while living in a world ruled by global capitalism. The possibility of a non-Occidentalist West is closely linked to the possibility of a noncapitalist future. Both possibilities aim for the same result, even though they use very different tools and struggles. The conception of a non-Occidentalist West translates itself into recognizing uncertainties and perplexities and turning them into the opportunity for emancipatory, political creativity. Until we confront the uncertainties and perplexities of our time, we are condemned to neo-isms and post-isms, that is to say, interpretations of the present that only have a past. Inspired by Lucian of Samosata, the distancing I proposed vis-à-vis the theories and disciplines constructed by orthopedic thinking is based on the fact that they have contributed

to the discrepancy between strong questions and weak answers that characterizes our time. Such a discrepancy translates itself into the uncertainty deriving
from the incapacity to grasp the inexhaustible diversity of human experience.
This incapacity also implies that aspiring to a better world cannot find support
in a theory of history that indicates that a better world is indeed necessary or
at least possible. To face this uncertainty, I have proposed two epistemological
suggestions based on two particularly rich traditions of Western modernity, both
marginalized and forgotten by the orthopedic thinking that has dominated for
the past two centuries: learned ignorance and the ecology of knowledges deriving therefrom, and the wager. They reveal that erudite knowledge has a naive
relationship with the knowledge it considers naive. They denounce the precariousness of knowledge (knowledge that does not know) and of acting (wagering
on the basis of limited calculations).

These proposals do not aim to eliminate the uncertainties of our time. Rather,
they aim to assume them completely and use them productively, turning from
constraint to opportunity. Learned ignorance, the ecology of knowledge, and
the wager represent a much broader rationality (because far more aware of their
limits) than the rationality that ended up being dominant. Because they were
marginalized and forgotten, they kept an openness vis-à-vis the non-Western
traditions and problematics that Western modernity lost by falling prey to orthopedic thinking. Because they were marginalized and forgotten, these traditions
had a fate similar to that of many non-Western ways of knowing, and so they are
today better prepared to learn from them and, together with them, to contribute
toward the ecologies of knowledge and interculturality.

Learned ignorance, the ecology of knowledges it leads to, and the wager do
not bring about a kind of social emancipation, let alone a typology of social
emancipations. What comes forth is simply reasonableness and the will to fight
for a better world and a more just society, a set of ways of knowing and precarious
calculations, animated by ethical exigencies and vital necessities. The struggle
for survival and liberation and against hunger and violence is the degree zero of
social emancipation; in some situations, it is also its maximum degree. Social
emancipation is somewhat like the *arte perfectoria* of Nicholas of Cusa's Idiot,
who makes wooden spoons without limiting himself to imitating nature (there is
no spoon in nature) but also without attaining the idea of spoonhood accurately
(the spoon's essence belongs to "divine art"). Social emancipation is thus every
action aiming at denaturalizing oppression (showing that, besides being unjust,
oppression is neither necessary nor irreversible) and conceiving of it in such a
manner that it can be fought with the resources at hand. Learned ignorance, the
ecology of knowledges, and the wager are the ways of thinking present in this
action. Indeed, we only have proof of their existence in the context of this action.

PART TWO

Toward Epistemologies of the South: Against the Waste of Experience

CHAPTER 4

Beyond Abyssal Thinking

From Global Lines to Ecologies of Knowledges

M ODERN WESTERN THINKING is an abyssal thinking.[1] It consists of a system of visible and invisible distinctions, the invisible ones being the foundation of the visible ones. The invisible distinctions are established through radical lines that divide social reality into two realms, the realm of "this side of the line" and the realm of "the other side of the line." The division is such that "the other side of the line" vanishes as reality, becomes nonexistent, and is indeed produced as nonexistent. Nonexistent means not existing in any relevant or comprehensible way of being. Whatever is produced as nonexistent is radically excluded because it lies beyond the realm of what the accepted conception of inclusion considers to be its other. What most fundamentally characterizes abyssal thinking is thus the impossibility of the copresence of the two sides of the line. To the extent that it prevails, this side of the line only prevails by exhausting the field of relevant reality. Beyond it, there is only nonexistence, invisibility, nondialectical absence.

In my previous work (Santos 1995), I have characterized Western modernity as a sociopolitical paradigm founded on the tension between social regulation and social emancipation. This is the visible distinction that founds all modern conflicts, in terms of both substantive issues and procedures. But underneath this distinction there is another one, an invisible one, upon which the former is founded. Such an invisible distinction is that between metropolitan societies and

---

1. I do not claim that modern Western thinking is the only historical form of abyssal thinking. On the contrary, it is highly probable that there are, or have been, forms of abyssal thinking outside the West. This chapter does not claim to characterize the latter. It merely maintains that, whether abyssal or not, non-Western forms of thinking have been treated in an abyssal way by modern Western thinking. This is to say that I do not engage here with either premodern Western thinking or the marginal or subordinate versions of modern Western thinking that have opposed the hegemonic version. I have dealt with some such versions in Chapter 3. Here I am only concerned with the hegemonic version of Western modernity.

colonial territories. Indeed, the regulation/emancipation dichotomy only applied to metropolitan societies. It would be unthinkable to apply it to colonial territories. The regulation/emancipation dichotomy had no conceivable place in such territories. There, another dichotomy would apply, the appropriation/violence dichotomy, which in turn would be inconceivable if applied on this side of the line. Because the colonial territories were unthinkable as sites for the unfolding of the paradigm of regulation/emancipation, the fact that the latter did not apply to them did not compromise the paradigm's universality.

Modern abyssal thinking excels in making distinctions and radicalizing them. However, no matter how radical such distinctions are and how dramatic the consequences of being on the either side of such distinctions may be, they have in common the fact that they belong to this side of the line and combine to make invisible the abyssal line upon which they are grounded. The intensely visible distinctions structuring social reality on this side of the line are grounded on the invisibility of the distinction between this side of the line and the other side of the line.

Modern knowledge and modern law represent the most accomplished manifestations of abyssal thinking. They account for the two major global lines of modern times, which, though being different and operating differently, are mutually interdependent. Each creates a subsystem of visible and invisible distinctions in such a way that the invisible ones become the foundation of the visible ones. In the field of knowledge, abyssal thinking consists in granting to modern science the monopoly of the universal distinction between true and false, to the detriment of two alternative bodies of knowledge: philosophy and theology. The exclusionary character of this monopoly is at the core of the modern epistemological disputes between scientific and nonscientific forms of truth. Since the universal validity of a scientific truth is admittedly always very relative, given the fact that it can only be ascertained in relation to certain kinds of objects under certain circumstances and established by certain methods, how does it relate to other possible truths that may claim an even higher status but cannot be established according to scientific methods, such as reason as philosophical truth or faith as religious truth?[2] These tensions between science, philosophy, and theology have thus become highly visible, but, as I contend, they all take place on this side of the line. Their visibility is premised upon the invisibility of forms of knowledge that cannot be fitted into any of these ways of knowing. I mean popular, lay, plebeian, peasant, or indigenous knowledges on the other side of the line. They vanish as relevant or commensurable knowledges because they are beyond truth and falsehood. It is unimaginable to apply to them not only the scientific true/false distinction but also the scientifically unascertainable truths of philosophy and theology that constitute

---

2. Although in very distinct ways, Pascal, Kierkegaard, and Nietzsche were the philosophers who most profoundly analyzed, and lived, the antinomies contained in this question, more recently, mention must be made of Karl Jaspers (1952, 1986, 1995) and Stephen Toulmin (2001).

all the acceptable knowledge on this side of the line. On the other side of the line, there is no real knowledge; there are beliefs, opinions, intuitions, and subjective understandings, which, at the most, may become objects or raw materials for scientific inquiry. Thus, the visible line that separates science from its modern others is grounded on the abyssal invisible line that separates science, philosophy, and theology, on one side, from, on the other, knowledges rendered incommensurable and incomprehensible for meeting neither the scientific methods of truth nor their acknowledged contesters in the realm of philosophy and theology.

In the field of modern law, this side of the line is determined by what counts as legal or illegal according to the official state or international law. The legal and the illegal are the only two relevant forms of existing before the law; for that reason, the distinction between the two is a universal distinction. This central dichotomy leaves out a whole social territory where the dichotomy would be unthinkable as an organizing principle, that is, the territory of the lawless, the a-legal, the nonlegal, and even the legal or illegal according to nonofficially recognized law.[3] Thus, the invisible abyssal line that separates the realm of law from the realm of nonlaw grounds the visible dichotomy between the legal and the illegal that organizes, on this side of the line, the realm of law.

In each of the two great domains—science and law—the divisions carried out by the global lines are abyssal to the extent that they effectively eliminate whatever realities are on the other side of the line. This radical denial of copresence grounds the affirmation of the radical difference that, on this side of the line, separates true and false, legal and illegal. The other side of the line comprises a vast set of discarded experiences, made invisible both as agencies and as agents, with no fixed territorial location. Actually, as I suggest above, originally there was a territorial location, and historically it coincided with a specific social territory: the colonial zone.[4] Whatever could not be thought of as either true or false, legal or illegal, was most distinctly occurring in the colonial zone. In this respect, modern law seems to have some historical precedence over science in the creation of abyssal thinking. Indeed, contrary to conventional legal wisdom, it was the global legal line separating the Old World from the New World that made possible the emergence of modern law and, in particular, of modern international law in the Old World, on this side of the line.[5] The first modern

---

3. In Santos (2002b), I analyze in great detail the nature of modern law and the topic of legal pluralism (the coexistence of more than one legal system in the same geopolitical space).

4. In this chapter, I take for granted the intimate link between capitalism and colonialism. See, among others, Williams (1994 [1944]); Arendt (1951); Fanon (1967a); Horkheimer and Adorno (1972); Wallerstein (1974); Dussel (1992); Mignolo (1995); Quijano (2000); Grosfoguel (2005); Maldonado-Torres (2007).

5. Imperialism is thus constitutive of the modern state. Unlike what the conventional theories of international law affirm, the latter is not a product of the preexisting modern state. The modern state and international law, national constitutionalism, and global constitutionalism are the products of the same historical imperial process. See Koskenniemi (2002); Anghie (2005); Tully (2007).

global line was probably the Treaty of Tordesillas between Portugal and Spain (1494),[6] but the truly abyssal lines emerge in the mid-sixteenth century with the amity lines.[7] The abyssal character of the lines manifests itself in the elaborate cartographic work invested in their definition, in the extreme precision demanded from cartographers, globe makers, and pilots, and in vigilant policing and the harsh punishment of violations. In its modern constitution, the colonial represents not the legal or illegal but rather the lawless. The maxim then becoming popular—"Beyond the equator there are no sins"—is echoed in the famous passage of Pascal's *Pensées* written in the mid-seventeenth century: "Three degrees of latitude upset the whole jurisprudence and one meridian determines what is true.... It is a funny sort of justice whose limits are marked by a river; true on this side of the Pyrenees, false on the other" (1966: 46).

From the mid-sixteenth century onward, the legal and the political debate among the European states concerning the New World focuses on the global legal line, that is, on the determination of the colonial, not on the internal ordering of the colonial. On the contrary, the colonial is the state of nature where civil society's institutions have no place. Thomas Hobbes explicitly refers to the "savage

---

6. The definition of abyssal lines occurs gradually. According to Carl Schmitt (2003: 91), the cartographic lines of the fifteenth century (the *rayas*, Tordesillas) still presupposed a global spiritual order in force on both sides of the division—the medieval *res publica christiana*, symbolized by the pope. This explains the difficulties confronting Francisco de Vitoria, the great Spanish theologian and jurist of the sixteenth century, in justifying land occupation in the Americas. Vitoria asks if the discovery is sufficient title for juridical possession of the land. His response is very complex, not just because it is formulated in late Aristotelian style but mainly because Vitoria does not see any convincing response that is not premised upon the superior power of the Europeans. This fact, however, does not confer any moral or statutory right over the occupied land. According to Vitoria, not even the superior civilization of the Europeans suffices as the fundamental basis of a moral right. For Vitoria, the conquest could only be sufficient ground for a reversible right to land, a *jura contraria*, as he says. That is, the question of the relationship between conquest and the right to land must be asked in the reverse: If the Indians had discovered and conquered the Europeans, would they have a right to occupy the land as well? Vitoria's justification of land occupation is still embedded in the medieval Christian order, in the mission ascribed to the Spanish and Portuguese kings by the pope, and in the concept of just war. See Carl Schmitt (2003: 101–125). See also Anghie (2005: 13–31). Vitoria's laborious argumentation reflects the extent to which the crown was at the time much more concerned with legitimating property rights than sovereignty over the New World. See also Pagden (1990: 15).

7. From the sixteenth century onward, cartographic lines, the so-called amity lines—the first one of which may have emerged as a result of the 1559 Cateau-Cambresis Treaty between Spain and France—dropped the idea of a common global order and established an abyssal duality between the territories on this side of the line and the territories on the other side of the line. On this side of the line, truce, peace, and friendship apply; on the other side, the law of the strongest, violence, and plunder. Whatever occurs on the other side of the line is not subject to the same ethical or juridical principles applying on this side of the line. It cannot, therefore, give rise to the kinds of conflicts that the violation of such principles originates. This duality allowed, for instance, the Catholic king of France to have an alliance with the Catholic king of Spain on this side of the line and, at the same time, to have an alliance with the pirates who were attacking the Spanish ships on the other side of the line.

people in many places of America" as the exemplars of the state of nature (1985 [1651]: 187), and Locke thinks likewise when he writes in *Of Civil Government*, "In the beginning all the world was America" (1946 [1690]: §49). The colonial is thus the blind spot upon which the modern conceptions of knowledge and law are built. The theories of the social contract of the seventeenth and eighteenth centuries are as important for what they say as for what they silence. What they say is that modern individuals, that is, metropolitan men, enter the social contract in order to abandon the state of nature to form civil society.[8] What they do not say is that a massive world region given over to the state of nature is thereby being created, a state of nature to which millions of human beings are condemned and left without any possibility of escaping via the creation of a civil society.

Western modernity, rather than meaning the abandonment of the state of nature and the passage to civil society, means the coexistence of both the civil society and the state of nature, separated by an abyssal line whereby the hegemonic eye, located in the civil society, ceases to see, and indeed declares as nonexistent, the state of nature. The present being created on the other side of the line is made invisible by its being reconceptualized as the irreversible past of this side of the line. The hegemonic contact converts simultaneity into noncontemporaneity (see Chapter 5). It makes up pasts to make room for a single homogeneous future (see Chapter 6). Therefore, the fact that the legal principles in force in the civil society, on this side of the line, do not apply on the other side of the line does not in any way compromise their universality.

The same abyssal cartography is constitutive of modern knowledge. Again, the colonial zone is, par excellence, the realm of incomprehensible beliefs and behaviors that in no way can be considered knowledge, whether true or false. The other side of the line harbors only incomprehensible magical or idolatrous practices. The utter strangeness of such practices led to denying the very human nature of the agents of such practices. On the basis of their refined conceptions of humanity and human dignity, the humanists reached the conclusion that the savages were subhuman. Do the Indians have a soul? was the question. When Pope Paul III answered affirmatively in his bull *Sublimis deus* of 1537, he did so by conceiving of the indigenous people's soul as an empty receptacle, an *anima nullius*, very much like the *terra nullius*.[9]

On the basis of these legal and epistemological abyssal conceptions, the universality of the tension between regulation and emancipation, applying on this side of the line, is not contradicted by the tension between appropriation and violence applying on the other side of the line. Appropriation and violence take different forms in the abyssal legal line and in the abyssal epistemological

---

8. On the different conceptions of the social contract, see Santos (2002b: 30–39).

9. According to the bull, "The Indians are truly men and ... are not only capable of understanding the Catholic Faith but, according to our information, they desire exceedingly to receive it." See "Sublimis Deus," Papal Encyclicals Online, www.papalencyclicals.net/Paul03/p3subli .htm (accessed on January 26, 2012).

line. But, in general, appropriation involves incorporation, co-optation, and assimilation, whereas violence involves physical, material, cultural, and human destruction. It goes without saying that appropriation and violence are deeply intertwined. In the realm of knowledge, appropriation ranges from the use of locals as guides[10] and of local myths and ceremonies as instruments of conversion to the pillaging of indigenous knowledges of biodiversity, while violence ranges from the prohibition of the use of native languages in public spaces and the forcible adoption of Christian names to conversion and the destruction of ceremonial sites and symbols and to all forms of racial and cultural discrimination. As regards law, the tension between appropriation and violence is particularly complex because of its direct relation to the extraction of value: the slave trade and forced labor, the instrumental use of customary law and authority in indirect rule, the pillaging of natural resources, the massive displacement of populations, wars and unequal treaties, different forms of apartheid and forced assimilation, and so on. While the logic of regulation/emancipation is unthinkable without the matricial distinction between the law of persons and the law of things, the logic of appropriation/violence only recognizes the law of things, of both human and nonhuman things. The almost ideal typical version of such a law is the law of the "Congo Free State" under King Leopold II of Belgium.[11]

There is therefore a dual modern cartography: a legal cartography and an epistemological cartography. The other side of the abyssal line is the realm beyond legality and illegality (lawlessness), beyond truth and falsehood (incomprehensible beliefs, idolatry, magic).[12] These forms of radical negation together result in a radical absence, the absence of humanity, modern subhumanity. The exclusion is thus both radical and nonexistent, as subhumans are not conceivably candidates for social inclusion.[13] Modern humanity is not conceivable without modern subhumanity.[14] The negation of one part of humanity is sacrificial in

---

10. As in the famous case of Ibn Majid, an experienced pilot who showed Vasco da Gama the maritime way from Mombassa to India (Ahmad 1971). Other examples can be found in Burnett (2002).

11. Different views on this "private colony" and on King Leopold can be read in Emerson (1979); Hochschild (1999); Dumoulin (2005); Hasian (2002: 89–112).

12. The deep duality of abyssal thinking and the incommensurability between the terms of the duality were enforced by well-policed monopolies of knowledge and law with a powerful institutional base—universities, research centers, scientific communities, law schools, and legal professions—and the sophisticated linguistic technology of science and jurisprudence.

13. The supposed externality of the other side of the line is, in effect, the consequence of its doubly belonging to abyssal thinking: as foundation and as negation of the foundation.

14. Fanon (1963, 1967a) denounced this negation of humanity with surpassing lucidity. The radicalism of the negation grounds Fanon's defense of violence as an intrinsic dimension of the anticolonial revolt. The contrast between Fanon and Gandhi in this regard, even though they both shared the same struggle, must be the object of careful reflection, particularly because they are two of the most important thinkers-activists of the last century. See Federici (1994); Kebede (2001).

that it is the condition of the affirmation of that other part of humanity that considers itself as universal.

My argument in this chapter is that this is as true today as in the colonial period. Modern Western thinking goes on operating through abyssal lines that divide the human from the subhuman in such a way that human principles do not get compromised by inhuman practices. The colonies provided a model of radical exclusion that prevails in modern Western thinking and practice today as it did during the colonial cycle. Today, as then, both the creation and the negation of the other side of the line are constitutive of hegemonic principles and practices. Today, as then, the impossibility of copresence between the two sides of the line runs supreme. Today, as then, the legal and political civility on this side of the line is premised upon the existence of utter incivility on the other side of the line. Guantánamo is today one of the most grotesque manifestations of abyssal legal thinking, the creation of the other side of the line as a nonarea in legal and political terms, an unthinkable ground for the rule of law, human rights, and democracy.[15] But it would be an error to consider it exceptional. There are many other Guantánamos, from Iraq to Palestine to Darfur. More than that, there are millions of Guantánamos in the sexual and racial discriminations both in the public and the private spheres, in the savage zones of the megacities, in the ghettos, in the sweatshops, in the prisons, in the new forms of slavery, in the black market for human organs, and in child labor and prostitution.

I argue, first, that the tension between regulation and emancipation continues to coexist with the tension between appropriation and violence to such an extent that the universality of the first tension is not contradicted by the existence of the second; second, that abyssal lines continue to structure modern knowledge and modern law; and, third, that these two abyssal lines are constitutive of Western-based political and cultural relations and interactions in the modern world-system. In sum, I argue that the metaphorical cartography of the global lines has outlived the literal cartography of the amity lines that separated the Old World from the New. Global social injustice is therefore intimately linked to global cognitive injustice. The struggle for global social justice must therefore be a struggle for global cognitive justice as well. In order to succeed, this struggle requires a new kind of thinking, a postabyssal thinking.

The Abyssal Divide between Regulation/Emancipation and Appropriation/Violence

The permanence of abyssal global lines throughout the modern period does not mean that they have remained fixed. Historically, the global lines dividing the

---

15. On Guantánamo and related issues, see, among many others, McCormack (2004); Amann (2004a, 2004b); Human Rights Watch (2004); Sadat (2005); Steyn (2004); Borelli (2005); Dickinson (2005); Van Bergen and Valentine (2006).

two sides have been shifting. But at any given historical moment, they are fixed and their position is heavily surveyed and guarded, very much like the amity lines. In the last sixty years, the global lines suffered two tectonic shake-ups. The first took place with the anticolonial struggles and the processes of independence.[16] The other side of the line rose against radical exclusion as the peoples who had been subjected to the appropriation/violence paradigm got organized and claimed the right to be included in the regulation/emancipation paradigm (Cabral 1979; Fanon 1963, 1967a; Gandhi 1951, 1956; Nkrumah 1965a). For a time, the appropriation/violence paradigm seemed to have come to an end, and so did the abyssal division between this side of the line and the other side of the line. Each of the two global lines (the epistemological and the juridical) seemed to be moving according to its own logic, though both of them in the same direction: their movements seemed to converge in the shrinking, and ultimately the elimination, of the other side of the line. However, this is not what happened, as shown by dependency theory, modern world-system theory, and postcolonial studies.[17]

In this chapter, I focus on the second tectonic shake-up of the abyssal global lines. It has been under way since the 1970s and 1980s, and it goes in the opposite direction. This time, the global lines are moving again, but in such a way that the other side of the line seems to be expanding, while this side of the line is shrinking. The logic of appropriation/violence has been gaining strength to the detriment of the logic of regulation/emancipation, to such an extent that the domain of regulation/emancipation is not only shrinking but becoming internally contaminated by the logic of appropriation/violence.

The complexity of this movement is difficult to unravel as it unfolds before our eyes, and our eyes cannot help being on this side of the line and seeing from inside out. To capture the full measure of what is going on requires a gigantic decentering effort. No single scholar can do it alone, as an individual. Drawing on a collective effort to develop an epistemology of the South, I surmise that this movement is made up of a main movement and a subaltern countermovement. The main movement I call the *return of the colonial and the return of the colonizer*, and the countermovement I call *subaltern cosmopolitanism*.

First, the return of the colonial and the return of the colonizer: the colonial is here a metaphor for those who perceive their life experiences as taking place on the other side of the line and rebel against this. The return of the colonial is the abyssal response to what is perceived as the threatening intrusion of the

---

16. On the eve of World War II, colonies and ex-colonies covered about 85 percent of the land surface of the globe.

17. The multiple origins and the subsequent variations of these debates can be traced in Memmi (1965); Dos Santos (1971); Cardoso and Faletto (1969); Frank (1969); Rodney (1972); Wallerstein (1974, 2004); Bambirra (1978); Dussel (1995); Escobar (1995); Chew and Denemark (1996); Spivak (1999); Césaire (2000); Mignolo (2000); Grosfoguel (2000); Afzal-Khan and Sheshadri-Crooks (2000); Mbembe (2001); Dean and Levi (2003).

colonial into metropolitan societies. Such a return comes in three main forms: the terrorist,[18] the undocumented migrant worker,[19] and the refugee.[20] In different ways, each carries along with her the abyssal global line that defines radical exclusion and legal nonexistence. For instance, in many of their provisions, the new wave of antiterrorism and immigration laws follow the regulatory logic of the appropriation/violence paradigm.[21] The return of the colonial does not necessarily require that she be physically present in the metropolitan societies. It suffices that she has a relevant connection with them. In the case of the terrorist, such a connection may be established by the secret services. In the case of the undocumented migrant worker, it will suffice that she be hired by one of the hundreds of thousands of sweatshops operating in the global South subcontracted by metropolitan multinational corporations. In the case of refugees, the relevant connection is established by their request to obtain refugee status in a given metropolitan society.

The colonial that returns is indeed a new abyssal colonial. This time, the colonial returns not just in the former colonial territories but also in the metropolitan societies. She is now intruding or trespassing on the metropolitan spaces that were demarcated from the beginning of Western modernity as this side of the line; moreover, she shows a level of mobility immensely superior to that of runaway slaves.[22] Under these circumstances, the abyssal metropolitan sees herself trapped in a shrinking space and reacts by redrawing the abyssal line. From her perspective, the new colonial resistance cannot but be met with the ordering logic of appropriation/violence. The time of a neat divide between the Old and New Worlds, between the metropolitan and the colonial, is over. The line must be drawn at as close a range as is necessary to guarantee security. What used to be unequivocally this side of the line is now a messy territory cut through by a meandering abyssal line. The Israeli segregation wall in Palestine[23] and the

18. Among many others, see Harris (2003); Kanstroom (2003); Sekhon (2003); C. Graham (2005); N. Graham (2005); Scheppele (2004a, 2004b, 2006); Guiora (2005).

19. See M. Miller (2002); De Genova (2002); Kanstroom (2004); Hansen and Stepputat (2004); Wishnie (2004); M. Taylor (2004); Silverstein (2005); Passel (2005); Sassen (1999). For the extreme right view on this topic, see Buchanan (2006).

20. Based on Edward Said's *Orientalism* (1978), Akram (2000) identifies a new form of stereotyping, which she calls neo-Orientalism, affecting the metropolitan evaluation of asylum and refugee claims by people coming from the Arab or Muslim world. See also Akram (1999); Menefee (2003–2004); Bauer (2004); Cianciarulo (2005); Akram and Karmely (2005).

21. On the implications of the new wave of antiterrorism and immigration law, see the articles cited in footnotes 23, 24, and 25 below and Immigrant Rights Clinic (2001); Chang (2001); Whitehead and Aden (2002); Zelman (2002); Lobel (2002); Roach (2002, focusing on the Canadian case); Van de Linde et al. (2002, focusing on some European countries); M. Miller (2002); Emerton (2004, focusing on Australia); Boyne (2004, focusing on Germany); Krishnan (2004, focusing on India); Barr (2004); N. Graham (2005).

22. See, for instance, David (1924); Tushnet (1981: 169–188).

23. See International Court of Justice (2004).

category of the "unlawful enemy combatant"[24] are probably the most adequate metaphors for the new abyssal line and the messy cartography to which it leads.

A messy cartography cannot but lead to messy practices. The paradigm of regulation/emancipation is becoming increasingly disfigured by the growing pressure and presence in its midst of the paradigm of appropriation/violence. However, neither the pressure nor the disfiguring can be fully acknowledged, precisely because the other side of the line was from the very beginning incomprehensible as a subhuman territory.[25] In many different ways, the terrorist and the undocumented migrant worker illustrate both the pressure of the appropriation/violence paradigm and the inability of abyssal thinking to acknowledge such pressure as something foreign to the paradigm of regulation/emancipation. It is increasingly evident that the just mentioned antiterrorist legislation, now being promulgated in many different countries following passage of UN Security Council Resolution 1566[26] and under strong pressure from US diplomacy, hollows out the civil and political content of basic constitutional rights and guarantees. As all this occurs without a formal suspension of such rights and guarantees, we are witnessing the emergence of a new state form, the state of exception, which, contrary to the old forms of state of siege or state of emergency, restricts democratic rights under the guise of safeguarding or even expanding them.[27]

More broadly, it appears that Western modernity can only spread globally to the extent that it violates all the principles upon which it has historically grounded the legitimacy of the regulation/emancipation paradigm on this side of the line. Human rights are thus violated in order to be defended; democracy is destroyed to safeguard democracy; life is eliminated to preserve life. Abyssal lines are being drawn in both a literal and a metaphorical sense. In the literal sense, these are the lines that define borders as fences[28] and killing fields, that divide the cities

---

24. See Dörmann (2003); Harris (2003); Kanstroom (2003); Human Rights Watch (2004); Gill and Sliedregt (2005).

25. As an illustration, legal professionals are called upon to accommodate the pressure by revising conventional doctrine, changing interpretation rules, and redefining the scope of principles and the hierarchies among them. A telling example is the debate on the constitutionality of torture between Alan Dershowitz and his critics. See Dershowitz (2002, 2003a, 2003b); Posner (2002); Kreimer (2003); Strauss (2004).

26. This antiterrorism resolution was adopted on October 8, 2004, following UN Security Council Resolution 1373, which was adopted as a response to the September 11 terrorist attacks on the United States. For a detailed analysis of the process of adoption of Resolution 1566, see Saul (2005).

27. I use the concept of state of exception to express a legal-political condition in which the erosion of civil and political rights occurs below the radar of the Constitution, that is, without formal suspension of those rights, as happens when a state of emergency is declared. See Scheppele (2004a); Agamben (2004).

28. A good example of the abyssal legal logic underlying the defense of the construction of a fence separating the southern US border from Mexico can be read in Glon (2005).

between civilized zones[29] and savage zones, and prisons between legal confinement sites and sites of brutal and lawless destruction of life.[30]

The other leg of the current main movement is the return of the colonizer. It involves resuscitating the forms of colonial ordering both in metropolitan societies, this time governing the life of common citizens, and in the societies once subjected to European colonialism. This is most notably the case with what I call the *new indirect rule*,[31] which emerges as the state withdraws from social regulation and public services are privatized. Powerful nonstate actors thereby get control over the lives and well-being of vast populations, be it the control of health care, land, potable water, seeds, forests, or the quality of the environment. The political obligation binding the legal subject to the *Rechtsstaat*, the modern constitutional state, which has prevailed on this side of the line, is being replaced by privatized, depoliticized contractual obligations under which the weaker party is more or less at the mercy of the stronger party. This latter form of ordering bears some disturbing resemblances to the ordering of appropriation/violence that prevailed on the other side of the line. I have described this situation as the rise of societal fascism, a social regime of extremely unequal power relations that grant to the stronger party a veto power over the life and livelihood of the weaker party.

Elsewhere I distinguish five forms of societal fascism.[32] Here I refer to them briefly because they clearly reflect the pressure of the logic of appropriation/violence upon the logic of regulation/emancipation. The first is the *fascism of social apartheid*. I mean the social segregation of the excluded through the division of cities into savage and civilized zones. The savage zones are the zones of Hobbes's state of nature. The civilized zones are the zones of the social contract, and they are under constant threat from the savage zones. In order to defend themselves, the civilized zones turn themselves into neofeudal castles, the fortified enclaves that are characteristic of the new forms of urban segregation—private cities, enclosed condominiums, gated communities. The division into savage and civilized zones in cities around the world—even in "global cities" like New

29. See Blakely and Snyder (1999); Low (2003); Atkinson and Blandy (2005); Coy (2006).

30. See Amann (2004a, 2004b); M. Brown (2005). A report by the European Parliamentary Temporary Committee on illegal CIA activity in Europe (November 2006) shows how European governments acted as the willing facilitators of CIA abuses, such as secret detention and rendition to torture. This lawless investigative field involved 1,245 overflights and stopovers by CIA planes in Europe (some of them involving prisoner transfers) and the creation of secret detention centers in Poland and Romania and probably also in Bulgaria, Ukraine, Macedonia, and Kosovo.

31. Indirect rule was a form of European colonial policy practiced largely in the former British colonies, where the traditional local power structure, or at least part of it, was incorporated into the colonial state administration. See Lugard (1929); Perham (1934); Malinowski (1945); Furnivall (1948); Morris and Read (1972); Mamdani (1996, 1999).

32. I analyze in detail the emergence of societal fascism as a consequence of the breakdown of the logic of the social contract in Santos (2002b: 447–458).

York and London, which, as has been shown (Sassen 1999), are the nodes of the global economy—is becoming a general criterion of sociability, a new hegemonic time-space that crosses all social, economic, political, and cultural relations and is therefore common to state and nonstate action. As far as the state is concerned, the division amounts to a double standard of state action in the savage and civilized zones. In the civilized zones, the state acts democratically, as a protective state, even if often inefficient and unreliable. In the savage zones, the state acts in a fascistic manner, as a predatory state, without the slightest regard, not even in appearance, for the rule of law.[33] The same police officers, all trained in the same academies and under the same regulations, solicitously help children cross the streets in civilized zones while killing youngsters at point-blank range in the savage zones, allegedly in self-defense.

The second form is *contractual fascism*. It occurs in the situations in which the power inequalities between the parties in the civil contract are such that the weaker party, rendered vulnerable for having no alternative, accepts the conditions imposed by the stronger party, however costly and despotic they may be. The neoliberal project of turning the labor contract into a civil-law contract like any other foreshadows a situation of contractual fascism. As mentioned above, this form of fascism occurs today frequently in situations of privatization of public services, such as health, welfare, utilities, and so on.[34] In such cases, the social contract that presided over the production of public services in the welfare state and the developmentalist state is reduced to the individual contract between consumers and providers of privatized services. In light of the often glaring deficiencies of public regulation, this reduction entails the elimination from the contractual ambit of decisive aspects of the protection of consumers, which, for this reason, become extracontractual. By claiming extracontractual prerogatives, the privatized service agencies take over functions of social regulation earlier exercised by the state. The state, whether implicitly or explicitly, subcontracts these agencies for carrying out these functions and, by so doing without the effective participation or control of the citizens, becomes complicit with the production of contractual fascism.

The third form of societal fascism is *territorial fascism*. It occurs whenever social actors with strong patrimonial or military capital dispute the control of the state over the territories wherein they act or neutralize that control by co-opting or

---

33. A good illustration of this dynamic is Caldeira's (2000) study on the geographic and social cleavages in São Paulo.

34. One of the most dramatic examples is the privatization of water and the social consequences resulting therefrom. See Bond (2000) and Buhlungu et al. (2006) for the case of South Africa; Oliveira Filho (2002) for the case of Brazil; Olivera (2005) and Flores (2005) for the case of Bolivia; Bauer (1998) for the case of Chile; Trawick (2003) for the case of Peru; Castro (2006) for the case of Mexico. For studies dealing with two or more cases, see Donahue and Johnston (1998); Balanyá et al. (2005); Conca (2005); Lopes (2005). See also Klare (2001); Hall, Lobina, and de la Motte (2005).

coercing the state institutions and exercising social regulation upon the inhabitants of the territory without their participation and against their interests.[35] In most cases, these are the new colonial territories inside states that almost always were once subjected to European colonialism. Under different forms, the original landgrabbing as a prerogative of conquest and the subsequent "privatization" of the colonies are at work in the reproduction of territorial fascism and, more generally, in the relationships between *terratenientes* and landless peasants. To territorial fascism are also submitted civilian populations living in armed conflict zones.[36]

The fourth form of societal fascism is the *fascism of insecurity*. It consists in the discretionary manipulation of the sense of insecurity of people and social groups rendered vulnerable by the precariousness of work or by destabilizing accidents or events. This results in chronic anxiety and uncertainty vis-à-vis the present and the future for large numbers of people, who thus reduce radically their expectations and become willing to bear huge burdens to achieve the smallest decrease of risk and insecurity. As far as this form of fascism is concerned, the lebensraum—the "vital space" claimed by Hitler for the German people, which justified annexations—of the new *Führers* is people's intimacy and their anxiety and uncertainty regarding the present and the future. It operates by putting in action the double play of retrospective and prospective illusions and is today particularly obvious in the domain of the privatization of social services, such as health care, welfare, education, and housing. The retrospective illusions consist in underscoring the memory of insecurity in this regard and the inefficiency of the state bureaucracy in providing social welfare. The prospective illusions, in turn, aim at creating expectations of safety and security produced in the private sector and inflated by the occultation of some of the risks and the conditions for the provision of services. Such prospective illusions proliferate today mainly in the form of health insurance and private pension funds.

The fifth form of societal fascism is *financial fascism*. This is perhaps the most vicious form of fascist sociability and therefore requires more detailed analysis. It is the type of fascism that controls the financial markets and their casino economy. It is the most pluralist in that the flows of capital are the result of the decisions of individual or institutional investors spread out all over the world and having nothing in common except the desire to maximize their assets. Precisely because it is the most pluralist, it is also the most vicious form of fascism, since its time-space is the most averse to any form of democratic intervention and deliberation. Highly significant in this regard is the reply of the stock market broker when asked what he considered to be the long term: "For me, the long term is the next ten minutes." This virtually instantaneous and global time-space, combined with the speculative logic of profit that sustains it, confers a huge discretionary

---

35. This is the case, for instance, of popular militias in Medellín (Colombia) and of the groups of emerald miners in the western part of Boyacá, Colombia. See Gutiérrez and Jaramillo (2003).

36. For the case of Colombia, see Santos and García Villegas (2001).

power to financial capital, strong enough to shake, in seconds, the real economy or the political stability of any country. The exercise of financial power is totally discretionary, and the consequences for those affected by it—sometimes entire nations—can be overwhelming.

The viciousness of financial fascism consists of the fact that it has become the model and operative criterion of the institutions of global regulation. I mention just one of them: the rating agencies, the agencies that are internationally certified to evaluate the financial situations of the different states and the risks or opportunities they may offer to foreign investors. The grades conferred are decisive for the conditions under which a given country or a firm in such a country may be eligible for international credit. The higher the grade, the better the conditions. These companies have extraordinary power. According to Thomas Friedman, "The post–cold war world has two superpowers, the United States and Moody's."[37] Friedman justifies his statement by adding, "If it is true that the United States of America can annihilate an enemy by using its military arsenal, the agency of financial rating Moody's has the power to strangle a country financially by giving it a bad grade" (Warde 1997: 10–11). These agencies' discretionary power is all the greater because they have the prerogative of making evaluations not solicited by the countries or firms in question.

In all its forms, societal fascism is a regime characterized by social relations and life experiences under extremely unequal power relations and exchanges that lead to particularly severe and potentially irreversible forms of exclusion. Such forms of social exclusion exist both within national societies and in the relations among countries. Societal fascism is a new form of the state of nature and it proliferates in the shadow of the social contract in two ways: postcontractualism and precontractualism. Postcontractualism is the process by means of which social groups and social interests up until now included in the social contract are excluded from the latter without any prospect of returning: workers and popular classes are expelled from the social contract through the elimination of social and economic rights, thereby becoming discardable populations. Precontractualism consists in blocking access to citizenship to social groups that before considered themselves candidates for citizenship and had the reasonable expectation of acceding to it—for instance, the urban youth living in the ghettos of megacities in the global North and global South.[38]

As a social regime, societal fascism may coexist with liberal political democracy. Rather than sacrificing democracy to the demands of global capitalism, it trivializes democracy to such a degree that it is no longer necessary, or even convenient, to sacrifice democracy to promote capitalism. It is therefore a pluralistic fascism, that is to say, a form of fascism that never existed. Indeed, I contend

---

37. Moody's is one of the four rating agencies certified by the Securities and Exchange Commission; the others are Standard and Poor's, Fitch Ratings, Duff, and Phelps.

38. An early and eloquent analysis of this phenomenon can be read in Wilson (1987).

that we may be entering a period in which societies are politically democratic and socially fascistic.

The new forms of indirect rule also comprise the second great transformation of property and property law in the modern era. Property, and specifically the property of the New World territories, was, as I mentioned in the beginning, the key issue underlying the establishment of modern, abyssal global lines. The first transformation took place when the ownership of things was expanded, with capitalism, into an ownership of the means of production. As Karl Renner (1965) describes so well, the owner of the machines became the owner of the labor of the workers operating the machines. Control over things became control over people. Of course, Renner overlooked the fact that in the colonies this transformation did not occur, since the control of people was the original form of the control of things, the latter including both human and nonhuman things. The second great transformation of property takes place, far beyond production, when the ownership of services becomes a form of control of the people who need them to survive. The new indirect rule gives rise to a form of decentralized despotism, to use Mahmood Mamdani's (1996: ch. 2) characterization of African colonial rule. Decentralized despotism does not clash with liberal democracy; rather, it makes the latter increasingly irrelevant to the quality of life of increasingly larger populations.

Under the conditions of the new indirect rule, rather than regulating social conflict among citizens, modern abyssal thinking is called upon to suppress social conflict and ratify lawlessness on this side of the line, as had always happened on the other side of the line. Under the pressure of the logic of appropriation/ violence, the very concept of modern law—the universally valid norm emanating from the state and coercively imposed by it if necessary—is thereby changing. As an illustration of the conceptual changes under way, a new type of law is emerging that is euphemistically called soft law.[39] Presented as the most benevolent manifestation of a regulation/emancipation ordering, it carries with it the logic of appropriation/violence whenever very unequal power relations are involved. It consists of law with which compliance is voluntary. Without surprise, it is being used, among other social domains, in the field of capital/labor relations,[40] and

---

39. A vast literature has developed over the last few years that theorizes and empirically studies novel forms of governing the economy that rely on collaboration among nonstate actors (firms, civic organizations, NGOs, unions, and so on) rather than on top-down state regulation. In spite of the variety of labels under which social scientists and legal scholars have pursued this approach, the emphasis is on softness rather than hardness, on voluntary compliance rather than imposition: "responsive regulation" (Ayres and Braithwaite 1992), "post-regulatory law" (Teubner 1986), "soft law" (Snyder 1993, 2002; Trubek and Mosher 2003; Trubek and Trubek 2005; Mörth 2004), "democratic experimentalism" (Dorf and Sabel 1998; Unger 1998), "collaborative governance" (Freeman 1997), "outsourced regulation" (O'Rourke 2003), or simply "governance" (Mac Neil, Sargent, and Swan 2000; Nye and Donahue 2000). For a critique, see Santos and Rodríguez-Garavito (2005: 1–26); Santos (2005: 29–63); Rodríguez-Garavito (2005: 64–91).

40. The other area is environmental protection.

its most accomplished version is the codes of conduct whose adoption is being recommended to the metropolitan multinationals entering outsourcing contracts with "their" sweatshops around the world.[41] The plasticity of soft law bears intriguing resemblances to colonial law, whose application depended, more than anything else, on the whims of the colonizer.[42] The social relations they regulate are, if not a new state of nature, a twilight zone between the state of nature and civil society, where social fascism proliferates and flourishes.

In sum, modern abyssal thinking, which on this side of the line has been called upon to order the relationships among citizens and between them and the state, is now, in the social domains that bear greater pressure from the logic of appropriation/violence, called upon to deal with citizens as noncitizens and with noncitizens as dangerous colonial savages. As societal fascism coexists with liberal democracy, the state of exception coexists with constitutional normalcy, civil society coexists with the state of nature, and indirect rule coexists with the rule of law. Far from being a perversion of some original normal rule, this is the original design of modern epistemology and legality, even if the abyssal line that from the very beginning has distinguished the metropolitan from the colonial has been displaced, turning the colonial into an internal dimension of the metropolitan.

Conclusion: Toward Postabyssal Thinking

In light of what I have just said, it seems that, if not actively resisted, abyssal thinking will go on reproducing itself, no matter how exclusionary and destructive the practices to which it gives rise. As I have shown in the previous chapters, political resistance thus needs to be premised upon an epistemological break: there is no global social justice without global cognitive justice. This means that the critical task ahead cannot be limited to generating alternatives. Indeed, it requires an alternative thinking of alternatives. A new postabyssal thinking is thus called for. Is it possible? Are there any conditions that, if adequately valued, might give it a chance? This inquiry explains why I pay special attention to the countermovement I mentioned above as resulting from the shake-up of the abyssal global lines since the 1970s and 1980s. Postabyssal thinking starts from the recognition that social exclusion in its broadest sense takes very different forms according to whether it is determined by an abyssal or a nonabyssal line, as well as that, as long as abyssally defined exclusion persists, no really progressive postcapitalist alternative is possible. During a probably long transitional period, confronting abyssal exclusion will be a precondition to address in an effective

---

41. See Rodríguez-Garavito (2005) and the bibliography cited there.

42. This type of law is euphemistically called soft because it is soft on those whose entrepreneurial behavior they are supposed to regulate (employers) and hard on those suffering the consequences of noncompliance (workers).

way the many forms of nonabyssal exclusion that have divided the modern world on this side of the line. A postabyssal conception of Marxism (in itself, a good exemplar of abyssal thinking) will claim that the emancipation of workers must be fought for in conjunction with the emancipation of all the discardable populations of the global South, which are oppressed but not directly exploited by global capitalism. It will also claim that the rights of citizens are not secured as long as noncitizens go on being treated as subhumans.[43]

The recognition of the persistence of abyssal thinking is thus the *conditio sine qua non* to start thinking and acting beyond it. Without such recognition, critical thinking will remain a derivative thinking that will go on reproducing the abyssal lines, no matter how antiabyssal it proclaims itself. Postabyssal thinking, on the contrary, is a nonderivative thinking; it involves a radical break with modern Western ways of thinking and acting. In our time, to think in nonderivative terms means to think from the perspective of the other side of the line, precisely because the other side of the line has been the realm of the unthinkable in Western modernity. The rise of the appropriation/violence ordering inside the regulation/emancipation ordering can only be tackled if we situate our epistemological perspective on the social experience of the other side of the line, that is, the nonimperial global South, conceived of as a metaphor for the systemic and unjust human suffering caused by global capitalism and colonialism. Postabyssal thinking can thus be summarized as learning from the South through an epistemology of the South. On its basis it is possible to struggle for a *subaltern insurgent cosmopolitanism* based on a subaltern cosmopolitan reason.

The use of the term *cosmopolitanism* to describe the global resistance against abyssal thinking may seem inadequate in the face of its modernist or Western ascendancy.[44] The idea of cosmopolitanism, like universalism, world citizenship, and the rejection of political and territorial borders, indeed has a long tradition in Western culture, from the cosmic law of Pythagoras and the philallelia of Democritus to the *Homo sum, humani nihil a me alienum puto* of Terence, from the medieval *res publica christiana* to the Renaissance humanists, and from Voltaire, for whom "to be a good patriot, it is necessary to become an enemy of the rest of the world" (2002: 145), to working-class internationalism. This ideological

---

43. Gandhi is arguably the thinker-activist of modern times who thought and acted most consistently in nonabyssal terms. Having lived and experienced with extreme intensity the radical exclusions typical of abyssal thinking, Gandhi did not swerve from his goal of building a new form of universality capable of liberating both the oppressor and the victim. As Ashis Nandy correctly insists, "The Gandhian vision defies the temptation to equal the oppressor in violence and to regain one's self-esteem as a competitor within the same system. The vision builds on an identification with the oppressed which excludes the fantasy of the superiority of the oppressor's lifestyle, so deeply embedded in the consciousness of those who claim to speak on behalf of the victims of history" (1987: 35).

44. The current debates on cosmopolitanism do not concern me here. In its long history cosmopolitanism has meant universalism, tolerance, patriotism, world citizenship, worldwide

tradition has often been put at the service of European expansionism, colonialism, and imperialism, the same historical processes that today generate globalized localisms and localized globalisms. The phrase "subaltern, insurgent cosmopolitanism," on the contrary, refers to the aspiration of oppressed groups to organize their resistance and consolidate political coalitions on the same scale as the one used by the oppressors to victimize them, that is, the global scale. Insurgent cosmopolitanism is also different from that invoked by Marx as meaning the universality of those who, under capitalism, have nothing to lose but their chains—the working class. In addition to the working class described by Marx, the oppressed classes in the world today cannot be encompassed by the "class-which-has-only-its-chains-to-lose" category. Insurgent cosmopolitanism includes vast populations in the world that are not even sufficiently useful or skilled enough to "have chains," that is, to be directly exploited by capital. It aims at uniting social groups on both a class and a nonclass basis, the victims of exploitation as well as the victims of social exclusion, of sexual, ethnic, racist, and religious discrimination. For this reason, insurgent cosmopolitanism does not imply uniformity, a general theory of social emancipation and the collapse of differences, autonomies, and local identities. Giving equal weight to the principles of equality and the recognition of difference, insurgent cosmopolitanism is no more than a global emergence resulting from the fusion of local, progressive struggles with the aim of maximizing their emancipatory potential *in loco* (however defined) through translocal/local linkages.

To the epistemological foundations of subaltern, insurgent cosmopolitanism I turn in the next three chapters.

---

community of human beings, global culture, and so on. More often than not, when this concept has been used—either as a scientific tool to describe reality or as an instrument in political struggles—the unconditional inclusiveness of its abstract formulation has been used to pursue the exclusionary interests of a particular social group. In a sense, cosmopolitanism has been the privilege of those who can afford it. The way I revisit this concept entails the identification of groups whose aspirations are denied or made invisible by the hegemonic use of the concept but who may be served by an alternative use of it. Paraphrasing Stuart Hall (1996), who raised a similar question in relation to the concept of identity, I ask, Who needs cosmopolitanism? The answer is simple: whoever is a victim of intolerance and discrimination needs tolerance; whoever is denied basic human dignity needs a community of human beings; whoever is a noncitizen needs world citizenship in any given community or nation. In sum, those socially excluded victims of the hegemonic conception of cosmopolitanism need a different type of cosmopolitanism. Subaltern cosmopolitanism is therefore an oppositional variety. Just as neoliberal globalization does not recognize any alternative form of globalization, so cosmopolitanism without adjectives denies its own particularity. Subaltern, oppositional cosmopolitanism is the cultural and political form of counterhegemonic globalization. It is the name of the emancipatory projects whose claims and criteria of social inclusion reach beyond the horizons of global capitalism. Others, with similar concerns, have also adjectivized cosmopolitanism: rooted cosmopolitanism (Cohen 1992), cosmopolitan patriotism (Appiah 1998), vernacular cosmopolitanism (Bhabha 1996; Diouf 2000), cosmopolitan ethnicity (Werbner 2002), or working-class cosmopolitanism (Wrebner 1999). On different conceptions of cosmopolitanism, see Breckenridge et al. (2002).

CHAPTER 5

Toward an Epistemology of Blindness

Why the New Forms of "Ceremonial Adequacy" neither Regulate nor Emancipate

Introduction

In his celebrated essay of 1898, Thorstein Veblen criticized classical economics for promoting an impoverished, tautological, or circular relation between facts and theory, a relation that he designated as "ceremonial adequacy" (1898: 382). Once the laws of the normal and of the natural are formulated, "according to a preconception regarding the ends to which, in the nature of things, all things bend" (1898: 382), either the facts corroborate such a concept of normality and the propensity to predefined ends and are thus established as relevant, or they do not, in which case they are discarded as abnormal, marginal, or irrelevant. Veblen's plea was for the replacement of this normative and illusory adequacy with a real one, the abandonment of the "metaphysics of normality and control-ling principles" for the observation of the real economic life process made of real economic actions by real economic agents.

With this plea, Veblen launched a debate in economics that has been with us ever since in all the social sciences and indeed in science as a whole. The debate can be formulated in the following terms: What counts as representation? And what are the consequences of misrepresentation? The most intriguing features of this debate are, on the one hand, that it is by far easier to establish the limits of a given representation than to formulate a general coherent representation of limits and, on the other hand, that the consequences of misrepresentation tend to be different from those predicted, thus confirming, if nothing else, the misrep-resentation of consequences. In other words, it has been much easier to criticize ceremonial adequacy than to create a credible alternative to it. Veblen illustrates

136

this condition very well. At the outset of his article, he mentions approvingly, and as an example to follow, the "eminent anthropologist" M. G. de Lapouge, whose work is given as a symbol of the evolutionary revolution going on in other sciences (Lapouge and Closson 1897: 373). If, however, we read the article by Lapouge and note the scientific results accepted by Veblen, we are confronted with a delirious racial anthropology in which the binary of dolichocephalic-blond and brachycephalic types account for such laws as the law of the distribution of wealth, the law of attitudes, the law of urban indices, the law of emigration, the law of marriages, the law of the concentration of dolichoids, the law of urban elimination, the laws of stratification, the law of intellectual classes, and the law of epochs.

Our evaluation of Lapouge's evolutionary science and of the way Veblen draws from it shows that the blindness of others, particularly of those in the past, is both recurrent and easy to establish. But if that is the case, whatever we say today about the blindness of others will probably be seen in the future as evidence of our own blindness. The dilemma can be formulated thus: If we are blind, why is it so difficult to accept our own blindness? And if indeed we are blind, what is the point of seeing at all? My contention is that the consciousness of our own blindness, which we are forced to exercise when unveiling the blindness of others, should be at the core of a new epistemological stance that calls for a plurality of knowledges and practices, since no knowledge or practice in isolation provides reliable guidance, and for an edifying, socially responsible, rather than technical, application of science, fully aware that the consequences of scientific actions tend to be less scientific than the actions themselves.

In this chapter I address the issue of the resilience of ceremonialism in our scientific management of adequacy. Accordingly, I concentrate on the two steepest slopes of the debate: the issues of the representation of limits and the misrepresentation of consequences. Concerning the first issue, the representation of limits, I argue that the most intractable difficulty lies in that, for Western modernity and for modern science, there are indeed no insurmountable limits. Accordingly, the representation of limits is as provisional as the limits it represents. Concerning the second issue, the misrepresentation of consequences, I argue that the project of modernity anticipated two mutually constituted consequences of modern science: social regulation and social emancipation. However, to the extent that the possibilities of modernity were reduced to those of capitalism, the two consequences were torn apart: some knowledges and social practices, by far the dominant ones, took social regulation as the primordial consequence of their endeavors, while subordinate knowledges and social practices took social emancipation as their privileged consequence. The problem, however, is that, in this paradigm, the regulation that does not emancipate does not regulate, and vice versa; the emancipation that does not regulate does not emancipate.

Knowledge-as-Regulation and Knowledge-as-Emancipation

Before I address the representation of limits and the misrepresentation of consequences I must situate them in a broader epistemological landscape, the project of Western modernity as an epistemological paradigm.

The project of Western modernity is organized around a discrepancy between social experience and social expectations; herein lies its utmost novelty. For the first time in Western history, experience does not have to, and indeed should not, coincide with expectations. Seen from the perspective of social experiences, social expectations are excessive, and vice versa; seen from the perspective of social expectations, social experiences are deficient. The normality and symmetry of this disjuncture are rendered by the twin pillars upon which Western modernity is based: social regulation and social emancipation. Each is constituted by three principles or logics.[1] The pillar of regulation is constituted by the principle of the state, formulated most prominently by Hobbes, the principle of the market, developed by Locke and Adam Smith in particular, and the principle of the community, which presides over Rousseau's political theory. The pillar of emancipation is constituted by three logics of rationality as identified by Weber: the aesthetic-expressive rationality of literature and the arts, the cognitive-instrumental rationality of science and technology, and the moral-practical rationality of ethics and law. The tensions between the two pillars, which derive from the play of excesses and deficits in the discrepancies between experience and expectations, are to be managed by the exercise of reason as a normal state of affairs designated as progress. The project of Western modernity thus aims at a harmonious and reciprocal development of both the pillar of regulation and the pillar of emancipation, whereby the harmonization of potentially incompatible social values, such as justice and autonomy, solidarity and identity, and equality and freedom, will be ensured.

The epistemological dimension of the paradigm of modernity matches the scope and structure of the double binding of social regulation and social emancipation. We know that any form of knowledge implies a trajectory or progress from point A, designated as ignorance, to point B, designated as knowing. Forms of knowledge are distinguished by the way they characterize both the two points and the trajectory that connects them. There is, therefore, neither ignorance in general nor knowing in general. Each form of knowledge recognizes itself in a certain kind of knowing to which it opposes a certain kind of ignorance, which in its turn is recognized as such only in contrast with that kind of knowing. All knowing is knowing of a certain ignorance, as all ignorance is ignorance of a certain knowing.

---

1. I develop this characterization of Western modernity in detail in Santos (1995).

The paradigm of modernity comprises two main forms of knowledge: knowledge-as-emancipation and knowledge-as-regulation. Knowledge-as-emancipation entails a trajectory between a state of ignorance that I call *colonialism* and a state of knowing that I call *solidarity*. Knowledge-as-regulation entails a trajectory between a state of ignorance that I call *chaos* and a state of knowing that I call *order*. While the former form of knowledge progresses from colonialism toward solidarity, the latter progresses from chaos toward order. In the terms of the paradigm, the mutual binding between the pillars of regulation and emancipation implies that these two forms of knowledge balance each other in a dynamic way. This means that the knowing power of order feeds the knowing power of solidarity, and vice versa. Knowledge-as-emancipation derives its dynamics from the excesses of order, while knowledge-as-regulation derives its dynamics from the excesses of solidarity (Santos 1995: 25).

I argue that this social and epistemological paradigm suffered a historical accident. Something happened that only retrospectively can be conceived of as inscribed in an evolutionary necessity: from the mid-nineteenth century onward, the possibilities for the implementation of the paradigm of modernity were reduced to those made available by world capitalism. This accident produced an enormous turbulence between social regulation and social emancipation, which eventually led to the cannibalization of social emancipation by social regulation; from being the other of social regulation, social emancipation was transformed into the double of social regulation. But since social regulation does not sustain itself without its other, its cannibalization of social emancipation led to a double crisis of regulation and emancipation, each feeding on the other. This is the situation in which we now find ourselves. At the epistemological level this historical process led to the total primacy of knowledge-as-regulation over knowledge-as-emancipation: order became the hegemonic way of knowing, while chaos became the hegemonic form of ignorance. Such an imbalance allowed knowledge-as-regulation to recodify knowledge-as-emancipation in its own terms. Thus, knowing in knowledge-as-emancipation became ignorance in knowledge-as-regulation (solidarity was recodified as chaos); conversely, ignorance in knowledge-as-emancipation became knowing in knowledge-as-regulation (colonialism was recodified as order). My argument is that the persistence of ceremonial adequacy and its problems, as concern both the representation of limits and the misrepresentation of consequences, have much to do with the conversion of order, as a way of knowing, into colonialist knowledge and with the concomitant conversion of solidarity, as a way of knowing, into chaotic ignorance. In my view, the way out of this situation in a context of paradigmatic transition consists of reassessing knowledge-as-emancipation, granting it primacy over knowledge-as-regulation. This implies, on the one hand, that solidarity be turned into the hegemonic form of knowing and, on the other, that a certain degree of chaos be taken in as a consequence of the relative negligence of knowledge-as-regulation.

The Representation of Limits

In the study of the representation of limits both in economics and in the social sciences in general, it will be helpful to consider the cases of sciences that have faced the issues of both representation and limits most dramatically, either because of the nature of the objects they study or because of the type of technical capabilities they have been designed to develop. I mean archaeology, involved in the study of objects and behaviors that are very distant in time; astronomy, involved in the study of objects that are very distant in space; cartography, concerned with the representation of spaces through maps; and photography, concerned with representation as reproduction. It will also be useful to consider an artistic activity, painting, which, at least since the Renaissance, has been haunted particularly by the question of representation.

Drawing freely on the procedures and strategies that these knowledges and practices have designed in order to overcome the dilemmas and fallacies of representation, I want to show, first, that such procedures, strategies, dilemmas, and fallacies are at the core of modern scientific knowledge as a whole and, second, that within the range of alternatives made possible by such procedures and strategies, the social sciences in general and mainstream economics in particular have chosen the alternatives least suited to promote solidarity as a form of knowing. Underlying my argument is the idea that such procedures and strategies are the metatechnologies that allow the scientist to produce recognizable and convincing knowledge and that such metatechnologies, which are internal to the scientific process, are as partisan and arbitrary as the technological interventions of science in social life. The key concepts in my analysis are the following: scale, perspective, resolution, and signature. All of them have been developed by the above-mentioned disciplines as they have confronted, in closest contact, the limits of representation and addressed the dilemmas emerging therefrom.

The Determination of Relevance

The first limit of representation concerns the question, What is relevant? The relevance of a given object of analysis lies not in the object itself but in the objectives of the analysis. Different objectives produce different criteria of relevance. If we should submit the choice of objectives to the open and potentially infinite scientific discussion that characterizes the analysis of scientific objects, we would never be able to establish a coherent criterion of relevance and carry out any intelligible scientific work. As long as we discuss objectives, we cannot agree on objects. Since the discussion is potentially infinite, the only way to make science possible at all is to postulate the equivalence or fungibility of alternative objectives. It is therefore by denying or hiding the hierarchy of relevance among objectives that modern science establishes the hierarchy of relevance among objects. The distortion is thus imminent and indeed unavoidable. The established relevance is a sociological, or better, a political, economic fact disguised as epistemological evidence. The invisibility of the disguise is premised on the credibility of the distortion. The distortion is made credible by creating, in a systematic way, credible illusions of correspondence with whatever is to be analyzed. Two procedures are used to produce such illusions: scale and perspective.

We do not observe phenomena. We observe scales of phenomena. Though scales are important to all the disciplines from which I am drawing, it is in cartography that scales are most central. Indeed, the main structural feature of maps is that in order to fulfill their function of representation and orientation, they inevitably distort reality. Jorge Luis Borges tells the story of the emperor who ordered the production of an exact map of his empire. He insisted that the map should be exact to the minutest detail. The best cartographers of the time were engaged in this important project. Eventually, they produced the map, and in fact it could not possibly be more exact, as it coincided point by point with the empire. However, to their frustration, it was not a very practical map, since it was of the same size as the empire (Borges 1974: 90).

To be practical, a map cannot coincide point by point with reality. However, the distortion of reality thus produced will not be considered inaccurate if the mechanisms by which the distortion of reality is accomplished are known and can be controlled. Maps distort reality through three specific mechanisms that, since they are used systematically, become intrinsic or structural attributes of any map. Such mechanisms are scale, projection, and symbolization. For the purposes of this chapter, I will limit myself to scales.[2]

Scale, as Mark Monmonier has defined it, "is the ratio of distance on the map to the corresponding distance on the ground" (1981: 4). Scale involves, then, a decision on more or less detail. "Since large-scale maps represent less land on a given size sheet of paper than do small-scale maps, large-scale maps can present more detail" (1981: 4). Since maps are "a miniaturized version" of reality (Keates 1982: 73), mapmaking involves the filtering of details, "the selection of both meaningful details and relevant features" (Monmonier 1981: 4). As P. C. Muehrcke puts it, "What makes a map so useful is its genius of omission. It is reality uncluttered, pared down to its essence, stripped of all but the essentials" (1986: 10).[3] One easily understands that the decision on scale conditions the

---

2. A detailed analysis of these cartographic mechanisms can be read in Santos (1995: 456–473).

3. On the roles and limits of maps, see, among others, Monmonier (1991, 1993, 2010, 2012); Campbell (1993); MacEachren (1994, 2004); Akerman and Karrow (2007).

decision on the use of the map, and vice versa: "Small-scale maps are not intended to permit accurate measurements of the width of roads, streams, etc., but rather to show with reasonable accuracy the relative positions of these and other features" (Monmonier 1981: 4).

Geography, which shares with cartography the concern for spaces and spatial relations, has also contributed important insights on scales, both scales of analysis and scales of action. As to the former, there are phenomena that can only be represented on a small scale, such as climate, whereas others, like erosion, for instance, can only be represented on a large scale. This means that the differences in scale are not simply quantitative but also qualitative. A given phenomenon can only be represented on a given scale. To change the scale implies changing the phenomenon. Each scale reveals one phenomenon and distorts or hides others.[4] As in nuclear physics, the scale creates the phenomenon. Some of the fallacious correlations in geography derive from the superimposition of phenomena created and analyzed on different scales. The scale is "a coherent forgetting" (Racine 1982: 126) that must be carried out coherently. Mediating between intention and action, scale applies also to social action. Urban planners as well as military chiefs, administrators, business executives, legislators, judges, and lawyers define strategies on a small scale and decide day-to-day tactics on a large scale. Power represents social and physical reality on a scale chosen for its capacity to create phenomena that maximize the conditions for the reproduction of power. The distortion and concealment of reality are thus presuppositions of the exercise of power.

Different scales of analysis create different patterns of regulation and promote different action packages. As regards *regulation patterns*, it must be borne in mind that representation and orientation are two antagonistic modes of imagining and constituting reality, one geared to identifying position, the other to identifying movement. Large-scale regulation is rich in details and features, describes behavior and attitudes vividly, contextualizes them in their immediate surroundings, and is sensitive to distinctions (and complex relations) between inside and outside, high and low, just and unjust. Large-scale regulation invites a pattern of regulation based on (and geared to) representation and position. On the contrary, small-scale regulation is poor in details and features, skeletonizes behavior and attitudes and reduces them to general types of action, and provides a sense of direction and schemes for shortcuts. In sum, small-scale regulation favors a pattern of regulation based on (and geared to) orientation and movement.

Besides having different regulation patterns, different scales of analysis also condition different *action packages*. An action package is a connected sequence of actions structurally determined by predefined boundaries. I identify two kinds

---

4. According to Monmonier, "Perhaps the most enigmatic problem in cartography is the generalization to a much smaller scale of thematic data, such as land use, mapped at a larger scale" (1985: 111).

of boundaries: those defined by range and those defined by ethics. According to range, we can distinguish two ideal types of action packages: tactical and strategic. According to ethics, we can also distinguish two ideal types of action packages: edifying and instrumental. In light of the previous examples, I would suggest that large-scale analysis and regulation invite tactical and edifying action packages, while small-scale analysis and regulation invite strategic and instrumental action packages. Social groups or classes that are predominantly socialized in one of these forms of analysis and representation tend to be specifically competent in the type of action package associated with it. In a situation in which large- and small-scale analysis and regulation intersect, the large-scale action package tends to be defensive and to regulate normal, routine interaction or, at the most, molecular struggles, while the small-scale action package tends to be aggressive and to regulate critical, exceptional situations, triggered by molar struggles. These tendencies may hold true irrespective of the class nature of the social groups involved in the specific action package.

Of all the social sciences, mainstream economics has been the most focused on orientation, with its greatest involvement in science-based intervention in social life. For that reason it has favored small-scale analysis, of which mathematical modeling is the most characteristic illustration. Small-scale analysis has been as prevalent in macro- as in microeconomics. As in the case of maps, small-scale analysis privileges a pattern of regulation geared to orientation and movement and an action package based on strategic and instrumental actions. The efficacy of the orientation is premised upon the vagueness of representation, that is, upon the negligence of details and contrasts, the dismissal of submerged meanings and practices, and disregard for the different durations of both declining and emergent qualities. In such a mode of representation, the uncertainty of the position is made irrelevant by the dynamics of the movement. Based on such a representation, the efficacy of the orientation depends on one condition: it must be sustained by extrascientific political forces powerful enough to promote movement to cover for the social costs of the negligence of position.

This means that the preference for small scale, and thus for orientation over representation, is an epistemological decision that, rather than sustaining itself, is grounded on a sociological, political economic fiat. The definition of the relevant features of a given course of action is determined by the regulation objectives, and not the other way around. Different objectives and thus different interests create different relevant facts.

This may be illustrated with the analysis of a given labor conflict in a factory producing for a transnational corporation through franchising or subcontracting. The factory code, that is, the production law of the workplace, as a form of local legality, regulates the relations in production in great detail in order to maintain workplace discipline, prevent labor conflicts, reduce their scope whenever they occur, and eventually settle them. The labor conflict is the nuclear object of the factory code because it confirms, *a contrario*, the continuity of the relations in production, which are the raison d'être of the factory code. In the wider context of national state labor law, the labor conflict is only a dimension, however important, of industrial relations. It is part of a broader network of social, political, and economic facts in which we easily identify, among others, political stability, the inflation rate, income policy, and power relations among labor unions, businesses, and government. In the still wider context of the transnational regulation of international franchising or subcontracting, the labor conflict becomes a minute detail in international economic relations, hardly worth mentioning.

Thus, the different regulatory orders operating on different scales translate the same social objects into different relevant objects. However, since in real life the different regulatory scales do not exist in isolation but rather interact in different ways—in our example the regulatory purposes of the three scales converge in the same social event—there may be the illusion that the three regulatory objects overlap point by point. In fact, they do not coincide at all. Workers and sometimes the employer tend to have a large-scale view of a given conflict, with all its details and relevant features, a concept molded by local regulation. Union leaders and sometimes the employer tend to see the conflict as a crisis in a process of continuous industrial relations. Their view is predominantly molded by national state regulation; consequently, their actions aim at a compromise between the medium-scale and the large-scale view of the conflict. For the transnational corporation, the labor conflict is a tiny accident in a globally designed investment and production system; if not promptly overcome, it can be easily circumvented simply by moving production to another country.

Transnational corporations favor the small-scale view of the conflict because this is the scale at which they organize their global operations. Together with the multilateral financial institutions, they are the small-scale actors par excellence, covering vast parts of the globe and most drastically reducing the amount of detail or contrast as a condition of operational efficacy. Mainstream economics tends also to favor the small-scale view of the conflict. The fact that this view converges with the view of the transnational corporations is, in epistemological terms, a coincidence and, in political-economic terms, the cover-up for a combination of interests. Mainstream economics creates the reality that maximizes the efficacy of the regulation it propounds.

The Determination of Degrees of Relevance

Once relevance is established, a further question must be asked: How relevant? In Western modernity and modern science, the degrees of relevance are established by another procedure operating in tandem with scale: perspective. Leon Battista Alberti (1404–1472) is considered the founder of one-point perspective in Renaissance painting, even though the mathematical laws of perspective were formulated for the first time by the Florentine architect Fillipo Brunelleschi

(1377–1446). In his treatise *De pictura* of 1435, Alberti compares the painted picture to an open window: "A picture, in his view, should be made to seem as if it were a pane of transparent glass through which we look into an imaginary space extending in depth" (Andrews 1995: 1). In order to achieve that, he devises a method for drawing a mathematically correct representation of space in which the relative size of objects at different distances and the apparent convergence of parallel lines will be as convincing to the eye in art as they are in nature (Gilman 1978: 17). As E. B. Gilman says, "In the fifteenth and early sixteenth centuries … perspective arises out of and gives expression to a sense of certainty about man's place in the world and his ability to understand that world" (1978: 29). The system of proportions between the objects to be painted and their images and between the distance of the observer's eye and the painting creates an intelligible world organized around the viewpoint of the spectator. The credibility of this "illusionistic" art (Gilman 1978: 23) lies in the mathematical precision of the individual's point of view. Renaissance perspective is both a show of confidence in human knowledge and the artistic counterpart of individualism.

However, this precision and this confidence are obtained at a very high price: the absolute immobility of the eye. The illusion is real on the condition that the painting is seen from a predetermined and rigidly fixed point of view.[5] If the spectator changes his place, the illusion of reality vanishes. Gilman is thus right when he says that "the very fullness and definition of perspective space implies the radical incompleteness of our vision, and the point of view becomes a drastic limitation, a set of blinders, as well as an epistemological privilege" (1978: 31).

The imaginative structure of proper perspective underlies, as I said, both modern art and modern science. It is also through perspective that degrees and proportions of scientific relevance can be established. There is, however, an important difference in the operation of perspective in art and science. In modern art the painter conceives of the spectator as his radical other. The painter paints for the ideal spectator. The painter imagines the spectator's gaze in order to deceive it effectively. The painter is the only one with access to reality, and both he and his spectator know that. The illusion of reality develops in tandem with the reality of the illusion. On the contrary, modern scientists see themselves as the ideal spectators; they put themselves at the center of the privileged point of view to observe the reality fully revealed to their gaze. Even though they do other things besides merely spectating—otherwise no scientific work would get done—these other things are the product of the spectator's mind. In other words, they are the spectator at work. As the creator is absorbed by the spectator, the reality of the illusion is cannibalized by the illusion of reality; as a consequence, the latter becomes the reality of reality. Accordingly, modern scientists believe

---

5. John Ruskin: "Perspective can, therefore, only be quite right by being calculated for one fixed position of the eye of the observer; nor will it ever appear *deceptively* right unless seen precisely from the point it is calculated for" (1913: 328).

in the illusions they create to an extent that the painter does not. Nor would scientists be as comfortable with the epithet "illusionistic science" to characterize their work as painters are with that of "illusionistic art" to characterize theirs.

This conflation of the creator with the spectator in modern science has had a crucial consequence. Because he or she always externalizes the spectator, the painter can make a distinction between the ideal spectator, the one eye of the viewer, and the significant spectator, his patron or *mecenas*. On the contrary, the scientist can make no such distinction because the scientist is always both the ideal and the significant spectator simultaneously. This makes it impossible to ask for and to question the significant spectator for whom the scientist, as a creator, works. The negative consequences of such unquestioning have grown with the conversion of science into a productive force and thus with the significant spectator's growing impact on, or even interference with, the work of the scientist.

Of all social sciences, mainstream economics has been the one in which the choice among alternative significant spectators has been most drastically reduced to a single one, the capitalist entrepreneur. As the latter's impact on scientific work grew, the invisibility of the reality of illusion allowed for the illusion of reality to become the entrepreneur's reality. The latter's preferences and limitations, rather than being blinders, became epistemological privileges. Consequently, a political economic fiat could be credibly smuggled into the scientist's epistemological claims. The efficacy of the orientation made possible by small-scale analysis was reinforced by the monopolistic appropriation of the significant perspective.

The Determination of Identification

I have so far dealt with the first limit of representation, the determination of relevance. The second limit of representation deals with the question, How to identify it? Once the relevant level of observation and analysis has been established, it is necessary to identify the relevant phenomena. Identification consists of two major démarches: detection and recognition. Detection has to do with the definition of the traits or features of a given phenomenon. Recognition consists of the definition of the parameters according to which the detected phenomena will be classified as a distinct element of a system of explanation or of interpretation. The procedure underlying both detection and recognition is *resolution*.

Resolution refers to the quality and details of a given identified phenomenon, be it a social behavior or an image. Resolution is central to photography, remote-sensing technologies, and archaeology. In photography, resolution or resolving power is the capability to image spatial detail. This capability may be referred either to the film or to the lens. The resolution of the film is determined by the size distribution of its silver halide grains (the larger the grains the poorer the resolution). The resolution of the lens is determined by its optical properties and size. The number of line-pairs per millimeter defines the level of resolution (Avery and Berlin 1992: 36). In remote-sensing technologies the most important type of resolution for my purposes here is spatial resolution: "It is the measure of the smallest object that can be resolved by the sensor or the area on the ground represented by each pixel. The finer the resolution, the lower the number" (ERDAS 1997: 15).[6] In archaeology the resolution refers to the homogeneity of events and behavior and their relation to the archaeological record (Gamble 1989: 23).

There are many degrees of resolution, but they are usually reduced to two: coarse-grain and fine-grain resolution. For instance, in photography, high-speed films operate with minimal lighting conditions but only incorporate large-diameter grains and, for that reason, have a lower resolution than low-speed films (Avery and Berlin 1992: 38). In archaeology, a coarse-grained assemblage is one where, at any one location, the correspondence between an event and the archaeological record it generated is poor; conversely, a fine-grained assemblage is one where the materials deposited reflect more precisely the activities that were carried out at those locations and in relation to the immediate environment (Gamble 1989: 23, 24). For my purposes here it is important to note that whenever a system of resolution is constituted by more than one component, the resolution level of the system is determined by the component with the lowest resolution. For instance, in photography the resolution system is constituted by two components, the film and the lens. If the two do not have the same level of resolution, the resolution level of the photography will be determined by the lowest-rated component (Avery and Berlin 1992: 37).

In my view, resolution, like scale and perspective, is at the core of modern science and operates at two different levels: the level of methodology and the level of theory. Both methods and theories are present in the scientific identification of objects to be analyzed, but methods predominate in the process of detection while theories predominate in the process of recognition. The quality of the scientific identification is thus determined by a system of resolution comprised of two components: methods and theories. It is commonly observed that the development of research methods has outpaced the development of theories, particularly in the social sciences. For that reason it is not surprising that it is still common to go back to the nineteenth-century founding fathers to look for theoretical guidance, whereas the research methods and the data-gathering techniques we use today are extremely more sophisticated than those available in the nineteenth century. This means that the resolution level of our methods is higher than the resolution level of our theories and, consequently, that while the quality of scientific detection tends to be fine grain, the quality of scientific

---

6. On the use of remote sensing in cartography, see Monmonier (1985: 89–100). As happens with scale and perspective, the determination of the type and level of resolution is both a technical and a political problem. Concerning the latter and just as an example, high-resolution remote-sensing systems can collect sensitive environmental data that polluters would prefer be kept from an alert and apprehensive public (Monmonier 1985: 185).

recognition tends to be coarse grain. In other words, our detection capabilities by far exceed our recognition capabilities.

Even though this discrepancy is inherent to all social sciences for reasons that deserve to be elucidated, mainstream economics is the one discipline in which the gap between detection resolution levels and recognition resolution levels is widest. Probably for the same reason, it is also the one in which the very existence of the gap has been most fiercely denied. As a result, because the level of resolution of identification is determined by the lowest-rated component, that is, by theory and thus by recognition resolution, mainstream economics operates and intervenes in social life in a coarse-grain mode but manages to legitimize its operation and intervention as if it were of fine-grain resolution quality.

The consequences of economics' interventions in society cannot but betray the excess of this claim. Among such consequences, the most negative can be designated as the *fallacy of exogeneity*. This consists of defining as relations among exogenous entities the internal transformation such entities undergo as their mutual endogeneity develops. Sam Bowles (1998) has exposed this fallacy in his analysis of market preferences. As Bowles (1998: 103) emphasizes, mainstream economics has cherished as one of its fundamental axioms the axiom of exogenous preferences, the celebrated minimalist conception of an undersocialized *homo economicus*, an individual actor with exclusively self-regarding and outcome-based preferences. Against this vision he convincingly argues in favor of the endogeneity of preferences, that is, the extent to which markets affect the preferences that are supposed to impact on them as external forces. In particular, he focuses on a group of preferences that he calls "nice traits"—"these are behaviors which in social interactions confer benefits on others" (1998: 92)—and shows how the markets may block or discourage the development of such traits.

In my view, it is not surprising that the fallacy of exogeneity should occur most specifically in markets. Contacts in markets are ephemeral and impersonal. Given the high resolution of methods, mainstream economics can detect, as individual and separate, entities or factors that keep minimal distances among themselves. The meaning of such distances—that is, the understanding of what might be separating entities or, on the contrary, uniting them—can only be provided by theory and recognition resolution, and since the latter is coarse grain it is unable to discriminate among contexts, networks, interpenetrations, and embeddedness. This explains why the endogeneity of preferences does not emerge clearly and is accordingly discarded.

The Impossibility of Duration

The third limit of representation blocking the road to unceremonial adequacy is that of time and time perception. Once relevance has been determined and the object identified, it is necessary to determine the object's temporal location. All

objects exist in time-spaces, and therefore neither their relevance nor their identification can be considered complete before their time-spaces are determined.
This determination is most difficult because, whereas in scales, resolution, and
perspective the distinction between subject and object operates unproblematically,
in the determination of time-space the subject and the object both exist in time-
space. To solve this difficulty, modern science has tried to neutralize differences
by hypostatizing the most elusive frame: the *hic et nunc*, the here and now, presence and simultaneity. Modern perspective has made possible such simultaneity
between subject and object, between painter and spectator. Through perspective,
simultaneity is attained scientifically, since once the viewer is immobilized by
the logic of the system, the space is totally unified. "Simultaneity in perceiving
a picture ... also requires a synchronization of what is represented; by grasping
the picture spatially as a unit we also assume the depicted events to be simultaneous" (Andrews 1995: 35). Disregarding time differences is thus a condition of
analytical confidence. However operational, this orientation toward presence
and simultaneity is totally arbitrary and vulnerable to the *fallacy of false contemporaneity*. This fallacy consists of assuming that the contemporaneity of a given
event or behavior is equal for all participants in it. When World Bank officials
meet with African peasants, it is assumed that the contemporaneity or coevality
of both groups is generated by the simultaneity of the encounter. The fact that the
peasants' present reality is conceived by them as a past present and by the World
Bank as a present past, however crucial, gets obscured and goes uncontrolled.
In this context there is no room to account for the noncontemporaneity of the
simultaneous or, most importantly, for different ways of being contemporaneous.

Of all the social sciences, mainstream economics is the most prone to navigate
in the fallacy of false contemporaneity. This is linked to the features of determination of relevance and identification characteristic of mainstream economics.
Starting with relevance, the privilege granted to small-scale analysis also means
that orientation and movement are privileged to the detriment of representation
and position. The compression of time is thus particularly drastic; duration cannot
be grasped, and residues become indistinguishable from emergent qualities. To
the extent that residues and emergences are still distinguishable, the orientation
bias of the small scale tends to be overzealous in the identification of obstacles to
movements and consequently to exaggerate the identification of observed features
as residues. While archaeology excels in finding residues in order to explain the
evolution of behavior patterns, mainstream economics excels in finding them
and discarding them as trash. It is ironic that much of what the archaeologists
of the twenty-second century will know about us will be revealed by the trash
we left behind.[7] This should alert us to the situatedness of our findings and the
relevance we ascribe to them. The epistemology of trash cannot be discarded as
easily as the trash to which it refers.

---

7. On this topic, see Deagan (1989).

Turning now to the determination of the degrees of relevance, I would like to show how the use of perspective by mainstream economics prevents the identification of durations, rhythms, sequences, tempos, synchronies, and nonsynchronies. As I mentioned above, what is characteristic of mainstream economics in this regard is the monopolistic appropriation of the significant spectator by the capitalist entrepreneur. The dramatic intensification thus produced of the significant other, smuggled in as the self, has two main consequences: a hyperspatialization of past times and fast-speed interventions.

The lessons from archaeology are particularly pertinent in this regard. The temporal construction of archaeological records can occur in two ways. The first, extremely rare, can be called the *Pompeii mode* (Binford 1981). It occurs whenever it is possible to determine rigorously the date on which different events and objects enter simultaneously into the archaeological record. Hiroshima will be the Pompeii of the archaeologists of the future. The second mode, much more common, can be called the *palimpsest mode*. It refers to situations in which the same archaeological layers consist of objects and residues from very different periods and times not susceptible to exact dating.

The hyperspatialization of past time in mainstream economics consists of an inherent bias in favor of the Pompeii mode, which, given its extreme rarity (e.g., a global oil shock, a world war, a global financial crash, etc.), implies the systematic misrepresentation of social palimpsests as social Pompeiis. This bias derives from the pressure to privilege clearly delimited, highly homogeneous and simultaneous findings.

The second consequence is fast-speed intervention. Highly spatialized simultaneous social fields call for fast-speed interventions, ones that maximize the orientation and movement preferences of the small scale. Fast-speed interventions, like fast-speed films, require very little exposure and can operate in virtually all conditions; however, also like fast-speed films, they have a very low resolution level; they are coarse-grain interventions. Their speed, together with the coarseness of their resolutions, makes such interventions highly intrusive, highly fallible, and highly destructive. The Rapid Rural Appraisals by World Bank economists throughout Africa and Asia are a good example of fast-speed interventions.[8]

These types of intervention, which indeed, irrespective of the names they bear, are much more common than we may imagine, symbolize the destructive side of scientific research. Since the very beginning modern science has assumed a posture that Joseph Schumpeter was to attribute later to capitalism: the capacity for creative destruction. In epistemological terms, such a posture resides in the very idea of scientific revolution conceived of as a radical break with and a departure from all previous knowledges. Gaston Bachelard (1972 [1938]) has formulated it

---

8. On the problem raised by the Rapid Rural Appraisals, see Chambers (1992); Richards (1995); Sapsford and Singer (1998).

better than anyone else with his concept of *rupture épistémologique*. By discarding all alternative knowledges, modern science has revealed itself as a waste maker, a condition that we, the few privileged inhabitants of consumer society, share as well. This is, by the way, another dimension of the above-mentioned epistemology of trash and, indeed, another aspect of a political economy of waste making in modern science. Two questions must be asked in this regard: How much waste do we have to make in order to produce scientific consequences? Who suffers most with the pollution we thereby produce?

Of all the social sciences, mainstream economics has been most involved in fast-speed intervention. For that reason it is most directly confronted with what I will call the *excavation dilemma*. Excavation is the core procedure of archaeological research. It is through excavation that one has access to the archaeological record. The excavation site is a well-delimited area where the systematic search for residues deposited underground takes place, a search that when successful is the only way to identify behavioral patterns and adaptive strategies in our most ancient past. The dilemma, however, is that once the excavation is conducted and the residue is collected, the archaeological work destroys the archaeological site forever, making it impossible to start all over again: once taken out of the deposits into which they were integrated, the collected objects cannot be put back in. The dilemma resides therefore in that an eventual advancement in knowledge necessarily entails a definitive and irreversible destruction: the destruction of the relations among objects and, with it, the elimination of any possible alternative knowledge about them.

This dilemma has been fully acknowledged by archaeologists, and strategies around it have been designed. For instance, according to R. J. Sharer and W. Ashmore, "Since the excavation process itself destroys an archeological site, it should be confined whenever possible to situations in which adequate planning, time and money are available to ensure the maximum useful knowledge about the past is recovered" (1987: 564). Similarly, Robert Dunnell considers that excavation "is expensive, destructive to the record and at best yields great detail about a few widely separate sites. . . . Excavation, once the hallmark of archaeology, will [in the next fifty years] be employed only when all other means of data acquisition have been exhausted" (1989: 65).[9]

In mainstream economics, on the contrary, this dilemma has never been acknowledged, despite the fact that it is dramatically present in most scientific interventions and, above all, in fast-speed interventions. As a consequence, and contrary to what happens in archaeology, no alternative research strategies have been designed. The blindness vis-à-vis this dilemma increases the possibility that the creative destruction of mainstream economics becomes just destructive destruction.

---

9. For a treatment of these methodological issues, see Meneses (2000).

The Determination of Interpretation and Evaluation

The final limit of representation has to do with interpretation and evaluation. It is through interpretation and evaluation that our research objects are integrated into the wider contexts of politics and culture, at which level science-based transformation occurs. Such integration is made possible by establishing links between social action and patterns of political and cultural formation. Because of the nature of the scientific object, archaeology is probably the science in which establishing such a link is the most central task. The term used by some archaeologists to designate such a link is *signature*. In my view this concept has heuristic capabilities far beyond archaeology. In archaeology, signature describes the link between behavior and distinctive patterns of residue formation (Gamble 1989: 22). Signature is thus about authorship, intelligibility, and purposefulness. This means that interpretation and evaluation are premised on the knowledge of the agents involved (authorship), their knowledge practices (intelligibility), and their projects (purposefulness).

This is a domain in which those limits of representation already dealt with converge to make the signature of reality—in the social sciences in general and in mainstream economics in particular—highly deficient. Concerning agents, the smaller the scale of analysis, the stronger the emphasis on orientation and movement. The representation of agents tends to privilege those that move and need orientation, that is, docile bodies. The smaller the scale, the higher the docility of the bodies. The one-point perspective reinforces this effect. The immobility of the spectator's eye, which is particularly intense in mainstream economics, can only guarantee the illusion of reality to the extent that mathematical proportions are strictly kept. The represented bodies have to be kept in a cage, be it an iron or a rubber one. Outside the cages there are no agents, whether friends or enemies. At the most, there are strangers, indifferent bodies. Docile bodies and strangers are thus the two possible categories of agents, hardly a fine-grain resolution of social agency.

The impact of perspective on the representation of knowledge practices is equally constraining. As Gilman (1978: 31) reminds us, the intelligibility of the world made possible by Renaissance perspective was obtained at an exacting price, the immobility of the eye and the blinders necessary to create the single view. This single view is what best characterizes modern science and its epistemological break both with common sense and all other alternative knowledges. The other side of the strength of the single view is its incapacity to recognize alternative views. Social practices are knowledge practices, but they can only be recognized as such to the extent that they are the mirror image of scientific knowledge. Whatever knowledge does not fit the image is discarded as a form of ignorance. The single view, rather than being a natural phenomenon, is the ur-product of the creative destruction of modern science. The epistemological privilege that modern science grants to itself is thus the result of the destruction of all alternative knowledges that could eventually question such privilege. It is, in other words, a product of what I called in a previous chapter *epistemicide*. The destruction of knowledge is not an epistemological artifact without consequences. It involves the destruction of the social practices and the disqualification of the social agents that operate according to such knowledges. In mainstream economics the particular intensity of the significant spectator has imposed an especially arrogant single view, and, as a consequence, the epistemicide has been broader and deeper.

Finally, the purposefulness in social action, that is, the agents' projects, is the domain in which the scientific signature of reality is most deficient. Projects are an anticipation of reality and as such imply a distance from current experience. Anticipation and distance have a specific temporality, the temporality of a bridge among noncontemporaneous courses of action through aspiration and desire. The fallacy of false contemporaneity analyzed above makes such a bridge a useless device, turning aspiration into conformism and desire into the desire of conformism. Moreover, the type of coarse-grain identification characteristic of modern science creates, as I mentioned above, a bias in favor of the proliferation of residues to the detriment of emergent qualities, a condition that leads to disqualifying as retrospective all the emergent qualities that do not fit the qualities of the project legitimated by science. The narrower the project, the wider the retrospective.

The limits of signature, whether of authorship, intelligibility, or purposefulness, are therefore strict, and, of course, the possibilities of interpretation and evaluation cannot exceed them. The result is an imaginative structure consisting of docile bodies and strangers, victims of successive epistemicides, navigating in a sea of residues "swept along into the future that others have laid out for them," like the temporally poor described by Jeremy Rifkin (1987: 166).

This signature of social practice is highly selective, and therefore the link it establishes between agents and patterns of behavior is at best speculative. As I have indicated, at each stage of the signature process, many alternatives are left out: alternative types of agents other than docile bodies and strangers, alternative knowledges other than scientific knowledge, alternative projects other than the project of the significant spectator. Dealing with discarded alternatives means dealing with nonexistent entities. There are at least two ways in which nonexistent entities may "occur" and, accordingly, two ways of trashing alternatives. First, there are alternatives that never occurred because they were prevented from emerging. Second, there are alternatives that did occur, but the types of scale, perspective, resolution, time compression, and signature used by science did not recognize them at all or took them for residues. Only a *sociology of absences* will be able to elucidate the limits of representation at work in each situation. In the first situation, where the alternatives did not occur, we are dealing with silences and unpronounceable aspirations; in the second situation, where the alternatives did occur, we are dealing with silencings, epistemicides, and trashing campaigns.

Possible alternatives are, in epistemological terms, the missing links, the incomplete records, black holes, voids. Modern science suffers in general from *horror vaccui* and whenever possible discards alternatives in order to eliminate epistemological disturbances. The objectivity and rigor of scientific knowledge is indeed a by-product of *horror vaccui*. Mainstream economics is, of all the social sciences, the most haunted by *horror vaccui*. The specific way it has dealt with the limits of relevance, identification, duration, and interpretation and evaluation makes *horror vaccui* look particularly threatening and destabilizing. On the other pole of the spectrum, we could locate archaeology, which, while sharing with all the other social sciences the same *horror vaccui*, takes a much more relaxed attitude toward it, trying to domesticate rather than eliminate it. Glenn Stone, for instance, speaks of negative evidence in these terms: "Negative evidence is a form of data. 'Data' are taken to be observations made of archeological phenomena, as opposed to the phenomena themselves.... Negative evidence refers to the failure to observe a given phenomenon (or lacunae in data sets)" (1981: 42). Stone thus proposes that the interpretation of such absences be an integral part of the archaeological analysis.

As I show in the two following chapters, performing the sociology of absences is a daunting task. It will prevent interpretation and evaluation from being based on very blurred, coarse-grain signatures of social life. Otherwise, rather than signatures, we end up with wandering names looking for docile bodies and strangers.

From the Epistemology of Blindness to the Epistemology of Seeing

An insight into the consequences of the epistemology of blindness is not, in itself, an insight into the epistemology of seeing. Therefore, I will start from the consequences of the epistemology of blindness and move later to delineate an epistemology of seeing.

The consequences of blindness manifest themselves as the misrepresentation of consequences. Such misrepresentation must be analyzed at two levels: the capacity to regulate and the capacity to emancipate. In general, modern science has represented the phenomena in ways that fit its regulatory imagination. In the case of mainstream economics, this seems to be particularly true, all the more so when regulation is disguised as deregulation. The specific social construction of agents, as both docile bodies and strangers, is in fact geared to making social regulation particularly easy. Docile bodies and strangers are about the easiest possible targets of social regulation. One can even say that the undersocialized *homo economicus* looks like a hero when compared either with docile bodies or strangers, the two versions of the oversocialized *homo sociologicus*. However, as I hope to have shown, the oversocialized *homo sociologicus* is not the opposite of the undersocialized *homo economicus*; it is rather its double. The *homo sociologicus* is the *homo economicus* in action.

The facility of regulation is merely apparent for the following two reasons, one having to do with agents and the other with actions. First, I have claimed that the tension between current experience and expectations about the future is one of the most distinctive characteristics of modern regulation. The agents constructed by the mainstream social sciences and particularly by mainstream economics are incapable of living through that tension. Docile bodies experience but do not have expectations, or, which is the same, their expectations mirror their current experiences one to one. On the other hand, strangers are indifferent both to experience and to expectations; they can live both separately and without any tension. In either case, the tension between experience and expectations is lost. Once this occurs, order, which is the point of knowing in knowledge-as-regulation, conflates with colonialism, the point of ignorance in knowledge-as-emancipation. In other words, it becomes the colonialist order, the degree zero of social emancipation. At the degree zero of emancipation, however, modern regulation cannot sustain itself, since it is the tension between regulation and emancipation that keeps it both alive and credible on this side of the abyssal line (see Chapter 4).

The facility of regulation is also only apparent for another reason: because of the types of social actions constructed by science. While modern regulation is based on the tension between experience and expectation, it is also based on the symmetry between action and consequences. Modern science has been entrusted with the task of producing and reproducing this symmetry. Indeed, what makes a given action scientific is the control it exerts over the consequences stemming from it. It is today well established that this symmetry, if ever it existed at all, has vanished forever. Our common experience is rather that of a growing asymmetry between the scientific capacity to act, which has increased exponentially, and the scientific capacity to predict consequences, which at best has stagnated. Accordingly, the actual consequences of a given scientific action tend to be far less scientific than the action itself.

The notion that consequences are therefore excessive in relation to scientific action is probably the manifestation of another fallacy of exogeneity, the exogeneity between actions and consequences. In terms of my previous analysis of the limits of representation particularly as regards mainstream economics, the picture of scientific action that emerges is one constructed by (1) a very small-scale determination of relevance combined with a single-view perspective in which the significant spectator carries a heavy weight, (2) a coarse-grain identification resolution based on an imbalance between detection methods and recognition theories, (3) a gross distortion of sequences and temporalities caused by imposing Pompeii premises on social palimpsests and false contemporaneity on noncontemporaneous (or differently contemporaneous) social layers, and (4) a poor capacity to decipher the signatures of social practices, concerning both agents and knowledge practices and projects. A scientific action thus constructed bears the imprints of its consequences, which the fallacy of exogeneity attributes then to external nonscientific causes. The "less-than-scientific" character of the consequences is inscribed in the very "scientific" character of the actions from which they derive. A scientific form of social regulation that cannot control the consequences of its operation cannot by any standard be considered a reasonable or reliable form of regulation.

Modern science has become the privileged form of knowledge-as-regulation, despite the fact that, as I have shown, the social regulation cautioned by it is neither reliable nor sustainable. On the other hand, modern science has totally deserted the other possibility of knowledge inscribed in the paradigm of modernity: knowledge-as-emancipation. Mainstream economics is also in this case the extreme version of a syndrome that involves modern science as a whole. The solution that mainstream economics has given to the problems confronting the limits of representation converged, as we saw above, on a view of social reality fit to be regulated by a type of order close to colonialism, that is, a type of order that transforms the other into a manipulable and fungible object. This is, as I have suggested, the degree zero, the point of ignorance of knowledge-as-emancipation. In this form of knowledge, as we know, the point of knowing is solidarity, the recognition of the other as an equal and as an equal producer of knowledge. The form of regulation that has come to prevail makes solidarity unthinkable, unnecessary, or even dangerous. After all, docile bodies do not need solidarity, and strangers do not deserve it. *Horror vaccui* has been operative in this regard also; if there are no other types of relevant agents, solidarity, rather than being a missing link, has no place in scientific discourse.

Toward an Epistemology of Seeing

In a period of self-reflexivity, one may ask if the insight into the epistemology of blindness is not in itself a blind insight. Not necessarily, is my answer. The potential for an epistemology of seeing lies in the above-mentioned tension, intrinsic to Western modernity, between knowledge-as-regulation and knowledge-as-emancipation. The latter, as I said, has been totally marginalized by modern science but has not vanished as a virtual alternative. In point of fact, it is present as a produced absence, and this is what makes possible the epistemology of blindness.

An epistemology of seeing is one that inquires into the validity of a form of knowledge whose point of ignorance is colonialism and whose point of knowing is solidarity. Whereas in the hegemonic form of knowledge we know by creating order, the epistemology of seeing poses the question of whether it is possible to know by creating solidarity. Solidarity as a form of knowledge is the recognition of the other both as an equal, whenever difference makes her or him inferior, and as different, whenever equality jeopardizes his or her identity. Having been oversocialized by a form of knowledge that knows by creating order in nature as well as in society, we cannot easily practice or even imagine a form of knowledge that knows by creating solidarity both in nature and in society. To overcome the difficulties, I propose, as a prolegomena to this new form of knowledge, three epistemological démarches: the epistemology of absent knowledges, the epistemology of absent agents, and revisiting representation and its limits.

The Epistemology of Absent Knowledges

When analyzing the limits of interpretation and evaluation in modern science above, I stressed that the sociology of absences is a crucial démarche to identifying the blinders that limit interpretation and evaluation. In the next chapter I dwell in detail on the sociology of absences. The latter, however, must be itself grounded on an epistemology of absences. To this I turn in this section. In order to identify what is missing and why, we must rely on a form of knowledge that does not reduce reality to what exists. I mean a form of knowledge that aspires to an expanded conception of realism that includes suppressed, silenced, or marginalized realities, as well as emergent and imagined realities. Once again, in a self-reflexive turn, we may ask if the knowledge that identifies such absences is not the same that legitimated the conditions that suppressed the possibility of alternative realities now being identified as absences. My answer is twofold. First, we will not know this until the consequences of this knowledge are evaluated in terms of the solidarity they are able to create. Second, there will be always absences that will not be noted. These constitute the void that, rather than being stigmatized by our *horror vaccui*, should be contemplated by our *captatio benevolentiae*.

The epistemology of absent knowledges starts from the premise that social practices are knowledge practices. The practices not based on science, rather than being ignorant practices, are practices of alternative, rival knowledges. There is no a priori reason to favor one form of knowledge against another. Moreover, none of them in isolation can guarantee the emergence and flourishing of solidarity. The objective will be rather the formation of constellations of knowledges geared to create surplus solidarity. This we may call a new common sense.

Modern science built itself against common sense, which it deemed superficial, illusory, and false. Common sense was the name given to all forms of knowledge that did not meet the epistemological criteria that modern science established for itself. The distinction between science and common sense was made possible by what I call the *first epistemological break*. It distinguishes between two forms of knowledge: truthful knowledge and false knowledge or common sense. However opposed, these two epistemic entities entail each other, since one does not exist without the other. They are indeed part of the same cultural constellation that in our time gives signs of closure and exhaustion. In sum, common sense is as modern as modern science itself. The distinction between science and common sense is thus made both by science and by common sense, but it has different meanings in each case. When made by science, it signifies the distinction between objective knowledge and mere opinion or prejudice. When made by common sense, it signifies the distinction between an incomprehensible and prodigious knowledge and an obvious and obviously useful knowledge. It is then far from being a symmetrical distinction. Further, when made from the point of view of science, the distinction has a power that is excessive in relation to the knowledge that makes it possible. Like all specialized and institutionalized knowledge, science has the power to define situations beyond what it knows about them. That is why science can impose, as an absence of prejudice, the prejudice of pretending to have no prejudices.

I propose the concept of a *double epistemological break* as a way out of this stalemate. By the double epistemological break I mean that, once the first epistemological break is accomplished (thus allowing modern science to distinguish itself from common sense), there is another important epistemological act to perform, and that is to break with the first epistemological break so as to transform scientific knowledge into a new common sense. In other words, the new constellation of knowledges must break with the mystified and mystifying conservative common sense, not in order to create a separate, isolated form of superior knowledge but rather to transform itself into a new emancipatory common sense. Knowledge-as-emancipation ought to become an emancipatory common sense itself; beyond the conservative prejudice and the incomprehensible prodigy, I propose a prudent knowledge for a decent life (Santos 2007b). The epistemology of absent knowledges tries to rehabilitate common sense, for it recognizes in this form of knowledge some capacity to enrich our relationship with the world. Commonsense knowledge, it is true, tends to be a mystified and mystifying knowledge, but, in spite of that, and despite its conservative quality, it does have a utopian and liberating dimension that may be enhanced by its dialogue with modern science. This utopian, liberating quality may be seen to flourish in many different characteristics of our commonsense knowledge.

Common sense collapses cause and intention; it rests on a worldview based on action and on the principle of individual creativity and responsibility. Common sense is practical and pragmatic. It reproduces knowledge drawn from the life trajectories and experiences of a given social group and asserts that this link to group experience renders it reliable and reassuring. Common sense is self-evident and transparent. It mistrusts the opacity of technological objectives and the esoteric nature of knowledge, arguing for the principle of equal access to discourse, to cognitive and linguistic competence. Common sense is superficial because it disdains structures that cannot be consciously apprehended, but for the same reason, it is expert at capturing the horizontal complexity of conscious relations, both among people and between people and things. Commonsense knowledge is nondisciplinary and nonmethodical. It is not the product of a practice expressly devised to create it; it reproduces itself spontaneously in the daily happenings of life. Common sense favors actions that do not provoke significant ruptures in reality. Common sense is rhetorical and metaphorical; it does not teach but persuades or convinces. Finally, common sense, in John Dewey's words, fuses use with enjoyment, the emotional with the intellectual and the practical.

These characteristics of common sense hold the virtue of foreknowledge. Left to itself, common sense is conservative. However, once transformed by knowledge-as-emancipation, it may be the source of a new rationality—a rationality comprised of multiple rationalities. For this configuration of knowledge to occur, it is necessary to duplicate the epistemological break. In modern science, the epistemological break symbolizes the qualitative leap from commonsense knowledge to scientific knowledge; in knowledge-as-emancipation, the most important leap is that from scientific knowledge to commonsense knowledge. Modern science taught us how to depart from existing conservative common sense. This is inherently positive but insufficient. Knowledge-as-emancipation will teach us how to build up a new, emancipatory common sense. Only thus will it be a clear knowledge that fulfills Ludwig Wittgenstein's dictum: "Whatever allows itself to be said, allows itself to be said clearly" (1973: §4.116). Only thus will it be a transparent science that does justice to Nietzsche's belief that "all commerce among men aims at letting each one read upon the other's soul, common language being the sound expression of that common soul" (1971: 99). By becoming common sense, knowledge-as-emancipation does not shun the knowledge that produces technology, but it does believe that, as knowledge must translate into self-knowledge, so technological development must translate into life-wisdom. Wisdom points out the markers of prudence to our scientific adventure, prudence being the acknowledgment and control of insecurity. Just as Descartes, at the threshold of modern science, acknowledged doubt rather than suffered it, we too, at the threshold of the new constellation of knowledges, should acknowledge insecurity rather than suffer it.

The emancipatory common sense is a discriminating common sense (or unequally common, if you like), constructed so as to be appropriated in a privileged way by oppressed, marginalized, or excluded social groups and actually strengthened by their emancipatory practice. This leads me to the second démarche toward an epistemology of seeing.

The Epistemology of Absent Agents

As we saw above, mainstream social sciences and especially mainstream economics have reduced the variety and wealth of social agency to two types of individuals, docile bodies and strangers, neither of which is fit to sustain a social practice based on knowledge-as-emancipation. The monopoly of subjectivity that they have conquered explains why, as I mention in the introduction, at the beginning of the twenty-first century the crisis of social regulation, rather than prompting the opportunity for a new surge of emancipatory ideas, forces, and energies, feeds on the symmetrical crisis of social emancipation.

As a result, the invention of a new emancipatory common sense based on a constellation of knowledges oriented toward solidarity must be complemented by the invention of individual and collective subjectivities able and willing to base their social practice on that constellation of knowledges. The epistemology of absent agents is thus a quest for destabilizing subjectivities, which, as I explained in Chapter 2, are subjectivities that rebel against conformist, routinized, repetitive social practices and are energized by experimenting with liminality, that is, with eccentric or marginal forms of sociability. Against a political economy of representation that proliferates residues, the epistemology of seeing proliferates emergent qualities grounded in different knowledge practices and lets them compete in the social fields, thus converting them into fields of social experimentation. The epistemology of blindness has promoted a construction of social practice based on the distinction between structure and agency. The apparent equality between the two terms of the distinction has been used to transform structure into a more or less iron-cage determination of agency. The result is the mediocrity of either docile bodies or strangers. The epistemology of seeing, on the contrary, will promote a construction of social practice based both on the distinction between conformist action and rebellious action and on the preference for the latter, characterized by me in Chapter 2 as *action-with*-clinamen.

The decentering of conformism and thus of docile bodies through rebellious action must be complemented by the decentering of indifference and the strangers it breeds. Though this may be controversial because it evokes Carl Schmitt's political theory, I think that against indifference, which is the hallmark of political liberalism, it is necessary to revive the friend/foe dichotomy. There is nothing authoritarian or antidemocratic in the dichotomy of friends and enemies, as long as the dichotomy is established by nonauthoritarian democratic means. Probably the most dilemmatic difficulty confronting critical theory today lies in the blurring of the distinction between friend and enemy. Critical theory has always presupposed a question—which side are we on?—and has been elaborated to provide answers to it. It is not surprising that assorted kinds of neopositivists have managed to delegitimize this question by trashing the normative claims that underlie it. Their hegemony in society at large targets the youth in particular, for whom it has become more and more difficult to identify alternative positions in relation to which it would be imperative to take sides. There is an increasing opacity to the enemy. Without enemies there is no need for friends. If there are no friends, there is no purpose in exercising solidarity.[10]

Revisiting the Limits of Representation

The limits of representation, which, as we saw, are particularly drastic in mainstream economics, derive their credibility from the scientific actions they make possible. By confronting these actions with their human consequences and

---

10. At its deepest roots, the crisis of the welfare state stems much less from a largely manipulated fiscal crisis than from the ideological inculcation of vanishing friends and their replacement by a sea of strangers, at best indifferent, at worst potentially dangerous.

appealing to alternative knowledges and agencies, the epistemology of absences questions the limits of representation of mainstream science. They thereby lose their monopoly of representation and are forced into a discursive competition with other knowledges and alternative forms of representation. Whenever this competition breaks out, the convincing power of the arguments can be derived not from logical principles but rather from pragmatic considerations, from the "last things" called for by W. James, that is, from the human consequences of alternative courses of action. Such competition, however, is not a competition about consequences. It is rather a competition about the linkages between consequences and the political economy of the analytical procedures that may sustain them in real life.

The epistemology of absences, both of absent knowledges and absent agents, enables us to revisit the limits of representation in mainstream social sciences: the limits of the representation of relevance, identification, duration, and interpretation and evaluation. Seen from the perspective of the constellation of emancipatory knowledges propounded here, they lose their dilemmatic nature. I will limit myself to indicate, in a brief note, some of the possible ways they can be overcome.

Concerning the limits of relevance, I propose two démarches: the *trans-scale* and the *curious perspective*. Since different knowledges privilege different scales of phenomena, the epistemology of seeing I am proposing here suggests that we learn how to translate among different scales. The limits of a representation on a given scale become more visible when we compare that representation with a representation on a different scale. Trans-scaling is thus a démarche that permits us to contrast limits of representation with the purpose of elucidating what is at stake in the choice among alternative criteria of relevance.

Trans-scaling presupposes a certain unlearning of current criteria of relevance determination. It invites us to consult social reality through different cognitive maps operating at different scales. The learning process consists of raising the consciousness of the limits—contrasting representation with orientation, position with movement—without getting paralyzed by it. A higher consciousness of limits is at the core of the kind of prudent knowledge I am proposing here, a form of knowledge that teaches us how to keep consequences under the control and within the sight of the actions that cause them.

Curious perspective is the search for a different angle from which the proportions and hierarchies established by normal perspective are destabilized and their claim of a natural, orderly, and faithful representation of reality accordingly subverted. In the seventeenth century, artists and art teachers began to criticize Alberti's proper perspective for being fully manifest and comprehensible. They then began to explore "how rules of perspective can magnify or diminish, multiply or distort the image" (Gilman 1978: 34). Their idea was that the illusion of reality was something not to take too seriously but rather to take as play and to play with. According to Gilman, "The world implied in the writings of later perspectivists is shifting, multifaceted, and ambiguous" (1978: 34). In my view, this curious perspective, both playful and unsettling, must be brought into play in the determination of degrees of scientific relevance. The criteria of relevance based on a supposedly mathematical and rigidly established perspective tend to be reified by their recurrent and unproblematic use. Reification means, in this context, the conversion of the illusion of reality into a compressed, credibly faithful reproduction of reality. On the contrary, the curious perspective reconstitutes the creative processes at the core of modern sciences, a production of illusions that, rather than imitating society, reinvents it.

Concerning the limits of identification, the epistemology of seeing invites us to shift our priorities from an excessive focus on what we already know too well, that is, methods-based detection, to a focus on what we know less, and indeed are knowing less and less, that is, theory-based recognition. Since this discrepancy is exclusive of modern science, the recourse to alternative knowledges will unsettle the resolution levels to which we are used. It is necessary to raise our demands to an ever finer-grain resolution only possible in the context of constellations of knowledges.

Another procedure to aim at is *multicontrasted resolution*. In remote-sensing photography, resolution is highly dependent upon target contrast. "A high-contrast target is one in which there is a large density difference between bright and dark areas" (Avery and Berlin 1992: 37). The improvement of the resolution level with which we analyze society may require the invention of highly contrasted social practices, even when the surface of such practices, as with the earth itself, is deceptively low contrast. The generation of high contrast and multicontrasted resolution is made possible by the trans-scaling and curious perspectives that are characteristic of cognitive processes inside constellations of knowledges called for by the epistemology of seeing.

Concerning the limits of the representation of duration, the procedures already indicated will help to discern that social reality is a more or less sedimented terrain, a geological construct made of different regulations composing different layers, all of them in force together but never in a uniform fashion, all of them in the same moment but always as a momentary convergence of different temporal projections. Reinhart Koselleck's conception of "the contemporaneity of the noncontemporaneous" (1985), which is derived from Martin Heidegger and Hans-Georg Gadamer, may be useful to capture the complexity and unevenness of social, political, legal, or epistemological copresence. Although in general all social sciences bring together in a given time-space different temporalities and spatialities, some social sciences—which we may call performative—emphasize the contemporaneity, that is to say, the uniqueness, of the encounter, while others—which we may call self-reflexive—emphasize the noncontemporaneous roots of what is brought together. Of all the social sciences, mainstream economics is the most performative. It reproduces the forms of power and knowledge that best suit its horizons of expectations. Whatever is brought into the analytical field (issues, social groups, cognitive maps, normative orderings) is somehow pulled by the roots, so as to become coeval with whatever else is brought together into analysis. The momentary and pragmatic suspension of noncontemporaneity apparently favors the elimination of hierarchies among social temporalities, thereby suggesting that there are different ways of being contemporaneous.

Like trans-scale, curious perspective, and multicontrasted resolution, *intertemporality* turns the question of duration into an extremely complex one. Probably for this reason, this is the question that mainstream economics has most caricatured by means of the kind of compression of time and flattening out of sequences in which it excels.

Finally, concerning the limits of interpretation and evaluation, the epistemology of seeing, by drawing our attention to both absent knowledges and absent agents, provides the key to understanding that the richer the parameters that define authorship, intelligibility, and purposefulness, the greater the need to submit narrowly defined technological applications of knowledge to political and ethical contestations. In the process we will move from a paradigm based on the technical application of science to a paradigm based on the edifying application of prudent knowledges, knowledges that transform research objects into solidary subjects and urge knowledge-based actions to navigate prudently within the sight of consequences.

Conclusion

Enlightened by the epistemologies of both blindness and seeing, it is possible to envisage the emergence of a prudent knowledge for a decent life, a knowledge that, by going from colonialism to solidarity, opens the space for a new kind of order, a noncolonialist or decolonial order bounding current experiences and expectations about the future, actions, and consequences. The ultimate aspiration is all too human, an aspiration that I call *advanced normality*: the aspiration to live in normal times whose normality does not derive from the naturalization of abnormality. The epistemological break proposed here is premised upon a break with the type of reason that lies at the core of hegemonic Western thinking, which in the next chapter I call *lazy reason*. To this I now turn.

CHAPTER 6

A Critique of Lazy Reason

Against the Waste of Experience and Toward the
Sociology of Absences and the Sociology of Emergences

Introduction

In this chapter, I engage in a critique of the hegemonic Western model of rationality, which after Gottfried Wilhelm Leibniz (1985 [1710]) I call *lazy reason*,[1] and propose the prolegomena to another model that I designate *subaltern cosmopolitan reason*, the reason that grounds the epistemologies of the South. The proposal is based on three procedures: the sociology of absences, the sociology of emergences, and the work of intercultural translation. The first two are dealt with in this chapter; the third will be addressed in Chapter 8.

I start from three hypotheses. First, the understanding of the world by far exceeds the West's understanding of the world. The Western understanding of the world is as important as it is partial. Second, the understanding of the world and the way it creates and legitimates social power have a lot to do with conceptions of time and temporality. Third, the most fundamental characteristic of the Western conception of rationality is that, on the one hand, it contracts the present and, on the other, it expands the future. The contraction of the present, brought about by a peculiar conception of totality, turns the present into a fleeting instant, entrenched between the past and the future.[2] By the same token,

---

1. In Chapter 4, I showed how laziness slides into predation. Here, I concentrate on the hegemonic model or form of Western modernity. As I mentioned in Chapter 3, throughout the historical trajectory of Western modernity there were several different models or versions, some dominant, some suppressed or marginalized. In the end, the disputes among them were decided on the basis of their adequacy for the historical objectives of capitalism and colonialism.

2. Paradoxically, and as I demonstrated in Chapter 2, the contraction of the present may occur through the infinite repetition of undifferentiated fleeting instants or moments. Once the bridges to the past and future are cut off, the instant can hardly be distinguished from the eternal, a kind of secular eternity.

the linear conception of time and the planning of history permit the future to expand infinitely. The larger the future, the more exhilarating the expectations vis-à-vis the experiences of today. In the 1940s, Ernst Bloch (1995: 313) wondered in perplexity, If we only live in the present, why is it so transient? The same perplexity lies at the core of this chapter.

I propose a subaltern cosmopolitan rationality that, in this phase of transition, must trace an inverse trajectory: to expand the present and contract the future. Only thus will it be possible to create the time-space needed to know and valorize the inexhaustible social experience under way in our world today. In other words, only thus will it be possible to avoid the massive waste of experience we suffer today. To expand the present, I propose a sociology of absences; to contract the future, a sociology of emergences. Because we live in a situation of bifurcation, as Ilya Prigogine (1997) and Immanuel Wallerstein (1999) show, the immense diversity of social experiences that these procedures reveal cannot be adequately accounted for by a general theory. Instead of a general theory, I propose a theory or procedure of translation, capable of creating mutual intelligibility among possible and available experiences without compromising their identity. This is the topic of Chapter 8.

In the preface to his *Theodicy*, Leibniz (1985 [1710]) mentions the perplexity that the sophism that the ancients called "indolent" or "lazy reason" had always caused: if the future is necessary and what must happen happens regardless of what we do, it is preferable to do nothing, to care for nothing, and merely to enjoy the pleasure of the instant. This form of reason is lazy because it gives up thinking in the face of necessity and fatalism, of which Leibniz distinguishes three kinds: *fatum Mahometanum*, *fatum Stoicum*, and *fatum Christianum*.

The laziness of the reason critiqued in this chapter occurs in four different ways: *impotent reason*, a reason that does not exert itself because it thinks it can do nothing against necessity conceived of as external to itself; *arrogant reason*, a kind of reason that feels no need to exert itself because it imagines itself as unconditionally free and therefore free from the need to prove its own freedom; *metonymic reason*, a kind of reason that claims to be the only form of rationality and therefore does not exert itself to discover other kinds of rationality or, if it does, it only does so to turn them into raw material;[3] and *proleptic reason*, a kind of reason that does not exert itself in thinking the future because it believes it knows all about the future and conceives of it as a linear, automatic, and infinite overcoming of the present.[4]

Under its various forms, lazy reason underlies the hegemonic knowledge, whether philosophical or scientific, produced in the West in the past two hundred

---

3. I use metonymy, a figure of speech related to synecdoche, to signify the part for the whole.

4. I use prolepsis, a common narrative device of anticipation, to signify knowledge of the future in the present.

years. The consolidation of the liberal state in Europe and North America, the Industrial Revolution and capitalist development, colonialism, and imperialism constituted the social and political context in which lazy reason evolved. Partial exceptions, like romanticism and Marxism, were neither strong nor different enough to become an alternative to lazy reason. Thus, lazy reason created the framework for the large philosophical and epistemological debates of the last two centuries and indeed presided over them. For example, impotent and arrogant reason shaped the debate between determinism and free will and later that between structuralism and existentialism. No wonder these debates were intellectually lazy. Metonymic reason, in turn, took over old debates, such as the debate between holism and atomism, and originated others, such as the *Methodenstreit* between nomothetic and ideographic sciences and between explanation and understanding. In the 1960s, metonymic reason led the debate over the two cultures launched by C. P. Snow (1959, 1964). In this debate, metonymic reason still considered itself as a totality, although a less monolithic one. The debate deepened in the 1980s and 1990s with feminist epistemology, cultural studies, and the social studies of science. By analyzing the heterogeneity of the practices and narratives of science, the new epistemologies further pulverized that totality and turned the two cultures into an unstable plurality of cultures. Metonymic reason, however, continued to lead the debates, even when the topic of multiculturalism was introduced and science started to see itself as multicultural. Other knowledges, neither scientific nor philosophical, particularly non-Western knowledges, have remained largely outside the debate until today.

As regards proleptic reason, the way it conceived of the planning of history dominated the debates on dialectical idealism and materialism and on historicism and pragmatism. From the 1980s onward, proleptic reason was contested mainly by the theories of complexity and chaos. Proleptic reason, based on the linear idea of progress, was confronted with the ideas of entropy and disaster, although no alternative has yet emerged from such confrontation.

The debate generated by the "two cultures" and the various third cultures thereby emerging—the social sciences (Lepenies 1988) or the popularization of science (Brockman 1995)[5]—did not affect the domination of lazy reason under any of its four forms: impotent reason (determinism, realism), arrogant reason (free will, constructivism), metonymic reason (*pars pro toto*, dualism), and proleptic reason (evolutionism, progress). There was therefore no restructuring of knowledge. Nor could there be, to my mind, because the indolence of reason manifests itself particularly in the way it resists changes of routine and transforms hegemonic interests into true knowledge. As I see it, in order for deep changes to occur in the structure of knowledge, it is necessary to change the form of reason

---

5. João Arriscado Nunes (1998/1999), addressing contemporary debates on this subject, illustrates how the new configuration of knowledges has to go beyond the "two cultures."

that presides over knowledge and its structure. In a word, lazy reason must be confronted.

In this chapter, I confront lazy reason in two of its forms: as metonymic and proleptic reason.[6] The two other forms have elicited more debate (on determinism or free will, realism or constructivism).

The Critique of Metonymic Reason

Metonymic reason is obsessed by the idea of totality in the form of order. There is no understanding or action without reference to a whole, the whole having absolute primacy over each one of its parts. There is therefore only one logic ruling the behavior of both the whole and each of its parts. There is thus homogeneity between the whole and its parts, the latter having no independent existence outside their relation to the whole. Possible variations in the movement of the parts do not affect the whole and are viewed as particularities. The most complete form of totality according to metonymic reason is dichotomy, because it combines symmetry and hierarchy most elegantly. The symmetry of parts is always a horizontal relation that conceals a vertical relation. It is so because, contrary to what is proclaimed by metonymic reason, the whole is less, not more, than the sum of its parts. The whole is indeed a part turned into a term of reference for the others. This is why all dichotomies sanctioned by metonymic reason contain a hierarchy: scientific culture/literary culture, scientific knowledge/traditional knowledge, man/woman, culture/nature, civilized/primitive, capital/labor, white/black, North/South, West/East, and so on and so forth.

All this is well known today and needs no further elaboration. I focus on its consequences.[7] The two main ones are the following. First, because nothing exists outside the totality that is or deserves to be intelligible, metonymic reason

---

6. For a first critique of lazy reason, see my quest for a new common sense in Santos (1995, 2004).

7. In the West, the critique of both metonymic reason and proleptic reason has a long tradition. To restrict myself to the modern era, it can be traced back to romanticism and appears under different guises in Kierkegaard, Nietzsche, phenomenology, existentialism, and pragmatism. The laziness of the debates lies in that the latter do not question, in general, the peculiar disembeddedness of knowledge as something set apart from and higher than the rest of reality. This is why, in my view, the most eloquent critiques come from those for whom metonymic and proleptic reason are not just an intellectual artifact or game but the generating ideology behind a brutal system of domination, that is, the colonial system. Gandhi (1929/1932, 1938, 1951, 1960, 1972), Fanon (1961), Martí (1963–1966), Nkrumah (1965b), and Memmi (1965) are some of the outstanding voices. In the colonial context, lazy reason lies behind what Quijano (2000), Dussel (2001), Mignolo (2000), and I (2010) call the "coloniality of power," a form of power that, rather than ending with the end of colonialism, has continued to be prevalent in postcolonial societies.

claims to be exclusive, complete, and universal, even though it is merely one of the logics of rationality that exist in the world and prevails only in the strata of the world comprised by Western modernity. Metonymic reason cannot accept that the understanding of the world is much larger than the Western understanding of the world. Second, according to metonymic reason, none of the parts can be conceived outside its relation with the totality. The North is not intelligible outside its relation to the South, just as traditional knowledge is not intelligible outside its relation to scientific knowledge or woman outside her relation to man. It is inconceivable that each of the parts may have its own life beyond the dichotomous relation, let alone be a different totality or part of a different totality. The understanding of the world promoted by metonymic reason is therefore not only partial but also very selective. Western modernity, controlled by metonymic reason, has a limited understanding not only of the world but also of itself.

Before I deal with the processes that sustain understanding and police its limits, I must explain how such a limited rationality ended up having such primacy in the last two hundred years. Metonymic reason is, together with proleptic reason, the response of the West, intent on the capitalist and colonialist transformation of the world, to its own cultural and philosophical marginality vis-à-vis the East. As Karl Jaspers and others have shown, the West constituted itself as a deserter from a founding matrix—the East (Jaspers 1951, 1976; Needham 1954–2008; Marramao 1995: 160).[8] This founding matrix is truly comprehensive because it encompasses a multiplicity of worlds (both earthly and nonearthly) and a multiplicity of times (past, present, future, cyclical, linear, simultaneous). Its holism has no need to claim totality or to subordinate parts to itself. It is an antidichotomic matrix because it does not have to control or police limits. On the contrary, the West, aware of its own eccentricity vis-à-vis this matrix, takes from it only what can encourage the expansion of capitalism and colonialism. Thus, the multiplicity of worlds is reduced to the earthly world and the multiplicity of times to linear time.

---

8. Jaspers considers the period between 800 and 200 BC as an "axial age," a period that lay down "the foundations upon which humanity still subsists today" (1951: 98). In this period, most of "the extraordinary events" that shaped humankind as we know it occurred in the East—in China, India, Persia, and Palestine. The West is represented by Greece, and as we know today, Greek classic antiquity owes much to its African and Eastern roots (Bernal 1987). See also Schluchter (1979). Joseph Needham, with his gigantic magnum opus *Science and Civilization in China*, represents the most ambitious attempt at confronting Western modernity with the limits of its metonymic reason. Before Jaspers and Needham, Schopenhauer was the Western philosopher who best understood the limits of the tradition he came from and felt the need to reach out to Eastern philosophies. Given the arrogance of lazy reason, this was probably one of the reasons why his classes were deserted by students who experienced much greater comfort in the well-policed boundaries of the philosophical system of Hegel, who was teaching at the same time at the same university, the University of Berlin.

Two processes preside over such a reduction. The reduction of the multiplicity of worlds to the earthly world comes about by means of secularization and laicization as analyzed by Max Weber (1958, 1963, 1968), Reinhart Koselleck (1985), and Giacomo Marramao (1995), among many others. The reduction of the multiplicity of times to linear time is achieved by replacing the rich soteriological idea that used to link the multiplicity of worlds (salvation, redemption, reincarnation, or metempsychosis) with such concepts as progress and revolution upon which proleptic reason came to be based. Based on this truncated conception of Eastern wholeness, the West took possession of the world in a productive way and turned the East into a stagnated, unproductive center. The angst caused by metonymic reason led Weber to counter the unproductive seduction of the East with the disenchantment of the Western world.

As Marramao (1995: 160) notes, the supremacy of the West, created from the margins, never turned culturally into an alternative centrality vis-à-vis the East. For this reason, the power of Western metonymic reason always exceeded the power of its foundation. This power is, however, undermined by a weakness that paradoxically grounds the very reason for its power in the world. This dialectic between power and weakness ended up translating itself into the parallel development of two opposite urges: (1) *Wille zur Macht* from Hobbes to Nietzsche, Carl Schmitt, and Nazism/fascism, and (2) the *Wille zur Ohnmacht* from Jean-Jacques Rousseau to Hans Kelsen, liberal democracy, and the rule of law. In each of these urges, totality is nonetheless present. Totality, because it is truncated, must ignore what it cannot contain and impose its primacy on its parts; further, the parts, to be maintained under its control, must be homogenized as parts. This explains why the totality in the weak power version of *Wille zur Ohnmacht* is allowed to impose itself powerfully and even violently on the non-Western world. Liberal democracy and the rule of law are imposed worldwide through the conditionalities of the International Monetary Fund and World Bank and, whenever convenient, through military intervention. Because it is unsure as to its foundations, metonymic reason does not insert itself in the world through argumentation and rhetoric. It does not explain itself; rather, it imposes itself by the efficacy of its imposition. Such efficacy manifests itself in a twofold way: by productive thought and by legislative thought. Instead of the reasonableness of argumentation, it resorts to productivity and coercion.

Grounded on metonymic reason, the transformation of the world cannot be based on or accompanied by an adequate understanding of the world. Inadequacy, in this case, meant violence, appropriation, destruction, and silencing for all those who, outside the West, were subjected to metonymic reason; in the West, it meant alienation, malaise, and uneasiness. Walter Benjamin (1972: 213–219) was witness to this uneasiness when he showed the paradox that has dominated life in the West ever since: the fact that the wealth of events translates itself into the poverty, rather than wealth, of our experience.[9] This paradox came to coexist with another: the fact that the vertigo of change frequently turns itself into a feeling of stagnation.

Today, and thanks to the rise of so many social movements grounding their activism, at least in part, on non-Western premises, it begins to be apparent that metonymic reason has contracted the world in the very process of expanding it according to its (metonymic reason's) own rules, thus causing the crisis of the idea of progress and hence the crisis of the idea of totality that grounds it. The abbreviated version of the world became possible because of a conception of the present time that reduces it to the fleeting instant between what no longer is and what is not yet. The brevity of the gaze conceals the abbreviation of the gazed upon. As such, what is considered contemporaneous is an extremely reduced part of the simultaneous. The gaze that sees a person plowing the land only sees in that person the premodern peasant. Koselleck (1985) acknowledges this much when he speaks of the contemporaneity of the noncontemporaneous (see Chapter 5). But Koselleck does not address the fact that in such asymmetry a hierarchy is hidden, namely, the superiority of those who establish the time that determines contemporaneity. The contraction of the present thus conceals most of the inexhaustible richness of the social experiences in the world. Benjamin identified the problem but not its causes. The poverty of experience is the expression not of a lack but rather of an arrogance: the arrogance to refuse to see, let alone valorize, the experience around us only because it is outside the reason that allows us to identify and valorize it. The critique of metonymic reason is therefore a necessary condition to recuperate the wasted experience. At stake is the expansion of the world through the expansion and diversification of the present. Only by means of a new time-space will it be possible to identify and valorize the inexhaustible richness of the world and the present. But this new time-space presupposes another kind of reason. Up until now, the aspiration of the expansion of the present was formulated by literary creators alone. One example among many is Franz Kafka's parable about the precariousness of modern man stuck between two formidable adversaries, the past and the future:

He has two antagonists: the first pushes him from behind, from his birth. The second blocks the road in front of him. He struggles with both. Actually the

---

9. Benjamin (1972: 214) thought that World War I had deprived the world of the social relations through which the older generations passed their wisdom on to the younger generations. A new world had emerged after the war, he argued, a world dominated by the development of technology, a world in which even education and learning ceased to translate themselves into experience. A new poverty has thus emerged, a lack of experience in the midst of hectic transformation, a new form of barbarism (1972: 215). He concludes his essay in this way: "We have become poor. Piece by piece we have relinquished the heritage of humankind, often deposited in a pawnshop for a hundredth of its value, only to get back the small change of the 'current balance'" [*Aktuelle*] (1972: 219, my translation).

first supports him in his struggle with the second, for the first wants to push him forward; and in the same way the second supports him in his struggle with the first; for the second of course is trying to force him back. But this is only theoretically so. For it is not only the two protagonists who are there, but he himself as well, and who really knows his intentions? However that may be, he has a dream that some time in an unguarded moment—it would require too, one must admit, a night darker than anything that has ever yet been—he will spring out of the fighting line and be promoted, on account of his experience of such warfare, as judge over his struggling antagonists. (1960: 298–299)

The expansion of the present lies in two procedures that question metonymic reason in its foundations. The first consists of the proliferation of totalities. The question is not to amplify the totality propounded by metonymic reason but rather to make it coexist with other totalities. The second consists of showing that any totality is made of heterogeneity and that the parts that comprise it have a life outside it. That is to say, their being part of a certain totality is always precarious, whether because the parts, besides being parts, always hold, at least in latency, the status of totality or because parts migrate from one totality to another. What I propose is a procedure denied by metonymic reason: to think the terms of the dichotomies regardless of the power articulations and relations that bring them together as a first step in freeing them of such relations and to reveal other alternative relations that have been obscured by hegemonic dichotomies—to conceive of the South as if there were no North, to conceive of woman as if there were no man, to conceive of the slave as if there were no master. Deepening the understanding of the power relations and radicalizing the struggles against them imply imagining the dominated as beings free from domination. The Afro-descendent activist, researcher, or artist who turns her activism, research, or art into a struggle against racism deepens her struggle by imagining what her citizen activism, research, or art might be if there were no racism, if she did not have to start from a specific identification that was imposed on her and oppresses her. The assumption underlying this procedure is that metonymic reason was not entirely successful when it dragged these entities into the dichotomies, because components or fragments not socialized by the order of totality were left out. These components or fragments have been wandering outside the totality like meteorites hovering in the space of order, not susceptible to being perceived and controlled by order until social movements become strong enough to bring them home and turn them into empowering resources for the struggles against invisibility and domination.

In this transition phase, in which metonymic reason, although much discredited, is still dominant, the enlargement of the world and the expansion of the present must begin by a procedure that I designate the *sociology of absences*. This consists of an inquiry that aims to explain that what does not exist is in fact actively produced as nonexistent, that is, as a noncredible alternative to what exists. From a positivistic point of view—which best embodies the metonymic reason in the realm of the social sciences—the empirical object of the sociology of absences is deemed impossible. The sociology of absences is a transgressive sociology because it violates the positivistic principle that consists of reducing reality to what exists and to what can be analyzed with the methodological and analytical instruments of the conventional social sciences. From the point of view of subaltern cosmopolitan reason, reality cannot be reduced to what exists because what exists is only the visible part of reality that modern abyssal thinking defines as being on this side of the line and within whose confines it elaborates its theories (see Chapter 4). Beyond that line, on the other side of the line, there is nothing of relevance, and it can therefore be easily dismissed or made invisible or irrelevant. In sum, whatever is on the other side of the line is produced as nonexistent. The sociology of absences is the inquiry into the workings of this abyssal line in our time.

The objective of the sociology of absences is to transform impossible into possible objects, absent into present objects. It does so by focusing on the social experience that has not been fully colonized by metonymic reason. What is there in the South that escapes the North/South dichotomy? What is there in traditional medicine that escapes the modern medicine/traditional medicine dichotomy? What is there in woman apart from her relation with man? Is it possible to see the subaltern regardless of the relation of subalternity? Could it be possible that the countries considered less developed are more developed in fields that escape the hegemonic terms of the dichotomy? In sum, is conceiving in an empowering way only possible on the other side of the line?

There is no single, univocal way of not existing. The logics and processes through which metonymic reason produces the nonexistence of what does not fit its totality and linear time are various. Nonexistence is produced whenever a certain entity is disqualified and rendered invisible, unintelligible, or irreversibly discardable. What unites the different logics of the production of nonexistence is that they are all manifestations of the same rational monoculture.

Five Modes of Production of Nonexistence

I distinguish five logics or modes of production of nonexistence.

The first derives from the *monoculture of knowledge and the rigor of knowledge*. It is the most powerful mode of production of nonexistence. It consists of turning modern science and high culture into the sole criteria of truth and aesthetic quality, respectively. The complicity that unites the "two cultures" resides in the fact that both claim to be, each in its own field, exclusive canons of knowledge production or artistic creation. All that is not recognized or legitimated by the canon is declared nonexistent. Nonexistence appears in this case in the form of ignorance or lack of culture.

The second logic resides in the *monoculture of linear time*, the idea that history has a unique and well-known meaning and direction. This meaning and direction have been formulated in different ways in the last two hundred years: as progress, revolution, modernization, development, and globalization. Common to all these formulations is the idea that time is linear and that ahead of time proceed the core countries of the world-system and, along with them, the dominant knowledges, institutions, and forms of sociability. This logic produces nonexistence by describing as backward whatever is asymmetrical vis-à-vis whatever is declared forward. It is according to this logic that Western modernity produces the non-contemporaneity of the contemporaneous and that the idea of simultaneity, by concealing the asymmetries of the historical times that converge into it, fails to recognize the possible different ways of being contemporaneous. As I argue in Chapter 5, the encounter between the African peasant and the officer of the World Bank on his field trip illustrates this condition. In this case, nonexistence assumes the form of residuum, which in turn has assumed many designations for the past two hundred years, the first being the primitive, closely followed by the traditional, the premodern, the simple, the obsolete, and the underdeveloped.

The third logic is the logic of social classification, based on the *monoculture of the naturalization of differences*. It consists of distributing populations according to categories that naturalize hierarchies. Racial and sexual classifications are the most salient manifestations of this logic. Contrary to what happens in the relation between capital and labor, naturalized social classification is based on attributes that negate the intentionality of social hierarchy. The relation of domination is the consequence, rather than the cause, of this hierarchy, and it may even be considered an obligation of whoever is classified as superior (for example, the white man's burden in his civilizing mission). Although the two forms of classification (race and sex) are decisive for the relation between capital and labor to stabilize and spread globally, racial classification was the one most deeply reconstructed by capitalism, as Immanuel Wallerstein and Etienne Balibar (1991) and most incisively Aimé Césaire (1955), Anibal Quijano (2000), Walter Mignolo (2000), Enrique Dussel (2001), Nelson Maldonado-Torres (2004), and Ramón Grosfoguel (2007), among others, have shown. According to this logic, nonexistence is produced under the form of an insuperable, because natural, inferiority. Inferior people are insuperably inferior and cannot therefore constitute a credible alternative to superior people.

The fourth logic of production of nonexistence is the *monoculture of logic of the dominant scale*. According to this logic, the scale adopted as primordial determines the irrelevance of all other possible scales. In Western modernity, the dominant scale appears under two different forms: the universal and the global. Universalism is the scale of the entities or realities that prevail regardless of specific contexts. For that reason, they take precedence over all other realities that depend on contexts and are therefore considered particular or vernacular. Globalization is the scale that since the 1980s has acquired unprecedented relevance in various social fields. It is the scale that privileges entities or realities that widen their scope to the whole globe, thus earning the prerogative to designate rival entities as local. According to this logic, nonexistence is produced under the form of the particular and the local.[10] The entities or realities defined as particular or local are captured in scales that render them incapable of being credible alternatives to what exists globally and universally.

Finally, the fifth logic of nonexistence is the *monoculture of the capitalist logic of productivity.* According to this logic, capitalist economic growth is an unquestionably rational objective. As such, the criterion of productivity that best serves this objective is unquestionable as well. This criterion applies both to nature and to human labor. Productive nature is nature at its maximum fertility in a given production cycle, not nature at its maximum fertility in a series of cycles of production that allow for its vital restorative cycles to be preserved. Similarly, productive labor is labor that maximizes generating profit likewise in a given production cycle; unpaid labor, plus all the other productive activities that guarantee the reproduction and flourishing of personal, family, and community life are not considered productive labor. According to this logic, nonexistence is produced in the form of nonproductiveness. Applied to nature, nonproductiveness is sterility; applied to labor it is sloth, indolence, or lack of qualification.

There are thus five principal social forms of nonexistence produced by metonymic reason: the ignorant, the residual, the inferior, the local, and the nonproductive. They are social forms of nonexistence because the realities to which they give shape are present only as obstacles vis-à-vis the realities deemed relevant, be they scientific, advanced, superior, global, or productive realities. They are therefore disqualified parts of homogeneous totalities that, as such, merely confirm what exists and precisely as it exists. They are what exists under irretrievably disqualified forms of existing.

The social production of these absences results in the subtraction of the world and the contraction of the present, hence in the waste of experience. The sociology of absences aims to identify the scope of this subtraction and contraction so that the experiences produced as absent may be liberated from those relations of production and thereby made present. To be made present means for them to be considered alternatives to hegemonic experience, to have their credibility discussed and argued for and their relations taken as an object of political dispute.[11] The sociology of absences aims thus to create a want and turn the lack of social experience into a waste of social experience. It thereby creates the conditions to

---

10. On the modes of the production of globalization, see Santos (1995, 2002a).

11. The sociology of absences does not wish to abolish the categories of ignorant, residual, inferior, local, or unproductive. Instead it wishes that they stop being ascribed according to one criterion alone, one that does not tolerate being questioned by any other alternative criterion. This monopoly is not the result of a work of argumentative reasonableness. Rather it results from an imposition that is justified only by the supremacy of whoever has the power to impose.

enlarge the field of credible experiences in this world and time, thus contributing to enlarging the world and expanding the present. The enlargement of the world occurs not only because the field of credible experiences is widened but also because the possibilities of social experimentation in the future are increased. The expansion of the present occurs as what is considered contemporaneous is augmented, as present time is laid out so that all experiences and practices occurring simultaneously may eventually be considered contemporaneous, even if each in its own way.

How does the sociology of absences work? It starts from two inquiries. The first one inquires about the reasons why such a strange and exclusive conception of totality could have acquired such primacy in the past two hundred years. The second inquiry aims to identify the ways to confront and overcome such a conception of totality as well as the metonymic reason that sustains it. The first inquiry was dealt with in Chapter 4. In this chapter, I focus on the second inquiry.

Homogeneous and exclusive totalities and the metonymic reason that sustains them can be superseded by confronting each one of the modes of production of absence mentioned above. Because metonymic reason shaped conventional social science, the sociology of absences cannot but be transgressive and, as such, is bound to be discredited. Nonconformity with such discredit and the fact that social movements have been acting out the sociology of absences with no need to name it[12] make it possible for the sociology of absences not to remain an absent sociology.

Five Ecologies against the Waste of Experience

The sociology of absences operates by substituting ecologies for monocultures. By ecology I mean sustainable diversity based on complex relationality. It is therefore a normative concept based on the following ideas. First, the value of diversity, complexity, and relationality must be recognized: nothing exists by itself; something or someone exists because something else or someone else exists. Second, complex and relational diversity means that the criteria that define diversity are themselves diverse. Third, the choice among them is a political one, and in order to respect diversity, it must be based on radical and intercultural democratic processes. Fourth, the robustness of the relations depends on nurturing diversity and exerting vigilance against monocultural temptations that come from both within and without, even if the distinction between what is within and what is without is intrinsically problematic. Corresponding to the five monocultures I distinguish five ecologies.

---

12. *Epistemologies of the South: Reinventing Social Emancipation* (forthcoming) treats the ways the social movements are acting out the sociology of absences and the sociology of emergences dealt with below.

The Ecology of Knowledges

The first logic, the logic of the monoculture of scientific knowledge and rigor, must be confronted with the identification of other knowledges and criteria of rigor and validity that operate credibly in social practices pronounced nonexistent by metonymic reason. I dedicate the next chapter to the ecology of knowledges.

The Ecology of Temporalities

The second logic, the logic of the monoculture of linear time, must be confronted with the idea that linear time is only one among many conceptions of time and that, if we take the world as our unit of analysis, it is not even the most commonly adopted. The predominance of linear time is the result not of its primacy as a temporal conception but of the primacy of Western modernity that embraced it as its own. Linear time was adopted by Western modernity through the secularization of Judeo-Christian eschatology, but it never erased, not even in the West, other conceptions of time such as circular time, cyclic time, glacial time, the doctrine of the eternal return, and still others that are not adequately grasped by the images of the arrow or circle. That is why the subjectivity or identity of a given person or social group at a given moment is a temporal palimpsest. It is made up of a constellation of different times and temporalities, some modern, some not, some ancient, some recent, some slow, some fast, and they are all activated in different ways in different contexts or situations. More than any other, the social movements of the indigenous and Afro-descendent peoples are witness to such temporal constellations.

Moreover, the different cultures and the practices they ground have different temporal codes and different intertemporal relations: the relation between past, present, and future; how early and late, short and long term, life cycle, and urgency are defined; how life rhythms, sequences, synchronies, and diachronies are accepted. Thus, different cultures create different temporal communities: some control time, some live inside time; some are monochronous, some are polychronous; some concentrate on the necessary minimal time to carry out certain activities, some on the necessary activities to fill up time; some privilege schedule-time, some event-time, thus underscoring different conceptions of punctuality; some valorize continuity, some discontinuity; for some time is reversible, for some it is irreversible; some include themselves in a linear progression, some in a nonlinear progression. The silent language of cultures is above all a temporal language.

The need to take into account these different conceptions of time derives from the fact, pointed out by Koselleck (1985) and Marramao (1995), that societies understand power according to the conceptions of temporality they hold. The most resistant relations of domination are those based on hierarchies among temporalities. Such hierarchies are constitutive of the world-system. They reduce much social experience to the condition of residuum. Experiences become residual because they are contemporary in ways that are not recognizable by the dominant temporality: linear time. They become disqualified, suppressed, or rendered unintelligible for being ruled by temporalities that are not included in the temporal canon of Western capitalist modernity.

The sociology of absences starts off from the idea that societies are made up of different times and temporalities and that different cultures generate different temporal rules. It aims to free social practices from their status as residuum, devolving to them their own temporality and thus the possibility of autonomous development. Once such temporalities are retrieved and acknowledged, the practices and sociabilities under them become intelligible and credible objects of political argumentation and debate. Let me offer an example: once liberated from linear time and devolved to its own temporality, the activity of the African or Asian peasant stops being residual and becomes contemporaneous with the activity of the high-tech farmer in the United States or the activity of the World Bank executive. By the same token, the presence or relevance of the ancestors in one's life in different cultures ceases to be an anachronistic manifestation of primitive religion or magic to become another way of experiencing contemporaneity.

The diversity of the temporal codes of the movements and organizations that fight in different parts of the world against the exclusion and discrimination produced or increased by neoliberal globalization encourages development of a different kind of temporal literacy, which I would call *intertemporality*. To build coalitions and organize collective actions among movements or organizations with different temporal rules is no easy task. Movements and organizations based on a monochronic, discontinuous schedule-time, conceived of as a controlled resource with linear progression, have difficulty understanding the political and organizational behavior of movements and organizations constituted in the light of a continuous, polychronous event-time, conceived of as a time that controls us and progresses in a nonlinear mode, and vice versa. Such difficulties can be overcome only through mutual learning, that is to say, through intertemporal literacy.

The Ecology of Recognition

The third logic of the production of absences is the logic of social classification. Although in all logics of production of absence the disqualification of practices goes hand in hand with the disqualification of agents, it is here that the disqualification affects mainly the agents and only secondarily the social experiences of which they are the protagonists. The coloniality of modern Western capitalist power consists of collapsing difference and inequality while claiming the privilege to ascertain who is equal or different. The sociology of absences confronts coloniality by looking for a new articulation between the principles of equality and difference, thus allowing for the possibility of equal differences—an ecology of differences comprised of mutual recognition. It does so by submitting hierarchy and difference to critical inquiry. It consists of deconstructing both difference (to what extent is difference a product of hierarchy?) and hierarchy (to what extent is hierarchy a product of difference?). The differences that remain when hierarchy vanishes become a powerful denunciation of the differences that hierarchy reclaims in order not to vanish.

Feminist, indigenous, and Afro-descendent movements have been at the forefront of the struggle for an ecology of recognition. The ecology of recognition becomes crucial as the social and cultural diversity of collective subjects fighting for social emancipation increases. The identification of various forms of oppression and domination, as well as the multiple forms and scales of the struggles against them (local, national, and transnational), confers a new visibility to the different and unequal dynamics of global capitalism, dynamics capable of generating different contradictions and struggles.

It has thus become obvious that the naturalization of differences is the consequence of ontological coloniality, meaning the coloniality of being (what counts as being, including human being), which in turn founds the coloniality of knowledge and power. That is why the Eurocentric conceptions of social regulation and social emancipation do not allow for the creation of circles of reciprocity comprehensive enough to found the new demand for balance between the principles of equality and of recognition of difference. It was on the basis of the denunciation of such denial of reciprocity that feminist, postcolonial, peasant, indigenous, ethnic, gay, and lesbian struggles fought for the creation of subaltern and insurgent public spheres. The struggle for the recognition of differences opened up new resistance repertoires geared up by the idea of strong citizenship, thus becoming a privileged forum for articulating economic with social and cultural redistribution. By enlarging the reciprocity circle—the circle of equal differences—the ecology of recognition creates a new exigency of reciprocal intelligibility. The multidimensionality of forms of domination and oppression gives rise to forms of resistance and struggle mobilizing different collective actors, vocabularies, and resources not always mutually intelligible, which may pose serious limitations to the redefinition of the political space. Hence, the need for intercultural translation as analyzed in Chapter 8.

The Ecology of Trans-scale

The sociology of absences confronts the fourth logic, the logic of global scale, by recuperating what in the local is not the result of hegemonic globalization and what in it may potentially lead to counterhegemonic globalization. There is no globalization without localization. What today is viewed as local is very often a localized globalism, that is, the result of the specific impact of hegemonic global-ization on a given social entity or condition. The localization of the German language is the result of the globalization of the English language, as much as the local conditions on the shores of Africa where toxic waste has been dumped is a product of neoliberal globalization. And long before globalization, colonialism was (and still is) the greatest producer of local conditions. By deglobalizing the local vis-à-vis hegemonic globalization, the sociology of absences also explores the possibility of counterhegemonic globalization based on alternative local/global articulations. This inquiry involves elucidating what in the local is not reduc-ible to the impact of hegemonic globalization and what in it is or may become a seed of resistance against the unequal power relations produced or favored by such globalization.

The sociology of absences in this domain requires resorting to what in the previ-ous chapter I called the curious perspective, the use of cartographic imagination, whether to see in each scale of representation not only what it reveals but also what it conceals or to deal with cognitive maps that operate simultaneously with different scales, thus allowing for the identification of new local/global articula-tions. Many of the emancipatory movements of the last decades started out by being local struggles fought against the social exclusion imposed or increased by neoliberal globalization. Only more recently have these movements developed local/global articulations in order to create counterhegemonic forms of global-ization. The World Social Forum is a vital (albeit embryonic) manifestation of this process (Santos 2006b).

As concerns the privilege granted to universalism as a measure for everything else considered not universal, the sociology of absences proceeds by excavating the long historical process of Western modernity. It interpellates those specific understandings of social and natural reality (social justice, success, dignity, respect, wealth, solidarity, community, cosmic order and harmony, spirituality, nature, well-being, East/West divide, and so forth) that gradually came to be invoked in very different contexts and always for the same purpose of ground-ing and legitimizing structures of power and domination. In so doing it also illuminates other specific understandings that, on the contrary, were in the same process confined to a given context and the range of their validity closely and often violently policed. In the latter case, the sociology of absences inquires into the possible presence of such understandings in the different regions of the globe that were subjected to European historical colonialism and capitalism (Europe included) and into the ways in which they may be present as empowering resources in the struggles of oppressed social groups against capitalism and colonialism. To the extent that their presence can be detected, they can be used as building blocks for the construction from below of self-consciously partial universalisms whose main function consists of showing the specific kind of particularism that is at work in Western-centric abstract universalism.

The Ecology of Productivities

Finally, in the domain of the fifth logic, the logic of capitalistic productivity, the sociology of absences consists of recuperating and valorizing alternative systems of production, popular economic organizations, workers' cooperatives, self-managed enterprises, solidarity economy, conceptions of property beyond private individual property, and so on, which have been hidden or discredited by the monopoly of capitalist productivity. I have in mind movements of peasants and indigenous peoples fighting for land and land property, urban movements fighting for housing, indigenous movements fighting for their historical territories and the natural resources meanwhile therein discovered, movements of lower castes in India fighting to protect their lands and forests, movements in favor of ecological sustainability, popular economic movements, movements against the privatization of water or welfare services, and movements against development megaprojects (such as, for instance, large dams forcing the displacement of many thousands of people). This is perhaps the most controversial domain of the sociology of absences, for it directly confronts the paradigms of development, of infinite economic growth, of the primacy of private property, and of the accumulation that sustains global capitalism. It shows that the specific concept of productivity that came to dominate was historically chosen not because of its intrinsic or innate value but rather because it served better than any other an economic paradigm based on greed and possessive individualism and not on cooperation and shared social prosperity.

The scale of these initiatives varies widely. There are microinitiatives carried out by marginalized social groups, both in the global South and in the global North, trying to gain some control over their lives and communities; there are proposals for economic and legal coordination at the international level aimed at guaranteeing the respect for basic patterns of decent work and environmental protection; there are initiatives for the control of global financial capital; there are efforts to build regional economies based on principles of cooperation and solidarity.

These alternative conceptions and practices of production and productivity share two main ideas. First, rather than embodying coherent projects of economic systems alternative to global capitalism, such practices are mainly the localized efforts of communities and workers to create pockets of solidary production, often with the support of networks and coalitions of transnational progressive advocacy. These alternatives are much less grand than those of twentieth-century socialism, and their underlying theories are less ambitious than the faith in the historical inevitability of socialism that dominated classical Marxism. As a matter of fact, the viability of such alternatives largely depends, at least in the short and medium run, on their capacity to survive under global capitalism. Aware as they are of their proper context, they nonetheless point to alternative forms of economic organization and give them credibility. The second idea is that these initiatives share a comprehensive conception of "economy" in which they include such objectives as democratic participation; environmental sustainability; social, sexual, racial, ethnic, and cultural equity; and transnational solidarity.

In this domain, the sociology of absences enlarges the spectrum of social reality through experimentation on realistic economic alternatives for building a more just society. By upholding organizational and political values opposed to global capitalism, economic alternatives broaden the principle of citizenship beyond the narrow limit defined by political liberalism and keep alive the promise of eliminating the current cohabitation of low-intensity democracy and economic despotism.

In each of the five domains, the objective of the sociology of absences is to disclose the diversity and multiplicity of social practices and confer credit to them in opposition to the exclusive credibility of hegemonic practices. The idea of multiplicity and nondestructive relations is suggested by the concept of ecology: the ecology of knowledges, the ecology of temporalities, the ecology of recognition, the ecology of trans-scale, and the ecology of productivities. Common to all these ecologies is the idea that reality cannot be reduced to what exists. It amounts to an ample version of realism that includes the realities rendered absent by silence, suppression, and marginalization—in a word, realities that are actively produced as nonexistent.

In conclusion, the exercise of the sociology of absences is counterfactual and takes place by confronting conventional scientific common sense. To be carried out it demands sociological imagination. I distinguish two types of imagination that, although they belong together, can be analyzed separately. The epistemological imagination allows for the recognition of different knowledges, perspectives and scales of identification and relevance, and analysis and evaluation of practices; the democratic imagination allows for the recognition of different practices and social agents. Both the epistemological and the democratic imagination have a deconstructive and a reconstructive dimension.

The Critique of Proleptic Reason

Proleptic reason is the face of lazy reason when the future is conceived of from the vantage point of the monoculture of linear time. The monoculture of linear time expanded the future enormously at the same time that it contracted the present, as we saw when metonymic reason was analyzed. Because the meaning and direction of history reside in progress and progress is unbounded, the future is infinite. Because it is projected according to an irreversible direction, however, the future is, as Benjamin clearly saw, an empty and homogeneous time.[13] The future is as abundant as it is empty; the future only exists, as Marramao (1995: 126) says, to become past. A future thus conceived need not be an object of thought, and in this consists the laziness of proleptic reason.

Whereas the objective of the critique of metonymic reason is to expand the present, the objective of the critique of proleptic reason is to contract the future. To contract the future means to make it scarce and hence the object of care. The future has no other meaning or direction but what results from such care. To contract the future consists of eliminating, or at least diminishing, the discrepancy between the conceptions of the future of society and the future of individuals. Unlike the future of society, the future of individuals is limited by the duration of their lives—or reincarnated lives, in cultures where metempsychosis is a matter of faith. In either case, the limited character of the future and the fact that it depends on the management and care of individuals makes it possible for the future to be reckoned with as an intrinsic component of the present. In other words, the contraction of the future contributes to the expansion of the present.

Whereas the expansion of the present is obtained through the sociology of absences, the contraction of the future is obtained through the sociology of emergences. The sociology of emergences consists of replacing the emptiness of the future (according to linear time) with a future of plural and concrete possibilities, utopian and realist at one and the same time and constructed in the present by means of activities of care.

To call attention to emergences is by nature speculative and requires some philosophical elaboration. The profound meaning of emergences can be observed in the most diverse cultural and philosophical traditions. As far as Western philosophy is concerned, emergences have been a marginal topic, one dealt with most eloquently by Ernst Bloch. The concept that rules the sociology of emergences is the concept of Not Yet (*Noch Nicht*) advanced by Bloch (1995). Bloch takes issue with the fact that Western philosophy has been dominated by the concepts of All (*Alles*) and Nothing (*Nichts*), in which everything seems to be contained in latency but from whence nothing new can emerge. Western philosophy is therefore a static philosophy. For Bloch (1995: 241), the possible is the most uncertain and the most ignored concept in Western philosophy. Yet only the possible permits the inexhaustible wealth of the world to be revealed. Besides All and Nothing, Bloch introduces two new concepts: Not (*Nicht*) and Not Yet (*Noch Nicht*). The Not is the lack of something and the expression of the will to surmount that lack. The Not is thus distinguished from the Nothing (Bloch 1995: 306). To say no is to say yes to something

---

13. "The concept of historical progress of mankind cannot be sundered from the concept of its progression through a homogeneous, empty time" (Benjamin 1968: 261). And he counterposes, "The soothsayers who found from time to time what it had in store certainly did not experience time as either homogeneous or empty" (1968: 264).

different. The Not Yet is the more complex category because it expresses what exists as mere tendency, a movement that is latent in the very process of manifesting itself. The Not Yet is the way in which the future is inscribed in the present. It is not an indeterminate or infinite future but rather a concrete possibility and a capacity that neither exists in a vacuum nor is completely predetermined. Indeed, it actively redetermines all it touches, thus questioning the determinations that exist at a given moment. Subjectively, the Not Yet is anticipatory consciousness, a form of consciousness that, although extremely important in people's lives, was completely neglected by Freud (Bloch 1995: 286–315). Objectively, the Not Yet is, on the one hand, capacity (potency) and, on the other, possibility (potentiality). Possibility has both a dimension of darkness insofar as it originates in the lived moment and is never fully visible to itself and a component of uncertainty that derives from a double want: (1) the fact that the conditions that render possibility concrete are only partially known, and (2) the fact that the conditions only exist partially. For Bloch, it is crucial to distinguish between these two wants: it is possible to know relatively well conditions that exist only very partially, and vice versa.

The Not Yet inscribes in the present a possibility that is uncertain but never neutral; it could be the possibility of utopia or salvation (*Heil*) or the possibility of catastrophe or damnation (*Unheil*). Such uncertainty brings an element of chance or danger to every change. This uncertainty is what, to my mind, expands the present while at the same time contracting the future and rendering it the object of care. At every moment, there is a limited horizon of possibilities, and that is why it is important not to waste the unique opportunity of a specific change offered by the present: carpe diem (seize the day). In accord with Marxism, which he in any case interpreted in a very creative way, Bloch thinks that the succession of horizons leads or tends toward a final state. I believe, however, that disagreeing with Bloch in this regard is irrelevant. Bloch's emphasis stresses the critique of the mechanical conception of matter, on the one hand, and the affirmation of our capacity to think and act productively upon the world, on the other. Considering the three modal categories of existence—reality, necessity, and possibility (Bloch 1995: 244, 245)—lazy reason focused on the first two and neglected the third one entirely. According to Bloch, Hegel is mainly responsible for the fact that the possible has been neglected by philosophy. For Hegel, because the possible is contained in the real, either it does not exist or is not different from what exists; in any case, it need not be thought of. Reality and necessity have no need of possibility to account for the present or future. Modern science was the privileged vehicle of this conception. For this reason, Bloch (1995: 246) invites us to focus on the modal category that has been most neglected by modern science: possibility. To be human is to have a lot ahead of you.

Possibility is the world's engine. Its moments are want (the manifestation of something lacking), tendency (process and meaning), and latency (what goes ahead in the process). Want is the realm of the Not, tendency the realm of the

Not Yet, and latency the unstable double realm of Nothing and All, for latency can end up either in frustration or hope.

The sociology of emergences is the inquiry into the alternatives that are contained in the horizon of concrete possibilities. Whereas the sociology of absences amplifies the present by adding to the existing reality what was subtracted from it by metonymic reason, the sociology of emergences enlarges the present by adding to the existing reality the realistic possibilities and future expectations it contains. In the latter case, the enlargement of the present implies the contraction of the future inasmuch as the Not Yet, far from being an empty and infinite future, is a concrete future, forever uncertain and in danger. As Bloch (1995: 311) says, next to every hope there is always a coffin. Caring for the future is imperative because it is impossible to armor hope against frustration, the advent against nihilism, redemption against disaster—in a word, because it is impossible to have hope without the coffin.

The sociology of emergences consists of undertaking a symbolic enlargement of knowledges, practices, and agents in order to identify therein the tendencies of the future (the Not Yet) upon which it is possible to intervene so as to maximize the probability of hope vis-à-vis the probability of frustration. Such symbolic enlargement is actually a form of sociological imagination with a double aim: on the one hand, to know better the conditions of the possibility of hope; on the other, to define principles of action to promote the fulfillment of those conditions.

The sociology of emergences acts both on possibilities (potentiality) and on capacities (potency). The Not Yet has meaning (as possibility) but no direction for it can end either in hope or disaster. Therefore, the sociology of emergences replaces the idea of determination with the idea of care. The axiology of progress is likewise replaced by the axiology of care. Whereas in the sociology of absences the axiology of care is exerted vis-à-vis already available alternatives, in the sociology of emergences the axiology of care is exerted vis-à-vis possible alternatives. Because of this ethical and political dimension, neither the sociology of absences nor the sociology of emergences is a conventional sociology. But they are not conventional for another reason: their objectivity depends on the quality of their subjective dimension. The subjective element of the sociology of absences is insurgent or subaltern cosmopolitan consciousness and nonconformism before the waste of experience. The subjective element of the sociology of emergences is anticipatory consciousness and nonconformism before a want whose fulfillment is within the horizon of possibilities. As Bloch (1995: 306) says, the fundamental concepts are not reachable without a theory of the emotions. The Not, the Nothing, and the All shed light on such basic emotions as hunger and want, despair and annihilation, and trust and redemption. One way or another, these emotions are present in the nonconformism that moves both the sociology of absences and the sociology of emergences. Both try to encourage collective actions of social change that always require emotional intelligence, be it enthusiasm or outrage. At its best, the emotional effects establish a balance between the two currents of personality, what I call the *cold current* and *warm current*. The cold current is the current concerned with knowledge of the obstacles and the conditions of change. The warm current is the current of the will to action, change, and overcoming the obstacles. The cold current prevents us from being deceived; if we know the conditions, we are not so easily conditioned. The warm current, on the other hand, prevents us from becoming easily paralyzed or disillusioned; the will to challenge sustains the challenge of the will. The balance of the two currents is difficult, whereas the imbalance, beyond a certain limit, is a factor of perversion. Excessive concern about being deceived risks changing the conditions into unsurpassable obstacles, thus leading to immobility and conformism. On the other hand, excessive concern about being disillusioned results in total aversion to all that is not visible or palpable, thus, by the same token, leading as well to immobility and conformism.

Whereas the sociology of absences acts in the field of social experiences, the sociology of emergences acts in the field of social expectations. As I mentioned earlier, the discrepancy between experiences and expectations is constitutive of Western modernity. Through the concept of progress, proleptic reason polarized this discrepancy so much that any effective linkage between experiences and expectations disappeared; no matter how wretched current experiences may be, they do not preclude the illusion of exhilarating expectations. The sociology of emergences conceives of the discrepancy between experiences and expectations without resorting to the idea of progress and seeing it rather as concrete and measured. Whereas proleptic reason largely expanded the expectations, thus reducing the field of experiences and contracting the present, the sociology of emergences aims at a more balanced relation between experience and expectation, which, under the present circumstances, implies dilating the present and shrinking the future. The question is not to minimize expectations but rather to radicalize the expectations based on real possibilities and capacities, here and now.[14]

Modernist expectations were grandiose in the abstract, falsely infinite and universal. As such, they have justified death, destruction, and disaster in the name of redemption ever to come. Against this disguised form of nihilism, which is as empty as the triumphalism of hegemonic forces, the sociology of emergences offers a new semantics of expectations. The expectations legitimated by the sociology of emergences are both contextual, because gauged by concrete possibilities, and radical, because, in the ambit of those possibilities and capacities, they claim a strong fulfillment that protects them, though never completely, from frustration and perversion. In such expectations resides the reinvention of social emancipation, or rather emancipations.

---

14. In Chapter 2, I argued for a new type of subjectivity that is able and willing to carry out the new articulation between current experiences and expectations about the future called for by the sociology of absences and the sociology of emergences.

By enlarging the present and contracting the future, the sociology of absences and the sociology of emergences contribute, each in its own way, to decelerating the present, giving it a denser, more substantive content than the fleeting instant between the past and the future to which proleptic reason condemned it. Instead of a final stage, they propose a constant ethical vigilance over the unfolding of possibilities, aided by such basic emotions as negative wonder provoking anxiety and positive wonder feeding hope.

The symbolic enlargement brought about by the sociology of emergences aims to analyze in a given practice, experience, or form of knowledge what in it exists as tendency or possibility. It acts both upon possibilities and capacities. It identifies signals, clues, or traces of future possibilities in whatever exists. Here too the point is to investigate an absence, but while in the sociology of absences what is actively produced as nonexistent is available here and now, albeit silenced, marginalized, or disqualified, in the sociology of emergences the absence is an absence of a future possibility as yet not identified and of a capacity not yet fully formed to carry it out. To fight the neglect suffered by the dimensions of society that appear as signs or clues, the sociology of emergences pays them "excessive" attention. Herein resides symbolic amplification. This is a prospective inquiry operating according to two procedures: to render less partial our knowledge of the conditions of the possible and to render less partial the conditions of the possible. The former procedure aims to understand better what in the researched realities turns them into clues or signs; the latter aims to strengthen such clues or signs. As the kind of knowledge underlying the sociology of absences, the one underlying the sociology of emergences is an argumentative kind of knowledge that, rather than demonstrating, persuades, rather than wishing to be rational, wishes to be reasonable. It is a kind of knowledge that evolves to the extent that it credibly identifies emergent knowledges or practices.

Conclusion

While the sociology of absences expands the realm of social experiences already available, the sociology of emergences expands the realm of possible social experiences. The two sociologies are deeply interrelated; the ampler the credible reality, the wider the field of credible clues and possible, concrete futures. The greater the multiplicity and diversity of the available and possible experiences (knowledges and agents), the more expanded the present and the more con-tracted the future. As increasingly revealed by social movements, diversity and multiplicity may give rise to intense social conflicts in such diverse domains as biodiversity (between biotechnology and intellectual property rights, on one side, and indigenous or traditional knowledges, on the other); medicine (between modern and traditional medicine); justice (between indigenous jurisdiction or traditional authorities and modern, national jurisdictions); agriculture (between agroindustrial and peasant technologies); environmental and other social risks (between technical and lay knowledge, between experts and common citizens, between corporations and communities); democracy (between liberal democracy and participatory or communitarian democracy, between individual rights and collective rights); religion (between secularism and state religion, between anthropomorphic gods and biomorphic gods, between institutionalized religiosity and spirituality); and development (between nature and mother earth, between megaprojects and peoples' livelihoods, between development imperatives and *buen vivir* or *sumak kawsay*, between alternative development and alternatives to development, between private property and individual titling of land, on one side, and communal or collective property and communal ancestral land, on the other).

CHAPTER 7

Ecologies of Knowledges

S TARTING FROM DIFFERENT positions, both postabyssal thinking and knowledge as emancipation (going from a point of ignorance called colonialism to a point of knowing called solidarity), as well as subaltern cosmopolitan reason, converge in the quest for epistemologies of the South based on learning from the anti-imperial South. The epistemologies of the South are built on two main procedures: ecologies of knowledges and intercultural translation. In this chapter I focus on ecologies of knowledges.

As I mentioned in the previous chapter, the ecology of knowledges confronts the logic of the monoculture of scientific knowledge and rigor by identifying other knowledges and criteria of rigor and validity that operate credibly in social practices pronounced nonexistent by metonymic reason. The central idea of the sociology of absences in this regard is that there is no ignorance or knowledge in general. All ignorance is ignorant of a certain kind of knowledge, and all knowledge is the overcoming of a particular ignorance. Learning a certain kind of knowledge may imply forgetting other kinds or indeed ignoring them. In other words, from the standpoint of the ecology of knowledges, ignorance is not necessarily an earlier stage or starting point. It may well be a point of arrival, the outcome of the forgetfulness or unlearning implied in a learning process. Thus, at every step of the ecology of knowledges, it is crucial to ask if what one is learning is valid and if what one already knows should be forgotten or unlearned and why. Ignorance is disqualifying when what one is learning is more valuable than what one is forgetting. Otherwise, ignorance amounts to Nicholas of Cusa's learned ignorance, which I analyzed in Chapter 3. The utopia of interknowledge consists of learning new and less familiar knowledges without necessarily having to forget the old ones and one's own. Such is the idea of prudence underlying the ecology of knowledges. The ecology of knowledges assumes that all relational practices involving human beings and human beings and nature entail more than one kind of knowledge, thus more than one kind of ignorance as well. From this epistemological standpoint, modern capitalist societies are characterized as favoring practices in which the forms of scientific knowledge prevail. This means that only ignorance of such forms is considered disqualifying. As a result of this privileged status granted to scientific practices, the latter's interventions in human and natural reality are favored. Any mistakes or disasters they may provoke are socially accepted and seen as an inevitable cost to be overcome or compensated for by new scientific practices.

Since scientific knowledge is not distributed in a socially equitable way, its interventions in the real world tend to serve the social groups having more access to such knowledge. Ultimately, social injustice is based on cognitive injustice. However, the struggle for cognitive justice will never succeed if it is based only on the idea of a more equitable distribution of scientific knowledge. Beyond the fact that such a distribution is impossible under the conditions of global capitalism, scientific knowledge has intrinsic limits concerning the kind of interventions it furthers in the real world.

In the ecology of knowledges, finding credibility for nonscientific knowledges does not entail discrediting scientific knowledge. It implies, rather, using it in a broader context of dialogue with other knowledges. In present conditions, such use of scientific knowledge is counterhegemonic. The point is, on the one hand, to explore alternative conceptions that are internal to scientific knowledge and have become visible through the pluralist epistemologies of various scientific practices (feminist epistemologies in particular) and, on the other, to advance interdependence among the scientific knowledges produced by Western modernity and other, nonscientific knowledges.

This principle of incompleteness of all knowledges is the precondition for epistemological dialogues and debates among different knowledges. What each knowledge contributes to such a dialogue is the way in which it leads a certain practice to overcome a certain ignorance. Confrontation and dialogue among knowledges are confrontation and dialogue among the different processes through which practices that are ignorant in different ways turn into practices that are also knowledgeable in different ways. All knowledges have internal and external limits. The internal limits concern restrictions regarding the kinds of intervention in the world they render possible. Such restrictions result from what is not yet known, but may eventually be known, by a given kind of knowledge. The external limits concern what is not and cannot be known by a given kind of knowledge. From the point of view of the ecology of knowledges, the external limits imply acknowledging alternative interventions only rendered possible by other kinds of knowledge. One of the specific features of hegemonic knowledge is that they only recognize internal limits. The counterhegemonic use of modern science constitutes a parallel and simultaneous exploration of its internal and external limits. For this reason, the counterhegemonic use of science cannot be restricted to science alone. It only makes sense within the ecology of knowledges.

Such an ecology of knowledges permits not only the overcoming of the mono-culture of scientific knowledge but also the idea that nonscientific knowledges are alternatives to scientific knowledge. The idea of alternatives presupposes the idea of normalcy, and the latter the idea of norm, and so, nothing further being specified, the designation of something as an alternative carries a latent connotation of subalternity. If we take biomedicine and traditional African medicine as an example, it makes no sense to consider the latter, predominant by far in Africa, as an alternative to the former. The important thing is to identify the contexts and the practices in which each operates and the way they conceive of health and sickness and overcome ignorance (as undiagnosed illness) through applied knowledge (as cure or healing).[1]

The ecology of knowledges does not entail accepting relativism. On the contrary, from the point of view of a pragmatics of social emancipation, relativism, considered as an absence of criteria of hierarchy among knowledges, is an unsustainable position, for it renders impossible any relation between knowledge and the meaning of social transformation. If all the different kinds of knowledge are equally valid as knowledge, every project of social transformation is equally valid or, likewise, equally invalid. The ecology of knowledges aims to create a new kind of relation, a pragmatic relation, between scientific knowledge and other kinds of knowledge. It consists of granting "equality of opportunity" to the different kinds of knowledge involved in ever broader epistemological arguments with a view to maximizing their respective contributions toward building "another possible world," that is to say, a more just and democratic society, as well as one more balanced in its relations with nature. The point is not to ascribe the same validity to every kind of knowledge but rather to allow for a pragmatic discussion among alternative, valid criteria without immediately disqualifying whatever does not fit the epistemological canon of modern science. The equality of opportunities to be granted to the different kinds of knowledge is not to be taken in the liberal sense, that is to say, as an equality of opportunities to achieve predetermined objectives. As understood here, an equality of opportunities implies that each kind of knowledge participating in the conversation of mankind, as John Dewey would say, brings along its own idea of "another possible world"; the discussion involved has little to do with alternative means to reach the same ends and more to do with alternative ends.

The ecology of knowledges focuses on the concrete relations among knowledges and on the hierarchies and powers generated among them. Actually, no concrete practice would be possible without such hierarchies. The ecology of knowledges challenges universal and abstract hierarchies and the powers that, through them, have been naturalized by history.

Concrete hierarchies should emerge from the validation of a particular intervention in the real world vis-à-vis other alternative interventions. Among the different kinds of intervention there may be complementarities or contradictions; at any rate, the debate among them must be presided over both by cognitive

---

1. There are still contexts and practices expressing "third" medical knowledges generated by the complementarity between the two kinds of medicine.

judgments and by ethical and political judgments. The objectivity presiding over the cognitive judgment of a given practice does not necessarily clash with the ethical-political evaluation of such a practice.

The impetus behind the ecology of knowledges resides in the fact that social struggles, particularly in the global South, are rendering visible social and cultural realities in which faith in modern science is weaker and the linkages between modern science and the objectives of colonial and imperial domination are more visible, while, at the same time, other kinds of nonscientific and non-Western knowledge persist in the social practices of large sectors of the population. These struggles do not necessarily discard scientific knowledge and hegemonic Western culture. They rather interrogate them, thereby generating possibly richer understandings than those provided by Northern epistemologies. This is what Roberto Retamar has in mind when he asserts, "There is only one type of person who really knows in its entirety the literature of Europe: the colonial" (1989: 28).

In the following I analyze some of the preceding considerations in greater detail.

The Ecology of Knowledges and the Inexhaustible Diversity of World Experience

The ecology of knowledges lies in the idea of radical copresence. Radical copresence means that practices and agents on both sides of the abyssal line are contemporaneous granted that there is more than one kind of contemporaneity. Radical copresence means equating simultaneity with contemporaneity, which can only be accomplished if the linear conception of time is abandoned (see Chapter 6). Only in this way will it be possible to go beyond Hegel (1970), for whom to be a member of historical humankind—that is, to be on this side of the line—meant to be a Greek and not a barbarian in the fifth century BC, a Roman citizen and not a Greek in the first centuries of our era, a Christian and not a Jew in the Middle Ages, a European and not a "savage" of the New World in the sixteenth century, and, in the nineteenth century, a European (including the displaced European of North America) and not an Asian, frozen in history, or an African, not even a part of history. The cultural context within which the ecology of knowledges is emerging is ambiguous. On the one hand, the idea of the sociocultural diversity of the world has been gaining acceptance within social movements in the last three decades, and that should favor the recognition of epistemological diversity and plurality as one of its dimensions. On the other hand, if all epistemologies share the cultural premises of their times, perhaps one of the most entrenched premises of abyssal thinking today remains the belief in science as the only valid and exact form of knowledge. José Ortega y Gasset (1942) proposes a radical distinction between beliefs and ideas, taking the latter to mean science or philosophy. The distinction lies in the fact that beliefs are an integral part of our identity and subjectivity, whereas ideas are exterior to us. While our ideas originate from uncertainties and remain associated with them, beliefs originate in the absence of doubt. Essentially, it is a distinction between being and having: we are what we believe, but we have ideas. A characteristic feature of our time is the fact that modern science belongs to the realm of both ideas and beliefs. Belief in science greatly exceeds anything scientific ideas enable us to accomplish. Therefore, the relative loss of epistemological confidence in science that pervaded the entire second half of the twentieth century was paralleled by a rising popular belief in science. The relationship between beliefs and ideas as related to science is no longer between two distinct entities but rather between two ways of experiencing science. This duality means that recognition of cultural diversity in the world does not necessarily signify recognition of the epistemological diversity in the world.

In this context, the ecology of knowledges is basically a counterepistemology. This implies renouncing any general epistemology. Throughout the world, there are not only very diverse forms of knowledge of matter, society, life, and spirit but also many and very diverse concepts of what counts as knowledge and the criteria that may be used to validate it. In this regard, what is valid for theory is valid for epistemology as well. In the transitional period into which we are entering, in which abyssal versions of totality and the unity of knowledge still prevail, we probably need a residual or negative general epistemological stance to move along: a general epistemology of the impossibility of a general epistemology.

Two main factors account for the emergence of the ecology of knowledges. The first of these is the strong political presence of peoples and worldviews on the other side of the line as partners in the global resistance to capitalism, that is, as significant agents of counterhegemonic globalization. The second factor is the unprecedented confrontation between radically different conceptions of alternative society, so much so that they cannot be brought together under the umbrella of a single totalizing alternative. Suffice it to mention the struggle of poor peasants against landgrabbing and agroindustrial monocultures around the world, or the struggles of indigenous peoples throughout Latin America against such megaprojects as dams or highways crossing national parks and the territories in which they live or against open pit mining on an unprecedented scale. They often confront progressive governments or workers' and miners' organizations for whom the revenues accruing from such "development of the productive forces" may allow for shared wealth and better social services. Or we can point to the new collective presences in the public sphere, such as the *indignados* in Europe or the people of the Occupy movement in the United States, confronting in their struggles (highly diversified in themselves) not just conservative governments at the service of global capital but also leftist parties and progressive social organizations for whom such struggles are utopian and counterproductive and end up being instrumental for dominant power structures. Counterhegemonic globalization excels in the absence of a single globally valid alternative. The ecology of knowledges aims to provide epistemological consistency for pluralistic, propositional thinking and acting.

This invites a deeper reflection on the difference between science as a monopolistic knowledge and science as part of an ecology of knowledges.

Modern Science as Part of an Ecology of Knowledges

As I mentioned above, scientific knowledge as a product of abyssal thinking is not socially distributed in an equitable manner; nor could it be insofar as it was originally designed to convert this side of the line into the subject of knowledge and the other side into an object of knowledge. The real-world interventions it favors tend to be those that cater to the social groups with greater access to scientific knowledge. As long as abyssal lines go on being drawn, the struggle for cognitive justice will not be successful if it is based solely on the idea of a more equal distribution of scientific knowledge. Apart from the fact that an equitable distribution is impossible under conditions of capitalism and colonialism, scientific knowledge has intrinsic limits in relation to the types of real-world intervention it makes possible.

The Internal Plurality of Scientific Practices[2]

The question of the *internal plurality of science* was raised, in the West, primarily by feminist epistemologies,[3] by social and cultural studies of science, and by the currents in the history and philosophy of science influenced by the latter.[4] In general, we designate them as epistemologies of the plurality of scientific practices. They look for a third way between the conventional epistemology of modern science and other, alternative ways of knowing. From their perspective, regardless of the emergent new sciences (the sciences of complexity), the dominant epistemology continues to be heavily dependent on positivism and its belief in the neutrality of modern science, its indifference to culture, its monopoly of valid knowledge, and its alleged exceptional capacity to generate the progress of humanity. At

---

2. In this section I rely on Santos, Meneses, and Arriscado (2007).

3. Feminist epistemologies—the plural is meant to address the diversity of positions on this matter within feminism—have been central to the critique of the "classical" dualisms of modernity, such as nature/culture, subject/object, and human/nonhuman, as well as the naturalization of hierarchies of class, sex/gender, and race (Soper 1995).

4. See, for instances of a still growing literature, Santos (1992, 1995, 2000, 2007b); Pickering (1992); Lynch (1993); Jasanoff et al. (1995); Galison and Stump (1996); Latour (1999); Kleinman (2000); Nunes and Gonçalves (2001); Stengers (2007).

the opposite pole there are the radical critics of modern science, of which they have a dystopian view, underscoring its destructive and antidemocratic nature, its pseudoneutrality put at the service of the dominant interests, and the sharp contrast between dramatic technological advance and stagnation, if not even retrogression, as regards the ethical development of humankind. The third way takes for granted that these two stances, however polarizing, ultimately share the same conception of science: scientific essentialism, scientific exceptionalism, self-referentiality, and representationalism. The third way emerges by opposing such a conception and trying to salvage what positive things modern science has created (Harding 1998: 92).

Third-way epistemologies have revealed that scientific research depends on a complex mix of science and nonscience constructs: the selection of topics, problems, theoretical models, methodologies, languages, images, and forms of argument. Through historical and ethnographic research, they have studied the material cultures of the sciences (Galison 1997; Kohler 2002; Keating and Cambrosio 2003), that is, the different ways in which scientists relate to institutional contexts, to their peers, to the state, to funding agencies and entities, and to economic interests or to public interest. They have highlighted the central significance of the conception of knowledge as a construction, as the interaction, through socially organized practices, of human actors, materials, instruments, ways of doing things, and skills, in order to create something that did not exist before, with new attributes, not reducible to the sum of the heterogeneous elements mobilized for its creation. Finally, they have scrutinized the conditions and limits of the autonomy of scientific activities, revealing their connections to the social and cultural contexts in which they are carried out. Through their analyses of the heterogeneity of practices and of scientific narratives, these approaches have exploded the presumed epistemological and praxiological unity of science and turned the opposition of the "two cultures" (the sciences and the humanities) as a structuring feature of the field of knowledge into a rather unstable plurality of scientific and epistemic cultures and configurations of knowledges.[5]

In the sixteenth and seventeenth centuries, there were already different positions concerning what was meant by science and scientific facts.[6] And yet, curiously enough, the various forms of inquiry that were to be identified with

---

5. For different approaches to this topic, see Galison and Stump (1996); Nunes (1998/1999, 2001); Wallerstein (2007); P. Wagner (2007); Stengers (2007).

6. This topic has attracted the attention of authors particularly interested in the historiography of the scientific revolution (e.g., Shapin 1996; Osler 2000). Such feminist historians of science as Londa Schiebinger (1989) or Paula Findlen (1995) have shown that the diversity of topics, methods, and conceptions of knowledge in the sixteenth and seventeenth centuries included the protagonism of women. As the sciences became institutionalized, many of the knowledges created by women were to be appropriated by an overwhelmingly male scientific community or simply discarded as ways of knowing.

modern science not only dealt with a wide range of topics and objects not yet linked to distinct disciplines or specialties but also allowed for different procedures: naturalist observation, description and classification of animals and minerals, controlled experimentation, mathematical resources, philosophical speculation, and so forth. Differentiation and specialization inside the sciences is therefore the result of a historical process that must be understood in the context of the distinction between science and technology, a distinction that is often still used to claim the intrinsic neutrality of science and locate the consequences of scientific research—whether desirable or undesirable—with its applications. The changes undergone over the last decades by the organization of scientific knowledge and its relationship to technological innovation and development in such fields as high-energy physics and molecular biology have led to significant reassessments of the historical record of that divide, which has shown evidence of many situations in the past in which technological innovation and development were inseparable from the activity of scientific research itself. The widely used expression "technoscience" was proposed as a way of describing the impossibility of a radical differentiation of science and technology.[7]

The attempt to reduce science to a single epistemological model inspired by Newtonian mechanics and based on mathematization as the ideal of scientificity[8] was belied by a diversification of situated practices coexisting and/or intertwined with an "ecology of practices" (Stengers 1996/1997) hosting a distinctive epistemological model but linked as well to specific spaces and times. In the course of more than three decades, the social studies of science produced a large set of empirical studies and theoretical and epistemological reflections on the situated characteristics of the production of scientific work. The recognition of the principles that legitimated the different practices constituted as sciences led not only to the claim of a diversity of models of scientificity but also to tensions between these models within the sciences themselves.

To insist on frontiers often meant preventing the consolidation of new disciplines or scientific fields. As it happens, however, some of the most innovative breakthroughs in scientific knowledge in the last decades occurred precisely "in between frontiers." I do not mean "interdisciplinarity," a kind of collaboration between disciplines that presupposes respecting borders. Unlike the policing typical of interdisciplinarity, the "frontier work" I have in mind, at its best, is capable of generating new objects, new questions, and new problems and, at its

---

7. On the relation between science and technology, see Latour (1987) and Stengers (1996/1997, 1997), as well as the work cited in note 5 on science and material culture. The essays in Santos (2007b) show how the impossibility of distinguishing science from technology is a crucial factor for understanding the global dynamics of knowledge and its concomitant inequalities, tensions, and conflicts.

8. The model was shaken by quantum physics and other convergent developments.

worst, of leading to the "colonization" of new spaces prey to knowledge under the "old" models.[9]

Could this "disunity" and diversity of science be simply the result of an epistemological pluralism, that is to say, various ways of looking at and manipulating the world, even if the world in itself is unique and homogeneous (the universe hypothesis)? Or could there be ontological causes for such diversity, a diversity resulting from the very heterogeneity of the world (the pluriverse hypothesis)? Be that as it may, epistemological diversity is not the simple reflection or epiphenomenon of ontological diversity or heterogeneity. There is no essential or definitive way of describing, ordering, and classifying processes, entities, and relationships in the world. The very action of knowing, as pragmatist philosophers have repeatedly reminded us, is an intervention in the world, which places us within it as active contributors to its making. Different modes of knowing, being irremediably partial and situated, will have different consequences and effects on the world. The very capacity of the modern sciences to create new entities and in this way to enact an ontological politics (Mol 2002)—with the effect, intentional or not, of increasing the heterogeneity of the world—seems to support this conception. It gives shape to a robust realism and to a strong objectivity, a clear awareness of the need to accurately and precisely identify the conditions in which knowledge is produced and how it is assessed on the basis of its observed or expected consequences. This allows for a rigorous account of the situatedness, partiality, and constructedness of all knowledges, while rejecting relativism as an epistemological and moral stance.[10]

The concept of construction is here a crucial resource to characterize the formation process of both knowledge and technological objects. To construct, from this perspective, means to put in relation and interaction, in the framework of socially organized practices, materials, tools, ways of making, and competencies, so as to create something that did not exist before, something having new properties and impossible to be reduced to the sum total of the heterogeneous elements mobilized to accomplish its creation. Thus, the opposition between the real and the constructed, so often invoked to lambast the social and cultural studies of science and technology, makes no sense whatsoever. That which exists—knowledge, technological objects, buildings, roads,

---

9. A particularly interesting example of this process concerns the history of biology during the last century, particularly as regards genetics, molecular biology, and development and evolution biology. On the epistemological and theoretical implications of this history, see, for instance, Lewontin (2000); Keller (1985, 2000); Oyama (2000); Oyama, Griffiths, and Gray (2001); Nunes (2001); Singh et al. (2001); Robert (2004). On the theoretical challenges and scientific practices in biology, see J. Ramalho-Santos (2007); M. Ramalho-Santos (2003).

10. See, on this, Dupré's proposal of a "promiscuous realism" (1993, 2003), which has strong affinities with pragmatist approaches (that of John Dewey in particular) earlier explored by Santos (1989).

cultural objects—exists because it is constructed through situated practices. The relevant distinction, as Bruno Latour reminds us, is not between the real and the constructed but between that which is well constructed, which successfully resists the situations in which its consistency, solidity, and robustness are put to the test, and that which is badly constructed, hence vulnerable to criticism or erosion. This is the difference that allows a distinction to be made between facts (well constructed) and artifacts (badly constructed).[11]

From this perspective, the practices of knowledge production imply working on the objects, whether to transform them into knowledge objects recognizable within the framework of what already exists or to redefine them as part of a broader redefinition of knowledge itself. Some objects are transformed when placed in new situations, whether by acquiring new properties without losing their own or assuming new identities, allowing for their reappropriation under new conditions. Other objects, while maintaining their own identity and stability, are distinctly appropriated in different situations and contexts—as is the case, for instance, with certain objects "shared" by biomedical research and clinical practice. However, in dealing with the unknown and with ignorance vis-à-vis the proprieties and future behavior of new objects—such as genetically modified organisms, prions, or climatic changes—the relation with the unknown and the ignorance involved in what is known and can be told contrasts with the cautious respect owed to what one does not know (Santos 1989). Invoking cautiousness (more on this below) when dealing with phenomena scarcely known entails not rejection of knowledge or intervention but rather the assumption of a specific risk: to put in question our convictions and our ignorance without reducing what one does not know to what one already knows and without proclaiming the irrelevance of what we cannot describe because we do not know it.

The definition of what an object is and the distinction between subject and object appear as one more factor of internal differentiation between the sciences. Some scientific practices are compelled to deal directly with the difficulties related to the distinction between subjects and objects. From biomedicine to the social sciences, including psychoanalysis, the definition of the objects of knowledge is not distinguished from a relation with the subjects constituted as its objects. To establish the frontier between subject and object becomes, thus, a move that compels us to work simultaneously on the various frontiers that trace the territories and the history of knowledge. We cannot discard the intersubjective relation and the "common" use of language or the interactional competencies shared by both scientists and laymen while members of collectives or societies if the "prime matter" for the production of knowledge is to be constituted. The internal tensions characterizing the history of the human

---

11. On this topic, see the contributions included in Santos (2007b). On the concept of construction as it is used in social and cultural studies of science, there is abundant bibliography. For two enlightening discussions, see P. Taylor (1995); Latour (1999).

sciences—including medicine and psychoanalysis—have to do as well with the definition of the frontier between subjects and objects. Other oppositions, such as explanation/understanding, attempt to ground an epistemological duality that, as we know today, does not agree well with the hybrid subjects/objects of human sciences.

Finally, following Sandra Harding (1998, 2006), within the third way between the conventional epistemology of modern science and other, alternative systems of knowledge, two approaches to the study of science and technology are possible: the post-Kuhnian approach, developed in the North, and postcolonial studies, mostly carried out in the global South. The former may be characterized according to the following topics: historical and cultural postulates have shaped the history of modern Western science; science progresses through conceptual discontinuities; the cognitive and technical core of modern science cannot be isolated from culture or politics; the sciences are, as they should be, de-unified; to conceive of science as a set of representations obscures the dynamics of intervention and interaction; every moment in the history of modern science shares the postulates of sexual difference in its time. The postcolonial approach, in turn, shares the post-Kuhnian characteristics but adds two more: in the North, the science produced in the North is deemed to be all of the science produced in the world; there is a causal relation between European expansion, colonialism, and the development of modern science. As I argue in Chapter 4, modern science, together with modern law, was the great designer of the abyssal line and the resulting invisibility of all that was on the other side of the line.

These two approaches conceive of science in a nonessentialist way, acknowledging that the frontiers separating them from other systems of knowledge are ambiguous; they consider that all systems of knowledge are systems of local knowledge; they valorize the cognitive diversity of science understood more in terms of technological virtuality than in representational terms; and, lastly, they think that the subject of scientific knowledge, far from being an abstract, homogeneous, culturally indifferent subject, is rather a very diversified set of subjects, with different histories, trajectories, and cultures and producing scientific knowledge having equally diversified objectives (Harding 1998: 104).

These approaches, which I have designated as plural epistemologies of scientific practices, are immersed in the *Weltanschauung* of diversity and plurality that characterizes the paradigmatic transition. To my mind, however, they do not go far enough in acknowledging diversity and plurality. Save for, in part, the postcolonial approaches, these epistemologies have confined themselves to science; when they refer to other systems of knowledge, they always do so from the standpoint of modern science because the other sociocultural component of the paradigmatic transition, hegemonic globalization, is not duly taken into account. Just as in classical science the unity of reality and knowledge went hand in hand with universalism, today diversity and plurality go hand in hand with hegemonic globalization.

Unlike universalism, which was the force of an idea representing itself as being imposed without the idea of force, hegemonic globalization is the force of an idea that asserts itself by the very idea of force, that is to say, by such imperatives of the free market as rating agencies, conditionalities imposed by multilateral financial agencies such as the World Bank or the International Monetary Fund, delocalization of businesses, landgrabbing, sweatshops throughout the global South, and so on. In other words, the relations of power, resistance, domination, and alternatives of hegemony and counterhegemony are constitutive of globalization. This is so because globalization is today the hegemonic marker of the terms of the sociohistorical conflict created by capitalism. Globalization is simultaneously conflict (the idea of force) and the terms of the conflict (the force of the idea). While at the end of the nineteenth century and the beginning of the twentieth the struggle against capitalism in the North was fought by a-critically accepting the unity of knowledge and universalism—as witness Karl Marx and Albert Einstein—today the struggles against capitalism and colonialism bring to the foreground the debate on the meaning of diversity and on the internal contradictions of globalization. Today the anticapitalist and colonialist struggles advance to the extent that the terms of the conflict change. There is, then, a capitalist, colonialist diversity and an anticapitalist, decolonial diversity, one hegemonic globalization and a counterhegemonic one. The mark of the conflicts among them traverses all the epistemological debates of our time. That is why it is so important to go from internal plurality to external plurality, from the internal discrimination of scientific practices to discriminating between scientific and nonscientific knowledges.

External Plurality: The Ecology of Knowledges

Intercultural and postcolonial approaches have allowed for the recognition of the existence of plural systems of knowledge that are alternative to modern science or that engage with it in new knowledge configurations. Accessibility to a plurality of ways of knowing and to new kinds of relations among them has been going on for some time with fertile results, especially in the global South, where the encounter between hegemonic and nonhegemonic knowledges is more unequal and the limits of each are more obvious. It is in these regions that nonhegemonic knowledges, conceived of as forms of self-knowledge, are mobilized to organize resistance against the unequal relations caused by capitalism, colonialism, and patriarchy.[12]

----

12. The epistemic debates around the production of knowledges are extremely diverse and fertile. See the analyses of Mudimbe (1988); Alvares (1992); Hountondji (1983, 2002); Dussel (2000, 2001); Visvanathan (1997, 2007); Mignolo (2000, 2003); Chakrabarty (2000); Lacey (2002); Meneses (2007); Xaba 2007.

Such subaltern self-reflexivity permits a double questioning: Why are all nonscientific knowledges considered local, traditional, alternative, or peripheral? Why does the relation of domination remain, even if the ideologies that ground it change (progress, civilization, modernization, globalization, governance)? The metamorphoses of the hierarchy concerning what is and is not scientific have thus varied, and they include the following dichotomies: monocultural/multicultural, modern/traditional, global/local, developed/underdeveloped, forward/backward, and so on. Each dichotomy reveals a measure of domination. As mentioned above, the dichotomy between modern and traditional knowledge is grounded on the idea that traditional knowledge is practical, collective, and strongly embedded in the local and reflects exotic experiences. But if one assumes that all knowledge is partial and situated, it is more appropriate to compare every kind of knowledge (including scientific knowledge) in terms of its capacity to fulfill certain tasks in social contexts shaped by particular logics (including logics that preside over scientific knowledge). This is the perspective that since the end of the nineteenth century has informed pragmatic philosophy and actually seems especially appropriate for the development of edifying applications of knowledge, including scientific knowledge.[13]

The epistemological difference that does not recognize the existence of other kinds of knowledge besides scientific knowledge contains and conceals other differences—capitalist, colonial, sexist differences. Postabyssal thinking and subaltern cosmopolitan reason reject mimesis—understood as the servile imitation of metropolitan culture—as the central mechanism of culture building (Said 1978, 1980), while promoting innovative and rebellious ways of knowing based on the constant reconstruction of both identity discourses and repertoires of social emancipation. Emancipatory interculturality presupposes recognition of a plurality of knowledges and distinct conceptions of the world and human dignity. The validity of the different knowledges and conceptions must obviously be assessed, but not on the basis of the abstract disqualification of some.

Throughout the centuries, constellations of knowledges have developed ways of mutual articulation. Today, more than ever, it is important to build a truly dialogic articulation between knowledges considered Western, scientific, and modern and those considered traditional, native, and local. Rather than going back to old traditions, we must recognize the fact that each technology carries with it the weight of its mode of seeing and being in nature and with other human beings (Nandy 1987). The future can thus be found at the crossroads of different knowledges and different technologies.

---

13. On this, see Santos (1992). In this essay, inspired by the pragmatism of William James and John Dewey, I defend a kind of science oriented toward edifying, as opposed to technical, applications (see also Toulmin 2001, 2007). Pratt (2002) has been arguing for the multicultural origin and capacity of incorporation of different cultural and cognitive contributions as characteristics of pragmatic philosophy. This kind of philosophy might generate an ampler range of reciprocity in Western philosophical and epistemological thinking.

The epistemic diversity of the world is open, since all knowledges are situated. The claim of the universal character of modern science is increasingly displayed as just one form of particularism, whose specificity consists of having the power to define all the knowledges that are its rivals as particularistic, local, contextual, and situational.

For an ecology of knowledges, knowledge-as-intervention-in-reality is the measure of realism, not knowledge-as-a-representation-of-reality. The credibility of cognitive construction is measured by the type of intervention in the world that it affords or prevents. Since any assessment of this intervention always combines the cognitive with the ethical-political, the ecology of knowledges makes a distinction between analytical objectivity and ethical-political neutrality. Nowadays, no one questions the overall value of the real-world interventions made possible by the technological productivity of modern science. But this should not prevent us from recognizing the value of other real-world interventions made possible by other forms of knowledge. In many areas of social life, modern science has demonstrated an unquestionable superiority in relation to other forms of knowledge. There are, however, other interventions in the real world that are valuable to us today in which modern science has played no part. There is, for example, the preservation of biodiversity made possible by rural and indigenous forms of knowledge, which, paradoxically, are under threat because of increasing science-ridden interventions (Santos, Meneses, and Nunes 2007). And should we not be amazed by the wealth of knowledges, ways of life, symbolic universes, and wisdoms for survival in hostile conditions that have been preserved based entirely on oral tradition? Does the fact that none of this would have been possible through science not tell us something about science?

Herein lies the impulse for copresence and for incompleteness. Since no single type of knowledge can account for all possible interventions in the world, all knowledges are incomplete in different ways. Incompleteness cannot be eradicated because any complete description of varieties of knowledge would necessarily not include the type of knowledge responsible for the description. There is no knowledge that is not known by someone for some purpose. All forms of knowledge uphold practices and constitute subjects. All knowledges are testimonial since what they know of reality (their active dimension) is always reflected back in what they reveal about the subject of this knowledge (their subjective dimension).

In a climate of ecology of knowledges, the quest for intersubjectivity is as important as it is complex. Since different knowledge practices take place on different spatial scales and according to different durations and rhythms, intersubjectivity entails also the disposition to know and to act on different scales (interscalarity) and under the articulation of different times and durations (intertemporality) (see Chapter 6). Most subaltern experiences of resistance are local or have been made local and therefore irrelevant or nonexistent by abyssal modern knowledge. However, since the resistance against abyssal lines must take place on a global scale, it is imperative to develop some kind of articulation among subaltern experiences through local-global linkages. In order to succeed, the ecology of knowledges must be trans-scalar.

Moreover, the coexistence of different temporalities or durations in different knowledge practices demands an expansion of the temporal frame. While modern technologies have tended to favor the time frame and duration of state action, understood both as public administration and as political life (the electoral cycle, for instance), the subaltern experiences of the global South have been forced to respond both to the shortest duration of immediate needs of survival and to the long duration of capitalism and colonialism. But even in subaltern struggles very different durations may be present. As an example, the same struggle for land in Latin America by impoverished peasants may include either the duration of the modern state, when, for example, in Brazil, the Landless Workers' Movement (MST) struggles for agrarian reform; or the duration of the slave trade, when the Afro-descendent peoples struggle to recover the *quilombos*, the land of the runaway slaves, their ancestors; or still a longer duration, the duration of colonialism, when the indigenous people struggle to recover their historical territories taken away from them by the *conquistadores*.

Relativizing the Distinction between the Internal and External Plurality of Knowledges: The Case of African Philosophy

The above distinction between the internal and external plurality of knowledges, despite its heuristic value, does raise some problems. The distinction is based on the idea that it is possible to define, unequivocally, the limits of each kind of knowledge. This would be the only way of knowing whether we are before a plurality among distinct knowledges (external plurality) or before variations within the same general kind of knowledge (internal plurality). We saw above how the epistemologies of scientific practices enlarged the field of the internal plurality of science immensely. Has internal plurality reached its possible maximum? By looking more closely, we realize that these epistemologies, however diverse, are confined to modern and contemporary scientific practices. When we compare them with the Chinese science studied by Joseph Needham (1954–2008), or with the Arabic or Islamic science of the Islamic golden age (c. 750–1258) studied by Seyyed Hossein Nasr (1976) and so many others, or still with the Gandhian science or Kadhi science, are we dealing with internal or external plurality?

An example taken from a different field of knowledge helps us to see that, in order to grasp the epistemological diversity of the world, we need not ascribe an absolute value to the distinction between internal and external plurality of knowledges. Let us start with the following question: Is a dialogue between Western philosophy and African philosophy an instance of internal or external plurality?[14] Since two philosophies are in question, it would seem that we have here an instance of internal plurality. Yet many Western and African philosophers alike think that it is not possible to refer to an African philosophy because there is only one philosophy, whose universality is not tarnished by the fact that until now it has been developed primarily in the West. Hence, whatever may be designated as African philosophy is, in fact, not philosophy and could only be compared to philosophy on the basis of external plurality. In Africa, this is the position taken by the modernist philosophers, as they are called. For other African philosophers, the traditionalist philosophers, there is an African philosophy that, since it is embedded in African culture, is incompatible with Western philosophy and should therefore follow its own autonomous line of development.[15] According to the latter authors, comparison or dialogue, to the extent that they are possible, imply external plurality, for with them we are faced with two totally distinct bodies of knowledge. It remains to be explained, however, why, despite the distinctions made, they are both called philosophy.

An explanation comes from those who support a third position. They maintain that there is not one philosophy but many and believe that mutual dialogue and enrichment is possible. They are the ones who often have to confront the problems of incommensurability, incompatibility, or reciprocal unintelligibility. They think, however, that incommensurability does not necessarily impede communication and may even lead to unsuspected forms of complementarity. It all depends on the use of adequate procedures of intercultural translation (see Chapter 8). Through translation, it becomes possible to identify common concerns, complementary approaches, and, of course, intractable contradictions.[16] According to this third position, it is possible to recognize internal plurality among knowledges distinguished by very profound differences, the type of differences that usually call for the recognition of external plurality. The wider the exercise of intercultural translation, the more likely the comparison is to become an internal one.

Two examples illustrate this. The Ghanaian philosopher Kwasi Wiredu (1990, 1996) claims that in the philosophy and language of the Akan, the ethnic group to which he belongs, it is not possible to translate the Cartesian precept *cogito, ergo sum*. This is because there are no words to express this idea. "Thinking," in

---

14. The same argument may be used in relation to a dialogue between religions.

15. On this subject, see Eze (1997); Karp and Masolo (2000); Hountondji (2002); Coetzee and Roux (2003); L. Brown (2004).

16. In this area, the problems are often associated with language, and language is, in fact, a key instrument in bringing about an ecology of knowledges. As a result, translation must operate on two levels, the linguistic and the cultural. Cultural translation will be one of the most challenging tasks facing philosophers, social scientists, and social activists in the twenty-first century. I deal with this issue in more detail in Santos (2004, 2006a).

Akan, means "measuring something," which does not make sense coupled with the idea of being. Moreover, the "being" of *sum* is also very difficult to explain because the closest equivalent is something like "I am there." According to Wiredu, the locative "there" "would be suicidal from the point of view of both the epistemology and the metaphysics of the *cogito.*" In other words, language enables certain ideas to be explained and not others. This does not mean, however, that the relationship between African and Western philosophy has to end there. As Wiredu has tried to show, it is possible to develop autonomous arguments on the basis of African philosophy, not only concerning the reason why it cannot express *cogito, ergo sum* but also concerning the many alternative ideas it can express that Western philosophy cannot.[17]

The second example is provided by H. Odera Oruka. It takes place between Western philosophy and the African concept of philosophical sagacity. The latter is an innovative contribution of African philosophy propounded by Odera Oruka (1990a, 1990b, 1998) and others.[18] It resides in a critical reflection on the world that has as its protoganists what Odera Oruka calls "sages," be they poets, traditional healers, storytellers, musicians, or traditional authorities. According to Odera Oruka, sage philosophy

> consists of the expressed thoughts of wise men and women in any given community and is a way of thinking and explaining the world that fluctuates between *popular wisdom* (well-known communal maxims, aphorisms, and general commonsense truths) and *didactic wisdom*, an expounded wisdom and rational thought of some given individuals within a community. While popular wisdom is often conformist, didactic wisdom is at times critical of the communal set-up and the popular wisdom. Thoughts can be expressed in writing or as unwritten sayings and argumentations associated with some individual(s). In traditional Africa, most of what would pass as sage-philosophy remains unwritten for reasons that must now be obvious to everyone. Some of these persons might have been partly influenced by the inevitable moral and technological culture of the West. Nevertheless, their own outlook and cultural well-being remain basically that of traditional rural Africa. Except for a handful of them, the majority of them are "illiterate" or semi-illiterate. (1990a: 28)

In other words, the idea of African philosophical sagacity is a form of knowledge so different from conventional philosophy that we cannot but be before an instance of external plurality. However, by calling for a redefinition of what we mean by philosophy, it may also be seen as pointing to an internal plurality within the now extremely expanded field of philosophy.

---

17. See Wiredu (1997) and a discussion of his work in Osha (1999).
18. On sage philosophy, see also Oseghare (1992); Presbey (1997).

The Ecology of Knowledges, Hierarchy, and Pragmatics

An epistemological pragmatics is above all justified because the life experiences of the oppressed are primarily made intelligible to them as an epistemology of consequences. In their life world, consequences are first; causes are second.

The ecology of knowledges is based on the pragmatic idea that it is necessary to reassess the concrete interventions in society and in nature that the different knowledges can offer. It focuses on the relations between knowledges and on the hierarchies that are generated between them, since no concrete practice would be possible without such hierarchies. However, rather than subscribing to a single, universal and abstract hierarchy among knowledges, the ecology of knowledges favors context-dependent hierarchies, in light of the concrete outcomes intended or achieved by different knowledge practices. Concrete hierarchies emerge from the relative value of alternative real-world interventions. Complementarity or contradictions may exist between the different types of intervention. Whenever there are real-world interventions that may, in theory, be implemented by different knowledge systems, the concrete choice of the form of knowledge must be informed by the principle of precaution, which, in the context of the ecology of knowledges, must be formulated as follows: preference must be given to the form of knowledge that guarantees the greatest level of participation to the social groups involved in its design, execution, and control and in the benefits of the intervention.

In this regard we should distinguish between two different situations. The first concerns the choice among alternative interventions in the same social domain in which different knowledges collide. In this case, the principle of precaution must result in judgments not based on abstract hierarchies between knowledges but stemming from democratic deliberations about gains and losses. The following example demonstrates the importance of this principle. In the 1960s, the millennia-old irrigation systems in the rice fields in several Asian countries were replaced by scientific irrigation systems as promoted by the prophets of the green revolution. In Bali, Indonesia, the traditional irrigation systems were based on ancestral religious, agrarian, and hydrological knowledges that were supervised by the priests of Dewi-Danu, the Hindu goddess of water (Callicott 2001: 89–90). They were replaced because they were deemed superstitious, being derived from what anthropologists have named the "rice cult." As it happens, the replacement had disastrous consequences for the rice culture, so disastrous indeed that the scientific systems had to be discarded and the traditional ones retrieved. The real tragedy, however, was that the alleged incompatibility between the two knowledge systems designed to perform the same intervention—the irrigation of the rice fields—resulted from an incorrect assessment of the situation caused precisely by abstract judgments (based on the universal validity of modern science) about the relative value of different knowledges. Years later, computational models—one of the fields of complexity sciences—demonstrated that the water sequences managed by the priests of Dewi-Danu were far more efficacious than those traced by scientific irrigation systems (Callicott 2001: 94).

The other case of alternative interventions based on different bodies of knowledges concerns interventions that do not take place in the same social domain. In this case, the decision among different and conflicting knowledges does not necessarily require the substitution of one type of intervention by another. It only calls for a decision about which social domain to intervene in and what kind of priority to establish. As I mentioned above, it is not reasonable to question today the general value of the interventions in the world made possible by modern science through its technological productivity. One may question many of its concrete options, be they the bombs that razed Hiroshima and Nagasaki or the destructive exploitation of natural resources. For instance, nobody questions the ability of modern science to transport men and women to the moon, even if the social value of such an enterprise may be called into question. In this domain, modern science shows an indisputable superiority vis-à-vis other kinds of knowledge. There are, however, other ways of intervening in reality that are precious to us today, to which modern science did not contribute at all, and which are rather the result of other kinds of knowledge. For example, as mentioned above, there is the preservation of biodiversity rendered possible by peasant and indigenous knowledges.

Orientations for Prudent Knowledge

The epistemological construction of an ecology of knowledges is no easy task. Suffice it to think of the many questions it raises. How is scientific knowledge to be distinguished from nonscientific knowledge? How is interknowledge constructed? How to distinguish between many nonscientific knowledges? What is the difference between Western and non-Western knowledge? If there are several Western knowledges, how to distinguish among them? If there are several non-Western knowledges, how to distinguish among them? From which perspective are the different knowledges to be identified? What are the possibilities and limits of recognizing a certain kind of knowledge from the viewpoint of another? What kinds of relations or articulations among the different knowledges are possible? What kinds of procedures may put these relations into practice? How are we to distinguish, in concrete and practical social struggles, the perspective and knowledge of the oppressed from those of the oppressors? None of these questions have unequivocal answers. A feature of the ecology of knowledges is that it constitutes itself through constant questions and incomplete answers. Herein resides its being a prudent knowledge. Below I summarize some of the findings so far. They can be conceived of as possible orientations for proceeding by and toward a prudent knowledge. The next chapter on intercultural translations will illustrate the copresence among differently incomplete knowledges.

1. *There is no global social justice without global cognitive justice. The struggle for cognitive justice will not be successful if it depends exclusively on a more equitable distribution of scientific knowledge.* Scientific knowledge has intrinsic limits as regards the kinds of social intervention it makes possible. Given the hegemony of conventional epistemology and the consequent monoculture of scientific knowledge, retrieving the presence and possible value of different knowledges is only possible through a sociology of absences and a sociology of emergences.

2. *The crises and disasters caused by the imprudent and exclusivist use of science are far more serious than acknowledged by the dominant scientific epistemology.* The crises and disasters might be avoided if nonscientific knowledges, which circulate in subordinate form in and out of scientific practices, are valorized, along with the social practices they sustain. In the ecology of knowledges, crediting nonscientific knowledges does not entail discrediting scientific knowledge. It merely implies the counterhegemonic use of the latter. It consists, on the one hand, of exploring alternative scientific practices made visible by the plural epistemologies of scientific practices and, on the other, of valorizing the interdependence between scientific and nonscientific knowledges.

3. *There is no kind of social knowledge that is not known by some social group toward a particular social objective. All knowledges sustain practices and constitute subjects.* All knowledges are testimonial because what they know about social reality (their active dimension) also reveals the kind of subjects of knowledge acting on social reality (their subjective dimension).

4. *All knowledges have internal and external limits.* The internal limits concern what a given knowledge does not yet know of social reality and of its possible intervention in it. The external limits concern interventions in social reality that are only possible on the basis of other kinds of knowledge. Hegemonic knowledges are characterized by knowing only their internal limits. The counterhegemonic use of modern science consists of the parallel exploration of the internal and the external limits.

5. *The ecology of knowledges is constructivist as concerns representation and realist as concerns intervention.* We do not have direct access to reality since we do not know reality save through the concepts, theories, values, and language we use. On the other hand, the knowledge we construct upon reality intervenes in it and has consequences. Knowledge is not representation; it is intervention. Pragmatic realism focuses on intervention rather than on representation. The credibility of the cognitive construction is measured by the kind of intervention in the world it provides, assists, or hinders. As the evaluation of such intervention always combines the cognitive and the ethicopolitical, the ecology of knowledges starts from the compatibility between cognitive and ethicopolitical values. Therein resides the distinction between objectivity and neutrality.

6. *The ecology of knowledges focuses on the relations among knowledges, on the hierarchies and powers emerging among them.* Starting the conversation among knowledges on the premise of equal opportunity granted to all of them is not

incompatible with concrete hierarchies in the context of concrete knowledge practices. The ecology of knowledges only fights the hierarchy established by universal and abstract cognitive power, naturalized by history and justified by reductionist epistemologies. Concrete hierarchies emerge from the evaluation of alternative interventions in social reality. Among the different kinds of intervention there may be complementarity or contradiction.

7. *The ecology of knowledges is ruled by the principle of precaution.* Whenever there are interventions in reality that may, in theory, be carried out by different knowledge systems, the concrete choices of kinds of knowledge to be privileged must be informed by the principle of precaution. Within the ecology of knowledges, this principle must be formulated thus: in equal circumstances, the kind of knowledge that guarantees more participation to the social groups involved in the conception, execution, control, and fruition of the intervention must be privileged.

8. *Knowledge diversity is not limited to the content and kind of its privileged intervention in social reality. It includes as well the ways in which it is formulated, expressed, and communicated.* The ecology of knowledges invites polyphonic and prismatic epistemologies: polyphonic, because the different knowledges have autonomous developments, different ways of producing and communicating knowledge, which explains why determining the relations among them tends to be a very complex task; prismatic, because the relation among knowledges changes according to the kind of social practices in which they intervene.

9. *The issue of incommensurability is not relevant only when the knowledges in question come from distinct cultures; it is an issue as well within the same culture.* As regards Western cultures, one of the most controversial topics has been how science delimits itself vis-à-vis other ways of relating to the world, ways deemed nonscientific or even irrational, such as the arts, the humanities, religion, and so on. Even the views critiquing the notion that scientific knowledge will increasingly get rid of the "irrational" elements—such us those of Thomas Kuhn (1970, 1977), Gaston Bachelard (1971 [1934], 1972 [1938], 1975 [1949], 1981), Georges Canguilhem (1988), and (to a certain extent) Michel Foucault (1980)—always base their paradigms, or epistemes, on discontinuities between science and other knowledges. Asserting such discontinuities requires, as Thomas Gieryn (1999) shows, a constant boundary-work involving a constant policing of borders and a persistent epistemological vigilance in order to contain and repel the imminent and insistent "attacks of irrationality."

We might ask, for instance, about the possible relations between poetry and science. I do not mean science as poetry but rather the epistemological value of poetry and a possible polyphonic epistemology involving poetry and science. Likewise, religious knowledge has its own epistemology that is generally considered incommensurable with scientific knowledge. The issue of the relation between religious and other knowledges acquires relevance when many social movements fighting today against oppression base their militancy on religious knowledge and on spirituality (Santos 2009).

10. *The ecology of knowledges aims to be a learned struggle against ignorant ignorance.* A distinct feature of hegemonic knowledge is its capacity to impose its knowledge and ignorance criteria on the rest of the knowledges. The ecology of knowledges allows us to have a broader view both of what we know and what we do not know. What we do not know is the product of our ignorance and not of ignorance in general.

11. *The history of the relation among different knowledges is central to the ecology of knowledges.* The long, historical duration of capitalism, colonialism, and patriarchy elucidates a past of unequal relations among knowledges. In many cases, those relations led to epistemicide. No exercise of the ecology of knowledges, however vast and deep, could erase that past. On the contrary, in the ecology of knowledges, history is an intense, constitutive part of the present. As T. Banuri (1990) asserts, what has affected the South most negatively since the beginning of colonialism is to have to concentrate its energies in adapting and resisting the impositions of the North.[19] Likewise concerned, Tsenay Serequeberhan (1991: 22) identifies the two challenges that confront African philosophy today. The first is a deconstructive challenge and consists of identifying the Eurocentric residua inherited from colonialism and present in various sectors of collective life, from education to politics, from law to culture. The second is a reconstructive challenge and consists of giving new life to the cultural and historical possibilities of the African legacy interrupted by colonialism and neocolonialism. The work of translation tries to catch these two moments: the hegemonic relations among experiences and what there is beyond such relations. In this double movement, the social experiences disclosed by the sociology of absences and the sociology of emergences are reconstructed in such a way as to offer themselves to relations of mutual intelligibility, without falling into reciprocal cannibalization.

12. *The ecology of knowledges aims to facilitate the constitution of individual and collective subjects combining sobriety in the analysis of facts with the intensification of the will against oppression.* Sobriety is called for by the multiplicity of cognitive perspectives on the reality of oppression. Oppression is always the product of a constellation of knowledges and powers. Hierarchies, too, act according to networks. The intensification of the will, in its turn, is the result of a deeper knowledge of human possibilities. The ecology of knowledges permits combining knowledges that privilege inner strength and *natura naturans* with

---

19. Banuri argues that the development of the "South" has been disadvantageous "not because of bad policy advice or malicious intent of the advisers, nor because of the disregard of neo-classical wisdom, but rather because the project has constantly forced indigenous people to divert their energies from the *positive* pursuit of indigenously defined social change, to the *negative* goal of resisting cultural, political, and economic domination by the West" (1990: 66, emphasis in the original).

knowledges (such as scientific knowledge) that privilege external strength and *natura naturata*.[20] The ecology of knowledges thus permits one to ground an imagination of the will that is incomprehensible to the conventional understanding of modern science.[21]

The ecology of knowledges does not occur only at the level of the logos. It occurs as well at the level of the mythos, at the level of the tacit presuppositions that render possible the horizon of possibilities of each knowledge and the dialogues between them. The idea of ferment is crucial here—linked to the élan vital, the field of forces of human energy that William James and Henri Bergson name technological spontaneity (Bloch 1995: 2:683), or to spirituality, as indigenous peoples simply name it. This polyphonic nature of the ecology of knowledges is aimed at promoting competent, rebellious subjectivities.[22] At stake is the formation of a spontaneity that founds a constituting will upon an attitude of suspicion vis-à-vis the social reality already constituted. The point is, in a word, to restore the harmony that Paracelsus, during the first Renaissance, identified between Archeus, the element of the will in the seed and the body, and Vulcanus, the natural force of matter.

The intensification of the will derives from a potentiality that can only be known through the sociology of emergences. In the ecology of knowledges, the will is guided by various compasses. There are neither absolute criteria nor monopolies of truth. To be guided by one compass alone would be a manifestation of ignorant ignorance in Nicholas of Cusa's terms. The contribution of each compass needs to be assessed regularly. The relative distance vis-à-vis exclusivist guides and vanguards is a factor of the consolidation of the will. That there are many compasses turns epistemological vigilance into a profound act of autoreflexivity.

13. *The ecology of knowledges signals the passage from a politics of movements to a politics of intermovements.* The concerns inspiring the exercises of the ecology of knowledges must be shared by diverse social groups that, in a given context, converge on the idea that their aspirations and interests can only be pursued successfully in articulation with other social groups, hence engaging other social groups' ways of knowing. The times and places of engagement must be suitable to the different groups or movements.

In this regard, another of Nicholas of Cusa's fruitful teachings that I analyzed in Chapter 3 comes to mind. In 1450 he composed three dialogues—"De Sapientia," "De Mente," and "De Staticis Experimentis"—in which the main character is the Idiot, a simple, illiterate man, a poor craftsman who makes wooden spoons. In the dialogues he engages in with the accredited philosopher (the humanist, the orator), the Idiot becomes the sage capable of solving the most complex problems of existence on the basis of the experience of his active life, to

---

20. On the technology of the will, see Bloch (1995: 2:675).
21. On the imagination and the crossing of knowledges, see Visvanathan (1997, 2007).
22. See the analysis of destabilizing subjectivities in Chapter 2.

which priority is given over contemplative life. As Leonel Santos says, "The Idiot is contrasted with the learned, erudite man, one who holds scholarly knowledge grounded in authors and authorities, wherefrom he draws his competence, but one who has lost the sense of use and autonomous cultivation of his own faculties" (2002: 73). The Orator provokes the Idiot: "How presumptuous of you, poor Idiot, to thus diminish the study of letters, without which no one progresses!" (2002: 78). The Idiot replies,

> It is not presumption, great Orator, that prevents me from remaining silent, but charity. Indeed, I see you devoted to the quest for wisdom with much futile toil.... The opinion of authority turned you, a free man by nature, into something rather like a horse tied to the manger by a tether and eating only what is served to him. Your knowledge feeds on the authority of those who write, it is limited to an alien, not natural pasture. (2002: 79)

And he adds, "But I tell you that wisdom cries out in the markets and its clamor resounds in the squares" (2002: 79). Wisdom expresses itself in the world and in mundane tasks, especially in those that are the world of reason and imply operations of calculation, measurement, and weighing (2002: 81).

In these extremely ironic dialogues, the Idiot is nothing but the propounder of Nicholas of Cusa's learned ignorance. The dialogues show that the great arguments among the schools of erudite knowledge lose their importance unless their relevance for practical life and experience is fully demonstrated. This decentering of ways of knowing has one other dimension. The field of practical interactions (that is to say, interactions having practical objectives) in which the ecology of knowledges takes place requires that the place where ways of knowing are interrogated and exchanged not be an exclusive place of knowledge, for instance, universities or research centers. The place of enunciation of the ecology of knowledges is any place where knowledge aims to turn into a transformative experience. That it is to say, it is every place situated beyond knowledge as a separate activity. Significantly, Nicholas of Cusa's dialogues take place at the barber's or in the humble craftsman's workshop. The philosopher is therefore compelled to argue in a territory that is not familiar to him and for which he was not trained—the territory of practical life. This is the territory where all practical relations are planned, opportunities calculated, risks measured, and pros and cons weighed. This is the territory of the artisanship of practices, the territory of the ecology of knowledges.

CHAPTER 8

Intercultural Translation

Differing and Sharing con Passionalità

T HE TWO MAIN procedures underlying the epistemologies of the South
are ecologies of knowledges and intercultural translation. In the previous
chapters I dealt with the first procedure. In the current chapter I deal with
the second one. At the core of ecologies of knowledges is the idea that different types
of knowledge are incomplete in different ways and that raising the consciousness
of such reciprocal incompleteness (rather than looking for completeness) will be a
precondition for achieving cognitive justice. Intercultural translation is the alternative both to the abstract universalism that grounds Western-centric general theories
and to the idea of incommensurability between cultures. The two are related and
account for the two "nonrelationships" of Western modernity with non-Western
cultures: destruction and assimilation.[1] They are "nonrelationships" in that both
refuse to consider non-Western cultures as relevant cultural alternatives in any conceivable sense. The latter are located on the other side of the line and can therefore
be either discarded as incomprehensible or turned into objects of appropriation
and violence. As understood here, intercultural translation consists of searching
for isomorphic concerns and underlying assumptions among cultures, identifying
differences and similarities, and developing, whenever appropriate, new hybrid
forms of cultural understanding and intercommunication that may be useful in
favoring interactions and strengthening alliances among social movements fighting,
in different cultural contexts, against capitalism, colonialism, and patriarchy and
for social justice, human dignity, or human decency. Intercultural translation questions both the reified dichotomies among alternative knowledges (e.g., indigenous
knowledge versus scientific knowledge) and the unequal abstract status of different
knowledges (e.g., indigenous knowledge as a valid claim of identity versus scientific

---

1. Military conquest, forced conversion, ideological indoctrination, linguistic repression,
and the profanation of sacred spaces are some of the many versions of the negation of the other
through imperial unilateralism. See Dallmayr (2006: 76).

knowledge as a valid claim of truth). In sum, the work of translation enables us to cope with diversity and conflict in the absence of a general theory and a commando politics. As shown below, it is a living process to be carried out both with arguments and with the emotions deriving from sharing and differing under an axiology of care. *Con passionalità* was Antonio Gramsci's apt expression (see below).

In the previous chapters I have described the political and intellectual climate justifying the need for intercultural translation from different perspectives. The emergence of counterhegemonic globalization, the rise of social movements anchored in non-Western cultural premises, the consequent distance vis-à-vis the Western critical tradition and political imagination, the collapse of the internationalism that throughout the twentieth century privileged the working class as a historical subject, and the related crisis of abstract universalism and general theories—all these factors converged in the call for intercultural translation. Intercultural translation raises a legion of questions. What types of relationships are possible between the different knowledges? How to distinguish incommensurability, incompatibility, contradiction, and complementarity? Where does the will to translate come from? Who are the translators? How to choose translation partners and issues? How to form shared decisions and distinguish them from imposed ones? What is the difference between intercultural translation and interlingual translation, and how are they related? How to make sure that intercultural translation does not become the newest version of abyssal thinking or of metonymic and proleptic reason, that is to say, a new version of imperialism and colonialism? How can we identify the perspective of the oppressed in cognitive terms? How can we translate this perspective into other knowledges and languages? In the search for alternatives to domination and oppression, how can we distinguish between alternatives to the system of oppression and domination and alternatives within the system; more specifically, how do we distinguish between alternatives to capitalism and alternatives within capitalism? In sum, how to fight against the abyssal lines using conceptual and political instruments that do not reproduce them? What would be the impact of a postabyssal conception of knowledge or of a subaltern cosmopolitan reason both upon social struggles and upon educational institutions?

I do not intend to answer all these questions in this chapter. I will limit myself to providing some examples of the work of translation in action, as they may shed some light on the questions themselves. But before that, let me start by briefly stating what I mean by intercultural translation and why it is important to reinventing social emancipation and insurgent political imagination. Viewed from the perspective of the epistemologies of the South, intercultural translation is also interpolitical translation, a procedure that promotes the intermovement politics at the source of counterhegemonic globalization. It is part and parcel of a political project and must be conducted in such a way as to maximize the latter's success. Intercultural translation is a tool to minimize the obstacles to political articulation among different social groups and movements fighting across the globe for social justice and human dignity when said obstacles are due to cultural difference and reciprocal unintelligibility.

Besides speaking different languages and coming from different historical trajectories, such groups and movements formulate their repertoires of struggle based not
only on the specific social and political contexts in which they operate but also on
different cultural premises and symbolic universes. In the last instance, only shared
cultural meanings turn demands into objectives worth fighting for. As part of an
interpolitical project, intercultural translation is therefore concerned both with why
translating is important and with the power relations involved in the work of translation. Intercultural translation, as I conceive of it in this chapter, is not a gesture of
intellectual curiosity or cultural dilettantism. It is rather an imperative dictated by
the need to broaden political articulation beyond the confines of a given locale or
culture.[2] Such need may initially be felt and voiced by a given group or movement,
but in order to lead to the concrete work of translation, it must be shared by some
other group or movement. Ideally, only equal power relations, that is, relations of
shared authority, fit the purposes of intercultural translation, since only then can
reciprocity among social groups or movements be obtained.[3] This ideal functions as
a normative standard in light of which the concrete practices of translation must be
evaluated. Inquiring into the social relations underlying intermovement translation
and striving for increasingly less unequal power relations are both constitutive of the
work of translation as understood here. As a living process, intercultural translation
aims at reciprocity instead of worrying about source cultures and target cultures,
cross-sourcing and cross-targeting. When in this chapter I address broader understandings of intercultural translation, I do so in order to illustrate the conditions for
interpolitical translation and to highlight the obstacles to their fulfillment.[4]

---

2. As a political project, the work of translation must confront the kind of political questions that, according to Lydia Liu, lie at the core of intercultural translation: "In whose terms,
for which linguistic constituency, and in the name of what kinds of knowledge or intellectual
authority does one perform acts of translation between cultures?" (1995: 1).

3. Though not concerned with the kind of intermovement politics I am focusing on here,
Tzvetan Todorov's conception of cross-cultural dialogue is close to the type of intercultural translation I have in mind. Todorov says that such a dialogue relies on a relationship "in which no one has
the last word" and where "no voice is reduced to the status of a simple object" or mere victim (1984:
247–251). Dallmayr (2006: 79) distinguishes three basic modalities of cross-cultural dialogue:
(1) pragmatic-strategic communication, (2) moral-universal discourse, and (3) ethical-hermeneutical dialogue; and as a subcategory: agonal dialogue or contestation. The ethical-hermeneutical
dialogue comes closest to my conception of intercultural translation. In this type of dialogue, "partners seek to understand and appreciate each other's life stories and cultural backgrounds, including
cultural and religious (or spiritual) traditions, storehouses of literary and artistic expressions, and
existential agonies and aspirations" (Dallmayr 2006: 79). There is, however, a major difference
between Dallmayr's approach and mine. My concern is not with ethics or hermeneutics per se but
rather with intermovement politics, that is, with the creation of conditions for thicker alliances
and aggregations of political interests. This also explains why I prefer the concept of translation to
the concept of dialogue. In reciprocal translation the focus is on working through differences in
order to identify the scope and the limitations of alliance building.

4. In my forthcoming *Epistemologies of the South: Reinventing Social Emancipation*, I present some exercises of intercultural translation that may facilitate and strengthen intermovement
politics in the future.

On Intercultural Translation as a Living Translation

It is not my purpose to engage in the numerous debates around translation, cultural translation, translatability, and translation as culture that have exploded in the humanities and social sciences since the 1980s, spawning entirely new research programs and disciplines such as translation studies. According to António Sousa Ribeiro,

> If, in every epoch, there are concepts that at a certain point in time achieve such a broad circulation that they seem able to name just by themselves the main determinants of the epoch, one such concept, nowadays, is the concept of translation. It can, in fact, be said without the least reservation that translation has become a central metaphor, one of the keywords of our time. Potentially, any situation where we try to relate meaningfully to difference can be described as a translational situation. (2004)

Similarly, Michaela Wolf states that "translation has long left the protected enclosure of the philological culture of translation, and is increasingly becoming a central category of cultural theory and the politics of culture" (2008).

Drawing on Gramsci's concept of "living philology" (*filologia vivente*),[5] I conceive of intercultural translation as a living process of complex interactions among heterogeneous artifacts, both linguistic and nonlinguistic, combined with exchanges that by far exceed logocentric or discourse-centric frameworks. According to Giorgio Baratta, Gramsci's living philology goes beyond texts and focuses on the concrete social and political conditions to which the texts are supposed to relate and on which they are to have an impact.[6] I will refer to the wealth of recent translation debates only insofar as they are relevant for the development of my argument in this book. Some clarifications are in order. I speak of intercultural translation rather than cultural translation because the cultural differences encountered in counterhegemonic globalization are more often intercultural than intracultural. But I am fully aware that in many instances it may not be easy to distinguish the two situations. Moreover, intracultural differences may at times lead to more intractable conflicts than intercultural ones. Intercultural translation is usually conceived of as a metaphor,[7] while linguistic translation refers to the traditional, literal sense of translating from one language into another. We do know, however, that with extensive and repetitive use, metaphors get literalized. On the other hand, interlingual translation cannot but imply cultural translation. Nonetheless, intercultural translation is far more encompassing as

---

5. See Gramsci (1975).
6. "A circular move from the empirical and the individual to the universal and the total, and vice-versa, without ever closing the circle or reaching a definitive or peremptory conclusion" (Baratta 2004: 18).
7. As Birgit Wagner (2011) suggests after Gramsci.

it involves linguistic and extralinguistic phenomena. I will enumerate now the topics of the cultural translation debates that are most relevant to the type of translational contact zone I am dealing with here.

Language is, of course, the central topic. For my analytical purposes, two major issues are at stake. The first concerns language difference, unequal linguistic competences, and the ways they impact upon the work of translation. The second issue is the place of language in intercultural translation, since the work of translation depends as well upon nonlinguistic and paralinguistic forms of communication, body language, gestures, laughter, facial expressions, silences, the organization and architecture of space, the management of time and rhythm, and so on. The second topic concerns translatability, which Walter Benjamin (1999) considered "the law governing translation" and Gramsci viewed as the difference that might blur or merely interfere with the supposedly universal contradiction in Marxist dialects. Translatability is the acknowledgment of a difference and the motivation to deal with it. Overlooking translatability amounts to making hegemony impossible. Hegemony is based on consent to ideas that lie beyond the confines of one's immediate life experience (and indeed may contradict it). Such consent, however, is only possible through an act of cultural and existential appropriation that brings ideas and life experiences closer together or makes the illusion of closeness more credible. Appropriation is the activation of difference in a movement from strangeness to familiarity. This activation is translatability at work. Born in Sardinia, Gramsci was keenly aware of both linguistic and cultural difference in his own country and was concerned that political thinking and discourse, often dependent on academic knowledge and universal theories such as Marxism, might not be properly understood by his addressees. Throughout the *Prison Notebooks*, he makes several harsh criticisms of the esoteric discourses of academia, which Gramsci (1975) called "philosophical and scientific Esperanto." Whatever could not be expressed in this Esperanto, he argued, was mere prejudice or superstition, if not sheer delusion (*delírio*).

The third topic concerns the asymmetries involved in the work of translation and how they can be reduced or even eliminated as the work of translation proceeds. How to create nonhierarchical communication and achieve shared meanings? This topic is particularly relevant for the kinds of translation I am concerned with here, for instance, translations as political projects aimed at reciprocal empowerment. Polycentrality is rarely a starting point. At best, it will be the point of arrival. A fourth, equally relevant topic concerns the changes that the identity of the participants in the work of translation undergoes as the work develops. Sharing meanings involves also sharing passions, feelings, and emotions. By the same token, communicating difference or even "staging a difference," as Homi Bhabha (1994) would say, has both communication and performativity dimensions that affect the translators' subjectivity as a whole. Both marking and unmarking differences get inscribed in the process of intersubjectivation and interidentification. As the subjects of translation change, so do the polarities that separate them. Reformulation and interpenetration are translation in action. A fifth topic, less debated in translational studies but crucial here, is the motivation behind translation. Wherefrom comes the pathos that generates the impulse for engaging in translation? How warm is the warm current of reason bringing together strangers with no certainty that, at the end of the work of translation, they will be less strange to each other, rather than the other way around? Gramsci's living philology (*filologia vivente*) implies the collective effort of translating by "an active and conscious sharing," that is to say, by *con passionalità*.[8] This concept is of the utmost importance since it underlines the emotions that embody the engagement and sharing of meanings and affections as the living process of translation proceeds.

Translation allows for mutual intelligibility among culturally diverse social experiences of the world, both those already available and other possible ones, in accordance with the sociology of absences and the sociology of emergences. By stressing the possibility of cultural communication, translation undermines the idea of original or pure cultures and stresses the idea of cultural relationality. Such concepts as equivocation, ambivalence, *mestizaje* or hybridity, and mimicry are central to intercultural translation. Because the latter is viewed and valued here for its possible contribution to intermovement politics, it is imperative to elucidate the historical relations among the different cultures involved, as well as the cultural and political inequalities they create, and to bear in mind that such inequalities are very much part of the present, even when the need for translation is reciprocally and equally felt. In Chapter 1, I addressed the power relations intervening in *mestizaje*, thereby distinguishing between colonial and decolonial *mestizaje*. The ambivalence of mimicry is that it affirms the difference in the very process of identifying the other. In the colonial context, race is the symbol of this difference and is, in fact, the cause of the failure of mimicry, since it does not allow for more than an incomplete presence. As Bhabha says, having India in mind, "to be Anglicized is *emphatically* not to be English" (1994: 87). And the same argument could be made in other colonial contexts.[9] Unlike Bhabha, I do not think that discrediting hegemonic representations and displacing antagonism is inherent in *mestizaje* or that the "third space" opened up by it is automatically empowering. Such a third space may be very disempowering indeed, as indigenous movements have eloquently shown in the last decades. While analyzing the baroque subjectivity in Chapter 1, I called attention to the limits of the subversion of domination it represents. The "virtues" of the third space depend on the concrete social relations that constitute it. The third space is the domain of the mediation and negotiation that are constitutive of intercultural

---

8. Gramsci (1975). According to Birgit Wagner (2011), Joseph Buttigieg, editor of the first two volumes of the American edition of *The Prison Notebooks*, is planning to use "empathy" to translate *con passionalità*.

9. For the Portuguese context, see Santos (2011).

translation. The political potential of the latter depends on the specific conditions of mediation and negotiation. The third space is what Viveiros de Castro calls the space of equivocation. According to him,

> To translate is to situate oneself in the space of the equivocation[10] and to dwell there. It is not to unmake the equivocation (since this would be to suppose it never existed in the first place) but precisely the opposite is true. To translate is to emphasize or potentialize the equivocation, that is, to open and widen the space imagined not to exist between the conceptual languages in contact, a space that the equivocation precisely concealed. The equivocation is not that which impedes the relation, but that which founds and impels it: a difference in perspective. To translate is to presume that an equivocation always exists; it is to communicate by differences, instead of silencing the Other by presuming a univocality—the essential similarity—between what the Other and We are saying. (2004: 10)

I prefer to conceive of the in-between space that makes translation possible as a contact zone, the translational contact zone. In general, contact zones are social fields in which different cultural life worlds meet, mediate, negotiate, and clash.[11] Contact zones are therefore zones in which rival normative ideas, knowledges, power forms, symbolic universes, and agencies meet in usually unequal conditions and resist, reject, assimilate, imitate, translate, and subvert each other, thus giving rise to hybrid cultural constellations in which the inequality of exchanges may be either reinforced or reduced. Complexity is intrinsic to the definition of the contact zone itself. Who defines who or what belongs to the contact zone and who or what does not? How to define the line that delimits the contact zone? Is

---

10. "Equivocation is not just a 'failure to understand,' but a failure to understand that understandings are necessarily not the same, and that they are not related to imaginary ways of 'seeing the world' but to the real worlds that are being seen.... The Other of the Others is always other. If the equivocation is not an error, an illusion or a lie, but the very form of the relational positivity of difference, its opposite is not the truth, but the univocal, as the claim to the existence of a unique and transcendent meaning. The error or illusion par excellence consists, precisely, of imagining that the univocal exists beneath the equivocal, and that the anthropologist is its ventriloquist" (Viveiros de Castro 2004: 12).

11. Pratt defines contact zones as "social spaces where disparate cultures meet, clash and grapple with each other often in highly asymmetrical relations of domination and subordination—like colonialism, slavery or their aftermaths as they are lived out across the globe today" (1992: 4). In this formulation, contact zones seem to involve encounters among cultural totalities. This does not need to be the case. The contact zone may involve selected and partial cultural differences, the ones that in a given time-space find themselves in competition to provide meaning for a given course of action. Moreover, as I have been claiming in this book, the unequal exchanges extend today far beyond colonialism and its aftermath, even though, as postcolonial studies have shown, colonialism continues to play a much more important role than one is ready to admit.

the difference between cultures or normative life worlds so wide as to make them incommensurable? How to approximate the cultural and normative universes so as to bring them "within visual contact," so to speak?

Paradoxically, because of the multiplicity of cultural codes present, the contact zone is relatively uncodified or substandard, a zone for normative and cultural experimentation and innovation. Moreover, to determine the equality or inequality of exchanges in the contact zone is never a simple task, since alternative concepts of equality are present and often in conflict. In the contact zones, the ideal of equality is the ideal of equal differences. The contact zones generated by intercultural translation, as understood here, are time-spaces of mediation and negotiation in which the inequality of translational relations are the main conditioning factor of the work of translation. The work of translation proceeds by reducing such inequality. The cultural constellations emerging from intercultural translation may be more or less unstable, provisional, and reversible.

As part of intermovement politics, the work of translation concerns both knowledges and practices, as well as their agents. There are different types of translation work. Some focus specifically on concepts or worldviews, others on alternative ways of constructing collective practices and agents. But in every instance, knowledges, practices, and agents work in tandem. When the focus is specifically on concepts and worldviews, I call the work of translation, after Raymond Panikkar (1979: 9), *diatopical hermeneutics*. It consists of interpretation work between two or more cultures to identify isomorphic concerns among them and the different responses thereby provided. For instance, concern with and aspiration to human dignity seem to be present, albeit in different ways, in different cultures. Diatopical hermeneutics is based on the idea that the topoi[12] of an individual culture, no matter how strong they may be, are as incomplete as the culture itself. Such incompleteness is not visible from inside the culture itself, since the aspiration to totality induces taking *pars pro toto*. The objective of diatopical hermeneutics is therefore not to achieve completeness—this being an unachievable goal—but, on the contrary, to raise the consciousness of reciprocal incompleteness to its possible maximum by engaging in the dialogue, as it were, with one foot in one culture and the other in another. Herein lies its *dia-topical* character.

According to Panikkar, in diatopical hermeneutics

the distance to be overcome is not merely temporal, within one broad tradition, but the gap existing between two human topoi, "places" of understanding and self-understanding, between two—or more—cultures that have not developed their patterns of intelligibility.... Diatopical hermeneutics stands

---

12. Topos is a key concept in Aristotelian rhetoric. It means the "commonplace," the notion or idea that—because it is self-evident in a given cultural context—is not argued about. On the contrary, it functions as a premise of argumentation.

for the thematic consideration of understanding the other without assuming that the other has the same basic self-understanding. The ultimate human horizon, and not only differing contexts, is at stake here. (1979: 9)

Seeking, among other things, to break out of the hermeneutic circle created by the limits of a single culture, diatopical hermeneutics attempts "to bring into contact radically different human horizons," traditions, or cultural locations (topoi) in order to achieve a true dialogue that bears in mind cultural differences. It is the art of arriving at understanding "by going through these different locations" (dia-topos).

As I mentioned before, to acknowledge the relativity of cultures does not imply the adoption of relativism as a philosophical stance. It does imply, however, the conception of abstract universalism as a Western peculiarity whose idea of supremacy does not reside in itself but rather in the supremacy of the interests that sustain it. The critique of universalism is related to the critique of the possibility of a general theory.[13] Diatopical hermeneutics presupposes, rather, what I designate *negative universalism*, the idea of the impossibility of cultural completeness. During the transition period we are in, still dominated by metonymic and proleptic reason, negative universalism is perhaps best formulated as a residual general theory: a general theory about the impossibility of a general theory.

The idea and feeling of want and incompleteness create motivation for the work of translation. Mikhail Bakhtin's description of cross-cultural dialogue comes to mind:

A meaning only reveals its depths once it has encountered and come into contact with another, foreign meaning: they engage in a kind of dialogue.... We seek answers to our own questions in [the foreign culture]; and [it] responds to us by revealing to us its new aspects and new semantic depths.... Such a dialogic encounter of two cultures does not result in merging or mixing. Each retains its own unity and open totality, but they are mutually enriched. (1986: 7)

In order to bear fruit, translation must be the crossing of converging motivations that have their origins in different cultures. Where does the motivation come from? It is imperative to distinguish between intellectual and political motivations. Throughout the modern period there are multiple examples of

---

13. A variation of universalism has been recently presented in the form of transversalism. Palencia-Roth (2006) claims that universal values are antithetical to transversal values. In axiological terms, transversal values are values that cross two or more cultures and are common to them without becoming universal values. If a cultural transversal is to remain transversal, it must retain its specificity. In my view, this is just a more elegant (and also more insidious) way of delivering the old claim of universalism. There are no values that, in themselves, are common to different cultures. They can only become so through cosmopolitan intercultural translation, that is, through procedures that, by their reciprocal and horizontal character, guarantee against top-down imposition and, in the end, against epistemicide.

intellectuals, sages, philosophers, and scientists, in both the global North and the global South, trying to reach out to other cultures in the search of answers that their culture does not provide. Sometimes it is an intellectual exercise aimed at disproving well-accepted truths concerning the uniqueness or precedence of a given culture. The most brilliant example in the twentieth century is certainly Joseph Needham's (1954–2008) gigantic effort of intercultural translation aimed at proving the lateness and derivativeness of modern science and Western civilization vis-à-vis the Chinese science and civilization. More often, the search is an act of soul-searching, an exercise of profound and existential self-reflectivity filled with anxiety inasmuch as whatever may be learned from other cultures must be digested,[14] disfigured, and transfigured in order to fit into new constellations of meaning. The Indian sociologist Shiv Visvanathan eloquently formulates the notion of want and motivation that I here designate as the work of translation. Says Visvanathan, "My problem is, how do I take the best of Indian civilization and at the same time keep my modern, democratic imagination alive?" (2000: 12). If we could imagine an exercise in diatopical hermeneutics conducted by Visvanathan and a European or North American scientist, it would be possible to think of the latter's motivation for dialogue formulated thus: "How can I keep alive in me the best of modern and democratic western culture, while at the same time recognizing the value of the world that it designated autocratically as noncivilized, ignorant, residual, inferior, or unproductive?" (2000: 12).

The second type of want and motivation is political, and it is the one that concerns me here. Its irreducible intellectual component is at the service of a political intent or project. What kind of political intent or project generates a want that by itself generates the motivation to reach out to another culture? At the pragmatic level, throughout the past decade the World Social Forum (WSF) has provided unequivocal evidence of the partial, local, or provincial character of political projects that were previously considered as universal and susceptible of universally intelligible and accepted formulations and validity. While revealing the extreme diversity (political, cultural, semantic, linguistic) of the social movements that resist neoliberal globalization all over the world, the WSF has remarked the need for articulation and aggregation among all these movements and organizations. In the absence of a top-down aggregation imposed by a grand theory or a privileged social actor, this would involve a giant effort of translation. What do the participatory budgeting practiced in many Latin American cities and the participatory democratic planning based on *panchayats* in Kerala and West Bengal in India have in common? What can they learn from each other? In what kinds of counterhegemonic global activities can they cooperate? The same questions can be asked of the peace movements and the anarchist movements, or of the indigenous movements and the *indignados* or Occupy movements, or even of the Landless Workers' Movement in Brazil and the Rio Narmada movement in India, and so on.

---

14. Recall here the anthropophagic movement of *Nuestra America* intellectuals as portrayed in Chapter 1.

When dealing more specifically with practices and agents, the work of translation focuses on mutual intelligibility among forms of organization and objectives of action. But, as I said, all types of the work of translation involve knowledges and practices as well as agents.[15] The work of translation aims to clarify what unites and separates different social groups or movements and practices so as to ascertain the possibilities and limits of articulation and aggregation among them. Because there is no single universal social practice or collective subject to confer meaning and direction to history, the work of translation becomes crucial to identify, in each concrete and historical moment or context, which constellations of practices carry more counterhegemonic potential. While the WSF generated the potential for intercultural translation, in Mexico the Zapatista indigenous movement acted out a very concrete example of the work of translation. It was an ephemeral but telling example of reaching out across cultural differences and translating among them. In March 2001, in its march to the capital of the country, the Zapatista movement became for a moment a privileged counterhegemonic practice inasmuch as it was capable of undertaking the work of translation between its objectives and practices and the objectives and practices of other Mexican social movements, from the civic and labor movements to the feminist movement. As a result of that work of translation, for example, the Zapatista leader chosen to address the Mexican Congress was Comandante Esther. With that choice, the Zapatistas wanted to signify the articulation between the indigenous movement and the women's liberation movement and thus deepen the counterhegemonic potential of both.

Learning from the South through Intercultural Translation

In the introduction I explained the reasons justifying my quest for achieving a distance vis-à-vis the Western Eurocentric critical tradition. Establishing such a distance involves both deconstructive and reconstructive démarches. In Chapters 1 through 5, I focused on deconstructive démarches, while in Chapters 6 and 7, I focused on reconstructive démarches. In this chapter I proceed with reconstruction at a deeper level, the level of intercultural translation. Depending on the types of intervening partners in the work of translation, I distinguish two major kinds of intercultural translation. The first is translation between Western and non-Western conceptions or practices; the second is the translation between different non-Western conceptions and practices.[16] As understood here, both kinds of translation aim at learning from the anti-imperial South, understood as a metaphor for the global, systemic, and unjust human suffering caused by

---

15.   The work of translation between modern biomedicine and traditional medicine is a good illustration of this. See Meneses (2007, 2010).

16.   There is also the possibility of translation among different Western conceptions and practices. The extent to which such translation is inter- or intracultural may be a topic for debate. This debate does not concern me here.

capitalism, colonialism, and patriarchy and for the resistance against the causes of such suffering. As I mentioned earlier, the anti-imperial South inhabits both the global South and the global North. Strengthening the anti-imperial South grounds the impulse to learn through intercultural translation, both from different knowledges and practices across the global South and from knowledges and practices in contact zones between the global North and the global South. These are two very different types of learning because both the sociology of absences and the sociology of emergences work very differently in each one of them. The modern history of unequal relations between the global North and the global South is such that questioning and challenging the contact zone as it presents itself must be the first task of the work of translation. Herein lies the decolonial nature of the encounters to be promoted.

Because it is a work of mediation and negotiation, the work of translation requires that the participants in the translation process defamiliarize themselves to a certain extent vis-à-vis their respective cultural backgrounds. In the case of North/South translations, which tend to be also Western/non-Western translations, the task of defamiliarization is particularly difficult because the imperial North has no memory of itself as other than imperial and, therefore, as unique and as universal. It would seem at first that there should be no such difficulty in the case of South/South translations. Nothing could be further from the truth. As a product of empire, the South is the house of the South where the South is not at home. That is to say, the construction of epistemologies of the South through intercultural translation must undergo a process of defamiliarization vis-à-vis both the imperial North and the imperial South. The imperial South is how the South relinquishes the possibility of representing itself other than as facilitating and desiring oppression by the imperial North. As Edward Said (1978) correctly stresses, imperial epistemology has represented the other as incapable of representing him- or herself. Vincent Tucker has also pointed out that "schools of thought such as Orientalism and disciplines such as anthropology speak for the 'other' often claiming to know those they study better than they know themselves"; he adds, "The other is reduced to a voiceless object" (1992: 20). By seeing through the lenses of the imperial North alone, the South could not but recognize itself as the imperial South. That is why today the global South is able to recognize itself as a victim of the imperial North much more easily than of the imperial South.[17] There is, however, one difference worth mentioning. In the global North

---

17. Novelists and poets in the South have been in the forefront of the struggle for a nonimperial South. Fredric Jameson argues that in the Third World novel the allegories are national rather than individual (as in the First World novel): "The story of the private individual destiny is always an allegory of the embattled situation of the public third world culture and society" (1986: 79). There is certainly a point in this observation, even though the term "third world culture and society" is very problematic for various reasons, including the reductionist intent of bringing the immense diversity of the novels in the global South into a single story.

the aspiration to an anti-imperial stance can only be imagined as a postimperial stance, since in the modern period imperialism was an original condition for the global North. In the case of the global South, on the contrary, it is possible to construct an anti-imperial stance by imagining a real or an invented precolonial, preimperial condition. As in other contexts,[18] the indigenous movements in Latin America illustrate the anticolonial, anti-imperial potential in claiming a precolonial memory. Such a reconstruction may not be necessarily progressive, but neither need it be necessarily reactionary. In order to be progressive it must consider itself as provisional in the sense that a full affirmation of anti-imperialism implies the very elimination of both the imperial North and the imperial South. To the extent that it is possible for the South to think of itself in terms other than the South, it will also be possible for the North to think of itself in terms other than the North.

Learning from the South is therefore the process of intercultural translation by means of which the anti-imperial South is constructed both in the global North and in the global South. As I have been emphasizing, the construction of an anti-imperial South is part and parcel of counterhegemonic globalization; thus, the work of translation, far from being an intellectual exercise, is rather a pragmatic instrument for mediation and negotiation. Its purpose is to overcome the fragmentation inherent in the extreme diversity of social experience of the world uncovered by the different ecologies highlighted in Chapters 6 and 7. The overall objective of the epistemologies of the South is to build a solid, consistent, and competent anti-imperial South. In this process, it is possible to distinguish three moments: rebellion, human suffering, and victim-aggressor continuity.[19] In each of them, intercultural translation will intervene in a specific way.

The *moment of rebellion* is when the imperial order is shaken, at least momentarily. The moment of rebellion of the oppressed signifies the weak link of imperial domination. In light of this, it is not surprising that its analysis is also a weak link of the conventional colonizing social sciences that constituted themselves and thrived on the imperial relation. For a convincing analysis of moments of rebellion, we should turn, for example, to the giant collection of studies on Indian society gathered by Ranajit Guha in the several volumes of *Subaltern Studies*.[20] Commenting on this formidable achievement in historical scholarship, Veena Das states precisely that the *Subaltern Studies* "make an important point in establishing the centrality of the historical moment of rebellion in understanding the

---

18. In Africa, see, for instance, Dioup (1974, 1996); wa Thiong'o (1986); Mudimbe (1988, 1994); S. B. Diagne (2001); M. Diagne (2005).

19. They are not phases, stages, or steps, as they may exist simultaneously. They represent different perspectives on the resistance against oppression and domination.

20. A series of collections of essays on South Asian history and society published during the 1980s under the editorship of Ranajit Guha. Among many studies, see one by Guha (1989) himself on colonialist historiography in India.

subalterns as subjects of their own histories" (1989: 312).[21] We are talking here about moments of defiance in which the representational order is confronted by an emerging new order. Interrogation of the representational order is the first impulse toward epistemologies of the South, thus allowing for emancipatory energies to recognize themselves as such. The moment of rebellion is therefore a moment of suspension that turns the imperial North into alienating power and the imperial South into alienating powerlessness. At such a moment, the oppressor's force begins to exist only to the extent that the victim's weakness permits: the oppressor's capacity is a function of the victim's incapacity; the will to oppress is a function of the will to be oppressed. This momentary reciprocity between oppressor and victim makes possible the rebellious subjectivity because the latter is, at least momentarily, in control of its own representation. Such subjectivity was memorably formulated by Gandhi when he imagined himself addressing the British like this: "It is not we who have to do as you wish, but it is you who have to do as we wish" (1956: 118).

The *moment of human suffering* is the moment of contradiction between the life experiences of the oppressed and the idea of a decent life. It is likewise the moment in which human suffering is translated into man-made suffering. It is a crucial moment, because hegemonic domination lies in the naturalization of human suffering as a fatality or necessity. The transformation of human suffering into man-made, unjust suffering requires, therefore, a great investment in oppositional representation and imagination. As Ashis Nandy says, "Our limited ethical sensibility is not a proof of human hypocrisy; it is mostly a product of our limited cognition of the human situation" (1987: 22). The perspective grounding the epistemologies of the South is the unjust human suffering together with the pathos of the will to resist against it.

As to the *moment of victim-aggressor continuity*, colonial discourse was certainly based on the polarity between the colonizer and the colonized, but it is important to underscore the continuity and ambivalence between the two since they are not independent of each other; nor is each one thinkable without the other. Gandhi was probably the first to formulate the moment of continuity when he clearly stressed that any system of domination brutalizes both the victim and the oppressor and that the oppressor also needs to be liberated. "All his life," says Nandy, "Gandhi sought to free the British as much as the Indians from the clutches of imperialism; the caste Hindu as much as the untouchable from untouchability" (1987: 35). Gandhi believed that the system of domination compels the victim to internalize the system's rules in such a way that there is no guarantee that, once the oppressor is defeated, domination will not continue to be exerted by the former victim, even if in different forms. The victim is a highly divided being concerning identification with or difference from the oppressor.

---

21. For a different view of the *Subaltern Studies* collective by someone who belonged to it, see Chakrabarty (1992).

I quote Nandy again: "The oppressed is never a pure victim. One part of him collaborates, compromises and adjusts; another part defies, 'non-cooperates,' subverts or destroys, often in the name of collaboration and under the garb of obsequiousness" (1987: 43).[22]

More recently, Frantz Fanon's and Albert Memmi's formulations are the most eloquent and forceful in this regard. According to both Fanon and Memmi, the link between colonizer and colonized is dialectically destructive and creative. It destroys and recreates the two partners of colonization. The chain that links colonizer and colonized is racism; the chain, however, is a form of aggression for the colonizer and a form of defense for the colonized[23] (Memmi 1965: 131). The most notorious ambivalence of the stereotype of the colonized as savage is the fact that it is also constituted of the opposite of its negative elements: the negro is simultaneously the savage and the most dignified and obedient servant; the incarnation of uncontrolled sexuality but also innocent as a child; mystic, primitive, and simpleminded and at the same time ingenious, a liar, and a manipulator of social forces (Bhabha 1994: 82).

By discovering the secrets of defiance against oppression, it becomes possible to struggle for an alternative world that does not produce reciprocal brutalization. In other words, the oppressor's liberation from dehumanization is only conceivable as a result of the victim's emancipatory struggle against oppression. Gustavo Gutierrez, the prominent theoretician of liberation theology, expresses this apparent asymmetry and paradox with great eloquence: "One loves the oppressors by liberating them from themselves. But this cannot be achieved except by resolutely opting for the oppressed, i.e. by combating the oppressive classes. It must be real and effective combat, not hate" (1991: 276).

In *Epistemologies of the South: Reinventing Social Emancipation* (forthcoming), I explore the potential of intercultural translation to learn from the South in an empowering way, that is, by making visible and credible non-Western knowledges and practices that were placed on the other side of the line by abyssal thinking. In this way the anti-imperial South may emerge. As mentioned above, I distinguish between North/South and South/South translations and will analyze some instances of possible translation in each case. None of these instances simply discards Western conceptions, even as each questions the latter's universality, thereby making room for other conceptions existing in other non-Western cultures. It rather brings them into a contact zone where mediation,

---

22. With reference to Gandhi, Rudolph (1996: 42) shows how the colonial encounter, disempowering as it is for the colonized, may, however, be subverted by the latter. The colonial subject, he comments, often proves to be more than the dough on which the imperial cookie cutter operates to create mentalities stuffed with imperial categories. Where the encounter stimulates the colonial subject to reformulate the cultural possibilities of his or her context, it can operate as a stimulus, even a goad, to cultural creativity and innovation.

23. On this, see the interesting collection of essays by Fanon (1967c). See also Maldonado-Torres (2010); Lewis Gordon (1995).

confrontation, and negotiation become possible and are carried out. The aim is to develop richer constellations of meaning whereby the anti-imperial South is empowered in its struggle against global capitalism, colonialism, and patriarchy.

Before I engage in the work of translation, I shall address, even if briefly, the question of the conditions and procedures of intercultural translation.

Conditions and Procedures of Translation

The work of translation is a collective intellectual and political work. It has a pathos as well, an emotional dimension, because it presupposes both a nonconformist attitude vis-à-vis the limits of one's knowledge and practice and the readiness to be surprised and to learn with and from the other's knowledge and practice in order to build collaborative actions of mutual advantage. Ecologies of knowledges and intercultural translation are the two central features of postabyssal thinking. Together they seek to create copresence across the abyssal lines. They cannot therefore rely on the contact zones generated by abyssal thinking since the latter are premised upon the logic of appropriation/violence. Ecologies of knowledges and intercultural translation can only proceed and flourish in subaltern cosmopolitan contact zones, that is, decolonial contact zones. The impulse for the creation of such zones comes from the social movements and organizations that, in a context of counterhegemonic globalization, engage in intermovement politics, that is, in political articulation across knowledges, practices, and agents with the purpose of strengthening the struggles against capitalism, colonialism, and patriarchy.

As I have already said, the work of translation is based on the idea of the impossibility of a general theory. Without this negative universalism, translation is a colonial kind of work, no matter how postcolonial it claims to be. The key questions are the following: What to translate? From what and into what to translate? Who translates? How to translate? When should translation take place? Why translate?

What to Translate?

The cosmopolitan contact zone starts from the assumption that it is up to each partner, as both knowledge and practice bearer, to decide what is put in contact with whom. Translational contact zones are always selective because movements and other social groups mobilize knowledges and practices that amply exceed those that are brought into the contact. Indeed, what is put in contact is not necessarily what is most relevant or central. On the contrary, the contact zones are frontier zones, borderlands, or no-man's-lands, where the peripheries or margins of knowledges and practices are the first to emerge. As the work of translation advances and intercultural competence deepens, it becomes possible to bring into the contact zone dimensions of knowing and acting considered more relevant.

In intercultural contact zones, it is up to each cultural practice to decide which aspects must be selected for intercultural confrontation. In every culture, there are features deemed too central to be exposed and rendered vulnerable by the confrontation in the contact zone, or aspects deemed inherently untranslatable into another culture. These decisions are part and parcel of the work of translation itself and are susceptible to revision as the work proceeds. If the work of translation progresses, it is to be expected that more features will be brought to the contact zone, which in turn will contribute to further the translation progress. In many countries of Latin America, particularly in those in which the constitution has recognized the intercultural or plurinational[24] character of the state, the indigenous peoples have been focusing their struggles on the right to control what in their knowledges and practices should or should not be the object of translation vis-à-vis the *sociedad mayor*.[25]

The issue of translatability is both less and more complex than is assumed in translation studies. It is less complex to the extent that translatability is not an intrinsic characteristic of what is at hand to be translated. It is above all an act of will, a fiat that draws the line between what is and what is not amenable to translation. Conversely, it is more complex because, as the will to translate changes according to reasons that reason ignores, the meeting ground is inherently unstable, precarious, and reversible. The issue of what is translatable is not restricted to the selection criterion adopted by each practice or knowledge in the contact zone. Beyond active selectivity, there is what we might call passive selectivity. It consists of what in a given culture has become unpronounceable because of the extreme oppression to which it was subjected during long periods. These are deep absences, made of an emptiness impossible to fill. In the case of longtime absences, it is possible that not even the sociology of absences may bring them to presence. The silences they produce are too unfathomable to become the object of translation work.

The question about what to translate stirs one more question that is particularly important in translational contact zones between different cultural universes. Cultures are monolithic only when seen from the outside or from afar. When looked at from the inside or at close range, they are easily seen to comprise various and often conflicting versions of the same culture. For example, when I speak of a possible intercultural dialogue on conceptions of human dignity, we can easily see that in Western culture there is not just one conception of human rights. Two at least can be identified: a liberal conception that privileges political

---

24. On this, see Santos and Exeni (2012); Santos and Grijalva (2012).

25. It would be wrong to assume that, once the range of the repertoire of translatable issues is agreed upon, the will to cross-translate will lead to transparent interactions and fully accurate representations of the other culture(s). In this regard it is prudent to follow Theo Hermans's recommendation: "I am recommending the pragmatic recognition of the impossibility of total description, and replacing the chimera of complete understanding with the critical inspection of the vocabularies we employ to conduct the cross-cultural hermeneutic exercise" (2003: 385).

and civic rights to the detriment of social and economic rights and a Marxist or socialist conception that stresses social and economic rights as a condition of all the others. I also show that, by the same token, in Islam it is possible to identify several conceptions of *umma*; some, more inclusive, go back to the time when the Prophet lived in Mecca; others, less inclusive, evolved after the construction of the Islamic state in Medina. Likewise, there are many conceptions of *dharma* in Hinduism.[26] They vary, for instance, from caste to caste. The more inclusive versions, holding a wider circle of reciprocity, are the ones that generate more promising contact zones; they are the most adequate to deepen the work of translation and diatopical hermeneutics.

To Translate from What into What?

The choice of knowledges and practices among which the work of translation occurs is always the result of a convergence of experiences and aspirations by the social actors. It may emerge as a reaction to a colonial or imperial contact zone. For example, biodiversity and ethnobotany constitute today an imperial contact zone between biotechnological knowledge and the knowledge of the shamans, traditional healers, or witch doctors in indigenous or rural communities of Latin America, Africa, and Asia. The indigenous movements and the international advocacy groups supporting them contest this contact zone and the powers that constitute it and fight for the creation of other, nonimperial contact zones where relations among the different knowledges may be more horizontal. This struggle brought a new acuteness to the translation between biomedical and traditional knowledges. To give an example from a totally different field, the labor movement, confronted with an unprecedented crisis, has been opening itself to contact zones with other social movements, namely, civic, feminist, ecological, and movements of migrant workers. In this contact zone, there is an ongoing translation work between labor practices, claims, and aspirations and the objectives of citizenship, protection of the environment, and antidiscrimination against women and ethnic or migrant minorities. Translation has slowly transformed the labor movement and the other social movements, thus rendering possible constellations of struggles that until a few years ago would be unthinkable.

It would be imprudent to assume that the reciprocal will to create a cosmopolitan translational contact zone leads "naturally" to horizontality and reciprocity in the ways cultures act as both sources and targets. Even though the work of translation proposed here is a decolonizing work, it carries on its shoulders a long past of brutally unequal relations between metropolitan and colonial cultures. As Michael Palencia-Roth (2006: 38) says, the comparative history of civilizations is often little more than a history of exploitation, conquest, colonization, and the

---

26. On the concept of *umma*, see, above all, Faruki (1979); An-Na'im (1995, 2000); Hassan (1996); on the concept of *dharma*, see Gandhi (1929/1932); Zaehner (1982).

exercise of power, in which the likelihood of the "dialogical"—a cross-cultural dialogue that neither points toward nor ends in the monologic hegemony of a single voice—is relatively rare. To undo this past is a task for generations, and the best that can be done at any given moment is to be fully aware of such a past and fully vigilant against its insidious workings in neutralizing the decolonial will and boycotting emancipatory projects. In light of this it is useful to bear in mind Richard Jacquemond's four hypotheses on "the problems of translating across power differentials" (2004: 125): a dominated culture will invariably translate far more of the hegemonic culture than the latter will of the former; when the hegemonic culture does translate works produced by the dominated culture, those works will be perceived and presented as difficult, mysterious, inscrutable, esoteric, and in need of a small cadre of intellectuals to interpret them, while a dominated culture will translate a hegemonic culture's works by trying to make them accessible to the masses; a hegemonic culture will only translate works by authors in a dominated culture that fit the former's preconceived notions of the latter; authors in a dominated culture who dream of reaching a larger audience will tend to write while having in mind their translation into a hegemonic language, and this will require some degree of compliance with stereotypes.[27] Though Jacquemond focuses on written texts, his hypotheses may be viewed as markers of epistemological vigilance in translational relations of other kinds.[28]

When to Translate?

In this case too, the cosmopolitan contact zone must be the result of a conjugation of times, rhythms, and opportunities. If there is no such conjugation, the contact zone becomes imperial and the work of translation a form of cannibalization. In the last three decades, Western modernity discovered the possibilities and virtues of multiculturalism. Accustomed to the routine of its own hegemony, Western modernity presumed that if it were to open itself up to dialogue with cultures it had previously oppressed, the latter would *naturally* be ready and available to engage in this dialogue—and indeed only too eager to do so. Such a presupposition has resulted in new forms of cultural imperialism, often under

---

27. See also Aveling (2006).

28. Jacquemond refers to the dominant culture as a stable culture that "tends to integrate imported texts by imposing its own conventions on them" (2004: 118). Such a culture leads to what Berman calls ethnocentric translation, based on two axioms: "We ought to translate the foreign work so that we do not 'feel' the translation, we ought to translate in a way that gives the impression that this is what the author would have written if he had written in the language of the translation" (1985: 53). This is another way of rendering the other culture invisible, or static, in sum, robbed of its agency. In such cases, cultural translation is a monologue rather than a dialogue, a conquest rather than a translation.

the guise of multiculturalism or toleration. This I call *reactionary multicultural-ism*. In contrast, I signal the emergence among social movements of a recipro-cally experienced, widespread sense that the advancement of counterhegemonic struggles is premised upon the possibility of sharing practices and knowledges globally and cross-culturally. Upon this shared experience it becomes possible to build the horizontal conjugation of times from which a cosmopolitan contact zone and the emancipatory work of translation may emerge.

As regards multicultural contact zones, the different temporalities that occur in them must still be taken into account. As I said previously, one of the principles of the sociology of absences consists of countering the logic of the monoculture of linear time with a pluralist constellation of times and durations in order to free the practices and knowledges that never ruled themselves by linear time from their status as residuum. The objective is to convert the simultaneity provided by the contact zone as much as possible into contemporaneity. This is not to say that contemporaneity annuls history but rather that history is made of different contemporaneities. This is an important caveat, particularly as regards contact zones of knowledges and practices in which extremely unequal relations of power led to a massive production of absences. In such situations, once a given knowledge or practice, absent before, is made present, the danger is there to believe that the history of that knowledge or practice starts with its presence in the contact zone. This danger has been present in many intercultural dialogues, mainly in those in which indigenous peoples have participated after their claims and rights started being recognized from the 1980s onward. The contact zone must be monitored by all the participants to prevent the simultaneity of contact from meaning the collapse of history.

Who Translates?

Knowledges and practices only exist as mobilized by given social actors. Hence, the work of translation is always carried out by them through their representa-tives and the rearguard intellectuals working together with them. The translators must have a profile similar to that of the *philosophical sage* identified by H. Odera Oruka (1990b) in his quest for African sagacity (see Chapter 7). They must be deeply embedded in the practices and knowledges they represent, having of both a profound and critical understanding. This critical dimension, which Odera Oruka designates as *didactic sageness*, grounds the want, the feeling of incompleteness, and the motivation to discover in other knowledges and practices the answers that are not to be found within the limits of a given knowledge or practice. Transla-tors of cultures must be good subaltern cosmopolitan intellectuals. They are to be found not necessarily among the leaders of social movements. They may be rank-and-file activists as well. As regards rearguard intellectuals, those trained in academic knowledges but solidarily involved with the social actors, their task is to retrain themselves in such a way as to be able constantly to translate academic knowledge into nonacademic knowledge, and vice versa, and to do so with *con passionalità*, as Gramsci would put it. In the near future, the decision about who translates is likely to become one of the most crucial democratic deliberations in the construction of counterhegemonic globalization.

How to Translate?

The work of translation is basically an argumentative work, based on the cosmopolitan emotion of sharing the world with those who do not share our knowledge or experience. The work of translation encounters multiple difficulties. The first difficulty concerns the premises of argumentation. Argumentation is based on postulates, axioms, rules, and ideas that are not the object of argumentation because they are taken for granted by all those participating in the argumentative circle. In general, they are called topoi, or commonplaces, and constitute the basic consensus that makes argumentative dissent possible.[29] The work of translation has no topoi at the outset because the available topoi are those appropriate to a given knowledge or culture, hence not accepted as evident by another knowledge or culture. In other words, the topoi that each knowledge or practice brings into the contact zone cease to be premises of argumentation and become arguments. As it progresses, the work of translation constructs topoi adequate to the contact zone and the translating situation. It is a demanding work, with no safety nets and ever on the verge of disaster. The ability to construct topoi is one of the most distinctive marks of the quality of the subaltern cosmopolitan intellectual, or sage.

The second difficulty regards the language used to conduct the argumentation. It is not usual for the knowledges and practices in presence in contact zones to have a common language or to have mastered the common language equally well. Furthermore, when the cosmopolitan contact zone is multicultural, one of the languages in question is often the language that dominated the colonial or imperial contact zone.[30] The replacement of the latter by a cosmopolitan contact zone may thus be boycotted by this use of the previously dominant language. The issue is not just that the different participants in the argumentative discourse may master the language unequally. The issue is that this language is responsible for the very unpronounceability of some of the central aspirations of the knowledges and practices that were oppressed in the colonial contact zone. If not explicitly

---

29. On topoi and rhetoric in general, see Santos (1995: 7–55).

30. "The use of English as a *lingua franca*, as is the case in so many international meetings around the world, can, it is true, mean no more than the creation of a 'neutral' space of communication, serving the instrumental purpose that resonates in the commonplace of the English language as the Esperanto of our time.... But English is the lingua franca of globalization because it is the language of Empire.... And the logic of empire, that of an all-encompassing centre governed by the goal of total assimilation, is essentially monolingual and monologic. Under such a unifying perspective, for which difference is not to be acknowledged or simply does not exist, translation is, in fact, irrelevant" (Ribeiro 2004).

questioned, the linguistic supremacy may carry with it conceptual and normative prevalence, thereby boycotting the work of translation.[31]

The third difficulty concerns the silences—not the unpronounceable but rather the different rhythms with which the different knowledges and social practices articulate words with silences and the different eloquence (or meaning) that is ascribed to silence by the different cultures. To manage and translate silence is one of the most exacting tasks of the work of translation.

Why Translate?

This last question encompasses all the others. Both ecologies of knowledges and intercultural translation are instruments geared to fulfill the core idea of the epistemologies of the South expounded in this book: global social justice is not possible without global cognitive justice.

The work of translation is the procedure we are left with to give meaning to the world after the latter has lost the automatic meaning and direction that Western modernity claimed to have conferred on it by defining history as lineal, by planning society, and by controlling nature. If we do not know if a better world is possible, what gives us the legitimacy or motivation to act as if we did? The need for translation resides in the fact that the problems that Western modernity purported to solve (liberty, equality, fraternity) remain unsolved and cannot be resolved within the cultural and political confines of Western modernity. In other words, in the transition period in which we find ourselves, we are faced with modern problems for which we have no modern solutions.

The work of translation undertaken on the basis of the sociology of absences and the sociology of emergences is a work of epistemological and democratic imagination, aiming to construct new and plural conceptions of social emancipation upon the ruins of the social emancipation of the modernist project. There is no guaranty that a better world may be possible or that all those who have not given up struggling for it conceive of it in the same way. The oscillation between banality and horror, which intrigued Max Horkheimer and Theodor Adorno (1969) so much, is now turned into the banality of horror. The possibility of disaster begins today to be obvious.

The situation of bifurcation mentioned by Ilya Prigogine (1997) and Immanuel Wallerstein (1999) is the structural situation in which the work of translation takes place. The objective of the translation work is to create constellations of knowledges and practices strong enough to provide credible alternatives to the current phase of global capitalism, characterized both by threatening on an

---

31. Having this in mind, D. A. Masolo (2003) suggests that the intellectual whose roots are in subaltern languages and cultures may be forced to resort to what he calls "polyrationalities," that is, the capacity to formulate the same basic concepts and arguments in different ways and in different languages, as well as in different cultural contexts.

unprecedented scale nature's restoration cycles and by subjecting to the mercantile logic ever ampler domains of social interaction. The work of translation operates upon a present that has been expanded by the sociology of absences and upon a future that has been contracted by the sociology of emergences. Through enhanced interknowledge, mediation, and negotiation, the field of political and social experiences to count and act upon is enlarged, thereby offering a broader view and a more realistic evaluation of the alternatives available and possible today. The possibility of a better future lies therefore not in a distant future but rather in the reinvention of the present as enlarged by the sociology of absences and by the sociology of emergences and rendered coherent by the work of translation. Through translation, the tension between experiences and expectations is recreated in a nonmodernist way, as the expanded present already contains the contracted future. Rather than a future-oriented present, we have a present-oriented future. The new nonconformity results from the verification that it would be possible to live in a much better world today. The capitalist and colonialist present is made of suppressed emergences and actively and invisibly produced absences. Thereby the future is set loose and made available for cathartic imaginations of a better society. Abyssal epistemology and abyssal law police minds as well as institutions in order to force the future out of the present. The absurdity of this modernist artifact emerges clearly out of the work of translation. Those involved in the work of translation wonder with Ernst Bloch why, if we only live in the present, it is so fleeting. In the intercultural contact zones, it is possible to enter in visual and existential contact with different kinds of present as experienced by different social actors. For some, the past is what is the future of others, and vice versa. And all of them are in the present working on building a new empowering, intercultural present. The urgent changes called upon to intervene in the present are civilizational changes as well. By operating through postabyssal thinking, the work of translation trains and empowers those in the contact zone to become competent destabilizing subjectivities and postinstitutional actors.

The work of translation permits the creation of meanings and directions that are precarious but concrete, short-range but radical in their objectives, uncertain but shared. The aim of translation between knowledges is to create cognitive justice. The aim of translation between practices and their agents is to create the conditions for global social justice from the standpoint of the democratic imagination. The work of translation creates the conditions for concrete social emancipations of concrete social groups in a present whose injustice is legitimated on the basis of a massive waste of experience. As the work of translation proceeds and expands, the vastness of such a waste becomes more visible, more absurd, and more revolting.

The new constellations of meaning made possible by the work of translation would be in themselves a waste of experience if they were not converted into new constellations of transformative practices. The practice of translation must lead to the practice of manifestos. I mean clear and unequivocal blueprints of alliances for collective action. Enhanced by interknowledge, mediation, and negotiation, common denominators turn into renewed mobilizing energies derived from a better sense of shared risks and shared possibilities on the basis of more *mestiza*, but no less authentic, identities. Herein lies the possibility of a bottom-up political aggregation, the alternative to a top-down aggregation imposed by a general theory or a privileged social actor.

Conclusion

I N MY *Toward a New Common Sense: Law, Science and Politics in the Paradigmatic Transition* (1995), I argued that the paradigmatic transition I was dealing with—from Western modernity as a sociocultural hegemonic paradigm toward another paradigm, or toward other paradigms impossible to name adequately— would occur both at the epistemological and the socio-politico-juridical level. In the book I am now concluding, I present the general outlines of the epistemological dimension of the transition. In *Epistemologies of the South: Reinventing Social Emancipation* (forthcoming), I will present the main contours of the social, political, and juridical dimensions of the same transition.

The idea of a paradigmatic transition may be questioned; it may even be suggested that our nonconformism before injustice and discrimination, however genuine, faces such long-lasting social processes that only a radical desire to put an end to them encourages us to speak of transitions that actually never happen. Consider the following quotation:

> If a man knew nothing about the lives of people in our Christian world and he were told "There is a certain people who have set up such a way of life, that the greater part of them, ninety-nine per cent, or thereabouts, live in ceaseless physical labor and oppressive need, and the rest one per cent lives in idleness and luxury now, if that one-hundredth has its own religion, science and art, what would that religion, science and art be like?" I think that there can only be one answer: "A perverted, a bad religion, science and art."

Was this written in the aftermath of the Occupy movement of the last three years? No, it was written by Leo Tolstoy in his diary on March 17, 1910 (1960: 66). In a tone breeding an even greater pessimism about the possibilities of emancipatory social transformation, Albert Camus blurted out in 1951, "After twenty centuries, the sum total of evil has not abated in the world. There has been no parousia, whether divine or revolutionary" (1951: 379).

I believe, however, that the idea of a paradigmatic transition need not be asserted or denied in absolute terms. Suffice it to bear in mind that it is a way to account for the transformations experienced as very profound in a given historical period, even if later on it may be possible to affirm that after all they did not change the status quo as much as they intended. Whether changes may be paradigmatic or subparadigmatic is of little importance. Of importance are the conditions under which they are experienced. There is no doubt today that one of the most significant changes of our time concerns the emergence on the global political scene of countries, peoples, and regions that for centuries were subjected to European colonialism and North American imperialism and that have come for the first time to lay claim to the conditions and priorities of the global agendas that up until now have been defined unilaterally by the global North. It may well be that this global South will end up reproducing, under new forms and with different kinds of discourses, the same social processes that for centuries were enacted by the global North. But, on the other hand, inside the global South there emerge social movements that are profoundly anticolonial and anti-imperial, resorting to discourses and practices of resistance to oppression and proposing alternatives that take off from non-Western presuppositions, be they ethical (ways of valuing and judging), political (ways of deliberating and of ruling and being ruled), cultural (ways of providing meaning), epistemological (ways of knowing), and even ontological (ways of being). These social movements give practical support to my main argument in this book: that there is no global social justice without global cognitive justice, that is to say, that there has to be equity between different ways of knowing and different kinds of knowledge. I offered this argument in conjunction with two other arguments: first, the understanding of the world by far exceeds the Western understanding of the world; second, the emancipatory transformations in the world may follow grammars and scripts other than those developed by Western-centric critical theory, and such diversity must be valorized.

The idea of cognitive justice points to a radical demand for social justice, a demand that includes unthinking the dominant criteria by which we define social justice and fight against social injustice. It implies, therefore, going to the roots of such criteria to question not only their sociopolitical determinations but also their cultural, epistemological, and even ontological presuppositions. These demands are today entering forcefully the agendas of resistance and alternative politics throughout the anti-imperial global South, and their sound is becoming increasingly more audible in the global North. This book aims at amplifying the intensity of this sound by exploring the different dimensions of the epistemological claims being made.[1] Of course, these claims have been there for a long, long time, and many even predate the colonial conquest. From the perspective of the epistemologies of the South, they can only be conceived of as emergent, in the sense that in recent times, and as a result of resistance and alternative politics

---

1. Jean Comaroff and John L. Comaroff (2012) reached me when my manuscript was ready to go to press. Although they focus on Africa alone as an exemplar of the global South, the purposes of our respective works converge somewhat. The same convergence exists with a very ambitious publishing project in which I also participated, coordinated by Corinne Kumar (2007a, 2007b, 2012, 2013).

in the global South, the pervasiveness of the epistemicide brought about by the Western-centric abyssal lines has been more efficiently exposed, the absences it has produced have become more forcefully present, and the new possibilities thereby opened up have grown more credible and promising. The exploration of such possibilities took two paths in this book. On the one side, I submitted the dominant epistemologies of the global North, which I called Northern epistemologies, to an exacting critique. This led me to highlight the complexity and internal diversity of what is conventionally referred to as Western modernity, which, at its best, takes the dominant conceptions for the totality and, at its worst, transforms Western modernity into a caricature all too easy to criticize. From different angles and perspectives I tried to show how dominant epistemologies have resulted in a massive waste of social experience and, particularly, in the massive destruction of ways of knowing that did not fit the dominant epistemological canon. This destruction I call *epistemicide*. On the other side, I defined the main traits of the epistemologies of the South as ways of knowing born in the struggle against capitalism, colonialism, and patriarchy. Such concepts as the sociology of absences, the sociology of emergences, ecologies of knowledges, and intercultural translation were central to this endeavor.

For no trivial reason this book started with an imaginary manifesto for good living/*buen vivir*. From the perspective of the epistemologies of the South, inquiries into ways of knowing cannot be separated from inquiries into ways of intervening in the world with the purpose of attenuating or eliminating the oppression, domination, and discrimination caused by global capitalism, colonialism, and patriarchy. Writing a theoretical book about the impossibility of separating theory and practice and writing it in a colonial language, even if acknowledging that many such ways of knowing may not even be pronounceable in colonial languages, seems to amount to a *contradictio in adjecto*. Hence the minifesto running hand in hand with the manifesto. The fertility of a contradiction does not lie in imagining ways of escaping it but rather in ways of working with and through it. If the time of paradigmatic transition has a name, it is certainly that of enabling contradictions. An enabling contradiction is a contradiction that recognizes the limits of thinking or action in a given period or context but refuses to view them at a distance or with reverence, as is typical of conformist thinking and action. An enabling contradiction is inflexible with the limits and rather comes as close as possible to them and explores their own contradictions as much as possible.

The enabling contradictions called for in this book have been of two kinds. On the one hand, different ways of knowing call for different forms of social agency, as well as for new grammars and objectives of social transformation. However, the need to intervene in translocal agendas, aggregate struggles, and the search for allies may call for some kind of cultural and epistemological hybridity, both as concerns what is to be done with whom and how to name it. I deal with intercultural translation in this book as a way of achieving this without compromising the cultural and political identity of the different social actors involved. On the other hand, the total investment in the present may also demand that the knowledges born in struggle engage with Western-centric conceptions and political instruments, be they democracy, human rights, or socialism, in order to design and carry out counterhegemonic, intercultural uses of such conceptions or instruments. Such conceptions are strangers but not complete strangers, since the struggles against them are also struggles with them. They are hybrids of strangeness and familiarity. The concrete workings of these enabling contradictions and their political productivity will be the analytical task of *Epistemologies of the South: Reinventing Social Emancipation.*

Working with and through contradictions is the other side of investing intensely in the present, conceived of as an expanded present both by the sociology of absences and the sociology of emergences. An intense investment in the present does not exclude the idea that another world is possible. On the contrary, it presupposes it but conceives of it as the measure and raison d'être of the nonconformism with an unjust present to be acted out in the present. The profile of such nonconformism fits the idea of rebellion rather than the idea of revolution. Finding no comfort in God or in the laws of history, such rebellion is a total investment in the present and in the concrete conditions in which concrete human beings live and are deprived of a dignified life. This total investment involves both the refusal of the present as it stands and the will not to escape from it. Those who cannot live with dignity in the present—the humiliated and the oppressed whose imagined voices were heard in the manifesto for good living/*buen vivir*—cannot afford to wait for imaginary futures. They represent the wounds of the present to be healed in the present. To quote Albert Camus one more time: "The real generosity toward the future consists of giving everything to the present" (1951: 380).

The only worthwhile utopia is, contradictorily enough, to be acted out here and now. Despite this, when we look into the mirror of our nonconformism, we tend to see the treacherous utopia of our present's future as if nothing or very little is accomplished now. Why is it so difficult to think that there is nothing else beyond our concrete present if it is so easy to prove that we only live and work in the present? Why is the immanence of the present less brilliant than the transcendence of the future? I have tried to show in this book that these questions will remain intractable as long as Northern epistemologies remain dominant. The future is a luxury that only those with a more or less secure present can afford. The trivialization of the present is always the other side of both the trivialization of the horror caused by so much unjust suffering and the trivialization of the struggles against it. For the epistemologies of the South and the knowledges born in struggle that they seek to validate, the present is the ground where the past and the future either irrupt or become meaningless verbiage, where past and future are freed from the linear-time cage, and the memory of the future is but the enabling vindication of a stolen or interrupted past.

This dense conception of contemporaneity—the conception of the present expanded by the sociology of absences and the sociology of emergences for which it calls—allows for a radically broader experience of the world as one's own. To experience the world as one's own is to experience the world as a set of problems in whose solution one can meaningfully participate. The Western-centric abyssal line has historically excluded large segments of populations and ideas from experiencing the world as their own and thus from actively participating in its transformation. They could not possibly be problem solvers since they themselves were the problem. At the beginning of the twentieth century, W. E. B. Du Bois denounced this brilliantly when in the first pages of *The Souls of Black Folk* (2008) he addresses the "negro problem" and asks how it feels to be a problem instead of having a problem. In 1952, Frantz Fanon published his "North African Syndrome," in which he makes the similar point that the North African, rather than having an illness, is converted by the colonial situation and European racism into a syndrome of his own: "The North African man who goes to see a doctor bears the dead weight of all his compatriots.... Threatened in his affectivity, threatened in his social activity, threatened in his membership in the community—the North African combines all the conditions that make a sick man" (1967b: 8, 13).[2] Inspired by these denunciations of the colonial ontologies from which so many supposedly universal theories of social transformation have derived, the epistemologies of the South proposed in this book are an invitation to a much larger experience of the world as one's own and thus to a much broader company in the task of transforming the world into a more equal and more diverse world, "a world in which different worlds will fit comfortably," to use the Neozapatista Subcomandante Marcos's slogan. The success of this task will decide the fate of the epistemologies of the South. They are there as long as the unequal relations between North and South, between West and East, go on ruling the world. The utopia of the epistemologies of the South is its own withering away.

---

2. "Le syndrôme nord africain" was first published in *L'Esprit* (Fevrier 1952): 237–251.

References

Abeele, Georges van der. 1992. *Travel as Metaphor*. Minneapolis: University of Minnesota Press.

Afzal-Khan, Fawzia, and Kalpana Sheshadri-Crooks. 2000. *The Pre-occupation of Postcolonial Studies*. Durham, NC: Duke University Press.

Agamben, Giorgio. 2004. *State of Exception*. Chicago: University of Chicago Press.

Ahmad, Ibn Majid Al-Najdi. 1971. *Arab Navigation in the Indian Ocean before the Coming of the Portuguese: Being a Translation of Kitab al-Fawa'id fi usul al-bahr wa'l-qawa'id of Ahmad b. Majid Al-Najdi, Together with an Introduction on the History of Arab Navigation, Notes on the Navigational Techniques and the Topography of Indian Ocean, and a Glossary of Navigational Terms by G. R. Tibbetts*. London: Royal Asiatic Society of Great Britain and Ireland.

Akerman, James, and Robert Karrow Jr., eds. 2007. *Maps: Finding Our Place in the World*. Chicago: University of Chicago Press for the Field Museum and the Newberry Library.

Akram, Susan Musarrat. 1999. "Scheherezade Meets Kafka: Two Dozen Sordid Tales of Ideological Exclusion." *Georgetown Immigration Law Journal* 14 (fall): 51–150.

———. 2000. "Orientalism Revisited in Asylum and Refugee Claims." *International Journal of Refugee Law* 12, no. 1: 7–40.

Akram, Susan Musarrat, and Maritza Karmely. 2005. "Immigration and Constitutional Consequences of Post-9/11 Policies Involving Arabs and Muslims in the United States: Is Alienage a Distinction without a Difference?" *U.C. Davis Law Review* 38, no. 3: 609–699.

Alberro, Solange. 1992. *Del gachupín al criollo*. Mexico City: El Colégio de Mexico.

Alexander, Jeffrey. 1982a. *Theoretical Logic in Sociology. Vol. 1: Positivism, Presuppositions and Current Controversies*. Berkeley: University of California Press.

———. 1982b. *Theoretical Logic in Sociology. Vol. 2: The Autonomies of Classical Thought: Marx and Durkheim*. Berkeley: University of California Press.

———. 1987. *Twenty Lectures*. New York: Columbia University Press.

———. 1995. *Fin de Siècle Social Theory*. London: Verso.

Alexander, Jeffrey C., and Kenneth Thompson. 2008. *A Contemporary Introduction to Sociology: Culture and Society in Transition*. Boulder, CO: Paradigm Publishers.

Alvares, Claude. 1992. *Science, Development, and Violence: The Revolt against Modernity*. New Delhi: Oxford University Press.

Amann, Diane Marie. 2004a. "Abu Ghraib." *University of Pennsylvania Law Review* 153, no. 6: 2085–2141.

———. 2004b. "Guantánamo." *Columbia Journal of Transnational Law* 42, no. 2: 263–348.

An-Na'im, Abdullahi A., ed. 1992. *Human Rights in Cross-cultural Perspectives: A Quest for Consensus*. Philadelphia: University of Pennsylvania Press.

———, ed. 1995. *Human Rights and Religious Values: An Uneasy Relationship?* Amsterdam: Rodopi.

———. 2000. "Human Rights and Islamic Identity in France and Uzbekistan: Mediation of the Local and Global." *Human Rights Quarterly* 22, no. 4: 906–941.

Anderson, Benedict. 1983. *Imagined Communities: Reflections on the Origin and Spread of Nationalism*. London: Verso.

Andrade, Oswald de. 1990 [1928]. *A Utopia Antropofágica*. São Paulo: Globo.

André, J. M. 1997. *Sentido, simbolismo e interpretação no discurso filosófico de Nicolau de Cusa*. Coimbra: Fundação Calouste Gulbenkian/JNICT.

Andrews, Lew. 1995. *Story and Space in Renaissance Art: The Rebirth of Continuous Narrative*. Cambridge: Cambridge University Press.

Anghie, Anthony. 2005. *Imperialism, Sovereignty and the Making of International Law*. Cambridge: Cambridge University Press.

Appiah, Kwame Anthony. 1998. "Cosmopolitan Patriots." In *Cosmopolitics: Thinking and Feeling beyond the Nation*, edited by P. Cheah and B. Robbins, 91–116. Minneapolis: University of Minnesota Press.

Arendt, Hannah. 1951. *The Origins of Totalitarianism*. New York: Harcourt.

Atkinson, Rowland, and Sarah Blandy. 2005. "International Perspectives on the New Enclavism and the Rise of Gated Communities." *Housing Studies* 20, no. 2: 177–186.

Aveling, Harry. 2006. "The Coloniser and the Colonised: Reflections on Translation as Contested Space." *Wacana: Jurnal Ilmu Pengetahuan Budaya* 8, no. 2: 162.

Avery, T. A., and G. L. Berlin. 1992. *Fundamentals of Remote Sensing and Airphoto Interpretation*. New York: Macmillan.

Ávila, Affonso. 1994. *O lúdico e as projecções do mundo barroco—II*. São Paulo: Perspectiva.

Ayres, Ian, and John Braithwaite. 1992. *Responsive Regulation: Transcending the Deregulation Debate*. New York: Oxford University Press.

Bachelard, Gaston. 1969. *The Poetics of Space*. Boston: Beacon.

———. 1971 [1934]. *Le nouvel ésprit scientifique*. Paris: Presses Universitaires de France.

———. 1972 [1938]. *La formation de l'ésprit scientifique*. Paris: J. Verin.

———. 1975 [1949]. *Le rationalisme appliqué*. Paris: Presses Universitaires de France.

———. 1981. *A epistemologia*. Lisbon: Edições 70.

Bakhtin, Mikhail. 1986. *Speech Genres and Other Late Essays*. Translated by V. W. McGee. Austin: University of Texas Press.

Balanyá, Belén, Brid Brennan, Olivier Hoedeman, Satoko Kishimoto, and Philipp Terhorst, eds. 2005. *Reclaiming Public Water: Achievements, Struggles and Visions from Around the World*. Amsterdam: Transnational Institute and Corporate Europe Observatory. Available at www.tni.org/books/publicwater.htm (accessed on October 11, 2012).

Bambirra, Vania. 1978. *Teoría de la dependencia: Una anticrítica*. Mexico City: Era.

Banuri, T. 1990. "Development and the Politics of Knowledge: A Critical Interpretation of the Social Role of Modernization Theories in the Development of the Third World." In *Dominating Knowledge: Development, Culture, and Resistance*, edited by F. Apfel Marglin and S. A. Marglin, 29–72. Oxford, UK: Clarendon Press.

Baratta, Giorgio. 2004. *As rosas e os cadernos*. Rio de Janeiro: DP&A Editora.

Barr, Bob. 2004. "USA PATRIOT Act and Progeny Threaten the Very Foundation of Freedom." *Georgetown Journal of Law and Public Policy* 2, no. 2: 385–392.

Baslar, Kemal. 1998. *The Concept of the Common Heritage of Mankind in International Law*. Dordrecht: Martinus Nijhoff.

Bauer, Carl J. 1998. *Against the Current: Privatization, Water Markets, and the State in Chile*. London: Kluwer.

Bauer, Laura Isabel. 2004. "They Beg Our Protection and We Refuse: U.S. Asylum Law's Failure to Protect Many of Today's Refugees." *Notre Dame Law Review* 79, no. 3: 1081–1116.

Beck, Ulrich. 1992. *The Risk Society: Towards a New Modernity*. London: Sage.

Becker, Marc. 2006. "Mariátegui, the Comintern, and the Indigenous Question in Latin America." *Science and Society* 70, no. 4: 450–479.

Benjamin, Walter. 1968. "Thesis on the Philosophy of History." In *Illuminations*. New York: Schocken.

———. 1972. "Erfahrung und Armut." In *Gesammelte Schriften* (II.1), edited by Rolf Tiedemann and Hermann Schweppenhäuser, 213–219. Frankfurt: Suhrkamp.

———. 1999. "The Task of the Translator: An Introduction to the Translation of Baudelaire's Tableaux Parisiens," translated by Harry Zohn. In *Translation Studies Reader*, edited by Lawrence Venuti, 75–82. New York: Routledge.

Berman, Antoine. 1985. "La traduction et la lettre ou l'auberge du lointain." In *Les tours de Babel: Essais sur la traduction*, edited by A. Berman, 33–150. Mauvezin, France: Trans-Europ-Repress.

Bernal, Martin. 1987. *Black Athena: The Afroasiatic Roots of Classical Civilization*. Vol. 1. New Brunswick, NJ: Rutgers University Press.

Bhabha, Homi K. 1994. *The Location of Culture*. London: Routledge.

———. 1996. "Unsatisfied: Notes on Vernacular Cosmopolitanism." In *Text and Nation*, edited by L. Garcia-Morena and P. C. Pfeifer, 191–207. London: Camden House.

Bilgrami, A. 2006. "Occidentalism, the Very Idea: An Essay on Enlightenment and Enchantment." *Critical Inquiry* 32, no. 3: 381–411.

Binford, L. R. 1981. "Behavioral Archaeology and the 'Pompeii Premise.'" *Journal of Anthropological Research* 37, no. 3: 195–208.

Blakely, Edward J., and Mary Gail Snyder. 1999. *Fortress America: Gated Communities in the United States*. Cambridge, MA: Brookings Institution, Lincoln Institute of Land Policy.

Blaser, Arthur. 1990. "The Common Heritage in Its Infinite Variety: Space Law and the Moon in the 1990s." *Journal of Law and Technology* 5: 79–99.

Bloch, Ernst. 1995. *The Principle of Hope*. Cambridge, MA: MIT Press.

Bloom, Harold. 1973. *The Anxiety of Influence*. New York: Oxford University Press.

———. 1994. *The Western Canon: The Books and School of the Ages*. New York: Harcourt.

Bond, Patrick. 2000. *Elite Transition: From Apartheid to Neoliberalism in South Africa*. London: Pluto.

Borelli, Silvia. 2005. "Casting Light on the Legal Black Hole: International Law and Detentions Abroad in the 'War on Terror.'" *International Review of the Red Cross* 87, no. 857: 39–68.

Borges, Jorge Luis. 1974. *Obras completas*. Buenos Aires: Emecé.

Bowles, Samuel. 1998. "Endogenous Preferences: The Cultural Consequences of Markets and Other Economic Institutions." *Journal of Economic Literature* 36: 75–111.

Boyne, Shawn. 2004. "Law, Terrorism, and Social Movements: The Tension between Politics and Security in Germany's Anti-terrorism Legislation." *Cardozo Journal of International and Comparative Law* 12, no. 1: 41–82.

Breckenridge, Carol, Sheldon Pollock, Homi Bhabha, and Dipesh Chakrabarty, eds. 2002. *Cosmopolitanism*. Durham, NC: Duke University Press.

Brockman, John. 1995. *The Third Culture*. New York: Simon and Schuster.

Brown, Lee M., ed. 2004. *African Philosophy: New and Traditional Perspectives*. New York: Oxford University Press.

Brown, Michelle. 2005. "'Setting the Conditions' for Abu Ghraib: The Prison Nation Abroad." *American Quarterly* 57, no. 3: 973–997.

Brunkhorst, Hauke. 1987. "Romanticism and Cultural Criticism." *Praxis International* 6: 397–415.

Buchanan, Patrick J. 2006. *State of Emergency: The Third World Invasion and Conquest of America*. New York: St. Martin's.

Buhlungu, Sakhela, John Daniel, Roger Southall, and Jessica Lutchman. 2006. *State of the Nation, 2005–2006*. Cape Town: HSRC Press.

Burnett, D. Graham. 2002. "'It Is Impossible to Make a Step without the Indians': Nineteenth-Century Geographical Exploration and the Amerindians of British Guiana." *Ethnohistory* 49, no. 1: 3–40.

Buruma, I., and A. Margalit. 2004. *Occidentalism: The West in the Eyes of Its Enemies*. New York: Penguin.

Cabral, Amílcar. 1979. *Unity and Struggle: Speeches and Writings of Amilcar Cabral*. New York: Monthly Review.

Caldeira, Teresa. 2000. *City of Walls: Crime, Segregation and Citizenship in São Paulo*. Berkeley: University of California Press.

Callicott, J. Baird. 2001. "Multicultural Environmental Ethics." *Daedalus* 130, no. 4: 77–97.

Callinicos, Alex. 1995. *Theories and Narratives: Reflections on the Philosophy of History*. Cambridge, UK: Polity.

Campbell, John. 1993. *Map Use and Analysis*. Dubuque, IA: Wm. C. Brown Publishers.

Camus, Albert. 1951. *L'homme révolté*. Paris: Gallimard.

Canguilhem, Georges. 1988. *Ideology and Rationality in the History of the Life Sciences*. Cambridge, MA: MIT Press.

Cardoso, Fernando Henrique, and Enzo Faletto. 1969. *Dependencia y desarrollo en América Latina*. Mexico City: Siglo XXI.

Carrier, J. G. 1992. "Occidentalism: The World Turned Upside-Down." *American Ethnologist* 19, no. 2: 195–212.

Cassirer, Ernst. 1960. *The Philosophy of the Enlightenment*. Boston: Beacon.

———. 1963. *The Individual and the Cosmos in Renaissance Philosophy*. Oxford, UK: Blackwell.

Castro, José Esteban. 2006. *Water, Power, and Citizenship: Social Struggle in the Basin of Mexico*. Basingstoke, UK; New York: Palgrave Macmillan.

Césaire, Aimé. 1955. *Discours sur le colonialisme*. Paris: Présence Africaine.

———. 1997. *Une tempête* [d'après *La tempête* de Shakespeare, adaptation pour un théâtre nègre]. Paris: Seuil.

———. 2000. *Discourse on Colonialism*. New York: New York University Press.

Chakrabarty, Dipesh. 1992. "Postcoloniality and the Artifice of History: Who Speaks for 'Indian' Pasts?" *Representations* 37, no. 1: 1–26.

———. 2000. *Provincializing Europe: Postcolonial Thought and Historical Difference*. Princeton, NJ: Princeton University Press.

Chambers, R. 1992. "Rural Appraisal: Rapid, Relaxed and Participatory," *IDS Discussion Papers* 311: 1–90.

Chang, Nancy. 2001. "The USA Patriot Act: What's So Patriotic about Trampling on the Bill of Rights?" *Guild Practitioner* 58, no. 3: 142–158.

Chen, X. 1992. "Occidentalism as Counterdiscourse: 'He Shang' in Post-Mao China." *Critical Inquiry* 18, no. 4: 686–712.

Chew, Sing, and Robert A. Denemark, eds. 1996. *The Underdevelopment of Development: Essays in Honor of Andre Gunder Frank*. Thousand Oaks, CA: Sage.

Cianciarulo, Marisa Silenzi. 2005. "The W Visa: A Legislative Proposal for Female and Child Refugees Trapped in a Post–September 11 World." *Yale Journal of Law and Feminism* 17, no. 2: 459–500.

Coetzee, Pieter Hendrik, and A. P. J. Roux, eds. 2003. *The African Philosophy Reader: A Text with Readings*. New York: Routledge.

Cohen, Mitchell. 1992. "Rooted Cosmopolitanism: Thoughts on the Left, Nationalism, and Multiculturalism." *Dissent* 39, no. 4: 478–483.

Collins, Randall. 1994. *Four Sociological Traditions*. Oxford: Oxford University Press.

———. 2008. *Violence: A Micro-sociological Theory*. Princeton, NJ: Princeton University Press.

Comaroff, Jean, and John L. Comaroff. 2012. *Theory from the South: Or, How Euro-America Is Evolving toward Africa*. Boulder, CO: Paradigm Publishers.

Conca, Ken. 2005. *Governing Water: Contentious Transnational Politics and Global Institution Building*. Cambridge, MA: MIT Press.

Condillac, Etienne Bonnor de. 1984 [1754–1755]. *Extrait raisonné du traité des sensations*. In *Traité des sensations: Traité des animaux*. Paris: Fayard.

Coronil, F. 1996. "Beyond Occidentalism: Toward Nonimperial Geohistorical Categories." *Cultural Anthropology* 11, no. 1: 51–87.

Coutinho, Afrânio. 1990. "O barroco e o maneirismo." *Claro Escuro* 4, no. 5: 15–16.

Coy, Martin. 2006. "Gated Communities and Urban Fragmentation in Latin America: The Brazilian Experience." *GeoJournal* 66, nos. 1–2: 121–132.

Cuin, C.-H., and F. Gresle. 1992. *Histoire de la sociologie.* Paris: La Découverte.

Dallmayr, Fred. 2006. "Modalities of Intercultural Dialogue." *Cultural Diversity and Transversal Values: East-West Dialogue on Spiritual and Secular Dialogues.* Paris: UNESCO.

Das, Veena. 1989. "Discussion: Subaltern as Perspective." In *Subaltern Studies VI: Writings on South Asian History and Society,* edited by Ranajit Guha, 310–324. Delhi: Oxford University Press.

David, C. W. A. 1924. "The Fugitive Slave Law of 1793 and Its Antecedents." *Journal of Negro History* 9, no. 1: 18–25.

De Genova, Nicholas P. 2002. "Migrant 'Illegality' and Deportability in Everyday Life." *Annual Review of Anthropology* 31: 419–447.

Deagan, Kathleen. 1989. "Tracing the Waste Makers." *Archeology,* special issue, 42, no. 1: 56–61.

Dean, Bartholomew, and Jerome M. Levi, eds. 2003. *At the Risk of Being Heard: Identity, Indigenous Rights, and Postcolonial States.* Ann Arbor: University of Michigan Press.

Deleuze, Gilles. 1968. *Différence et répétition.* Paris: Presses Universitaires de France.

Dershowitz, Alan. 2002. *Why Terrorism Works: Understanding the Threat, Responding to the Challenge.* New Haven, CT: Yale University Press.

———. 2003a. "Reply: Torture without Visibility and Accountability Is Worse Than with It." *University of Pennsylvania Journal of Constitutional Law* 6, no. 2: 326.

———. 2003b. "The Torture Warrant: A Response to Professor Strauss." *New York Law School Law Review* 48, nos. 1–2: 275–294.

Desroche, Henri. 1975. *La société festive: Du fouriérisme aux fouriérismes pratiqués.* Paris: Seuil.

Diagne, Mamoussé. 2005. *Critique de la raison orale: Les pratiques discursives en Afrique Noire.* Niamey/Paris/Dakar: CELHTO/Karthala/IFAN.

Diagne, Souleymane Bachir. 2001. *Reconstruire le sens: Textes et enjeux de prospectives africaines.* Dakar: CODESRIA.

Dickinson, Laura. 2005. "Torture and Contract." *Case Western Reserve Journal of International Law* 37, no. 5-3: 267–275.

Diouf, Mamadou. 2000. "The Senegalese Murid Trade Diaspora and the Making of a Vernacular Cosmopolitanism." *Public Culture* 12, no. 3: 679–702.

Dioup, Cheik Anta. 1967. *Antériorité des civilisations nègres: Mythe ou vérité historique.* Paris: Présence Africaine.

———. 1974. *African Origins of Civilization—Myth or Reality.* Chicago: Lawrence Hill.

———. 1996. *Towards the African Renaissance: Essays in Culture and Development, 1946–1960.* London: The Estate of Cheikh Anta Diop and Karnak House.

Donahue, John, and Barbara Johnston, eds. 1998. *Water, Culture, and Power: Local Struggles in a Global Context.* Washington, DC: Island.

Dorf, Michael, and Charles Sabel. 1998. "A Construction of Democratic Experimentalism." *Columbia Law Review* 98, no. 2: 267–473.

Dörmann, Knut. 2003. "The Legal Situation of Unlawful/Unprivileged Combatants." *International Review of the Red Cross* 85, no. 849: 45–74.

Dos Santos, Theotonio. 1971. *El nuevo carácter de la dependencia.* Buenos Aires: S. Ediciones.

Du Bois, W. E. B. 2008. *The Souls of Black Folk.* New York: Oxford University Press.

Dumoulin, Michel. 2005. *Léopold II: Un roi génocidaire?* Bruxelles: Académie Royale de Belgique, Classe des Lettres.

Dunnell, Robert. 1989. "Hope for an Endangered Science." *Archeology,* special issue, 42, no. 1: 63–66.

Dupré, John. 1993. *The Disorder of Things: Metaphysical Foundations of the Disunity of Science.* Cambridge, MA: Harvard University Press.

———. 2003. *Darwin's Legacy: What Evolution Means Today.* Oxford: Oxford University Press.

Dupuy, René-Jean. 1974. *The Law of the Sea.* Dobbs Ferry, NY: Oceana.

Dussel, Enrique. 1992. *1492: El encubrimiento del otro: Hacia el origen del "mito de la modernidad."* Bogotá: Anthropos.

———. 1995. *The Invention of the Americas: Eclipse of "the Other" and the Myth of Modernity.* New York: Continuum.

———. 2000. *Ética de la liberación en la edad de la globalización y de la exclusión.* Madrid: Trotta.

———. 2001. *Hacia una filosofía política crítica.* Bilbao: Desclee de Brouwer.

Echeverría, Bolívar. 1994. *Modernidad, mestizaje, cultura, ethos barroco.* Mexico City: UNAM, El Equilibrista.

———. 1996. *Benjamin: Messianism y utopia.* Mexico City: UNAM.

———. 2011. *Antología: Crítica de la modernidad capitalista.* La Paz: Vicepresidencia del Estado Plurinacional de Bolivia.

Emerson, Barbara. 1979. *Leopold II of the Belgians: King of Colonialism.* London: Weidenfeld and Nicolson.

Emerton, Patrick. 2004. "Paving the Way for Conviction without Evidence—a Disturbing Trend in Australia's Anti-terrorism Laws." *Queensland University of Technology Law and Justice Journal* 4, no. 92: 1–38.

Epicurus. 1926. *Epicurus' Morals.* Collected and faithfully englished by Walter Charleton. London: Peter Davies.

ERDAS. 1997. *ERDAS Field Guide.* Atlanta: Erdas International.

Escobar, Arturo. 1995. *Encountering Development: The Making and Unmaking of the Third World.* Princeton, NJ: Princeton University Press.

———. 1999. "After Nature: Steps to an Anti-essentialist Political Ecology." *Current Anthropology* 40, no. 1: 1–30.

Eze, Emmanuel Chukwudi, ed. 1997. *Postcolonial African Philosophy: A Critical Reader.* Oxford, UK: Blackwell.

Falk, Richard. 1995. *On Humane Governance: Toward a New Global Politics.* University Park: Pennsylvania State University Press.

Fanon, Frantz. 1961. *Les damnés de la terre.* Preface by Jean Paul Sartre. Paris: Maspero.

———. 1963. *The Wretched of the Earth.* Preface by Jean-Paul Sartre. New York: Grove.

———. 1967a. *Black Skin, White Masks.* New York: Grove.

———. 1967b. "The 'North African Syndrome.'" In *Toward the African Revolution.* Translated by Haakon Chevalier. New York: Grove.

———. 1967c. *Toward the African Revolution.* New York: Grove.

Faruki, Kemal A. 1979. *The Constitutional and Legal Role of the Umma.* Karachi: Ma'aref.

Federici, Silvia. 1994. "Journey to the Native Land: Violence and the Concept of the Self in Fanon and Gandhi." *Quest* 8, no. 2: 47–69.

Findlen, Paula. 1995. "Translating the New Science: Women and the Circulation of Knowledge in Enlightenment Italy." *Configurations* 2: 167–206.

Flores, Carlos Crespo. 2005. *La guerra del agua de Cochabamba: Cinco lecciones para las luchas anti neoliberales en Bolivia.* Available at www.aguabolivia.org (accessed on October 11, 2012).

Foucault, Michel. 1980. *Power and Knowledge.* New York: Pantheon.

Fourier, Charles. 1967. *Théorie des quatre mouvements et des destinées generals.* Paris: Jean-Jacques Pauvert, Editeur.

Frank, Andre Gunder. 1969. *Latin America: Underdevelopment or Revolution.* New York: Monthly Review.

Freeman, Jody. 1997. "Collaborative Governance in the Administrative State." *UCLA Law Review* 45, no. 1: 1–98.

Freyre, Gilberto. 1946. *The Masters and the Slaves.* New York: Alfred A. Knopf.

Fukuyama, F. 1992. *The End of History and the Last Man.* London: Penguin.

Furnivall, John Sydenham. 1948. *Colonial Policy and Practice: A Comparative Study of Burma and Netherlands India.* Cambridge: Cambridge University Press.

Galison, Peter. 1997. *Image and Logic: A Material Culture of Microphysics.* Chicago: University of Chicago Press.

Galison, Peter, and David J. Stump, eds. 1996. *The Disunity of Science: Boundaries, Contexts, and Power.* Stanford, CA: Stanford University Press.

Gamble, C. 1989. *The Paleolithic Settlement of Europe.* Cambridge: Cambridge University Press.

Gandhi, Mahatma. 1929/1932. *The Story of My Experiments with Truth.* Vols. 1 and 2. Ahmedabad: Navajivan.

———. 1938. *Hind Swaraj.* Ahmedabad: Navajivan.

———. 1951. *Selected Writings of Mahatma Gandhi.* Boston: Beacon.

———. 1956. *The Gandhi Reader.* Bloomington: Indiana University Press.

———. 1960. *Discourses on the Gita.* Ahmedabad: Navajivan.

———. 1972. *Satyagraha in South Africa.* Ahmedabad: Navajivan.

Gandler, Stefan. 2010. "The Concept of History in Walter Benjamin's Critical Theory." *Radical Philosophy Review* 13, no. 1: 19–42.

García Linera, Álvaro. 2009. *La potencia plebeya: Acción colectiva y identidades indígenas obreras y populares en Bolivia.* Bogotá: Siglo del Hombre.

Gibbon, Edward. 1928. *The Decline and Fall of the Roman Empire.* London: J. M. Dent and Sons.

Giddens, Anthony. 1993. *New Rules of Sociological Method.* Cambridge: Polity.

———. 1995. *Politics, Sociology and Social Theory.* Cambridge: Polity.

Gieryn, Thomas F. 1999. *Cultural Boundaries of Science: Credibility on the Line.* Chicago: University of Chicago Press.

Gill, Terry, and Elies van Sliedgret. 2005. "A Reflection on the Legal Status and Rights of 'Unlawful Enemy Combatant.'" *Utrecht Law Review* 1, no. 1: 28–54.

Gilman, E. B. 1978. *The Curious Perspective: Literary and Pictorial Wit in the Seventeenth Century.* New York: Yale University Press.

Gilroy, Paul. 1993. *The Black Atlantic: Modernity and Double Consciousness.* Cambridge, MA: Cambridge University Press.

Glon, Justin C. 2005. "Good Fences Make Good Neighbors: National Security and Terrorism—Time to Fence in Our Southern Border." *Indiana International and Comparative Law Review* 15, no. 2: 349–388.

Goody, J. 2006. *The Theft of History.* Cambridge: Cambridge University Press.

Gordon, Lewis. 1995. *Fanon and the Crisis of European Man: An Essay on Philosophy and the Human Sciences.* London: Routledge.

Gordon, Linda, ed. 1991. *Women, the State and Welfare.* Madison: University of Wisconsin Press.

———. 2007. *The Moral Property of Women: A History of Birth Control Politics in America.* Champaign-Urbana: University of Illinois Press.

Gouldner, Alvin Ward. 1970. *The Coming Crisis of Western Sociology.* New York: Avon.

Graham, Chadwick M. 2005. "Defeating an Invisible Enemy: The Western Superpowers' Efforts to Combat Terrorism by Fighting Illegal Immigration." *Transnational Law and Contemporary Problems* 14, no. 1: 281–310.

Graham, Nora. 2005. "Patriot Act II and Denationalization: An Unconstitutional Attempt to Revive Stripping Americans of Their Citizenship." *Cleveland State Law Review* 52, no. 4: 593–621.

Gramsci, Antonio. 1975. *Quaderni del carcere*. Edited by Valentino Gerratana. 4 vols. Torino: Einaudi.

Gregory, D. 2006. *Violent Geographies: Fear, Terror, and Political Violence*. London: Routledge.

Grosfoguel, Ramón. 2000. "Developmentalism, Modernity, and Dependency Theory in Latin America." *Nepantla: Views from the South* 1, no. 2: 347–374.

———. 2005. "The Implications of Subaltern Epistemologies for Global Capitalism: Transmodernity, Border Thinking and Global Coloniality." In *Critical Globalization Studies*, edited by William Robinson and Richard Applebaum, 283–292. London: Routledge.

———. 2007. "The Epistemic Decolonial Turn: Beyond Political Economy Paradigms." *Cultural Studies* 21, nos. 2–3: 211–223.

Grotius, Hugo. 1964. *De jure belli ac pacis libri tres*. Vol. 2. New York: Oceana.

Guha, Ranajit. 1989. "Dominance without Hegemony and Its Historiography." In *Subaltern Studies VI: Writings on South Asian History and Society*, edited by Ranajit Guha, 210–309. Delhi: Oxford University Press.

Guiora, Amos N. 2005. "Legislative and Policy Responses to Terrorism: A Global Perspective." *San Diego International Law Journal* 7, no. 1: 125–172.

Gurvitch, Georges. 1969. "La multiplicité des temps sociaux." In *La vocation actuelle de la sociologie*. Vol. 2: *Antécédents et perspective*. Paris: Presses Universitaires de France.

Gutiérrez, Gustavo. 1991. *A Theology of Liberation*. New York: Orbis.

Gutiérrez Sanín, Francisco, and Ana María Jaramillo. 2003. "Pactos paradoxais." In *Reconhecer para libertar: Os caminhos do cosmopolitismo multicultural*, edited by Boaventura de Sousa Santos, 249–287. Rio de Janeiro: Civilização Brasileira.

Hall, David, Emanuele Lobina, and Robin de la Motte. 2005. "Public Resistance to Privatization in Water and Energy." *Development in Practice* 15, nos. 3–4: 286–301.

Hall, Stuart. 1996. "Who Needs Identity?" In *Questions of Cultural Identity*, edited by S. Hall and P. du Gay, 1–17. London: Sage.

Hansen, Thomas, and Finn Stepputat. 2004. *Sovereign Bodies: Citizens, Migrants, and States in the Postcolonial World*. Princeton, NJ: Princeton University Press.

Haraway, Donna. 1989. *Primate Visions*. New York: Routledge.

Hardin, Garrett. 1968. "The Tragedy of the Commons." *Science* 162: 1243–1248.

Harding, Sandra. 1998. *Is Science Multicultural? Postcolonialisms, Feminisms, and Epistemologies*. Bloomington: Indiana University Press.

———. 2006. *Science and Social Inequality: Feminist and Postcolonial Issues*. Urbana: University of Illinois Press.

Harris, George C. 2003. "Terrorism, War and Justice: The Concept of the Unlawful Enemy Combatant." *Loyola of Los Angeles International and Comparative Law Review* 26, no. 1: 31–36.

Hasian, Marouf Arif. 2002. *Colonial Legacies in Postcolonial Contexts*. New York: Peter Lang.

Hassan, Riffat. 1996. "Religious Human Rights and the Qur'an." In *Religious Human Rights in Global Perspective: Religious Perspectives*, edited by J. Witte Jr. and J. D. van der Vyver, 361–386. The Hague: Martinus Nijhoff Publishers.

Hedström, Peter. 2005. *Dissecting the Social: On the Principles of Analytical Sociology*. Cambridge: Cambridge University Press.

Hegel, Georg Wilhelm Friedrich. 1970. *Vorlesungen über die Philosophie der Geschichte*. Edited by Eva Moldenhauer and Karl Markus Michel. Frankfurt am Main: Suhrkamp.

Hermans, Theo. 2003. "Cross-cultural Translation Studies as Thick Translation." *Bulletin of the School of Oriental and African Studies* 66, no. 3: 385–386.

Hirschman, Albert. 1977. *The Passions and the Interests*. Princeton, NJ: Princeton University Press.

Hobbes, Thomas. 1985 [1651]. *Leviathan*. London: Penguin.

Hochschild, Adam. 1999. *King Leopold's Ghost: A Story of Greed, Terror, and Heroism in Colonial Africa*. Boston: Houghton Mifflin.

Holloway, John. 2002. *Change the World without Taking the Power: The Meaning of Revolution Today*. London: Pluto.

Homans, Peter. 1993. *Jung in Context*. 2nd ed. Chicago: University of Chicago Press.

Horkheimer, Max, and Theodor Adorno. 1969. *Dialektik der Aufklärung: Philosophische Fragmente*. Frankfurt: S. Fischer Verlag.

———. 1972. *Dialectic of Enlightenment*. New York: Herder and Herder.

Hountondji, Paulin J., ed. 1983. *African Philosophy: Myth and Reality*. Bloomington: Indiana University Press.

———. 2002. *Struggle for Meaning: Reflections on Philosophy, Culture, and Democracy in Africa*. Athens: Ohio University Press.

Human Rights Watch. 2004. *The United States' "Disappeared": The CIA's Long-Term "Ghost Detainees."* A Human Rights Watch Briefing Paper, October 2004. New York: Human Rights Watch.

Huntington, Samuel. 1993. "The Clash of Civilizations?" *Foreign Affairs* 72, no. 3: 22–49.

———. 1997. *The Clash of Civilizations and the Remaking of World Order*. New York: Touchstone.

Immigrant Rights Clinic (NYU). 2001. "Indefinite Detention without Probable Cause: A Comment on INS Interim Rule 8 C.F.R. 287.3." *New York University Review of Law and Social Change* 26, no. 3: 397–430.

International Court of Justice. 2004. "Legal Consequences of the Construction of a Wall in the Occupied Palestinian Territory—Advisory Opinion." The Hague, July 9. Available at cij.org /docket/index.php?pr=71&code=mwp&p1=3&p2=4&p3=6 (accessed on October 11, 2012).

Jacquemond, Richard. 2004. "Towards an Economy and Poetics of Translation." In *Cultural Encounters in Translation from Arabic*, edited by Said Faiq, 117–127. Bristol, UK: Multilingual Matters.

Jameson, Fredric. 1986. "Third World Literature in the Era of Multinational Capitalism." *Social Text* 15: 65–88.

Jasanoff, Sheila, Gerald E. Markley, James Peterson, and Trevor Pinch, eds. 1995. *Handbook of Science and Technology Studies*. Thousand Oaks, CA: Sage.

Jaspers, Karl. 1951. *Way to Wisdom: An Introduction to Philosophy*. New Haven, CT: Yale University Press.

———. 1952. *Reason and Anti-reason in Our Time*. New Haven, CT: Yale University Press.

———. 1976. *The Origin and Goal of History*. Westport, CT: Greenwood.

———. 1986. *Basic Philosophical Writings*. Athens: Ohio University Press.

———. 1995. *The Great Philosophers*. New York: Harcourt Brace.

Joas, Hans, and Wolfgang Knöbl. 2009. *Social Theory: Twenty Introductory Lectures*. Cambridge: Cambridge University Press.

Jones, C. P. 1986. *Culture and Society in Lucian*. Cambridge, MA: Harvard University Press.

Joyner, Christopher. 1986. "Legal Implications of the Concept of the Common Heritage of Humankind." *International and Comparative Law Quarterly* 35: 190–199.

Kafka, Franz. 1960. "He." In *Description of a Struggle and the Great Wall of China*. Translated by Tania and James Stern, 290–299. London: Secker and Warburg.

Kanstroom, Daniel. 2003. "Unlawful Combatants in the United States—Drawing the Fine Line between Law and War." *American Bar Association's Human Right Magazine* (Winter). Available at www.abanet.org/irr/hr/winter03/unlawful.html (accessed on October 11, 2012).

———. 2004. "Criminalizing the Undocumented: Ironic Boundaries of the Post–September 11th Pale of Law." *North Carolina Journal of International Law and Commercial Regulation* 29, no. 4: 639–670.

Karp, Ivan, and Dismas Masolo, eds. 2000. *African Philosophy as Cultural Inquiry*. Bloomington: Indiana University Press.

Karsenti, Bruno. 2005. *La societé en personnes: Etudes durkheimiennes*. Paris: Economica.

Keates, J. S. 1982. *Understanding Maps*. London: Longman.

Keating, P., and A. Cambrosio. 2003. *Biomedical Platforms: Realigning the Normal and the Pathological in Late-Twentieth-Century Medicine*. Cambridge, MA: MIT Press.

Kebede, Messay. 2001. "The Rehabilitation of Violence and the Violence of Rehabilitation." *Journal of Black Studies* 31, no. 5: 539–562.

Keller, Evelyn Fox. 1985. *Reflections on Gender and Science*. New Haven, CT: Yale University Press.

———. 2000. *The Century of the Gene*. Cambridge, MA: Harvard University Press.

Kiss, Alexandra. 1985. "The Common Heritage of Mankind: Utopia or Reality?" *International Journal* 40: 423–441.

Klare, Michael. 2001. *Resource Wars: The New Landscape of Global Conflict*. New York: Metropolitan Books.

Kleinman, Daniel L., ed. 2000. *Science, Technology and Democracy*. New York: SUNY Press.

Kohler, Robert E. 2002. *Landscapes and Labscapes: Exploring the Lab-Field Border in Biology*. Chicago: University of Chicago Press.

Koselleck, Reinhart. 1985. *Futures Past: On the Semantics of Historical Time*. Translated by Keith Tribe. Cambridge, MA: MIT Press.

Koskenniemi, Martti. 2002. *The Gentle Civilizer of Nations: The Rise and Fall of International Law, 1870–1960*. Cambridge: Cambridge University Press.

Kreimer, Seth. 2003. "Too Close to the Rack and the Screw: Constitutional Constraints on Torture in the War on Terror." *University of Pennsylvania Journal of Constitutional Law* 6, no. 2: 278–374.

Krishnan, Jayanth K. 2004. "India's Patriot Act: POTA and the Impact on Civil Liberties in the World's Largest Democracy." *Law and Inequality: A Journal of Theory and Practice* 22, no. 2: 265–300.

Kuhn, Thomas S. 1970. *The Structure of Scientific Revolutions*. Chicago: University of Chicago Press.

———. 1977. *The Essential Tension*. Chicago: University of Chicago Press.

Kumar, Corinne, ed. 2007a. *Asking We Walk: The South as New Political Imaginary*. Vol. 1. Bangalore: Streelekha Publications.

———, ed. 2007b. *Asking We Walk: The South as New Political Imaginary*. Vol. 2. Bangalore: Streelekha Publications.

———, ed. 2012. *Asking We Walk: The South as New Political Imaginary*. Vol. 3. Bangalore: Streelekha Publications.

———, ed. 2013. *Asking We Walk: The South as New Political Imaginary*. Vol. 4. Bangalore: Streelekha Publications.

Lacey, H. 2002. "Alternatives to Technoscience and the Values of Forum Social Mundial." Paper delivered at the Second World Social Forum (Workshop on Technoscience, Ecology and Capitalism), Porto Alegre, Brazil, January–February.

Lapouge, M. G. de, and Carlos Closson. 1897. "The Fundamental Laws of Anthropo-sociology." *Journal of Political Economy* 6, no. 1: 54–92.

Lash, Scott. 1999. *Another Modernity, a Different Rationality*. Oxford, UK: Blackwell.

Latour, Bruno. 1987. *Science in Action*. Cambridge, MA: Harvard University Press.

———. 1999. *Pandora's Hope: Essays on the Reality of Science Studies*. Cambridge, MA: Harvard University Press.

Leibniz, Gottfried Wilhelm. 1985 [1710]. *Theodicy: Essays on the Goodness of God, the Freedom of Man, and the Origin of Evil*. La Salle, IL: Open Court.

León, Antonio García de. 1993. "Contrapunto entre lo barroco y lo popular en el Vera Cruz colonial." Paper presented at International Colloquium Modernidad Europea, Mestizaje Cultural y Ethos Barroco, Universidad Nacional Autónoma de Méjico, Mexico City, May 17–20.

Lepenies, Wolf. 1988. *Between Literature and Science: The Rise of Sociology*. Translated by R. J. Hollingdale. Cambridge: Cambridge University Press.

Lewontin, Richard. 2000. *It Ain't Necessarily So: The Dream of the Human Genome and Other Illusions.* New York: New York Review of Books.

Liu, Lydia H. 1995. *Translingual Practice: Literature, National Culture, and Translated Modernity—China, 1900–1937.* Stanford, CA: Stanford University Press.

Lobel, Jules. 2002. "The War on Terrorism and Civil Liberties." *University of Pittsburgh Law Review* 63, no. 4: 767–790.

Locke, John. 1946 [1690]. *The Second Treatise of Civil Government and a Letter Concerning Toleration.* Introduction by J. W. Gough. Oxford, UK: B. Blackwell.

———. 1956. *An Essay Concerning Human Understanding.* Oxford, UK: Clarendon.

Lopes, Paula Duarte. 2005. "Water with Borders: Social Goods, the Market and Mobilization." PhD diss., Johns Hopkins University.

Low, Setha. 2003. *Behind the Gates: Life, Security, and the Pursuit of Happiness in Fortress America.* New York: Routledge.

Löwy, Michael. 2005a. *Fire Alarm: Reading Walter Benjamin's "On the Concept of History."* London and New York: Verso.

———. 2005b. "Introdução: Nem decalque nem cópia: O marxismo romântico de José Carlos Mariátegui." In *Por um socialismo indo-americano: Ensaios escolhidos*, edited by J. C. Mariátegui, 7–24. Rio de Janeiro: UFRJ.

Lucian of Samosata. 1905. *The Works of Lucian of Samosata.* Translated by H. W. Fowler and F. G. Fowler. 4 vols. Oxford, UK: Clarendon.

Lucretius. 1950. *Lucretius on the Nature of Things.* New Brunswick, NJ: Rutgers University Press.

Lugard, Frederick D. 1929. *The Dual Mandate in British Tropical Africa.* London: W. Blackwood.

Lynch, Michael. 1993. *Scientific Practice and Ordinary Action: Ethnomethodology and Social Studies of Science.* Cambridge: Cambridge University Press.

Mac Neil, Michael, Neil Sargent, and Peter Swan, eds. 2000. *Law, Regulation and Governance.* Ontario: Oxford University Press.

MacEachren, Alan. 1994. *Some Truth with Maps: A Primer on Symbolization and Design.* Washington, DC: Association of American Geographers.

———. 2004. *How Maps Work, Representation, Visualization and Design.* New York: Guilford.

Maier, Charles. 1993. "A Surfeit of Memory? Reflections on History, Melancholy and Denial." *History and Memory* 5, no. 2: 136–152.

Maldonado-Torres, Nelson. 2004. "The Topology of Being and the Geopolitics of Knowledge: Modernity, Empire, Coloniality." *City* 8, no. 1: 29–56.

———. 2007. "On the Coloniality of Being: Contributions to the Development of a Concept." *Cultural Studies* 21, nos. 2–3: 240–270.

———. 2010. "The Time and Space of Race: Reflections on David Theo Goldberg's Interrelational and Comparative Methodology: A Review of the Threat of Race: Reflections on Racial Neoliberalism." *Patterns of Prejudice* 44, no. 1: 77–88.

Malinowski, Bronislaw. 1945. "Indirect Rule and Its Scientific Planning." In *The Dynamics of Culture Change: An Inquiry into Race Relations in Africa*, edited by Phyllis M. Kaberry, 138–150. New Haven, CT: Yale University Press.

Mamdani, Mahmood. 1996. *Citizen and Subject: Contemporary Africa and the Legacy of Late Colonialism.* Princeton, NJ: Princeton University Press.

———. 1999. "Historicizing Power and Responses to Power: Indirect Rule and Its Reform." *Social Research* 66, no. 3: 859–886.

Mandell, B. R. 2007. "Adoption." *New Politics* 11, no. 2, whole no. 42.

Maravall, José Antonio. 1990. *La cultura del barroco: Análisis de una estructura histórica.* Barcelona: Ariel.

Mariátegui, José Carlos. 1974a [1925]. *Ensayos escogidos.* Lima: Universo.

———. 1974b [1925–1927]. *La novela y la vida.* Lima: Amanta.

Marramao, Giacomo. 1995. *Poder e secularização: As categorias do tempo*. São Paulo: Editora da Universidade Estadual Paulista.

Martí, José. 1963–1966. *Obras completas*. 25 vols. La Habana: Editorial Nacional de Cuba.

Masolo, Dismas A. 2003. "Philosophy and Indigenous Knowledge: An African Perspective." *Africa Today* 50, no. 2: 21–38.

Mbembe, Achille. 2001. *On the Postcolony*. Berkeley: University of California Press.

McCormack, Wayne. 2004. "Military Detention and the Judiciary: Al Qaeda, the KKK and Supra-state Law." *San Diego International Law Journal* 5: 7–72.

Memmi, Albert. 1965. *The Colonizer and the Colonized*. New York: Orion.

Menefee, Samuel Pyeatt. 2003–2004. "The Smuggling of Refugees by Sea: A Modern Day Maritime Slave Trade." *Regent Journal of International Law* 2: 1–28.

Meneses, Maria Paula. 2000. *New Methodological Approaches to the Study of the Acheulean from Southern Mozambique*. Rutgers University, UMI Dissertation Services.

———. 2007. "'When There Are No Problems, We Are Healthy, No Bad Luck': For an Emancipatory Conception of Health and Medicines." In *Another Knowledge Is Possible: Beyond Northern Epistemologies*, edited by Boaventura de Sousa Santos, 352–379. London: Verso.

———. 2010. "Traditional Doctors, Leaders of the Association of Traditional Doctors of Mozambique." In *Voices of the World*, edited by Boaventura de Sousa Santos, 257–300. London: Verso.

Merleau-Ponty, Maurice. 1968. *Résumés de Cours: Collège de France, 1952–1960*. Paris: Gallimard.

Mignolo, Walter. 1995. *The Darker Side of Renaissance: Literacy, Territoriality, and Colonization*. Ann Arbor: University of Michigan Press.

———. 2000. *Local Histories/Global Designs: Coloniality, Subaltern Knowledges, and Border Thinking*. Princeton, NJ: Princeton University Press.

———. 2003. *Histórias locales/diseños globales*. Madrid: Akal.

Miller, C. L. 2003. "Reading Cusanus: Metaphor and Dialectic in a Conjectural Universe." *Studies in Philosophy and the History of Philosophy* 37. Washington, DC: Catholic University of America Press.

Miller, Marc L. 2002. "Immigration Law: Assessing New Immigration Enforcement Strategies and the Criminalization of Migration." *Emory Law Journal* 51, no. 3: 963–976.

Mol, Annemarie. 2002. *The Body Multiple: Ontology in Medical Practice*. Durham, NC: Duke University Press.

Monmonier, Mark. 1981. *Maps: Distortion and Meaning*. Washington, DC: Association of American Geographers.

———. 1985. *Technological Transition in Cartography*. Madison: University of Wisconsin Press.

———. 1991. *How to Lie with Maps*. Chicago: University of Chicago Press.

———. 1993. *Mapping It Out: Expository Cartography for the Humanities and Social Sciences*. Chicago: University of Chicago Press.

———. 2010. *No Dig, No Fly, No Go: How Maps Restrict and Control*. Chicago: University of Chicago Press.

———. 2012. *Lake Effect: Tales of Large Lakes, Arctic Winds, and Recurrent Snows*. New York: Syracuse University Press.

Montaigne, Michel de. 1958. *Essays*. Harmondsworth, UK: Penguin.

Morris, H. F., and James S. Read. 1972. *Indirect Rule and the Search for Justice: Essays in East African Legal History*. Oxford, UK: Clarendon.

Mörth, Ulrika, ed. 2004. *Soft Law in Governance and Regulation: An Interdisciplinary Analysis*. Cheltenham, UK: E. Elgar.

Mudimbe, Valentin Y. 1988. *The Invention of Africa: Gnosis, Philosophy, and the Order of Knowledge*. Bloomington: Indiana University Press.

———. 1994. *The Idea of Africa*. Bloomington: Indiana University Press.

Muehrcke, P. C. 1986. *Map Use*. Madison, WI: JP Publications.

Nandy, Ashis. 1987. *Traditions, Tyranny, and Utopias: Essays in the Politics of Awareness*. Oxford: Oxford University Press.

Nasr, Seyyed Hossein. 1976. *Western Science and Asian Cultures*. New Delhi: Indian Council for Cultural Relations.

Needham, Joseph. 1954–2008. *Science and Civilization in China*. 6 vols. Cambridge: Cambridge University Press.

Nicholas of Cusa. 1985. *On Learned Ignorance (De docta ignorantia)*. Minneapolis: Arthur J. Banning Press. Available at http://cla.umn.edu/sites/jhopkins/DI-I-12-2000.pdf (accessed on October 11, 2012).

Nietzsche, Friedrich. 1971. "Rhétorique et langage." Edited and translated by Jean-Luc Nancy and Philippe Lacoue-Labarthe. *Poétique* 5 (March): 99–144.

———. 1973. *The Portable Nietzsche*. Edited by Walter Kaufmann. New York: Viking.

Nkrumah, Kwame. 1965a. *Consciencism: Philosophy and Ideology for Decolonization and Development with Particular Reference to the African Revolution*. New York: Monthly Review.

———. 1965b. *Neo-colonialism: The Last Stage of Imperialism*. New York: International Publishers.

Nunes, João Arriscado. 1998/1999. "Para além das 'duas culturas': Tecnociências, tecnoculturas e teoría crítica." *Revista Crítica de Ciências Sociais* 52/53: 15–59.

———. 2001. "A síndrome do Parque Jurássico: História(s) edificante(s) da genética num mundo 'sem garantias.'" *Revista Crítica de Ciências Sociais* 61: 29–62.

Nunes, João Arriscado, and Maria E. Gonçalves, eds. 2001. *Enteados de Galileu? A semiperiferia no sistema mundial da ciência*. Porto, Portugal: Afrontamento.

Nye, Joseph, and John Donahue, eds. 2000. *Governance in a Globalizing World*. Washington, DC: Brookings Institution.

O'Rourke, Dara. 2003. "Outsourcing Regulation: Analyzing Non-governmental Systems of Labor Standards Monitoring." *Policy Studies Journal* 31: 1–29.

Odera Oruka, H. 1990a. "Cultural Fundamentals in Philosophy." *Quest* 4, no. 2: 21–37.

———. 1990b. "Sage-Philosophy: The Basic Questions and Methodology." In *Sage Philosophy: Indigenous Thinkers and Modern Debate on African Philosophy*, edited by H. Odera Oruka, 27–40. Leiden: Brill.

———. 1998. "Grundlegende Fragen der Afrikanischen 'Sage-Philosophy.'" In *Vier Fragen zur Philosophie in Afrika, Asien und Lateinamerika*, edited by F. Wimmer, 35–53. Wien: Passagen.

Oliveira Filho, Abelardo. 2002. *Brasil: Luta e resistência contra a privatização da água*. Report to PSI InterAmerican Water Conference, San José, July 8–10, 2002. Available at www.psiru.org/Others/BrasilLuta-port.doc (accessed on October 11, 2012).

Olivera, Oscar. 2005. *Cochabamba! Water War in Bolivia*. Cambridge, MA: South End.

Ortega y Gasset, J. 1942. *Ideas y creencias*. Madrid: Revista de Occidente.

———. 1987. *El tema de nuestro tempo*. Madrid: Alianza.

Ortiz, Fernando. 1973. *Contrapunteo cubano del tabaco y el azucar*. Barcelona: Ariel.

Oseghare, Antony S. 1992. "Sagacity and African Philosophy." *International Philosophical Quarterly* 32, no. 1: 95–104.

Osha, Sanya. 1999. "Kwasi Wiredu and the Problems of Conceptual Decolonization." *Quest* 13, nos. 1–2: 157–164.

Osler, Margeret, ed. 2000. *Rethinking the Scientific Revolution*. Cambridge: Cambridge University Press.

Oyama, Susan. 2000. *Evolution's Eye: A Systems View of the Biology-Culture Divide*. Durham, NC: Duke University Press.

Oyama, Susan, Paul E. Griffiths, and Russell D. Gray, eds. 2001. *Cycles of Contingency: Developmental Systems and Evolution*. Cambridge, MA: MIT Press.

Pacem in Maribus XX. 1992. *Ocean Governance: A Model for Global Governance in the 21st Century.* Malta: International Ocean Institute.

Pagden, Anthony. 1990. *Spanish Imperialism and the Political Imagination.* New Haven, CT: Yale University Press.

Palencia-Roth, Michael. 2006. "Universalism and Transversalism: Dialogue and Dialogics in a Global Perspective." In *Cultural Diversity and Transversal Values: The East-West Dialogue on Spiritual and Secular Dynamics,* edited by UNESCO, 38. Paris: UNESCO.

Panikkar, Raymond. 1979. *Myth, Faith, and Hermeneutics.* New York: Paulist.

Pardo, Arvid. 1968. "Whose Is the Bed of the Sea?" *American Society, International Law Proceedings* 62: 216–229.

Pascal, B. 1966. *Pensées.* London: Penguin.

Passel, Jeffrey S. 2005. *Estimates of the Size and Characteristics of the Undocumented Population (US).* Washington, DC: Pew Hispanic Center.

Pastor, Alba, Eduardo Pen Aloza, and Victor Valerio Ulloa. 1993. *Aproximaciones al mundo barroco latinoamericano.* Mexico City: Universidad Nacional Autonoma de Mexico.

Payoyo, Peter. 1997. *Cries of the Sea: World Inequality, Sustainable Development and the Common Heritage of Humanity.* Dordrecht: Martinus Nijhoff.

Perham, Margery. 1934. "A Re-statement of Indirect Rule." *Africa: Journal of the International African Institute* 7, no. 3: 321–334.

Pickering, Andrew, ed. 1992. *Science as Practice and Culture.* Chicago: University of Chicago Press.

Polanyi, Karl. 1957 [1944]. *The Great Transformation.* Boston: Beacon.

Posner, Richard. 2002. "The Best Offense." *New Republic,* September 2.

Pratt, Mary Louise. 1992. *Imperial Eyes: Travel Writing and Transculturation.* London: Routledge.

Pratt, Scott L. 2002. *Native Pragmatism: Rethinking the Roots of American Philosophy.* Bloomington: Indiana University Press.

Presbey, Gail M. 1997. "Who Counts as a Sage? Problems in the Further Implementation of Sage Philosophy." *Quest: Philosophical Discussions* 11, nos. 1–2: 53–65.

Prigogine, Ilya. 1980. *From Being to Becoming.* San Francisco: Freeman.

———. 1997. *The End of Certainty: Time, Chaos, and the New Laws of Nature.* New York: Free Press.

Prigogine Ilya, and Isabelle Stengers. 1979. *La nouvelle alliance: Metamorphose de la science.* Paris: Gallimard.

Pureza, José Manuel. 1998. *O património comum da humanidade: Rumo a um direito internacional da solidariedade?* Porto, Portugal: Afrontamento.

———. 2005. "Defensive and Oppositional Counter-hegemonic Uses of International Law: From the International Criminal Court to the Common Heritage of Humankind." In *Law and Globalization from Below: Towards a Cosmopolitan Legality,* edited by Boaventura Santos and C. Rodríguez-Garavito, 267–280. Cambridge: Cambridge University Press.

———. 2009. "Democracia limitada y paz liberal: Anotaciones al 'totus orbis' en tiempo de globalización neoliberal." In *La calidad de la democracia: Las democracias del siglo XXI,* edited by A. Guerra and J. F. Tezanos, 431. Madrid: Sistema.

Quijano, Anibal. 2000. "Colonialidad del poder y classificacion social." *Journal of World-Systems Research* 6, no. 2: 342–386.

Racine, J. B., C. Raffestin, and V. Ruffy. 1982. "Escala e ação: Contribuições para uma interpretação de mecanismo de escala prática da geografia." *Revista Brasileira de Geografia* 45, no. 1: 123–135.

Ramalho-Santos, João. 2007. "Science on the Edge: Some Reproductive Biology Paradigms." In *Cognitive Justice in a Global World: Prudent Knowledge for a Decent Life,* edited by Boaventura de Sousa Santos, 251–269. Lanham, MD: Lexington.

Ramalho-Santos, Miguel. 2003. "Células estaminais como densidades autopoiéticas." In *Conhecimento prudente para uma vida decente: Um discurso sobre as ciências revisitado,* edited by Boaventura de Sousa Santos, 471–480. Porto, Portugal: Afrontamento.

Rawls, Anne Warfield. 2004. *Epistemology and Practice: Durkheim's "The Elementary Forms of Religious Life."* Cambridge: Cambridge University Press.

Renner, Karl. 1965. *Die Rechtsinstitute des Privatrechts und ihre soziale Funktion: ein Beitrag zur Kritik des Burgerlichen Rechts.* Stuttgart: Gustav Fischer.

Retamar, Roberto Fernández. 1989. *Caliban and Other Essays.* Minneapolis: University of Minnesota Press.

Ribeiro, António Sousa. 1995. "Walter Benjamin, pensador da modernidade." *Oficinas do CES* 41. Available at www.ces.uc.pt/publicacoes/oficina/ficheiros/41.pdf (accessed on June 27, 2013).

———. 2004. "The Reason of Borders or a Border Reason?" *Eurozine.* Available at www.eurozine.com/articles/article_2004-10-05-ribeiro-bs.html (accessed on October 11, 2012).

Ribeiro, Darcy. 1996. *Mestiço é que é bom.* Edited by Oscar Niemeyer, Antônio Callado, Antonio Houaiss, Eric Nepomuceno, Ferreira Gullar, Zelito Vianna, and Zuenir Ventura. Rio de Janeiro: Revan.

Richards, P. 1995. "Participatory Rural Appraisal: A Quick and Dirty Critique." *PLA Notes* 24: 13–16.

Rifkin, Jeremy. 1987. *Time Wars: The Primary Conflict in Human History.* New York: Simon and Schuster.

Ritzer, George, ed. 1990. *Frontiers of Social Theory.* New York: Columbia University Press.

———, ed. 1992. *Metatheorizing.* Newbury Park: Sage.

———. 2010. *Globalization: A Basic Text.* Malden, MA: Wiley-Blackwell.

Roach, Kent. 2002. "Did September 11 Change Everything? Struggling to Preserve Canadian Values in the Face of Terrorism." *McGill Law Journal* 47, no. 4: 893–847.

Robbins, B. 2007. "Not without Reason: A Response to Akeel Bilgrami." *Critical Inquiry* 33: 632–640.

Robert, Jason Scott. 2004. *Embryology, Epigenesis, and Evolution: Taking Development Seriously.* Cambridge: Cambridge University Press.

Rodney, Walter. 1972. *How Europe Underdeveloped Africa.* London: Bogle-L'Ouverture.

Rodríguez-Garavito, César A. 2005. "Nike's Law: The Anti-sweatshop Movement, Transnational Corporations, and the Struggle over International Labor Rights in the Americas." In *Law and Globalization from Below: Towards a Cosmopolitan Legality*, edited by Boaventura de Sousa Santos and C. Rodríguez-Garavito, 64–91. Cambridge: Cambridge University Press.

Rousseau, Jean-Jacques. 1973 [1762]. *The Social Contract and Discourses.* London: J. M. Dent and Sons.

Rudolph, Lloyd I. 1996. "Contesting Civilizations: Gandhi and the Counter-culture." In *Facets of Mahatma Gandhi.* Vol. 4: *Ethics, Religion and Culture*, edited by Subrata Mukherjee and Sushila Ramswamy, 41–93. New Delhi: Deep and Deep Publications.

Ruskin, John. 1913. *Proserpina; also, Ariadne Florentina; The Opening of the Crystal Palace; St. Mark's Rest; Lectures on Art; The Elements of Perspective.* Boston: D. Estes.

Sadat, Leila Nadya. 2005. "Ghost Prisoners and Black Sites: Extraordinary Rendition under International Law." *Case Western Reserve Journal of International Law* 37, no. 5-3: 309–342.

Said, Edward. 1978. *Orientalism.* New York: Vintage.

———. 1980. *The Question of Palestine.* New York: Vintage.

Sales, Sally. 2012. *Adoption, Family and the Paradox of Origins: A Foucauldian History.* Basingstoke, UK: Palgrave Macmillan.

Santos, Boaventura de Sousa. 1989. *Introdução a uma ciência pós-moderna.* Porto, Portugal: Afrontamento.

———. 1992. "A Discourse on the Sciences." *Review* XV, no. 1: 9–47.

———. 1995. *Toward a New Common Sense: Law, Science and Politics in the Paradigmatic Transition.* New York: Routledge.

———. 1998. "Why Is It So Difficult to Construct a Critical Theory?" *Zona Abierta* 82–83: 219–229.

———. 2000. *A crítica da razão indolente: Contra o desperdício da experiência.* Porto, Portugal: Afrontamento.

———. 2002a. "The Processes of Globalisation." *Eurozine.* Available at www.eurozine.com /articles/2002-08-22-santos-en.html (accessed on October 11, 2012).

———. 2002b. *Toward a New Legal Common Sense: Law, Globalization, and Emancipation.* London: Butterworths, 2002.

———. 2004. "A Critique of Lazy Reason: Against the Waste of Experience." In *The Modern World-System in the Longue Durée,* edited by Immanuel Wallerstein, 157–197. London: Paradigm Publishers.

———, ed. 2005. *Democratizing Democracy: Beyond the Liberal Democratic Canon.* London: Verso.

———. 2006a. *A gramática do tempo.* Porto, Portugal: Afrontamento.

———. 2006b. *The Rise of the Global Left: The World Social Forum and Beyond.* London: Zed.

———, ed. 2007a. *Another Knowledge Is Possible: Beyond Northern Epistemologies.* London: Verso.

———, ed. 2007b. *Cognitive Justice in a Global World: Prudent Knowledge for a Decent Life.* Lanham, MD: Lexington.

———. 2008. "The World Social Forum and the Global Left." *Politics and Society* 36, no. 2: 247–270.

———. 2009. "If God Were a Human Rights Activist: Human Rights and the Challenge of Political Theologies." *Law, Social Justice and Global Development* 1. Festschrift for Upendra Baxi.

———. 2010. "From the Postmodern to the Postcolonial—and Beyond Both." In *Decolonizing European Sociology: Transdisciplinary Approaches,* edited by Encarnación Gutiérrez Rodríguez, Manuela Boatca, and Sérgio Costa, 225–242. Farnham, UK: Ashgate.

———. 2011. "Portugal: Tales of Being and Not Being." *Portuguese Literary and Cultural Studies* 19/20: 399–443.

Santos, Boaventura de Sousa, and Flávia Carlet. 2010. "The Movement of Landless Rural Workers in Brazil and Their Struggles for Access to Law and Justice." In *Marginalized Communities and Access to Justice,* edited by Yash Ghai and Jill Cottrell, 60–82. Abingdon, UK: Routledge.

Santos, Boaventura de Sousa, and José Luis Exeni, eds. 2012. *Justicia indígena, plurinacionalidad e interculturalidad en Bolivia.* Quito: Ediciones Abya Yala y Fundación Rosa Luxemburg.

Santos, Boaventura de Sousa, and Mauricio García Villegas. 2001. *El caleidoscopio de las justicias en Colombia.* Bogotá: Ediciones Uniandes y Siglo del Hombre.

Santos, Boaventura de Sousa, and Agustin Grijalva, eds. 2012. *Justicia indígena, plurinacionalidad e interculturalidad en Ecuador.* Quito: Ediciones Abya Yala y Fundación Rosa Luxemburg.

Santos, Boaventura de Sousa, Maria Paula Meneses, and João Arriscado Nunes. 2007. "Opening Up the Canon of Knowledge and Recognition of Difference." In *Another Knowledge Is Possible: Beyond Northern Epistemologies,* edited by Boaventura de Sousa Santos, xvix–lxii. London: Verso.

Santos, Boaventura de Sousa, and César Rodríguez-Garavito. 2005. *Law and Globalization from Below: Towards a Cosmopolitan Legality.* Cambridge: Cambridge University Press.

Santos, Leonel Ribeiro dos. 2002. "A sabedoria do idiota." In *Coincidência dos opostos e concórdia: Caminhos do pensamento em Nicolau de Cusa,* edited by João Maria André and Mariano Alvarez Gómez, 67–98. Coimbra, Portugal: Faculdade de Letras.

Sapsford, D., and H. Singer. 1998. "The IMF, the World Bank and Commodity Prices: A Case of Shifting Sands?" *World Development* 26, no. 9: 1653–1660.

Sarmiento, Domingo. 1966. *Facundo, civilización y barbarie.* Mexico City: Porrúa.

Sassen, Saskia. 1999. *Guests and Aliens.* New York: New Press.

Saul, Ben. 2005. "Definition of 'Terrorism' in the UN Security Council: 1985–2004." *Chinese Journal of International Law* 4, no. 1: 141–166.

Scheppele, Kim Lane. 2004a. "Law in a Time of Emergency: States of Exception and the Temptations of 9/11." *University of Pennsylvania Journal of Constitutional Law* 6, no. 5: 1001–1083.

———. 2004b. "Other People's Patriot Acts: Europe's Response to September 11." *Loyola Law Review* 50, no. 1: 89–148.

———. 2006. "North American Emergencies: The Use of Emergency Powers in Canada and the United States." *International Journal of Constitutional Law* 4, no. 2: 213–243.

Schiebinger, Londa. 1989. *The Mind Has No Sex: Women in the Origins of Modern Science*. Cambridge, MA: Harvard University Press.

Schluchter, Wolfgang. 1979. *Die Entwicklung des okzidentalen Rationalismus: Analyse von Max Webers Gesellschaftsgeschichte*. Tübingen: Mohr.

Schmitt, Carl. 2003. *The Nomos of the Earth in the International Law of the Jus Publicum Europaeum*. New York: Telos Press.

Schopenhauer, Arthur. 2007 [1851]. *Parerga and Paralipomena: A Collection of Philosophical Essays*. New York: Cosimo Classics.

Schumpeter, Joseph. 1962 [1942]. *Capitalism, Socialism and Democracy*. New York: Harper and Row.

Sekhon, Vijay. 2003. "Civil Rights of Others: Antiterrorism, the Patriot Act, and Arab and South Asian American Rights in Post-9/11 American Society." *Texas Forum on Civil Liberties and Civil Liberties* 8, no. 1: 117–148.

Serequeberhan, Tsenay. 1991. "Introduction." In *African Philosophy: The Essential Readings*, edited by T. Serequeberhan, xvii–xxii. New York: Paragon.

Shapin, Steven. 1996. *The Scientific Revolution*. Chicago: University of Chicago Press.

Sharer, R. J., and W. Ashmore. 1987. *Archaeology: Discovering Our Past*. Palo Alto, CA: Mayfield.

Silverstein, Paul A. 2005. "Immigrant Racialization and the New Savage Slot: Race, Migration, and Immigration in the New Europe." *Annual Review of Anthropology* 34: 363–384.

Singh, R. S., C. B. Krimbas, D. B. Paul, and J. Beatty, eds. 2001. *Thinking about Evolution: Historical, Philosophical, and Political Perspectives*. Cambridge: Cambridge University Press.

Sloterdijk, P. 1987. *Critique of Cynical Reason*. Minneapolis: University of Minnesota Press.

Snow, C. P. 1959. *The Two Cultures and the Scientific Revolution*. New York: Cambridge University Press.

———. 1964. *The Two Cultures and a Second Look*. Cambridge: Cambridge University Press.

Snyder, Francis. 1993. *Soft Law and Institutional Practice in the European Community*. EUI Working Papers Law, 93/95. Florence: European University Institute.

———. 2002. "Governing Globalization." In *Transnational Legal Processes: Globalization and Power Disparities*, edited by M. Likosky, 65–97. London: Butterworths.

Soper, Kate. 1995. *What Is Nature? Culture, Politics and the Non-human*. Cambridge: Cambridge University Press.

Spivak, Gayatri Chakravorty. 1999. *A Critique of Postcolonial Reason: Toward a History of the Vanishing Present*. Cambridge, MA: Harvard University Press.

Steinberg, Michael, ed. 1996. *Walter Benjamin and the Demands of History*. Ithaca, NY: Cornell University Press.

Stengers, Isabelle. 1996/1997. *Cosmopolitiques*. 7 vols. Paris: La Découverte.

———. 1997. *Sciences et pouvoirs: La démocratie face à la technoscience*. Paris: La Découverte.

———. 2007. "Becoming Civilized: Beyond the Great Divide." In *Cognitive Justice in a Global World: Prudent Knowledge for a Decent Life*, edited by Boaventura de Sousa Santos, 135–152. Lanham, MD: Lexington.

Steyn, Johan. 2004. "Guantanamo Bay: The Legal Black Hole." *International and Comparative Law Quarterly* 53: 1–15.

Stone, G. D. 1981. "The Interpretation of Negative Evidence in Archaeology." *Atlal (University of Arizona, Department of Anthropology) Occasional Papers* 2: 41–53.

Strauss, Marcy. 2004. "Torture." *New York Law School Law Review* 48: 201–274.

Tapié, Victor. 1988. *Barroco e classicismo.* Lisbon: Presença.

Taylor, Margaret H. 2004. "Dangerous by Decree: Detention without Bond in Immigration Proceedings." *Loyola Law Review* 50, no. 1: 149–172.

Taylor, Mark, and Esa Saarinen. 1994. *Imagologies: Media Philosophy.* New York: Routledge.

Taylor, Peter J. 1995. "Building on Construction: An Exploration of Heterogeneous Constructionism, Using an Analogy from Psychology and a Sketch from Socioeconomic Modeling." *Perspectives on Science* 3, no. 1: 66–98.

Teubner, Gunther. 1986. "Transnational Politics: Contention and Institutions in International Politics." *Annual Review of Political Science* 4: 1–20.

Todorov, Tzvetan. 1984. *The Conquest of America: The Question of the Other.* Translated by Richard Howard. New York: Harper and Row.

Tolstoy, Leo. 1960. *Last Diaries.* New York: G. P. Putnam's Sons.

Toulmin, Stephen. 1990. *Cosmopolis: The Hidden Agenda of Modernity.* New York: Free Press.

———. 2001. *Return to Reason.* Cambridge, MA: Harvard University Press.

———. 2007. "How Reason Lost Its Balance." In *Cognitive Justice in a Global World: Prudent Knowledge for a Decent Life,* edited by Boaventura de Sousa Santos, ix–xv. Lanham, MD: Lexington.

Trawick, Paul B. 2003. *The Struggle for Water in Peru: Comedy and Tragedy in the Andean Commons.* Stanford, CA: Stanford University Press.

Trubek, David, and James Mosher. 2003. "New Governance, Employment Policy, and the European Social Model." In *Governing Work and Welfare in a New Economy,* edited by G. Teubner, 33–58. Berlin: De Gruyter.

Trubek, David, and Louise G. Trubek. 2005. "Hard and Soft Law in the Construction of Social Europe: The Role of the Open Method of Co-ordination." *European Law Journal* 11, no. 3: 343–364.

Tuck, Richard. 1979. *Natural Rights Theories: Their Origin and Development.* Cambridge: Cambridge University Press.

Tucker, Vincent. 1992. "The Myth of Development." *Occasional Papers Series* 6, Department of Sociology, University College, Cork.

Tully, James. 2007. "The Imperialism of Modern Constitutional Democracy." In *Constituent Power and Constitutional Form,* edited by M. Loughlin and N. Walker, 315–338. Oxford: Oxford University Press.

Turner, Charles. 2010. *Investigating Sociological Theory.* London: Sage.

Turner, Jonathan. 2010a. *Theoretical Principles of Sociology.* Vol. 1: *Macrodynamics.* New York: Springer.

———. 2010b. *Theoretical Principles of Sociology.* Vol. 2: *Microdynamics.* New York: Springer.

Tushnet, Mark. 1981. *The American Law of Slavery, 1810–1860.* Princeton, NJ: Princeton University Press.

Unger, Roberto. 1998. *Democracy Realized.* London: Verso.

Van Bergen, Jennifer, and Douglas Valentine. 2006. "The Dangerous World of Indefinite Detentions: Vietnam to Abu Ghraib." *Case Western Reserve Journal of International Law* 37, no. 5-3: 449–508.

Van de Linde, Erik, Kevin O'Brien, Gustav Lindstrom, Stephan de Spiegeleire, Mikko Vayrynen, and Han de Vries. 2002. *Quick Scan of Post 9/11 National Counter-terrorism Policymaking and Implementation in Selected European Countries.* Research project for the Netherlands Ministry of Justice. Leiden: RAND Europe.

Veblen, T. 1898. "Why Is Economics Not an Evolutionary Science?" *Quarterly Journal of Economics* 12: 56–81.

Venn, Couze. 2001. *Occidentalism: Modernity and Subjectivity.* London and Thousand Oaks, CA: Sage.

Vico, Giambattista. 1961 [1725]. *The New Science of Giambattista Vico.* Garden City, NY: Anchor.

Visvanathan, Shiv. 1997. *A Carnival for Science: Essays on Science, Technology and Development.* Oxford: Oxford University Press.

———. 2000. "Environmental Values, Policy, and Conflict in India." Paper presented at the seminar "Understanding Values: A Comparative Study on Environmental Values in China, India and the United States," Carnegie Council, New York, April 14. Available at www .carnegiecouncil.org/publications/articles_papers_reports/709.html/_res/id=sa_File1/709 _visvanathan.pdf (accessed on October 11, 2012).

———. 2007. "The Heuristics of a Dissenting Imagination." In *Another Knowledge Is Possible: Beyond Northern Epistemologies*, edited by Boaventura de Sousa Santos, 182–218. London: Verso.

Viveiros de Castro, E. 2004. "Perspectival Anthropology and the Method of Controlled Equivocation." *Tipití* 2, no. 1: 3–22.

Voltaire. 1950. *Voltaire's England.* London: Folio Society.

———. 2002 [1752]. *Philosophical Dictionary.* Edited by Theodore Besterman. London: Penguin Books.

wa Thiong'o, Ngu gi. 1986. *Decolonising the Mind: The Politics of Language in African Literature.* London: James Currey.

Wagner, Birgit. 2011. *Cultural Translation: A Value or a Tool? Let's Start with Gramsci!* FORUM: Postkoloniale Arbeiten/Postcolonial Studies. Available at www.goethezeitportal.de/fileadmin /PDF/kk/df/postkoloniale_studien/wagner_cultural-translation-gramsci.pdf (accessed on October 11, 2012).

Wagner, Peter. 2007. "On Wars and Revolutions." In *Cognitive Justice in a Global World: Prudent Knowledge for a Decent Life*, edited by Boaventura de Sousa Santos, 87–104. Lanham, MD: Lexington.

———. 2012. *Modernity: Understanding the Present.* Cambridge, UK: Polity.

Wagner, Seidman, ed. 1992. *Post-modernism and Social Theory.* Cambridge, UK: Blackwell.

Wallerstein, Immanuel M. 1974. *The Modern World-System.* New York: Academic Press.

———. 1999. *The End of the World as We Know It: Social Science for the Twenty-First Century.* Minneapolis: University of Minnesota Press.

———. 2004. *World-Systems Analysis: An Introduction.* Durham, NC: Duke University Press.

———. 2007. "The Structures of Knowledge, or How Many Ways May We Know." In *Cognitive Justice in a Global World: Prudent Knowledge for a Decent Life*, edited by Boaventura de Sousa Santos, 129–134. Lanham, MD: Lexington.

Wallerstein, Immanuel, and Etienne Balibar. 1991. *Race, Nation, Class: Ambiguous Identities.* New York: Verso.

Warde, Alan. 1997. *Consumption, Food and Taste: Culinary Antinomies and Commodity Culture.* London and Thousand Oaks, CA: Sage.

Wardell, M. L., and S. P. Turner, eds. 1986. *Sociological Theory in Transition.* London: Allen and Unwin.

Weber, Max. 1958. *The Protestant Ethic and the Spirit of Capitalism.* New York: Scribner.

———. 1963. *The Sociology of Religion.* Boston: Beacon.

———. 1968. *Economy and Society: An Outline of Interpretive Sociology.* New York: Bedminster Press.

Weinstein, Fred, and Gerald Platt. 1969. *The Wish to Be Free: Society, Psyche, and Value Change.* Berkeley: University of California Press.

Weiss, Edith. 1989. *Natural Law and Justice.* Cambridge, MA: Harvard University Press.

Werbner, Richard. 2002. "Cosmopolitan Ethnicity, Entrepreneurship and the Nation: Minority Elites in Botswana." *Journal of Southern African Studies* 28, no. 4: 731–753.

White, Mary V. 1982. "The Common Heritage of Mankind: An Assessment." *Case Western Reserve Journal of International Law* 14: 509–542.

Whitehead, John W., and Steven H. Aden. 2002. "Forfeiting Enduring Freedom for Homeland Security: A Constitutional Analysis of the USA Patriot Act and the Justice Department's Anti-terrorism Initiatives." *American University Law Review* 51, no. 6: 1081–1133.

Williams, Eric. 1994 [1944]. *Capitalism and Slavery*. Chapel Hill: University of North Carolina Press.

Wilson, William Justus. 1987. *The Truly Disadvantaged: The Inner City, the Underclass and Public Policy*. Chicago: University of Chicago Press.

Wiredu, Kwasi. 1990. "Are There Cultural Universals?" *Quest* 4, no. 2: 5–19.

———. 1996. *Cultural Universals and Particulars: An African Perspective*. Bloomington: Indiana University Press.

———. 1997. "African Philosophy and Inter-cultural Dialogue." *Quest* 11, nos. 1–2: 29–41.

Wishnie, Michael J. 2004. "State and Local Police Enforcement of Immigration Laws." *University of Pennsylvania Journal of Constitutional Law* 6, no. 5: 1084–1115.

Wittgenstein, L. 1973. *Tractatus Logico-Philosophicus*. Frankfurt: Suhrkamp.

Wolf, Michaela. 2008. "Translation—Transculturation: Measuring the Perspectives of Trans-cultural Political Action," translated by Kate Sturge. Europäisches Institut für Progressive Kulturpolitik. April. Available at http://eipcp.net/transversal/0608/wolf/en (accessed on October 11, 2012).

Wölfflin, Heinrich. 1979. *Renaissance and Baroque*. Ithaca, NY: Cornell University Press.

Wrebner, Pnina. 1999. "Global Pathways: Working Class Cosmopolitans and the Creation of Transnational Ethnic Worlds." *Social Anthropology* 7, no. 1: 17–37.

Xaba, Thokozani. 2007. "Marginalized Medical Practice: The Marginalization and Transformation of Indigenous Medicines in South Africa." In *Another Knowledge Is Possible: Beyond Northern Epistemologies*, edited by Boaventura de Sousa Santos, 317–351. London: Verso.

Yngvesson, Barbara. 1996. "Negotiating Motherhood: Identity and Difference in 'Open Adoptions.'" *Law and Society Review* 31, no. 1: 31–80.

Zaehner, R. C. 1982. *Hinduism*. Oxford: Oxford University Press.

Zappala, M. O. 1990. *Lucian of Samosata in the Two Hesperias: An Essay in Literary and Cultural Translation*. Potomac, MD: Scripta Humanistica.

Zelman, Joshua D. 2002. "Recent Developments in International Law: Anti-terrorism Legislation—Part One: An Overview." *Journal of Transnational Law and Policy* 11, no. 1: 183–200.

Zieck, Margoleine. 1992. "Reference to Extraterrestrial Realms." *Verfassung und Recht in Übersee* 25: 161–198.

Index

Abeele, Georges van der, 79
absent agents, 157, 159–161, 163
absent knowledges, 157–159, 161, 163
abyssal line(s), 70–71, 86–87, 119–121,
    121n6, 122, 124, 127–128, 133–134, 193,
    202, 238, 240
abyssal thinking, 95, 109n7, 118–135, 172,
    188, 191, 193, 226–227, 234
Acosta, Alberto, 30
action packages, 142–143
action-with-*clinamen,* 97–98, 160
adjectives, 33–34, 134–135n44
adoption, 85–86
Adorno, Theodor, 233
advanced normality, 163
African philosophy, 202–204, 209
Africa Water Network, 29
Afro-descendents, 10, 21, 34, 84, 108, 176,
    202; and political movements, 21, 27, 65,
    108, 171, 178
agency, 160
agent(s), 120, 122, 136, 152–155, 159–161,
    163, 177, 191–192, 219, 222, 227, 234
ALBA. *See* Bolivarian Alternative for the
    Americas (ALBA)
Alberti, Leon Battista, 144–145, 161
Allende, Salvador, 64
alternative societies, 23–24, 28, 35, 108,
    192
amelioration, 74
American century, 48–50
Americanization, 49
American university, 53, 66
Amerindian peoples, 52
amity lines, 121n7, 124–125
ancestral territories, 29
Andrade, Oswald de, 51, 52, 55–56, 60, 62,
    64, 66, 68
Angelus Novus (Klee), 73–76, 87, 88
anthropophagy, 52, 56, 60, 66

anti-imperialism, 26, 42, 54, 188, 222–227,
    237
antiquity, 101, 102
antiterrorism laws, 126, 127
appropriation/violence dichotomy, 119,
    122–134
archaeology, 140, 146–147, 149, 150, 151,
    152, 154
Argentina, 35, 54, 64, 68
Ariel (*The Tempest*), 68–69
arrogance, 53, 85, 103, 110, 170
arrogant reason, 165, 166
artifacts, 197, 215
artifice, 60–61
Ashmore, W., 151
astronomy, 140
atomism, 166
authorship, collective, 5, 7
autonomy, 45, 49, 55, 57, 106, 138, 194
axial age, 168n8
axiology of care, 184
Aymara, 40, 40n21

Bachelard, Gaston, 79, 150–151, 208
Bakhtin, Mikhail, 220
Balibar, Etienne, 173
Banuri, T., 209, 209n19
baroque ethos, 56–64, 217
Benjamin, Walter, 49, 74–75, 81, 88, 89, 95,
    96, 169–170, 170n9, 182, 216
Bergson, Henri, 80n11, 210
Berlin Wall, 24, 28
Bernal, Martin, 85, 168n8
Bernini, Gian Lorenzo, 59
Bhabha, Homi, 216, 217, 226
bifurcation, 59, 82, 165, 233
biodiversity, 4, 30, 67, 95, 123, 186, 201,
    206, 229
biology, 195, 196n9
blindness, 137, 154–156, 160

minifesto for intellectual-activists, 3–17

misrepresentation, 136–137; of consequences, 136–138

modernity: capitalism and, 102; history of, 72–73, 88; paradigm of, 138–139; Western, 3, 5, 11, 22, 44–46, 71–72, 74, 85, 109, 122, 127–128, 138, 176, 179, 212, 236, 238

modern science. *See* science

Monmonier, Mark, 141–142, 147n6

monocultural diversity, 13

monoculture, 15; of the capitalistic logic of productivity, 174; of linear time, 173, 181–182; of logic of the dominant scale, 173–174; of the naturalization of differences, 173; of scientific knowledge and rigor, 172, 188, 189–190

Montaigne, Michel de, 63

Montecristi constitution, 64

Moody's, 131

Morales, Evo, 8, 35, 64

motherhood, 85–86

MST. *See* Landless Workers' Movement

Mujica, José, 35

multicontrasted resolution, 162

multiculturalism, 166, 230–231

Multi-Donor Trust Fund, 31n14

multinational corporations, 25, 133, 144

The Mystical Ecstasy of Santa Teresa (Bernini), 59

Nandy, Ashis, 225–226

Nasr, Seyyed Hossein, 202

National Amazonian Park, 30

nation-state, 81, 94

natural law, 77–78

natural resources, 23, 95, 123

nature, 23, 25; messianic, 95–96; protection of, 30–33; state of, 50, 122, 128, 133

Nazism, 169

Needham, Joseph, 102, 168n8, 202, 221

negative evidence, 154

negative universalism, 220, 227

Negri, Toni, 38

neocolonialism, 101, 209

neoculture, 60

neodevelopmentalist state, 24–25

neoliberalism, 25, 36–37, 54, 83, 84, 93

neo-Orientalism, 126n20

Neoplatonism, 110

Neozapatismo, 28

neuroscience, 84

new historicism, 85

new indirect rule, 128, 132–133

new/old, 30–33

New World, 121–122

Nicaragua, 64

Nicholas of Cusa, 99, 103, 109–111, 115, 188, 210–211

Nietzsche, Friedrich, 72, 81, 86, 97, 169

99 percent movement, 4

noncolonial languages, 40–41

nonconformity, 9, 32, 75, 88–89, 91, 112, 175, 184, 227, 234, 236, 239

noncontemporaneity, 122

nonexistence, 118; modes of production of, 172–175; social forms of, 174

non-Occidentalist West, 99–115

nonstate actors, 128

North America, 48–49

North American Free Trade Agreement (NAFTA), 54

Northern epistemologies, 69, 191, 238

Not Yet, 10, 12, 33, 182–184

novelty, 31–33

Nuestra America, 48–69; baroque ethos and, 56–64; century of, 51; deterritorialization of, 66–68; founding ideas of, 51–56; limits of, 64–66

objects, 197–198

Occidentalism, 99–103

Occupy movement, 36, 50, 108, 192, 221, 236

Odera Oruka, H., 204, 231

Odyssey (Homer), 79–80

oikos, 79

oil resources, 30, 31

old/new, 30–33

one-point perspective, 144–145

ontological coloniality, 178

oppression, 4, 10, 21, 40, 45, 89–90, 113, 209–210, 226, 228, 237

options. *See* roots/options equation

organization, 39–40

Orientalism, 100–101, 223

orientation, 143

Ortega y Gasset, José, 105, 114, 191–192

orthopedic thinking, 105–107, 108, 109, 110, 111, 114, 115

About the Author

Boaventura de Sousa Santos is Professor of Sociology at the University of Coimbra (Portugal) and Distinguished Legal Scholar at the University of Wisconsin–Madison. He is director of the Center for Social Studies at the University of Coimbra and has written and published widely on the issues of globalization, sociology of law and the state, epistemology, social movements, and the World Social Forum. He has been awarded several prizes, most recently the Science and Technology Prize of Mexico, 2010, and the Kalven Jr. Prize of the Law and Society Association, 2011. Among his many books in English are *The Rise of the Global Left: The World Social Forum and Beyond* (Zed Books 2006) and *Law and Globalization from Below: Towards a Cosmopolitan Legality* (co-editor; Cambridge University Press 2005).

Printed in Great Britain
by Amazon